National Security
in the 1980s:
From Weakness
to Strength

NATIONAL SECURITY

IN THE 1980s:

FROM WEAKNESS TO STRENGTH

W. Scott Thompson, *Editor*
Kenneth L. Adelman
Richard R. Burt
Miles M. Costick
Robert F. Ellsworth
Fred Charles Iklé
Geoffrey T. H. Kemp
Edward N. Luttwak
Charles Burton Marshall
Paul H. Nitze
Sam Nunn
Henry S. Rowen
Leonard Sullivan, Jr.
William R. Van Cleave
Francis J. West, Jr.
Albert Wohlstetter
Elmo R. Zumwalt, Jr.

Institute for Contemporary Studies
San Francisco, California

Inquiries, book orders, and catalog requests should be addressed to the Institute for Contemporary Studies, Suite 811, 260 California Street, San Francisco, California 94111—415—398—3010.

Library of Congress Catalog Number 80—80648
ISBN 0—917616—38—3 (paper).
ISBN 0—87855—412—2 (cloth) available through Transaction Books, Rutgers—The State University, New Brunswick, NJ 08903.

CONTENTS

III

The Politics of Strength

IV

An American Strategy for the 1980s

V

Epilogue

CONTRIBUTORS

KENNETH L. ADELMAN
Senior Political Scientist, Strategic Studies Center,
SRI International; Adjunct Professor,
Defense Intelligence School

RICHARD R. BURT
National Security Affairs correspondent,
New York Times, *Washington Bureau*

MILES M. COSTICK
President, Institute on Strategic Trade

ROBERT F. ELLSWORTH
Managing Director, Robert Ellsworth and Company

FRED C. IKLÉ
Chairman, Conservation Management Corporation

GEOFFREY T. H. KEMP
Associate Professor of International Politics,
Fletcher School of Law and Diplomacy

EDWARD N. LUTTWAK
Senior Fellow, Center for Strategic and International Studies;
Research Professor, Georgetown University

CHARLES BURTON MARSHALL
Former Professor of International Politics, Johns Hopkins
School of Advanced International Studies

PAUL H. NITZE
Chairman of Policy Studies, Committee on the Present Danger;
Chairman, Advisory Council, Johns Hopkins School of
Advanced International Studies

SAM NUNN
U.S. Senator (D—Georgia)

HENRY S. ROWEN
Professor of Public Management, Graduate School of Business,
Stanford University

LEONARD SULLIVAN, JR.
Consultant, Center for National Security Research,
Systems Planning Corporation

W. SCOTT THOMPSON
Associate Professor of International Politics, Fletcher School
of Law and Diplomacy

WILLIAM R. VAN CLEAVE
Professor of International Relations and Director of the Defense
and Strategic Studies Program, University of Southern California

FRANCIS J. WEST, JR.
Director of Strategic Research, Naval War College

ALBERT WOHLSTETTER
University Professor and Fellow of the Center for Policy Studies,
University of Chicago

ELMO R. ZUMWALT, JR.
Admiral, U.S. Navy (Ret.), former Chief of Naval Operations.

PREFACE

In the fall of 1976 the institute undertook its first venture into foreign and military policy with the publication of *Defending America: Toward a New Role in the Post-Détente World*. Organized in collaboration with Basic Books (New York), that study expressed the growing alarm of a number of observers who were concerned about the ongoing Soviet military buildup combined with a growing post-Vietnam U.S. isolationism.

The themes expressed in *Defending America* gained a growing audience for the next couple of years, and by 1979 the Carter White House implicitly acknowledged the problem by calling for a small real increase in the defense budget. Inflation, however, eliminated the increase last year, and political leadership on the issue all but disappeared as the military and strategic imbalance was increasingly aggravated.

Toward the end of 1979 the seizure of hostages in Iran and the Soviet invasion of Afghanistan combined to change fundamentally the nature of the debate. In the wake of those events, it was no longer possible to ignore the growing threat. But although President Carter expressed a strong change of heart in his 1980 State of the Union message, his *policies* have changed almost not at all: the defense budget—to pick one important indication—is unchanged from what it was before the incidents in Iran and Afghanistan.

The most important point is that those incidents did not change the underlying situation, which has been readily apparent to observers for several years. The question has never been *whether* such crises would occur, but *when*. For this reason, in the fall of 1979 the institute asked W. Scott Thompson to organize a sequel to *Defending America*—to assemble a group of authors who would undertake a systematic study of the ways in which U.S. foreign and military policy ought to be reoriented, fundamentally. While *Defending America* was a critique, this project was organized to set forth a positive agenda for policy. For this purpose a number of authors who had contributed to the earlier book were recruited: Edward N. Luttwak, Charles Burton Marshall, Paul H. Nitze, and Albert Wohlstetter, in addition to Thompson. The new project was designed to recommend a whole range of policy options, from short-term quick fixes to longer-term military and diplomatic strategies.

At a special conference at Belmont House in Baltimore, Maryland, the authors met with other experts and with media representatives to discuss problems and chapters with independent observers, including some from the administration. The discussions were then transcribed and included in the book to enrich its content and to ensure that contrary opinion would be represented. They appear, following the order of the chapters, at the end of the last three major sections.

In judging the results, it becomes clear why the American public has recently been preoccupied with foreign policy. It is especially clear that the post-Vietnam period is over and that U.S. policymakers have yet to chart a new course in foreign policy. The development of new strategies will no doubt be worked out over the coming months in the course of the presidential campaign, and into the next administration.

This book presents one set of military and strategic options which deserve a major hearing in the coming debate.

H. Monroe Browne
President,
Institute for Contemporary Studies

10 May 1980
San Francisco, California

I

The Politics
of Weakness

enduring purposes." Edward Luttwak, in his chapter, argues further that strategy connects "diverse issues into a systematic pattern for things" and then crafts plans "for dealing with the whole."

If we envisage the means or tools of national survival—strategy, in other words—on a continuum, a symbolic soldier will be on one end and a diplomat on the other. The objectives of statecraft, or *foreign policy*, at whose service strategy works, will almost always benefit from a mixture somewhere in between the two poles. Excessive reliance on the soldier, certainly in a democracy, will cost the policy its public support. But too much faith in the diplomat or in the political tools of foreign policy, in the absence of sufficient military power, leads to weakness—and then possibly war, as happened to England in the 1930s; for appeasement, in the absence of countervailing strength, only fed Hitler's appetite.

This is also a book about the absence of strategy in contemporary America, or the failure to use both diplomat and soldier in judicious mixture. The book is thence about the construction of a national strategy from the position of relative weakness into which this once powerful country has been led through the neglect of strategy. For, as did England earlier, we have neglected the soldier. As Admiral Zumwalt demonstrates through a fresh analysis in the next chapter, our defenses have declined precariously in relation to those of our adversary, and we too—like the British before us—watch as our weakness and good intentions are exploited.

Ironically, as recently as the 1960s America's strategy was nearer the soldier's end of the continuum. It was from the Pentagon that fresh thinking emanated. Military power was the watchword of the New Frontier's faith, the backdrop against which the world was to be made safe for diversity and a principal means through which this would be effected. The United States in fact had strategic superiority then and was in no manner directly threatened; the prudent buildup of our forces that ensued was, luckily, to provide our margin for security into the 1970s. But the diplomat's end of the continuum might have had further emphasis as the nation sank further into the morass of an Asian war which it lacked the stomach to fight with vigor.

That war illustrates perfectly the problems that can occur when policy and strategy are unsynchronized and disconnected (at least in the popular perception) from the values of the nation they serve. Whatever one's view of whether the war could have been won,[1] the real point is that the public was asked to support a war's military aims, televised in all their gore, whose political aims it did not understand. The cost was much less the defeat of the Republic of Vietnam — and serious repercussions in other parts of the Third World—than the cost to American will, what Clausewitz considers the key variable of war, something which stands "like an obelisk toward which the principal streets of a town converge." Fighting for any cause thenceforth was considered dubious; indeed, America's moral worthiness to defend a worthy end was increasingly questioned by the nation's intellectual elite, whose spokesmen would soon hold high office.

Thus the tilt from soldier to diplomat went about as far in the opposite direction from the 1960s as it had ever gone in U.S. history, or for that matter in anybody's history. Military power was now universally taken to have been oversold, as the defense budget gradually declined until the end of the decade. Vietnam was brushed from memory despite persistent horrors in Southeast Asia, reminding the nation of some of the issues for which it had fought.

Henceforth, in the new view, America was to erase the memory of its period of military overextension; armed forces were to be treated as a necessary evil, not to be confused with real policy tools, which were economic aid and culture along with human rights. The study of national security was limited to arms control and disarmament. Foundations now began their massive subsidy of arms control centers, which tended to become sources of pressure on administrators and senators for more and more arms control and disarmament measures. But in responding, policymakers failed to consider adequately whether such pressure was mutual to the United States and to the Soviet Union, so on our side arms control became a substitute for strategy and key figures both inside and outside the government appeared undisturbed by the consequent asymmetry. The head of a major foundation, in one of the most revealing admissions of the period, boasted that his institution's money was doing "double duty" because the Soviet Union carried out none of its own such studies but received all those his foundation had sponsored. The obvious intelligence benefit gained by the Soviet Union, much less the irony of its lack of interest in arms control study, passed him by.

In this new policy fashion, it was only the "cold warriors" who took sides between the two superpowers. At the learned public centers of foreign policy discussion, and most of all in academe, intellectuals set the pace for the nation's withdrawal from even consideration of the cautious use of force.[2] The study of national strategy, never an American specialty, was all but abandoned: "It was the very notion of strategy that waned," Edward Luttwak writes herein.

The new strategists argued that international relations were being driven by new forces, ones where, happily, American advantages were great. Economic forces were what had come to matter, they emphasized; and anyway, Third World countries in particular wanted our goods, not our guns. The world, they argued, was too interdependent for war, and no country, it once again developed, was more interdependently tied up in the international system than the United States.

In the 1960s the United States had slowed down, then ultimately stopped, its missile production and devised a theory, "Mutual Assured Destruction" or MAD, to rationalize a policy whereby military superiority was foregone. Both sides accordingly would have merely enough forces to survive a surprise first strike and still be able to retaliate massively against the enemy's cities, presumably with the better hidden—but relatively small and inaccurate—submarine-launched missiles. The theory, of course, depended on both sides playing the game. We would teach the Soviet Union this "higher strategic logic," Paul Warnke (1977, p. 26) assured us, and it would then stop its relentless, mistaken, arms buildup.

But if it didn't, it wouldn't make much difference—the new theorists argued. In an essay that was to lay important foundations for administration policy at the end of the 1970s, Walter Slocum (who became head of the Pentagon's SALT task force under President Carter) argued that "even nuclear monopoly, much less first strike superiority over a lesser nuclear power, does not give its possessor the dominating political influence which comparison of strictly military capabilities would imply" (Slocum 1971). He was assuming, of course, that the Soviets, possessing the sorts of advantages that the United States had hitherto held (including a nuclear monopoly), would behave as benignly as we had. These arguments provided support for Senator McGovern's 1972 campaign proposal that the defense budget can be cut by $30 billion.

The Soviet buildup continued inexorably, nonetheless, but if it was remarked upon in the mid-1970s, it was with condescension or passing regret. William Bundy, than whom few had held more hawkish views in the 1960s, wrote in 1974 that "we must in effect say to the Soviet Union: 'what you are doing is a colossal diversion of resources that should be employed for your people and for others. Neither we nor others will let you obtain the power advantages you apparently seek in this crude way.' "

The thinking of academe, the media, and other opinion makers had badly misjudged reality. As Americans spoke of determinative economic forces, General Giap sent his more

traditional forces across an internationally sanctified demar-
cation zone; these soldiers conquered first South Vietnam
and then Laos and Cambodia. Shortly thereafter, while the
Western guard was down following our Vietnamese defeat,
over 20,000 Cuban troops went to Angola to settle the raging
conflict there, a conflict in which America had backed the
much more broadly based and larger parties. It was to
become a familiar scene.

As the new wisdom spoke of the diminishing importance of
alliances and military bases (as in fact the new policy concurrently began chastising our allies for their "human
rights" violations), the Soviet Union moved about the globe
picking up new allies and gaining access to new facilities.
Moscow's choice of such new friends as Uganda's former dictator Idi Amin and Mengistu Mariam of Ethiopia showed
that the Soviet Union had somewhat fewer scruples in the
human rights field.

And as the notion spread in America that force was being
outmoded in the discourse of nations, non-Communist Third
World countries were breaking all canons of their political
movements as they too invaded or otherwise struck at neighbors in defiance of their covenants. Ironically, the morally
most outspoken states of Asia and Africa, India and
Tanzania, were the first in their continents to invade neighboring countries in conventional formation.

Moreover, the interdependence on which we put such great
faith suddenly became—after the 1973 Middle East war—
symbolic of our great dependence, a dependence, in particular, on a far-away region hard by the Soviet Union's southern
flank. We were also suddenly realizing that interdependence
cut both ways; violence, revolution, coups, all manner of
destabilizing behavior harmful to our interests and favorable
to our adversary's reverberated throughout the interdependent world. Violence, it appeared, had a demonstration
effect, as Japanese terrorists learned violent tactics for use
in the Middle East from watching IRA soldiers on television.

But the greatest irony of all pertained to the unthinkable itself—strategic nuclear conflict between the superpowers. For nuclear war had never been remotely possible prior to the time in the mid-1970s when Moscow achieved at least parity with the United States—unless one assumes that America would have launched a surprise attack on the Soviet Union. Moscow had simply lacked the power to wage war on the United States, but the dramatic steps it had taken to remedy that deficiency now began to make nuclear war thinkable *precisely when the new conventional wisdom was defining it out of existence.* Our defenses were up when we were strong; now that we were becoming relatively weak, a host of theories rationalizing weakness took hold.

U.S. REALISTS AND NATIONAL SECURITY

Not everyone in the United States fell into the trap of the conventional wisdom—indeed the genesis of this book goes back to an effort five years ago to remedy the problem. By mid-1975 many of our serious strategists had begun looking closely at the *real* strategic logic in light of the new balance of forces emerging. They saw irrefutable evidence that Soviet missiles were aimed not at our cities, as would be required by MAD, but at our missiles themselves—at our means of defense. Indeed, the closer we looked at Soviet doctrine the more evidence we found that they considered MAD to be an inhuman strategy, one in which nuclear forces were aimed at helpless people in vulnerable cities rather than at military targets. The Soviets simply weren't playing the MAD game.

Thus if current trends were not corrected, we could calculate that the Soviets by the early 1980s at the latest would have the ability to destroy virtually all American land-based missiles, the half of our submarines that are in port at any one time, and all our bombers at base (something they could do with their nearby ship- and submarine-based missiles which could hit our bombers after only several minutes' warning). As the first object of a Soviet attack would surely be the destruction of America's highly vulnerable command-and-control network, it remained doubtful that we could then communicate with the other half of our submarines, those at sea, thus rendering the United States almost defenseless. Even assuming, optimistically, that communications with the submarines survived, one had to remember that submarine missiles are useful only against "soft" targets like population centers. With America reduced to its twenty submarines at sea and facing an enemy still in possession of much of its massive strategic capability, would a U.S. president order the destruction of any Soviet cities and the small percentage of the Soviet population not out of range or unprotected by their vast civil defense system, probably doing far less damage than was inflicted on Russia in all of World War II? Surely not, when a devastating Soviet counterthrust could simply wipe out America. "Mutual Assured Destruction," the cavalier strategy on which our civilian strategists had built their doctrine, was made even more absurd by this deadly logic.[3]

In light of these developments, a most extraordinary gathering of some of the nation's senior defense strategists was held at Strategic Air Command (SAC) headquarters in Omaha in the blistering cold of December 1975. It was the first time that so diverse and wide-ranging a group of experts had gathered at so high a level of secrecy to assess what most of them, in their individual arenas, were coming to see as worrying trends in the balance of forces. But few had had the chance to compare notes across a wide board of corresponding indicators from other services or areas, still less to make a general net assessment of our abilities, writ large, to stand up to the Soviet Union—something where the whole (our overall capability) would be greater than the sum of the parts, given the synergistic tendency of large systems in interaction.

A number of the authors in this volume took part in the conference at SAC. Albert Wohlstetter was there, alerting everyone to the alarming relative decline of our defense budget and noting the consistency with which we continued to underestimate the rate at which the Soviets were outstripping or catching up with us in pertinent defense categories. Henry Rowen looked at NATO and at the decline of our alliance systems in general. Paul Nitze circulated a then-unpublished essay which argued that the Soviet Union, as foreshadowed above, would soon have a "theoretical war-winning capability" against the United States, a judgment of some military precision and based on the most careful assessment of a range of indicators; the essay, after publication, was to kick off the great strategic controversy that culminated in the 1979 Strategic Arms Limitation Talks II (SALT II) debate.

Some of the analysts present were cautiously optimistic, nonetheless; none saw disaster on the immediate horizon, and most agreed that we had time enough to remedy the essential problems. As we said, reassuring ourselves, the U.S. Air Force would soon have a splendid new bomber, the B−1; Pentagon leaders were talking of (and would soon act on) speeding up development of the MX missile and the deployment of the new Trident submarine. For the European front we had the neutron bomb. We talked of our highest priority for the year—turning the budget around, that is, making it the first year without a cut in real dollars in defense spending since 1968. By the end of the 1970s—though Soviet momentum would continue to give us problems and Moscow would no doubt by then have achieved genuine superiority, it would not be of a crushing sort—a return to parity would be clearly in sight.

Throughout 1976, following the SAC conference, it increasingly looked as if national security could once again be discussed constructively, not in the context of domestic pressures but in the context of the *genuine needs* posed by the actual threat to the nation; in other words, the world as it was rather than as we wished it to be. Although we were still only devoting a third as much of our economy's output to defense as was our principal adversary, we did increase the budget in 1976 and were narrowing the gap slightly. We were charging ahead on the MX missile and on many another front. More important still, public opinion polls showed that real support for defense increases existed, which is why congressmen were voting more money for programs.

It was in such a context that the Institute for Contemporary Studies sponsored its first study in this area, *Defending America* (1977). It was composed, in effect, of unclassified further thoughts on many of the subjects discussed at SAC. It was the first published volume attempting to study the whole subject of the "correlation of forces," as the Soviets like to call it, or strategy in all its dimensions—not just the "bean counting" of missile numbers, but the overall state of the balance including alliance relationships, power projection, technology transfer, and so forth. It was a prescient book in many ways, and most of its essays still stand as analyses of the basic dilemmas in our defense posture.

THE U.S. DEFENSE POSTURE

By the time *Defending America* appeared in the spring of 1977, backsliding on an enormous scale had occurred in our defense thinking and planning, adding fuller force to the reminder in that book of Hegel's fear that the owl of Minerva always comes at dusk. The great educational process of 1975–1976 had been a truly nonpartisan process in which mainstream Republicans and Democrats contributed equally and were willing to share the blame for past deficiencies, which was in truth appropriate. Policymakers had let our defenses slide, owing to the growing demands for Great Society programs and to the escalating antiwar movement. But the learning process might well not have occured. For suddenly new leaders, whose attitude was not that of the managers of the early to mid-1970s, were in charge of national security. This new leadership was not reacting, it was initiating, and it had a new philosophy so to speak: the politics of weakness.

Great changes are usually comprehended only after normalcy returns. Thus it is that few Americans took the full measure of the changes that came in our national security policy between 1977 and 1980, until after the Afghan affair in which the President of the United States suddenly had revealed to him, he said, the nature of Soviet intentions. But in the meantime the guiding lines of our national security policy could be boiled down to a reliance on the good faith (and good intentions) of our adversaries, the momentum of détente, SALT, our economic and technological superiority, and most important of all, the benefits to flow from deemphasizing American military strength.

The ideological foundation of the administration's defense policy lay in the belief, already cited, that Moscow would not gain politically from substantial nuclear advantages—in other words, that military and political power was substantially decoupled. Critics had argued that the American land-based Minuteman missile was becoming vulnerable to a Soviet first strike. But in response, Secretary of Defense Harold Brown could argue in his first annual defense report that "the vulnerability of Minuteman is a problem, but even if we did nothing about it, it would not be synonymous with the vulnerability of the United States, or even a strategic deterrent" (U.S. Department of Defense 1978, p. 64). Thus the administration could justify a cutback of 50 percent in the development budget of a follow-on missile, the MX, and postpone (in the event, until late 1979) the decision whether to go ahead with this missile, which by the late 1980s was to match the capability of those fourth-generation Soviet missiles deployed—starting in the mid-1970s—well over a decade earlier.

Some theorists promoted American nuclear inferiority even as a wholly positive policy. One member of President Carter's National Security Council (NSC) staff argued publicly against American superiority: "I suspect we would occasionally use it as a way of throwing our weight around in some very risky ways. . . . It is in the U.S. interest to allow the few remaining areas of strategic advantage to fade away" (cited by Lehman 1979). And one senior sovietologist at the U.S. State Department argued widely that if the Soviet Union were more militarily powerful than the United States the world would be safer; it then would not feel insecure and threatened, whence flowed the real danger. Finally, in a reaction that was to become generalized in some administration circles, two White House NSC staffers said "So what?" to the assertion that their policies would lead to Communist takeovers in the area of the Persian Gulf and along the oil lanes to Europe and America; they indeed, facetiously only in part, proclaimed (as noted elsewhere) the "So What Carter Doctrine of Foreign Policy" (see Thompson 1978, pp.63–64).

STRATEGY FROM WEAKNESS

The decade of the 1970s, a decade mostly of lost dreams and wishful thinking, ended with the hard punch of reality—the Christmas invasion of Afghanistan.

Who invited 40,000 Russian soldiers complete with their Quisling into Afghanistan? Answer: President Carter, the American congress and American opinion—and those American allies who have dared not believe, and have done little to remedy or reverse, the crumbling of America's willingness to exercise its power, or thus the *Economist* (5 January 1980, p. 7) put it. Those who had long seen Moscow's intentions as benign now hurried to insist that the Soviet Union had indeed done something dastardly, but that it was a wholly new leaf in their books. But those who had all along worried about the downward trend in American defense capabilities were not those learning new things about the Soviet Union as a result of the invasion.

The authors of the present study met a few days before the invasion with about a dozen other defense specialists and journalists (including some critics) at Belmont House in the Maryland countryside to discuss the first drafts of these chapters. The authors and most of the discussants assumed that a move of some sort, massive and definitive, would occur before long. Some of them were long on record on this point. The transcript, where Afghanistan is mentioned, could thus be used unedited. So the invasion could not have been a new leaf. All manner of precedent existed, from operations in Angola and Ethiopia, or from North and South Yemen where the Soviets had gained practice in assassinating presidents the year before. More worrisome, the invasion took place in a country near the Persian Gulf, cutting in half the mileage between Soviet-controlled forward bases and the gulf whose control so many of us had long been warning was the true goal of Soviet policy.

Although this book was planned and the discussion among its authors took place before the events which appeared to have settled the American public's debate on defense in favor of greater vigilance, its purpose remains the same. That is to provide within one cover the latest and best thinking on what our national security dilemma is, where we should look for solutions, and what sort of strategy we can adopt in service of a policy designed to rebuild Western confidence and strength. There are no certain answers, but we think we know the direction in which the nation must look, and we have tried to establish some benchmarks for performance against which it is already apparent that the current administration's performance falls far short.

Paul Nitze says herein that few have looked at the art of conducting strategy from weakness. "It is also true that if one looks at history, no country has emerged as being a great country that hasn't lived through periods of great weakness and shown that it can conduct strategy from weakness and recover." Recognizing where we are is our first responsibility. And then devising a strategy for extricating ourselves, the next. For what came out of our discussions at Belmont House—and what is underlined anew by every action of our national leaders—is the fact of the absence of a national strategy. We hope this book helps to lay out the issues involved in rebuilding a national strategy within the framework of prudent policy.

The direction, let it be clear, is not toward a pell-mell race to subordinate every question of policy to the need for stronger defense—that is to say, to neglect the diplomat while concentrating exclusively on the soldier. Nonetheless, because we have fallen so far behind in defense, the most urgent attention will have to be paid to constructing guns for the soldier and ships for the sailor—while thinking out what the balance in our overall national strategy should be— before the soldiers and sailors could conceivably be asked to fight. Our task must be to restore a strategic concept of peace and end our commitment to a peace secured only by continuing retreat.

2

ELMO R. ZUMWALT, JR.

Heritage of Weakness: An Assessment of the 1970s

Reversals in U.S.–USSR military balance since World War II. The Soviet buildup of strategic nuclear arms. Post-Vietnam apathy toward U.S. defense budgets. Tactical and conventional forces in Europe, Asia, and the Third World. The political advantages of growing Soviet strength. U.S. economic power. A national strategy is needed—now.

The central consensus of U.S. security policy is that national security and prosperity are tightly linked to the security and prosperity of Western Europe and Japan. After World War II the United States built a strategic nuclear deterrent, formed the North Atlantic Treaty Organization (NATO), allied itself with Japan and other western Pacific allies, and rebuilt Europe's and Japan's war-devastated economies. These policies were an immense success. Our strategic superiority and conventional capabilities to reinforce allies guaranteed the security of Western Europe and Japan, with the consequence that the world would soon witness the "economic miracles" of their recovery.

In the Third World, America's vast military, technological, and economic superiority was apparent. Deployed U.S. forces inhibited Soviet adventurism, promoted stability, and prevented the West's isolation. Economic cooperation with Western Europe and Japan helped to promote the smooth flow of trade and capital. An economically open world ensured mutual prosperity and linked the Third World to the West.

But by the 1970s these strengths had given way to weakness. The United States failed to match the Soviet Union's investments in military power. The Soviets achieved an exploitable nuclear superiority. Growing Soviet conventional and tactical nuclear forces now have the capability to overrun NATO and to cut sea lines of communication critical to the free world. The buildup of the Soviet Pacific Ocean fleet and the fortification of the Kurile Islands threaten Japan's security.

The Soviets' emerging capacity to project power on a global scale (including the skillful use of proxy forces) has made it much more difficult and costly for the United States to maintain stability in the Third World. Since Vietnam , the nation has been less willing to make the attempt to preserve stability. Yet the West remains dependent on imports of oil and other mineral resources. Instability in the Third World, then, is a clear and present threat to Western prosperity.

In short, both the security and prosperity of the industrialized democracies are hostage to the Soviet military
buildup and to increased Soviet activism in the Third World.
This chapter compares that buildup with what has happened
to U.S. military power and then assesses the economic and
political implications of the "balance" for the enduring competition with the Soviet Union.

ASSESSMENT OF THE U.S.–USSR MILITARY BALANCE

We must begin with a harsh truth: In the 1970s Soviet
defense outlays steadily increased while those of the United
States declined. It is difficult to estimate Soviet defense expenditures precisely, but serious estimates agree. The dollar
value of Soviet military expenditures now exceeds U.S. military spending by 25 to 50 percent (see Figure 1).

Between 1970 and 1978 the Soviet Union increased real
defense expenditures by at least 4 percent a year. Real U.S.
defense expenditures declined steadily from 1970 to 1977. In
the 1970s Soviet military expenditures totaled nearly 30 percent more than ours. Soviet procurement of strategic forces
was more than two and one-half times that of the United
States. Soviet general purpose force acquisitions exceeded
ours by 50 percent. These diverging trends in military spending have a predictably adverse impact when our military
strength is compared to that of the Soviet Union.[1]

Strategic Balance

The results are especially apparent in the strategic nuclear
balance. The Soviets drew abreast the United States in the
number of strategic launchers in 1971—a simple measure of

the strategic balance. They now surpass us, 2,582 against 2,141 (Figure 2).[2]

Figure 1
U.S. and Soviet Defense:
A Comparison of U.S. Outlays with Estimated
Dollar Costs of Soviet Activities

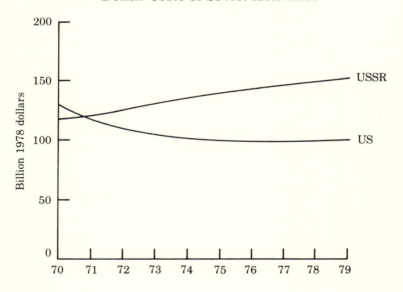

If SALT II (Strategic Arms Limitation Talks II) is ratified, the Soviet Union by 1985 will have, in comparison to the United States, twice the area destruction capability, twice the throw weight, thrice the megatonnage, and quintuple the ICBM/SLBM (intercontinental ballistic missile/sea-launched ballistic missile) hard target kill capability, plus at least equal accuracy. The United States may have an advantage in independently targeted warheads. But the Soviets are rapidly adding warheads and, according to the latest intelligence, they may have as many or more than the United States by 1985.

Figure 2
U.S./USSR Strategic Balance:
Total Strategic Launchers

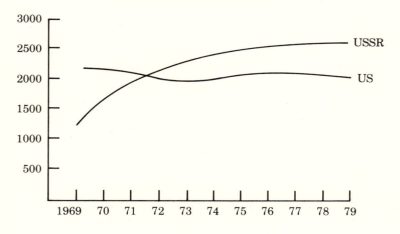

To the extent that our obsolescent B−52s can get off their bases and arrive close enough to launch their cruise missiles, to the extent those cruise missiles can penetrate to their targets through unconstrained Soviet air defenses, and to the extent no allowance is necessary for the offsetting capabilities of their Backfire bombers, we will have a continuing—in fact, growing—superiority in what is called delayed countermilitary potential. But this will not be sufficient to offset the other factors.

The United States has phased out most of its continental air defense capabilities. The Congress has forced the virtual deactivation of the U.S. antiballistic missile (ABM) defenses permitted under the ABM treaty. The U.S. Navy has never been permitted to ask for equipment, men, or funds for the purpose of developing antisubmarine warfare (ASW) capabilities designed to attack Soviet SLBMs.

The USSR has persistently put more emphasis on active defensive capabilities than has the United States. The Soviet Union has devoted a truly enormous effort to air defenses. It has deployed 12,000 surface-to-air missiles (SAMs) and approximately 2,700 interceptor fighters. It has deployed thousands of inter-netted air defense radars and ground-control-interceptor centers. It is deploying a new high capability mobile phased-array radar/missile system called the SAX–10. It has recently been reported that the SAX–10 is being deployed on surface ships, thus affording the Soviets the beginnings of a capability to deploy a forward barrier defense against our bomber aircraft.

The Soviet Union has maintained and somewhat improved those ABM capabilities it had earlier deployed in the Moscow area. It is significantly increasing the capabilities of its phased-array ABM "early warning" radars around the periphery of the USSR. This is permitted under the ABM treaty on the assumption that such a network, being close to the periphery, could be destroyed with limited effort in the event of war. It is also assumed that even more powerful radars in the Moscow area could, with greater effort, be destroyed. However, the large Soviet phased-array radar deployments, when coupled with the development of a transportable phased-array ABM radar and high-acceleration interceptor combination, could give the USSR a reasonably rapid breakout toward an important "damage limiting" ABM capability, particularly against U.S. SLBM reentry vehicles (RVs).

Even more important are the civil defense aspects of the problem. Many who have carefully studied the situation concur that a well-executed civil defense program—to evacuate most of the population of Moscow and Leningrad would take several days—can reduce fatalities by a factor of five to ten and can also substantially reduce industrial damage and the time necessary for economic recovery. There is now little doubt that the Soviet Union is working on civil defense much harder than was realized as recently as two years ago.

It was reported in 1979 that the executive branch would request an expansion of the U.S. civil defense program to include work to enable more rapid evaluation of our urban population in the event of a crisis. Approval of such a program could have been of major importance. Later, however, the president reversed his position. It should be noted, however, that our program, had it been approved, would have cost about one-tenth of what the executive branch estimates the Soviets are spending on civil defense.[3]

When one takes all factors into account, including the fact that the initiative is apt to be theirs—that their command, control, and wartime intelligence facilities are substantially harder and more diverse; that they have more and harder hard targets; that their active defenses and their civil defense preparations are substantially greater than ours—it is quite evident that strategic parity is slipping away from us and that the Soviets can be expected to achieve meaningful strategic superiority, probably by 1982 and most certainly by 1985, unless we take the most urgent steps to reverse current trends.

More complex measures of the strategic balance thus give us the same picture as Figure 2. The Soviets have been ahead since the early or mid-1970s and are getting further ahead.[4]

The higher megatonnage and increasing accuracy of Soviet warheads give the Soviets a significant counterforce against our land-based missiles. With this they will have the capability to launch a first strike capable of disarming America's land-based missile force, a reality that no strategic arms agreement will change (Nitze 1979b). The Soviets will achieve this capability in the early 1980s.

It is argued, of course, that despite the annihilation of our land-based missile force our deterrent would remain effective; that we would strike against Soviet cities by sea-based missiles and long-range bombers. But we must remember that Soviet strategy envisages warfighting. The Soviet leaders would be emboldened in confrontations with the United States by their calculation that the low average yield of our remaining weapons would render damage levels "acceptable." They believe that an effective civil defense plan (city evacuation, dispersal of industry, etc.) would limit casualties to 3 or 4 percent of their population. Though this figure is probably a bit low, the Soviets seem to believe it. The loss of our land-based missile force, the low average yield of our sea-based missile force, and a potentially low level of fallout (resulting from the U.S. decision in the 1960s to reduce the "continuing radiation" potential in exploded U.S. warheads) might well hold down Soviet casualties.

But the story with U.S. cities is much different. They would be exposed to a second strike by the Soviets' remaining land, sea, and air-launched strategic forces against which we have little or no defense. The higher megatonnage of the Soviet weapons (and their failure to reduce the "continuing radiation" levels of their exploded warheads) would guarantee horrendous American casualties. Thus, in a future crisis, a U.S. president may be faced with a stark alternative: strike first—to avoid loss of the land-based missiles but in a strike which would be incapable of destroying more than 65 percent of Soviet ICBMs and incapable of gaining poststrike strategic nuclear advantage—or yield without a fight.

How did we come to such a pass in such a vital military capability? There were faulty perceptions of the Soviet

Union and its strategic doctrine. We long failed to recognize that the Soviets aimed at an ability to fight and survive a war with strategic nuclear weapons. U.S. reliance on deterrence by an assumed "mutual assured destruction" also contributed, as did the mistaken notion that Soviet programs were mere reactions to ours. With these views, our leaders not unnaturally limited the size of our forces and slowed the development of new weapons. These mistakes were compounded by an unwillingness to devote sufficient resources to defense when other national problems demanded attention and while the Vietnam war and Watergate crises generated a public antipathy toward adequate defense budgets. Finally, the American arms control community sees strategic arms limits as an end; the Soviets see arms limits as a means of achieving nuclear superiority.

Tactical Nuclear Balance

This balance is particularly important in Europe. Tactical nuclear weapons are generally embedded in conventional forces, making it difficult to compare U.S. and Soviet tactical nuclear forces. Nevertheless, in 1979 the USSR, in comparison to NATO tactical nuclear weapons, had two to three times the number of theater nuclear systems, six times the area destructive potential, ten times the throw weight, and twenty-five times the megatonnage (Nitze 1979b). This balance, too, has been shifting against the United States.

Table 1 demonstrates the two- to three-fold advantage that the Warsaw Pact enjoys over NATO in the numbers of nuclear capable systems that could be employed in a European war. Table 1 also shows that the Warsaw Pact enjoys a more than 50 percent edge in the number of warheads available. These advantages are likely to grow if the Soviets continue to introduce rapidly the SS–20, a mobile intermediate range ballistic missile (IRBM) that can hit targets in Europe from the Soviet Union.

Table 1
U.S. and Soviet Theater Nuclear Systems in Europe

	USSR/Pact	U.S./NATO	Ratio: Pact to NATO
Delivery vehicles			
Missiles	1,213	326	3.72
Aircraft	4,151	1,679	2.47
Total	5,364	2,005	2.68
Tactical nuclear warheads			
Missiles	978	232	4.22
Aircraft	1,266	1,179	1.07
Total	2,244	2,411	1.59

Source: International Institute for Strategic Studies (1979, pp. 118–19). Figures exclude U.S. Navy Poseidon missiles, not a tactical system, which had to be taken off Soviet strategic targets in the early 1970s and directed against Warsaw Pact targets to partially relieve NATO's tactical nuclear defensive.

The December 1979 NATO decision to deploy 572 Pershing II and cruise missiles to Western Europe constitutes a minor political plus for NATO but does not redress NATO's tactical nuclear disadvantages.

Conventional Force Balance

Our inferior strategic and tactical nuclear forces are particularly worrisome in view of the increasing strength of Soviet conventional forces.

Striking the balance of conventional forces is difficult; nevertheless, the trends of the 1970s are clear—the Soviets have achieved conventional military superiority. During the 1970s the size of U.S. conventional forces declined steadily and our qualitative *advantages*, despite many technological developments on our side, declined as well. Meanwhile, most Soviet forces were growing impressively in size and capability.

The number of men in the armed forces is one measure that indicates overall conventional force capability. As Figure 3 shows, Soviet military manpower has grown steadily since the mid-1960s. Manpower strength in the United States exceeded that of the Soviets while we were engaged in Southeast Asia, but is now nearly 25 percent below the 1964 level. In 1979 Soviet forces numbered 1.6 million men more than ours—80 percent larger. This confers immense potential advantages. (The enormous military manpower of the People's Republic of China [PRC] is often cited as an offset to Soviet manpower advantages over NATO. But Moscow has added to its Warsaw Pact forces while compensating for PRC manpower along the Siberian border.)

To mold manpower into effective fighting forces requires deployable units, armed with appropriate weapons and provided with the necessary training, support, and leadership. These dimensions make the comparison of conventional forces difficult. But the charts of Figure 4 indicate the trends in the balance of general purpose force capabilities (Collins 1978).

In each of the main force categories—land forces, tactical air, and naval forces—the Soviets have some important advantages. Their deployable ground force is three times the size of ours. Similar comparisons of the equipment for ground forces such as tanks and artillery show large and growing Soviet advantages. Tactical air combat strengths

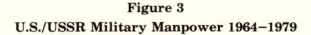

Figure 3
U.S./USSR Military Manpower 1964–1979

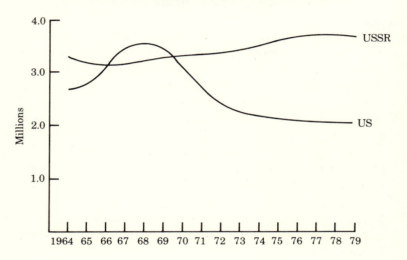

favor the Soviets by a two-to-one edge; only in sea-based tactical air does the United States have an advantage. Naval forces are even more difficult to compare. Submarine forces are shown in Figure 4 because of their importance in Soviet general purpose naval forces. They pose the most severe threat to our sea lines of communication. It is true that the United States has an overwhelming advantage in aircraft carriers and sea-based aviation, but the Soviets have an

Figure 4
Trends in U.S. and USSR General Purpose Forces

Deployable Ground Forces Manpower
(in thousands)

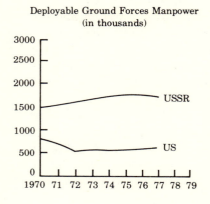

Combined Tactical Air
Combat Strength

Attack Submarines

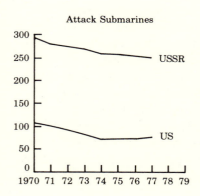

Strategic Airlift Aircraft

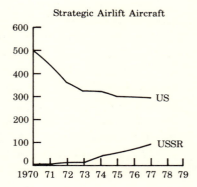

Source: Collins (1978).

overwhelming advantage in long-range land-based aviation with antiship cruise missiles—backed up with increasingly global access to client states' airfields. This advantage is further enhanced by the asymmetries of geography, which place most critical theaters (the Persian Gulf, in particular) close by Russia and far from the United States. And in their surface forces the Soviets outnumber us in warships and embarked cruise missiles. In my judgment, *the Soviet naval and air forces are clearly capable of gaining control of the Western Pacific and the Eastern Mediterranean in a fight with the United States.* U.S. control of the North Atlantic in a major war would be doubtful.

Note that the United States is still ahead in strategic airlift, reflecting a long-recognized need to be ready to support our allies overseas. Not shown is our clear advantage in amphibious and marine troops assault capability. But in another important component of mobility, merchant shipping, the United States is falling further and further behind the Soviets with each passing year.

These comparisons have stressed numbers of forces. Numbers do not tell the whole story, but they tell a vital one. They affect perceptions of U.S. strength and of commitment by political leaders and their constituencies around the world. And the perceptions relate to real advantages that larger forces provide. They can fight in several places at once. They can attack without lengthy and visible concentration of forces. They can saturate defenses. They can absorb losses and fight longer. Outcomes of war games, fleet exercises, and analytical calculations confirm that a conventional war at sea with the USSR would probably lead to our defeat.

Europe

On a smaller but more pertinent scale, the erosion of U.S. military strength is evident when comparing the East-West balance in Europe. In 1962 the total number of U.S. forces in

Europe was 434,000; the number is now about 300,000. On the other hand, the Soviet Union has increased the number of divisions in Eastern Europe from 26 in 1967 to 31 today, while adding some 25 divisions to the Chinese front. The Soviet divisions in Eastern Europe are also larger now than in 1967. Indeed, Warsaw Pact forces today enjoy a significant edge over NATO forces in men, tanks, and tactical aircraft. While NATO has been improving the quality of its forces, the Warsaw Pact has done more. Although NATO forces retain the edge in some areas like tactical aircraft, Soviet weapons in such other areas as surface-to-air missiles, some armored vehicles, and artillery are superior. However, the introduction of new weapons like precision-guided missiles and anti-tank and air-defense missiles may cut down the Warsaw Pact's advantage in tanks and planes. But these weapons alone are not NATO's salvation. Without adequate numbers, without adequate maneuver capability, without the ability to counterattack, with scandalously inadequate logistic support, NATO remains inferior. The balance in Europe has shifted against the West.

What practical options do these advantages in tactical nuclear and conventional forces in Europe open to the Soviets?

The first, most obvious, and most dangerous is a disarming first strike with theater nuclear weapons against Western Europe. Given the number, accuracy, and yield of those weapons they now possess, Soviet leaders might feel confident of achieving success while suffering only small losses themselves. They might calculate that they could destroy a very substantial portion of NATO's nuclear storage and delivery systems (including French and British weapons) along with most of NATO's reserve and conventional munitions. This result could be achieved with a sudden surprise attack. The experience of the Czech invasion in 1968 suggests that final Soviet preparations could be concealed from NATO even during a period of building international tensions. They could also attack NATO command and control centers, leaving Western Europe's cities more or less intact as hostages against an answering nuclear blow from NATO.

In this situation Soviet leaders could reasonably hope that the political will of NATO's European members would disintegrate. After all, NATO's options would be stark indeed: their nuclear counterforce capabilities would be devastated, their capacity to fight for long at the conventional level would be sharply reduced, and to mount countervalue nuclear strikes against the USSR would seem to invite suicide.

And what of the political will of the United States in the face of these Soviet actions? The Soviets would almost certainly assure the United States that their war objectives were confined to the European theater and back up that claim with an explicit threat to launch an all-out nuclear attack on the United States if we interfered. After all, they would explain, U.S. casualties in Europe had been purposely held to a minimum and the remaining Americans there were at their mercy. More fundamentally, the Soviets would explain that Europe was in the Soviet sphere and not that of the United States. "A nuclear war would be pointless; the United States would gain nothing and could lose everything," they would tell us.

These are not very attractive prospects for NATO, but they are one potential consequence of being on the short side of the military balance in Europe. The scenario can be varied, of course, and no doubt will be as Soviet conventional superiority continues to grow.

A second likelier option is a nonnuclear attack against NATO. The Soviets realize that a more desirable course would be to defeat NATO with a conventional force blitzkrieg *before* NATO political authorities could fire the alliance's nuclear arsenal. Recent changes in the structure of the Soviet forces in Europe are designed to achieve that objective while also improving the capacity of those forces to fight in a nuclear environment.

The third and likeliest option is the use of the threat (of their capabilities to carry out the first two options) to achieve, without fighting, the dissolution of NATO and Finlandization of Western Europe.

Asia

In the Pacific, naval forces weigh more heavily in the overall conventional force balance. The general picture of the naval balance is reflected in naval deployments to the Pacific: ours decline as theirs grow.

The Soviets have added at least one new major surface ship and one submarine to their Pacific force every year over the last decade. Their fleet now has 70 major combatants, 75 submarines (3 nuclear-powered), and more than 350 naval aircraft. With the addition of vertical takeoff lift (VTOL) aircraft carriers, the Soviets have added a whole new dimension to their naval warfare capabilities in the Pacific.

The U.S. Seventh Fleet, on the other hand, has declined by a third since 1970. Three years ago a carrier task group was withdrawn, leaving the fleet with about 45 ships: 2 carriers, 3 cruisers, 15 destroyers and frigates, 10 amphibious ships, 15 auxiliary ships, and about 4 submarines. Because of its responsibilities in both the western Pacific and the Indian Ocean, the fleet is stretched very thin. Today the United States could not meet simultaneous contingencies against Soviet-supported forces in the Persian Gulf and the Korean peninsula, for example. In the event of war in Europe, the need to transfer some U.S. ships from the Pacific to the Atlantic means that we would be unable to keep open the sea lanes to Japan.

Since naval forces provide our visible presence in Asia, the Soviet naval preponderance there raises serious questions. Japan may see itself potentially cut off from both the sources for its raw materials and the markets for its finished products. The enormity of the economic consequences of such a predicament could induce the Japanese to seek a separate accommodation with the Soviets.

Soviet naval superiority in Southeast Asia as a result of access to Vietnam's bases has flanked and weakened the PRC.

Third World

The Soviet Union began to project conventional military force in the Third World in the late 1960s employing growing airlift, naval, and sealift forces, military advisors, advanced logistic depots, and proxy forces. The Soviet Union clearly created an important new threat to Western interests during the 1970s—a capability to project military power into areas far from the Soviet Union to help accomplish Soviet foreign policy goals.

Medium-range and long-range transport aircraft have given the Soviets the ability to airlift arms, munitions, and personnel to distant parts of the globe. A new aircraft, the Il–76, substantially increases their airlift capability. The Soviets have also created three new airborne divisions, presumably for use in the Third World. The introduction of a new armored vehicle which can be dropped by parachute enhances the effectiveness of these airborne forces.

Soviet long-range naval aviation and worldwide client state bases have given Moscow a capability to cut sea lanes and to project power. The introduction of *Kiev*-class aircraft carriers has now added a capability to project sea-based air power. The size of the Soviet naval infantry has doubled in the past decade. The Soviets' newest amphibious ship is a large, fully capable, amphibious warfare unit. Further, the Soviets continue to add new roll on/roll off ships to their merchant fleet. These ships, now numbering over twenty, can deliver military equipment quickly and efficiently to underdeveloped ports or even over the beach. All Soviet merchant ships contribute to naval capabilities. In addition, the Soviets have been able to employ Cuba's armed forces as proxies.

In some areas of the globe, i.e., the eastern Mediterranean and northeast Asia, Soviet projection capabilities are now clearly superior to ours. In other areas their projection capabilities are still inferior to ours—if we have the will to employ them. If we examine the balance several hundred miles from the USSR: our marine corps far outnumbers the Soviet naval infantry; the transport capacity of the U.S. amphibious fleet is three times that of the Soviets; our thirteen large aircraft carriers outclass the Soviets' smaller VTOL versions; the U.S. Navy has a much greater capacity for sustaining combat at sea than the Soviet Navy; Soviet air transports have a shorter range and lift capability and cannot be refueled in flight; in terms of ton miles per day, Soviet airlift capacity is only half that of the United States.

If we were called upon to intervene in an area where Soviet land lines to the area are available—say, in the Persian Gulf—it would be a difficult matter. The secretary of defense has declared: "The United States would defend its oil interests in the Middle East if necessary."[5] However, there is no NATO plan to react to an interruption of the oil flow. Nor is NATO participation likely. So we would probably have to act alone. Our forces would have to move quickly and in sufficient numbers to overcome the Soviet Union's advantages in manpower and in geographical proximity. Given our limited force levels, we could not call on armored forces; they could not deploy quickly, and if they could their use would weaken our European force.

The proposed quick reaction force (still unfunded) of 100,000 men—if it comes into being at all—is likely to be composed of airborne troops and marines with tactical air support. A division's personnel could be airlifted to the Persian Gulf area in about a week. Unless their equipment is prepositioned at sea, it could take the marines as long as a

month to arrive by sea.[6] Offsetting this future U.S. reliance
on airlifted forces is the Soviet capability, flying from USSR
and Afghani airfields, to destroy all pro-U.S. facilities within
a 600-mile radius of Dhahran on the first day. Most important, there is good reason to doubt whether U.S. "light"
forces would be effective (even without Soviet force opposition) against heavily armed proxies in the Mideast (Iraq,
Syria), a region where war has been dominated by armored
units; some recent studies show Iraq conquering Kuwait and
Saudi Arabia without Soviet assistance—before the U.S.
Marines could be anywhere near the oil fields.

Summary

Clearly, the U.S. military capabilities declined during the
1970s. Just as clearly, Soviet power grew. Soviet force-building efforts have been long underway and now have an impressive momentum. The shift of the strategic balance to
Soviet superiority could be disastrous; dominance at the ultimate level of violence gives them freedom to act politically.
Their current European tactical nuclear forces and their
growing conventional forces there and in other regions allow
them to support friends and coerce enemies.

POLITICAL IMPACT OF SOVIET
MILITARY ADVANTAGES

If the military balance continues to shift against us in the
1980s, the political effects will be dire indeed. Who can
seriously question that the Soviet Union's increasing weight
in the military balance now threatens the cohesion of our
alliances with Western Europe and Japan? If current trends
are not reversed, is not America's implicit alliance with
China likely to be short-lived? Wouldn't Soviet activities in

the Third World become even more intense? One doesn't need any special insight to answer these questions. The evidence is all around us and new reports appear daily.

Europe

Some in Europe, like the eminent and thoughtful Frenchman Raymond Aron, described the Soviet Union as having the "most powerful army on the planet." The result, according to Aron (1979, p. 22), is that Europeans no longer put their trust

in NATO, in conventional forces, or in the American nuclear umbrella. They, rather, trust the prudence of the Bolsheviks, sensitive to the incalculable perils of massive attack against Western Europe, and to the importance of economic aid they receive from the West.

The Soviets have hardly been reluctant to exploit this attitude for their benefit. Brezhnev recently tried to intimidate the Western Europeans into dropping plans for modernizing NATO's theater-nuclear forces.

Brezhnev threatened NATO with warnings of unspecified "consequences" if such plans were implemented. To mask the threatening nature of the warnings, he announced a meaningless withdrawal to the Soviet Union of 20,000 Soviet troops and 1,000 tanks from positions in Eastern Europe. Although NATO has so far refused to be intimidated, Brezhnev's action demonstrates (and Dutch and Belgian reluctance to support the tactical nuclear reinforcement of NATO confirms its effectiveness) that the Soviets intend to exploit the fact of their military power to weaken NATO.

Asia

In Asia, the growing Soviet Pacific fleet and the declining size of the U.S. fleet are causing Japanese leaders to question American ability to defend their country. Political leaders in

Japan, South Korea, North Korea, and China perceive a "diminishing American presence and an increasing Soviet presence," according to Makota Momoi, a staff member of the Japanese government's Defense Research Institute. Momoi (*Los Angeles Times*, 9 April 1978, p. 1) claims that "The American commitment to Japan is now a limited commitment. It is no longer the unlimited commitment Japan once thought it was."

Just as the Soviets have attempted to exploit their military muscle to intimidate the Europeans, they have also pressured the Japanese. In response to Sino-Japanese negotiations for a peace treaty, the Soviets conducted naval exercises off Japan and fortified the Kurile Islands. In effect, Moscow was signaling the Japanese in no uncertain terms not to line up actively with the Chinese against the Soviet Union.

According to Momoi, the "diminishing U.S. presence and an increasing Soviet presence" in the Pacific is also being noted in China. Vice Premier Li Hsien Nien told the author in July 1977 that the PRC was concerned about U.S. indecisiveness and, in some quarters, "the Munich mentality."[7] Vice Premier Teng Hsiao-ping in January 1978 said that the U.S. military strength vis-à-vis the Soviet Union and our willingness to back our allies concerned China more than did normalization of relations. The United States did normalize ties with China and China's relations with the Soviet Union have worsened. However, the Chinese probably remain concerned that "advocates of appeasement" in the West "hope they can divert the Soviet Union to the East to free themselves from this Soviet peril at the expense of the security of other nations."[8] If the Chinese conclude that the United States lacks the ability or the will to oppose Moscow effectively, they may well be tempted to make amends with the Soviet Union. If this were to happen, not the least result could be the shift to the European theater of some or all of the forty-six Soviet divisions now on the Chinese border.

Third World

The Soviets have long been eager to exploit Third World crises for their own political benefit. An undercurrent of anti-Americanism continues to bubble up. Since 1967 they have employed their navy skillfully to produce positive benefits.[9] Now they are beginning to use airlift and other military capabilities as well. With each success they gain the opportunity for further activity. Cuban cooperation has given them wide options for projecting their power. Examples of Soviet activism in the Third World are legion: Afghanistan, Angola, Cambodia, Ethiopia, Iran, Iraq, Oman, Somalia, South-West Africa, Syria, Vietnam, Yemen, Zimbabwe-Rhodesia. These Soviet moves present the most immediate threat to U.S. interests.

Moscow's willingness and ability to exploit Third World crises have complicated U.S. efforts to maintain stability in the Third World. Washington's difficulties in maintaining strong ties with the oil-rich states of the Persian Gulf in face of Soviet activism are particularly evident. Soviet successes in Ethiopia and South Yemen have obviously weakened the confidence of Saudi Arabia and other Persian Gulf states in the U.S. willingness to protect them. As one Saudi minister put it (*New York Times*, 20 March 1979, p. A8), "Why is the United States stepping from one fiasco to another? In Ethiopia, in Somalia, in Afghanistan the United States left the field to the Russians without as much as an attempt to stop them." This, in turn, has complicated U.S. efforts to secure a Mideast peace settlement and to assure continuing access to Mideast oil. Feeling the need to accommodate pro-Soviet states like Iraq and Syria, the Saudis, after the peace treaty between Egypt and Israel, went along with much more stringent sanctions against Egypt than originally expected.

Soviet activism clearly complicated U.S. efforts to maintain stability in Iran. Soviet radio broadcasts helped inflame

popular feeling. In warning the United States against inter-
vening on behalf of the legal government of Iran, the Soviets
were flexing their military muscle in an attempt to intimidate the United States. Even though the United States did
not get involved in the Iranian revolution, Moscow's warnings and U.S. inaction represented a Soviet political victory
in the eyes of many in the Persian Gulf area. If we had
decided to become involved, we clearly would have had to
take Mr. Brezhnev's warnings into account. Soviet military
might gives such warnings a weight that prudent decision-
makers cannot ignore.

Soviet arms shipments to Syria, Iraq, Libya, and the
Palestine Liberation Organization (PLO) made it very
difficult for the United States to achieve further progress
toward a peace in the Mideast. Soviet actions in Afghanistan
have been especially disturbing. They gave direct military
support to revolutionaries in a bloody coup against an established government. They proved willing to intervene with
combat troops on behalf of a new Marxist government facing
popular unrest. The availability of this kind of support
means that the attitudes of governments like Libya and
Afghanistan toward accommodation and reconciliation will
be tough and unyielding at best. The emergence of a
neutral—and still less, a pro-Western—government becomes most unlikely.

In the Persian Gulf, the government of South Yemen gives
the Soviets a toehold on the Arabian peninsula. The South
Yemenis in the past have supported the Dhofar rebels
against the conservative government of Oman. In 1979
South Yemen launched a military attack on North Yemen,
acting as willing agent of Soviet subversion in the area. The
lesson was not lost on North Yemen; after accepting U.S.
arms to halt the invasion, it sought and won rapprochement
and arms from Moscow. Across the Red Sea, the Soviets support the Marxist-oriented military government of Ethiopia.
Although still attempting to suppress the guerrilla warfare

of the Eritreans and the Somalis, the Ethiopians give the Soviets a large pool of potential proxies for intervention in Africa and the Persian Gulf. For example, if revolutionaries operating out of South Yemen engineered the overthrow of the Saudi government, Ethiopian proxies with Soviet help could be used to sustain a hypothetical revolutionary government. (It was reported that a small number of Ethiopian troops were in the People's Democratic Republic of Yemen during the Yemeni border war in March 1979.)

In southern Africa, the Soviets have succeeded in complicating Western efforts to achieve a smooth transition from the white-dominated minority governments to majority rule. Through pro-Marxist governments like those of Mozambique and Angola, the Soviets have influenced the succession struggle with arms and training.[10] They have also encouraged the guerrilla struggle in Namibia (South-West Africa). So far, however, the Soviets do not appear eager to play a direct military role in these struggles. The Cubans are hampered by their inability to extricate themselves from Angola. At this time the Soviets probably lack a proper invitation, for the Africans remain wary of Soviet aims. The Soviets may also fear South African intervention in the Zimbabwe-Rhodesian struggle if they act. Therefore, the British government has had time to achieve what appears to be a transition to majority rule, though it may scarcely mark the end of the guerrilla war.

However, the ultimate problem for the West lies with the Republic of South Africa. South Africa's mineral resources are a great economic stake. South Africa's military capabilities and 20 percent white population probably guarantee the current regime's survival to the end of the century. (After all, the struggle in Zimbabwe-Rhodesia, with only a 5 percent white population, has been going on for fourteen years.) Western access to South Africa's mineral resources, however, may be impeded by a protracted guerrilla war which the Soviets are likely to support with arms aid and military training.

In Southeast Asia, the growing economies of Taiwan, South Korea, Hong Kong, Singapore, Malaysia, and Thailand have been an unexpected source of strength for the United States following the Vietnamese war. Their prosperity, however, is fragile. Dependent on exports for growth, they are vulnerable to dislocations in the international economy that might result from instability in the Persian Gulf. Social and political tensions generated by industrial growth would be exacerbated by a decline in growth. They could trigger unrest for the area's generally authoritarian regimes.

With the help of Vietnam, the Soviet Union could exploit such unrest and sustain any radical government that might emerge out of it. Vietnam has become the preeminent military power in Southeast Asia. However, it is now tied down by war in Cambodia and the threat of war with China. Vietnam also faces severe economic difficulties and political problems related to the absorption of South Vietnam. These many difficulties increase Vietnam's dependence on the Soviet Union for political, military, and economic support. Moscow thus might find the Vietnamese willing to support Soviet efforts to exploit political unrest in Southeast Asia. This fact and Vietnam's concern to destroy all Cambodian opposition could tempt Vietnam to invade Thailand.

In the Caribbean, the Soviets almost certainly will continue to probe U.S. reaction to incremental steps in their military presence in Cuba. The Soviets probably recognize, however, that their scope for action remains limited. They understand that Cuba is still an extraordinarily sensitive issue for the United States. They are therefore not likely to encourage too much Cuban activism in the Caribbean or Central America. More likely, Castro will confine his activities to subversion. Nevertheless, Cuba's acquisition of Soviet short-range transports is a worrisome development since it gives Castro the capacity to airlift troops to trouble spots.

Summary

The trends in the military balance have clearly given the Soviets an exploitable superiority, an advantage they have been using as a shield to protect their political and sublimited aggressions at every opportunity. Our primary alliances with NATO and Japan are long-established relationships with major industrial areas. They are now badly shaken but will not be easily destroyed. But the United States must show leadership in these relationships. They will not endure indefinitely if the United States proves unwilling or unable to reverse the perilous trends in military capabilities. Nor will they endure if the United States lacks the will to counter direct Soviet pressures on our allies or indirect pressures from Soviet adventurism or anti-American sentiments in the Third World.

The Soviet drive for dominance can be seen most clearly in Asia and Africa. Sometimes Soviet activism in these areas seems piecemeal and opportunistic. This appearance should not distract our attention from the brilliance of that very strategy — probing on many fronts with prompt exploitation of opportunities thus revealed. The result is a determined and long-term effort to reduce our ability and our will to resist Soviet expansion. The immediate focus is on the Persian Gulf, long a traditional Soviet interest and a prize of immense value in the East-West competition. The Soviets see success here as the best way to achieve their overriding strategic political goal of Finlandization of NATO. The next most important Soviet goals seem to be (1) to deny the West's access to the resources of Southern Africa, (2) to achieve a significant foothold in South America. The 1970s have seen major moves directly and through Cuban proxies.

So far these have not been answered directly by the Western alliance.

Though the Soviet's proximate goals are in the Third World, their ultimate goal is the subjugation of the free world. They aim to achieve this by threatening our access to raw materials and breaking down our alliance. They have vast military capabilities, but they threaten us more by indirection and subversion than by direct attack. Consequently the political effects of the changing military balance become of paramount importance.

ECONOMIC ASSESSMENT

The military and political developments of the 1970s illustrate the nature of the struggle between the United States and the Soviet Union. The fundamental rivalry is, so far, an indirect one whose end is not in sight. In this competition the United States and the Soviet Union invest economic power in military forces for global political effect.

To assess staying power in this unending competition, it is necessary to examine economic strengths and weaknesses. Can the massive Soviet efforts of the 1970s be sustained in the 1980s? Are higher U.S. military expenditures economically supportable? The answers to these questions depend on many factors—resources, technology, economic organization, and the willingness to apply economic power to national security purposes.

Economic strength is the United States' great advantage. If we can pull ourselves together and apply our economic strength appropriately, we can reverse the trends of the 1970s. This will require not only renewed military strength, but coordinated economic and diplomatic moves as well.

Economic Strength

The best way to gauge the strength of a nation's economy is to evaluate its total production, called its gross national product (GNP). By this measure, the U.S. economy is the largest in the world; the Soviets are second, well ahead of Japan. Over the long haul, the Soviets have been closing the gap. Soviet GNP in 1955 was 40 percent of ours; by 1965 it was half ours; today Soviet GNP is about 60 percent of U.S. GNP (Figure 5).

The implication of this narrowing gap is that the Soviet economy has been the faster growing. Soviet economic growth exceeded ours throughout the 1950s and 1960s. By the late 1970s, however, the U.S. economy was growing at a slightly faster rate. Both nations, though, faced a slowdown in the growth.

These aggregate differences in GNP conceal some important details. First, in the United States about 70 percent of output goes to consumption; in the Soviet Union just over 50 percent is consumed. Second, the Soviets have been allocating about 30 percent of their output to investment while investment in the United States uses only 15 to 17 percent of GNP. As a result, the amount the Soviets invest is greater than U.S. investment in recent years. Finally, the United States devotes a much smaller share of its total output to defense—5 percent versus about 15 percent for the Soviet Union.

Soviet Economic Potential

The slowdown in Soviet growth reflects serious economic problems. Earlier rapid growth was fueled by Russia's vast natural resources. But the costs of natural resources have been rising, the best sources have been used up, and more remote supplies must be developed. Energy costs are rising and the Soviets face serious energy problems in the 1980s. Agriculture continues to lag. The Soviet labor force cannot

Figure 5

U.S./USSR: Trends in Relative Size of GNP

(Soviet GNP as percent of U.S. GNP)

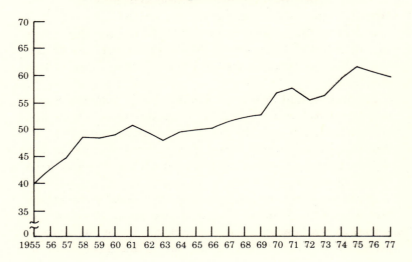

Source: Edwards, Huges, and Noren (1979, p. 383).

be expanded further; well over 90 percent of the working age population is employed and the size of the young adult population will decline in the 1980s. As a consequence of all this, productivity has declined and growth has slowed. The Soviet system seems unable to put new technology to use to alleviate these problems. Soviet economic growth is likely to slow further in the 1980s.

On top of this, Soviet economic managers are pressed to provide more consumer goods. A Soviet citizen consumes less than half the goods and services a U.S. citizen does. But though more resources have been put into consumption programs, the results have been disappointing; no significant increase in the availability of consumer goods has been achieved.

Given these economic problems, can the Soviets sustain the momentum of the military programs in the 1980s? A "command economy" such as the Soviet Union will produce what its leaders demand. Soviet leaders want "guns, butter, and growth," but butter clearly takes a back seat to guns and growth. Soviet leaders exert enough control over Soviet society to maintain those priorities in spite of consumer pressures.[11]

Soviet management skill may be weak, but the country's leaders remain determined. There is no sign that the Soviet drive for world supremacy is abating nor is there evidence of slackening in the efforts of Soviet defense industries. The Soviets have long borne the burden of a defense establishment that takes a share of output two to three times larger than that of the United States. Official forecasts predict that Soviet defense spending will continue to increase in real terms:

Soviet defense spending—and spending for military procurement in particular—will continue to increase in real terms at least through 1985. . . .

[Moreover,] we project a continuing across-the-board improvement in force capabilities as new, costly weapon systems are introduced.

These will include new land- and sea-based strategic missiles, tactical and air defense aircraft and missiles, ground forces armaments, and general purpose naval ships. . . .

We think it unlikely that economic problems will force the Soviets to reverse their commitment to continuing improvement in their military forces.[12]

There is no reason to doubt the accuracy of this assessment. We cannot count on Soviet economic problems to reduce the threat to our security. We must do that ourselves.

U.S. Economic Potential

The United States emerged from World War II with its industry intact and it dominated the world economy for twenty-five years. American generosity contributed to our leadership, but most of our influence flowed from the diversity and the technical superiority of the products and services that poured forth from American industry.

Our economic superiority began to erode in the 1970s. Improvement in labor productivity virtually disappeared and economic growth began to slow. Efficient competitors appeared in the international scene. Inflation and unemployment became chronic problems that economic management seems unable to overcome.

Increasing dependence on foreign oil underlined the erosion of U.S. economic power during the 1970s. Our inability to put a coherent policy into effect leaves open a major economic vulnerability, one that our enemies are already exploiting. We are now—and for the unforeseeable future will continue to be—vulnerable to the embargo weapon.

This vulnerability is not limited to oil, though that is the weakest point. We also import a high proportion of other raw materials—aluminum, chromium, cobalt, manganese, nickel, tin, and titanium, for example. Access to these raw materials—at reasonable prices—is necessary to keep our industrial economy functioning.

To preserve our economic strength, we must insure our access to the energy and minerals of the Third World. To accomplish this requires that we contain Soviet military presence and political activism there. This calls not only for larger U.S. military forces, but also for the will to employ them when our interests are being challenged. If we are going to acquire and operate larger forces—and we must—we shall need to devote a larger share of our nation's economic output to national security programs.

Can we do so? We have in the past, and we can do so again. The proportion of GNP devoted to defense has fallen steadily (Table 2). The defense outlay in the 1980 budget is less than 5 percent of GNP for the first time since before the Korean War. And it is a smaller portion of the federal budget than at any time since Pearl Harbor.

Table 2
Proportion of GNP Allocated to U.S. Defense

Year	Defense as Percent of GNP
1964	8.2
1968	9.3
1975	6.0
1980	4.9
1984 (projected)	4.7

The Soviets recognize the power of our economy. They know that if we are aroused we have the capacity to regain military superiority. They recognize that as a great threat to their drive for world power. And so they proceed accordingly. They probe and push and stall and negotiate and feed our delusions. They move cautiously so as not to push America into rearmament. We must recognize a more subtle threat and arm against it.

If the proportion of GNP allocated to national defense could be set at a pre–1975 level—7 percent—about $50 billion more would be available to meet the vital military needs detailed elsewhere in this volume. This would clearly be a good investment. It would yield a high return in protection for our citizens and our interests. The military capabilities acquired would pay off in more certain access to the raw materials our economy needs. But, most important of all, a substantial boost in defense spending would signal our allies or enemies alike that the United States has the staying power for a long conflict.

CONCLUSION

As the Chinese curse would have it, the 1980s promise "interesting times." The trends in nuclear and conventional forces are moving against the United States. The shift in military power towards the Soviet Union threatens to weaken our alliances with Western Europe and Japan. It has also encouraged Soviet adventurism in the Third World, where we have vital political and economic stakes.

Indeed, it is in the Third World where the danger is most immediate. For the time being, the United States is dependent on petroleum and other mineral resources in Third World regions. Our allies in Western Europe and Japan are even more dependent. Soviet adventurism in Southern

Africa—and especially in the Persian Gulf area—threatens our access to those resources. This activism may well grow as Soviet economic difficulties increase in the 1980s.

In the coming decade, leadership in the Soviet Union will pass to a new generation. This generation may well be less cautious and even more impressed with Soviet power than Moscow's present leadership. The Soviet Union's new leaders may be tempted to use their military power directly or through intimidation to gain greater access to Mideast oil resources in order to ease energy shortages at home.

In doing so they might underestimate our will and capacity to resist such a direct threat to the West's security and prosperity and thereby precipitate a general conflict. Or our own perception of our weakness might make deterrence or resistance seem futile. If so, our allies may see no choice except accommodation with the Soviet Union. Western economic cooperation and economic growth would collapse into cutthroat competition. A new dark age, presided over by the Soviet Union, would have begun.

II

Quick Fixes

3

FRED CHARLES IKLÉ

Preparing for Industrial Mobilization: The First Step toward Full Strength

The U.S.–USSR gap in military investment. Possibilities of changing the present trends in defense spending. Reasons behind the neglect of U.S. military potential—economic strength, a "short war," expansion possibilities. Improving the nation's capability for industrial mobilization.

Economic instability caused by deficit spending constitutes a much greater threat from within to both the security and survival of our liberties than does the military threat of communism from without.

> Senator John McClellan in May 1950, when the defense budget amounted to 4.8 percent of GNP.

To me, the greatest threat to our national security today is not the condition of our defense establishment and is not those threats which we can perceive from abroad. The greatest threat to our national security is inflation.

> Senator Edmund Muskie in September 1979, when the defense budget amounted to 4.9 percent of GNP.

For more than a decade the Soviet Union has gained militarily in relation to the United States—not only in nearly every category of armaments, but also in the geography of military power by acquiring outposts and transit rights throughout the world. Some years ago these trends were grimly argued among defense specialists. But more recently they have become widely reported to the general public—in the measured statements of our secretary of defense, in congressional hearings, in cover stories of mass circulation, in weeklies, on television.

Recent events in the Persian Gulf have further stimulated public concern and have even awakened the Carter administration to acknowledge the Soviet threat. Nonetheless, the American body politic at this time apparently is not choosing a defense policy that would arrest the continuing decline in our relative military strength. Moreover, no major effort is visible in either the executive branch or the legislative branch of the U.S. government to close the U.S.–Soviet gap in military investment, let alone to recover some of the lost ground.

WHILE PRESENT TRENDS CONTINUE

A somewhat obscure mixture of personal attitudes and political motivations in this country account today for what might be called a decision by default, an implicit consensus not to change the trends of the continuing decline in America's relative power. The legacy of Vietnam and the turbulent 1970s, concern over inflation and high taxes, the seeming remoteness of military statistics which (though not necessarily disputed) do not seem to impact on our daily lives, and the generally optimistic view about the military balance reflected by the commander in chief—all these factors combine today to make unlikely an increase in our defense effort large enough to close the U.S.–Soviet gap in military investment. Hence, short of some precipitating event that would lead to a new political consensus, the arithmetic of the arms balance will get worse before it gets better. At this time, one cannot predict whether the 1980 elections, in and by themselves, might produce a sufficient change.

Let us look at the arithmetic for a moment. Let us assume that the pro-defense mood in Congress becomes somewhat stronger than today so that, rather than the 3 to 5 percent increase debated in 1979/1980, a cumulative 10 percent real increase in the defense budget will be voted on each year. If we further assume that only 1 percent of this increase would be added to personnel and operations and maintenance (O&M) expenditures, our military investment would grow at a 9 percent annual compound rate. If this trend continued for ten years, our annual military investment by 1990 would be 2.4 times larger than today. According to the Central Intelligence Agency (CIA) estimates, the Soviets are now spending twice as much on military investment as we and are increasing their defense expenditures by 4 percent annually. Let us assume the optimists are right in that Soviet military investment will taper off, increasing by only 2 percent annually—despite our own increasing effort. If these trends obtained, the Russians in 1990 would still spend slightly more than we to buy new arms.

In other words, even with optimistic assumptions about changes in present trends, the gap in military investment in favor of the Russians would not be closed for another ten years. Throughout the 1980s the Soviet Union would continue to gain in ready military power relative to the United States. Such a development is bound to result in a major crisis.

HOW PRESENT TRENDS MIGHT CHANGE

The present level of U.S. defense spending, relative to several economic time series, is very low. It is at the lowest point since fiscal year (FY) 1940 as a percent of all public spending and at the lowest point since 1947–1948 as a percent of gross national product (GNP). Hence, given the necessary political decision, our defense spending could increase substantially. At the peak after the North Korean attack it was three times higher than today relative to GNP; at the World War II peak it was nine times higher than today.

What kind of crises might provoke the political decision for such a massive expansion of our defense effort, yet leave the United States with sufficient economic and industrial assets to undertake the expansion?

A nuclear attack on targets in the United States, even if designed as a counterforce strike, would probably make it physically impossible to organize and carry out a substantial defense expansion. Moreover, the Soviets might be able to use their residual nuclear strength to prevent any large-scale mobilization effort. To prevent such a nuclear attack, our deterrent forces must be ready. Mobilization would come too late.

But there are many possible crises that could provoke a major defense expansion in the United States. If adequate in scope and timing, moreover, such an expansion could provide the means to regain lost ground and to restore the peace. Broadly speaking, three types of crises could provide the provocation for a massive expansion in U.S. defense production:

(1) *A dramatic realization that the Soviet Union has stepped up the arms buildup; for example, an open abrogation of the anti-ballistic missile (ABM) treaty.*   In the 1930s the German arms buildup led to a gradual but substantial increase in British defense expenditures from 15 percent of government expenditures in 1935 to 43 percent in 1939; but the last step-up was reached in response to the violation of the Munich agreement. In 1937, the year that Neville Chamberlain became prime minister, British defense spending reached the same percentage of government outlays that it now absorbs in the United States.

(2) *Local Soviet-supported aggression, without major fighting between U.S. and Soviet forces.*   The example of this contingency is, of course, the North Korean attack in 1950. That triggering event had a double impact. On the one hand, our involvement in the Korean war required troops and materiel; on the other hand, the provocative nature of the attack led to a sudden change in the American perception of the global Soviet military threat.

When the Chinese entered the Korean war, in November 1950 the Truman administration and Congress came to see the strengthening of our global military capability as even more important than at the beginning of the Korean war. The second Supplemental Defense Bill in December 1950, which added another $18 billion to the defense budget and the Atomic Energy Commission ($55 billion in current dollars), served not just the needs of the troops in Korea. Moreover, the expansion also went beyond the objective of building up ready forces worldwide. It was seen instead as a way of building up the industrial mobilization capability for a *future* still larger expansion in the event we should have to fight what was then called World War III.

The contrast with our arms programs during the war in Vietnam is instructive. During the decade following the outbreak of the Korean war we steadily improved our global military posture; during the Vietnam decade we permitted it to decline. Among the factors that account for this difference, one is worth noting here. Prior to the Korean war high-level government studies (the NSC–68 exercise) concluded that U.S. military strength was inadequate and that a large U.S. buildup was needed across the board. By contrast, during the years when the Vietnam war began to heat up, the administration and Congress predominantly held the view that our global military posture—in particular, our strategic forces—was sufficient but that we had to shift military strength to fight Khrushchev's "wars of liberation." In short, the predispositions prior to Korea favored an expansion; hence the sudden North Korean attack could serve as the catalyst. The predispositions in the early phase of our involvement in Vietnam favored a contraction of our defense effort. The requirements for our forces in Vietnam thus were in part met by curtailing our strategic program and by drawing down other U.S. forces.

With today's deep and widespread concern about the global military balance, the preconditions might well exist for a political decision rapidly to expand. The predisposition in the United States for a massive expansion of the defense effort may well have been strengthened late in 1979 by the two dramatic crises in the Middle East: the seizure of the American embassy in Iran and the Soviet invasion of Afghanistan that began on Christmas Day. But as of January 1980 it appears that the invasion of Afghanistan will not have caused a political decision for a substantial increase in the defense effort. There are at least two obvious differences with the attack on North Korea: (1) the American presence and role in Afghanistan has been considerably less significant than it was in South Korea prior to the 1950 attack; (2) in Afghanistan, Soviet influence was increased stepwise (it was already substantial prior to the Christmas Day invasion), but on the Korean peninsula the communists had been completely excluded from the southern half.

(3) *A major conventional war involving U.S. and Soviet forces.* The extraordinarily successful mobilization after the attack on Pearl Harbor was greatly facilitated by the two years of partial mobilization that preceded it (in response to British arms purchases, lend and lease, and anticipatory measures by the Roosevelt administration). Today our European allies vigorously reject the notion that a post-attack industrial mobilization could help overcome an initial defeat in a major North Atlantic Treaty Organization (NATO) contingency. They fear deterrence of a conventional attack would be weakened by anything that contradicted the present declaratory posture of a short-term conventional defense backed up by the threat of nuclear escalation.

A Soviet planner, however, may look differently at the risks. To him, the recent growth in Soviet nuclear strength may promise either successful deterrence of any nuclear escalation by NATO or escalation dominance for the Soviet Union. By contrast, the prospect that the United States would launch an all-out mobilization, possibly in concert with Japan and China, might seem to jeopardize the gains of territorial conquests in continental Western Europe.

CURRENT NEGLECT OF OUR INDUSTRIAL MOBILIZATION CAPABILITY

The case for examining and improving America's capability

massively to expand defense production is lost between two extreme assumptions. Either it is assumed that the greater strength of our economy could unquestionably be marshalled to redress any serious military imbalance should "détente" break down or should arms control agreements be violated; or it is assumed that "the war" (any large war?) would start so suddenly and end so quickly—resulting either in our total destruction or in a new era of peace and stability—that the mobilization of our industrial strength would come too late. And even though these assumptions are contradictory, they are often found together.

The first assumption reflects an optimistic bias. It takes for granted that the economy and industrial assets of the United States (or of the Western alliance as a whole) could make up for any possible military weaknesses on our side, since the present size and future potential of our economic assets exceed those of the Soviet empire. In this view, our nation's economic strength is often regarded as an insurance against the breakdown of détente. In the hearings on Strategic Arms Limitation Talks (SALT), for instance, when skeptical senators worried about the possibility that the Soviets might violate the agreement, defenders of the treaty argued that a significant violation would be discovered soon enough for the United States to react and that the Soviets would have to fear—and would, in the end, lose—an all-out arms race that they thus provoked.

The notion that our economic potential, in the last resort, will help preserve the peace is a comforting thought. It must account in part for the relaxed attitude of many in the administration and in Congress toward the continuing discrepancy between the defense effort of the United States and the military buildup of the Soviet Union. Yet despite the importance of this idea, it is rarely fully articulated, much less seriously studied.

The second reason for neglecting the massive military potential of the American economy lies in a peculiar habit of thinking that has become common among our defense planners. It is the habit of assuming a "short war." Evidently our defense planning takes seriously the assumption that our forces must be able to fight a nonnuclear war against Soviet forces (or against a middle-sized power backed by the Soviets), since about three-quarters of our defense budget are devoted to such a contingency. Yet according to present planning and preparations we would run out of supplies before stepped-up defense production could reach the front lines. So what could be done about this gap between existing reserves and new production?

In the past our military planners would have answered that our superior strategic forces would come into play well before our supplies were exhausted. Our nuclear superiority would either help us end the war on satisfactory terms or, failing that, would destroy the aggressor. Hence, when this view of the world still seemed to make sense, we could reason with ourselves that our supplies for a conventional war in Europe did not have to last till new production could meet the needs of our troops. Our conventional defense had to create a "pause" only, a "firebreak" until the Soviet Union would be forced to retreat for fear of nuclear war.

But for the coming era when Soviet nuclear forces will be superior, what will happen when our conventional forces run out of supplies? In the Pentagon this question lies buried under mountains of studies of the "short war," a conventional war that begins with only a few weeks or months of warning and ends in sixty or ninety days. Based on these planning assumptions, it is concluded that the mobilization of American industry would come too late; the war would have ended before Detroit could mass-produce new tanks. One is reminded of a bridge builder whose bridge fails to span the river. When asked whether he does not need additional timbers to complete the job, he answers that none are needed since he is planning for a "short bridge."

How is it possible that "short war" planning could result in such a starkly illogical neglect of our industrial mobilization capacity? The answer probably lies in the changed strategic context. Part of our military thinking simply has not yet adapted to our loss of strategic superiority. The notion seems to linger in the back of our minds that when push comes to shove in a conventional war, the "nuclear deterrent" would somehow bail us out. This notion is particularly inappropriate today for a conflict in the Middle East, in which U.S. forces would be outgunned by superior Soviet conventional strength.

As our forces would be pushed into retreat, surely we would neither initiate nuclear Armageddon nor capitulate. Instead, the president would ask Congress to increase the defense budget perhaps by 200 percent, just as Harry Truman did in the summer of 1950 when our forces in Korea were pushed back to a narrow foothold at the port of Pusan. And Congress would almost certainly go along, if it did not urge an even larger defense expansion on the president.

OUR CAPABILITY TO EXPAND DEFENSE PRODUCTION

A national decision for a two-fold or several-fold increase in our defense effort seems exceedingly unlikely short of a dramatic external event that would trigger a reassessment of the external threat and would change beliefs in Congress and the media as to what the nation can and should afford for defense. Both in 1941 and in 1950 the triggering event was preceded by a public debate about the need for an increased defense effort. In 1949–1950 popular sentiment ran strongly in favor of increasing defense—the North Korean attack acted like a crystal falling into a saturate solution.

For any major program of defense expansion we have to consider the options open to the Soviet Union to counter our program. To begin with, the Soviets might accelerate their own arms buildup (unless such acceleration has already occurred and has triggered our expansion). Particularly dangerous would be a program enhancing the potential for strategic attack, such as an ABM system. Furthermore, the Soviets might try to impede our efforts to expand defense production by interrupting scarce supplies in the Third World through sabotage or through political pressure on supplier countries.

Unfortunately, the Soviets today would have a head start in expanding arms production. They have far more hot production lines and a larger defense plant. Under present conditions it might take the United States up to two years of an all-out effort to begin to pull ahead in an industrial "mobilization race."

The U.S. capability rapidly to expand defense production, however, could be substantially improved, even within the present budgetary constraints that Congress prefers to maintain for national security outlays. A program to enhance our latent capability for industrial mobilization would have several components.

Administrative and Legal Preparations

First, as the driving motor there has to be an administrative and legal structure. Ideally, this structure should be in place "the morning after" the emergency began—that is to say, as soon as a majority in Congress is agreed that the country urgently must expand its defense production. In 1941, when that decision was reached by 8 December, mobilization could proceed as rapidly as it did because of the trial and error period that preceded it. For two years the Roosevelt administration had experimented with different schemes for administering priorities and allocating scarce resources.

Similarly, the Korean expansion was facilitated by assets left from World War II; not only standby plants and equipment, but also a cadre of managers experienced in industrial mobilization.

A key question for the administrative structure for an industrial mobilization period is the mechanism chosen to allocate economic resources. What mix of monetary incentives, mandatory priorities, price controls, and rationing should be chosen to shift resources to defense production? The Defense Production Act of 1950, as amended, and the National Emergencies Act of 1976 would cover some of the legal requirements, but they do not go far enough. Regulatory restrictions and environmental and health laws would have to be relaxed or suspended to permit a faster expansion in industrial production. The mobilization efforts of World War II and the Korean war did not have to contend with impact statements for new plant construction, with present severe air pollution and water discharge standards, and with many of the regulations affecting hiring and recruiting. The more cohesive the nation's political reaction and the greater its sense of urgency, the more far-reaching could be the special legal and administrative arrangements to enhance the country's capacity to mobilize.

Plants, Tools, and Prototypes

Standby preparations for production facilities present considerable difficulties. They can absorb a lot of money and easily become obsolescent. Presently, some $200 million are being spent annually on the Planned Production Program of the Department of Defense. But this program, according to several studies, is badly out-of-date.

Imaginative institutional incentives are needed to provide for greater industrial readiness, both through rapid expansion of defense industries and through the conversion of civilian industry. One suggestion is to develop special prototypes of weapons systems that could be more easily mass produced than the systems appropriate for the much lower present defense budgets.

Raw Materials and Manpower

Several West European countries are far ahead of the United States in providing emergency stockpiles for their industry. Instead of relying exclusively on government stockpiles, these countries require or encourage industry to maintain their own stockpiles. This policy has several advantages: it is cheaper, more easily updated, and tends to locate the stockpiles where they will be needed. Especially for oil, current U.S. policy fails to make the most of privately held stockpiles, the volume of which exceeds by far the strategic petroleum reserve.

Manpower might not be a critical problem, except for special skills. By expanding to the maximum number of shifts, defense industry could use the same plants and skilled cadres to roughly double production. Since the outbreak of the Korean war, the percentage of the labor force in manufacturing has declined from 33.7 percent to 23.6 percent in 1975. This might mean a greater elasticity of supply, allowing for the expansion of manufacturing at the expense of service industry.

A STRATEGY BUILDING ON THE U.S. POTENTIAL FOR DEFENSE EXPANSION

With a substantially higher defense budget, the appropriate national strategy would be different than with the present budget. New missions would become possible; different weapon systems could be produced. For example, various anti-ballistic missile systems would become feasible. Outer space systems might become more important. Continental air defense might be revived. Part of the preparations to improve our potential for expansion, therefore, must consist of the development of new strategies that would make sense for a three-fold, five-fold, or still higher level of effort.

Since the contingency that would provoke the defense expansion cannot be predicted, flexible strategic concepts for the expansion are desirable. In some situations we may want to emphasize conventional force expansion; in others, nuclear strategic. Also, the strategic concepts should be flexible enough to exploit new opportunities — e.g., new technology, unanticipated foreign support, newly discovered enemy weaknesses.

Advance work on alternative strategic concepts for an expanded defense effort can guide the preparedness program for industry, inspire new research and development, and save time if and when the emergency arises. The expansion after June 1950 was speeded up, apparently because of the prior conceptual work on NSC–68.

A vastly improved capability to expand defense production should become part and parcel of our overall security policy. It would not only help reduce the time needed for industrial mobilization in an all-out emergency, but would make Soviet leaders more cautious about initiatives that could trigger our expansion. Improving our expansion capability is a first step we could take now to regain the necessary military strength for a major crisis. Politically it is probably a more realistic step today than an immediate increase in the defense budget that would be large enough to close the military investment gap between us and the Russians.

4

GEOFFREY T. H. KEMP

Defense Innovation and Geopolitics: From the Persian Gulf to Outer Space

The need for access to scarce resources. U.S. military inadequacies. The linkage between strategic NATO theaters. India's position. Vacillation and indecision in U.S. foreign and arms transfer policies. Technological expansion into the oceans, the polar regions, and outer space. The use of imaginative planning in long-term security policies.

It is now well established that one of the most serious threats to Western security is the possibility that access to Persian Gulf oil will be restricted in the decade ahead. In the wake of the Soviet invasion of Afghanistan and the U.S. crisis with Iran over the kidnapping of fifty American hostages, the dire consequences of a cutoff or major decline in this source of supply have become apparent even to the most dedicated proponents of détente. By the early months of 1980 the Carter administration thus began, belatedly, to talk about the military implications of the crisis and to propose some remedies for dealing with the problem.

This chapter addresses the question of strategic access to scarce resources and of the need for *any* U.S. administration to act decisively in both the short- and long-term time frames to ensure that the United States and its Western allies take drastic steps to reduce their dependency upon those insecure overseas resources vital to industrial survival. In the short run there are several innovative policies an administration should adopt beyond increasing the size, configuration, and readiness of U.S. rapid deployment forces. Imaginative approaches towards alliance responsibilities, Western relations with Middle East and West Asian countries, and a new, more dynamic, arms transfer policy can help to overcome some of the inherent disadvantages the West faces in challenging the Soviet and radical threats. However, in the long run the United States should not plan on relying upon geographically remote, inherently insecure sources for raw materials but should now seek to develop radical new geopolitical approaches to the resource question. This will mean exploiting to a much greater extent the one remaining military advantage the Western world has over the Soviet Union—innovative, advanced technology.

ALLIED RESPONSIBILITIES AND POWER PROJECTION TO THE PERSIAN GULF

Over the past ten years a series of events have occurred which have made it more difficult for the United States and the Western powers to project military forces into the Persian Gulf. The reasons for this have to do with the growth of Soviet power projection and the growth of the military capabilities of local states, some equipped with sophisticated armaments (i.e., Syria, Iraq). A third, more negative reason has to do with the decline of U.S. and allied base rights in Africa, the Middle East, and Southeast Asia, rights which are essential if a serious military presence in the gulf is to be considered.

While there is little we can do to prevent the growth of Soviet power projection and the rearmament and military buildup of local powers, there are things we can do to increase our own capabilities to overcome some of these constraints. The decision to go ahead with the rapid deployment force is the most obvious short-term military solution. Yet analysis of the requirements for a rapid deployment force point to the discrepancy between our ability to assemble a force to deter local conflict in peacetime or crisis and our ability to field military forces capable of deterring—and if necessary, fighting—the Soviet Union. In both the peacetime and wartime scenarios, two serious constraints have emerged irrespective of whether we have combat forces: the inadequacy of our airlift and sealift and the inadequacy of our logistical infrastructure and basing facilities.

If we assume worst-case scenarios, i.e., Soviet invasion of Pakistan or military intervention in the Persian Gulf, then a gloomy future looms on the horizon. Furthermore, there is little we can do about the worst case in the short run, even if all the programs currently being requested by the administration are forthcoming (e.g., a new CX long-range transport aircraft and new logistics ships to carry equipment for marine forces). One cannot build a new fleet of airplanes in two years. Neither can we arm and rely upon the remaining pillar of our Persian Gulf policy—namely, Saudi Arabia—to the point where its military forces can do the job for us.

We must reassess radically our strategic concepts and the relationship between our interests in such theaters as the Persian Gulf and the southern flanks of NATO (North Atlantic Treaty Organization). This requires that we face the fact that Europe and Japan depend more upon the Persian Gulf oil and southern African minerals than we do. Yet they know and we know that only the United States can provide the basic forces for any Western military capability in these regions. The first innovation should be *that the Western alliance must "redraw" the maps of its strategic theaters to indicate the growing linkages between them.* In the case of the Middle East, it becomes apparent that a new strategy towards the region is essential if the growth of Soviet power along its southern front is to be blocked. Geopolitically, this means that the artificial distinction between NATO's boundaries—which end at the Turkish border and the Tropic of Cancer—and the Middle East must, for purposes of wartime contingencies, be removed. (No one expects NATO to "redraw" its formal map of responsibilities in peacetime; this would be unacceptable politically, given the wide divergence of opinion and interests among the members of the allegiance.)

In considering wartime and crisis scenarios in this area, our ability to provide a credible military posture will depend upon access to such allies and friends as Turkey, Egypt, and Israel, and upon their cooperation. Access to these countries and their facilities could make up for many of the current deficits in our own military capabilities. This requires, in turn, that the administration rethink its position on the Greek-Turkish crisis and the Arab-Israeli dispute and that it forcefully communicate its views to our allies and to the U.S. Congress. While consensus within the Western alliance concerning the status of Jerusalem or Cyprus is unlikely, we must urge that the Europeans and the Japanese face *their* realities, for without political consensus our military options do not add up to very much.

There are two reasons why such an initiative is of utmost importance to a new administration. The first, pessimistic, reason relates to the Soviet Union's capacity, in the last resort, to divide the Western world by exercising *control* over the Middle East oil. This possibility has at last gained widespread currency in the wake of the Afghanistan invasion and reflects the most serious danger to the alliance since World War II. The second, more optimistic, reason is that the Western alliance and its friends have considerable ready assets which could be quickly brought to bear against the Soviet Union and its radical supporters if political agreement can be reached on the need to do something. These assets are economic, political, and military.

In military options, Britain and France still own or have access to important facilities in the Indian Ocean and along the East African coast which could be of invaluable help in a crisis. Both countries also have military forces which could be deployed to the area. Britain has extensive and recent operational experience in fighting in Yemen and Oman, and France continues to deploy one of the largest flotillas of her ships in the Indian Ocean. The local countries friendly to the West could bring together many assets in any coalition effort. Israeli armed forces and infrastructure are obvious political assets. However, Egyptian and Pakistani forces could add greatly to the problems the Soviet Union and its friends would have to face. Operationally, the broader alliance could redistribute some of its responsibilities, with Japan taking upon itself a greater burden of maritime defense in the Pacific and with the Europeans assuming more important missions in the western Mediterranean, leaving the United States more flexibility in earmarking forces for the eastern Mediterranean, the Indian Ocean, and the Persian Gulf.

At the political level, a new strategy would suggest that a U.S. administration seriously reconsider the utility of UN Resolution 242 as the model for an eventual solution to the Arab-Israeli conflict. The Iranian debacle has shown that settlement of the Arab-Israeli conflict based upon the premises of Resolution 242 will not in itself be sufficient to bring peace and tranquility to Israel's immediate neighbors, let alone to the Arab world and the Persian Gulf. The underriding sources for discontent throughout this entire area go much deeper than the status of Jerusalem or the Israeli occupation of the Golan Heights. It thus is a real question whether now is the ideal time for Israeli withdrawals from other occupied territory just as these assets are growing in value. For it should be recognized that while we, as an alliance, need Saudi oil and will need it for the calculable future, the most important countries who can help us from a military point of view are Turkey, Egypt, and Israel. Indeed, we would be extremely foolish to rely upon the future stability and good graces of the Saudi regime to assist in our military planning and to guarantee our access to oil. We have to face up to the fact that the Saudi regime may fall and that our only recourse will be to intervene to restore a pro-Western government or face inevitable blackmail.

Improve and Strengthen Strategic Relations with India

The dilemma in which we find ourselves in the Persian Gulf is in part due to the fact that we have such a precarious set of relationships with the most important countries around the Indian Ocean littoral. A case in point is India. U.S.-Indian relations have always been temperamental and the reelection of Mrs. Ghandi did not help matters. Yet the fact remains that in our support of Pakistan over the years we have backed a country that has lost all the wars it has fought against India. Pakistan is much smaller than India in terms of population and resources. The country faces the prospect of further instability and possible dismemberment in the years ahead, and has been governed by a motley group of authoritarian leaders including the current government which, until the Soviet invasion of Afghanistan, displayed growing hostility towards the United States. India, on the other hand, commands a vital strategic position in the Indian Ocean—Persian Gulf region and, with the exception of its conflict with China in 1962, it has won all the wars it has fought since 1948. Despite occasional political traumas at home, it has retained a relatively stable political system, given its fundamental poverty, and has managed to overcome some of its more severe shortages of food and energy. It also has a treaty of friendship with the Soviet Union and has been hostile towards many American actions in the Third World.

In the wake of the current Persian Gulf crisis, the continuing oil dependency, and fears about the growing spread of nuclear weapons, a new and more affirmative policy towards India could well bring useful rewards, especially if the situation throughout the Middle East continues to deteriorate. The major obstacles to such an initiative relate to the United States' continuing need—in view of the situation in Afghanistan—to support Pakistan with new arms, the negative reactions this generates in India, and the close relationship between Pakistan, the United States, and China. On the other hand, Soviet advances into western Asia at the expense of Pakistan could not be regarded with indifference by Indian leaders no matter how antagonistic they were toward Pakistan. This is thus an appropriate time to remind the Indians that their long-term security will be better served by resisting Soviet adventurism in the region and by actively seeking greater cooperation with the United States,

Pakistan, and China. The United States can assist in nurturing such developments by ensuring that its arms supplies to Pakistan do not include weapons more appropriate for fighting India than for defending against attacks from Afghanistan (heavy tanks would fall into this category). The United States should also make much greater efforts to sell arms to India and thereby help to wean India away from its dependency upon the Soviet Union for advanced military technology.

For in the last resort we should not forget the military potential that India brings to bear either as a friend or as an enemy. Its army and air force are well trained; its navy is growing; the Indian nuclear program has clearly a superior potential to that rumored to exist in Pakistan. India also has an embryonic space program and is relatively self-sufficient in energy. A new initiative towards India does not have to be at the expense of Pakistan or China, for India and its neighbors have more to fear over the long run from Soviet military power than from any conceivable threat posed by the Western countries.

New U.S. Arms Transfer Policies

When Mr. Carter became president in 1977, he forcefully reiterated his election campaign pledge and vowed that he would take steps to slow down the pace of U.S. arms transfers on the grounds that there was something fundamentally wrong with a country that preached arms control yet was the world's largest arms supplier. The guidelines for the Carter policy were spelled out in the president's statement made in May 1977. After making exceptions for transfers to NATO, Australia, Israel, Japan, and New Zealand, the president established a set of controls which were to be binding except in special circumstances which would qualify for a presidential exception. The controls included a ceiling for the dollar volume of U.S. transfers, a commitment that the United States would not be the first to introduce new sophisticated weapons into local regions, that sale of advanced weapons to any region would be prohibited until such weapons were operational with U.S. forces, that development or modification of advanced weapons solely for export would not be permitted, that tight controls would be placed upon coproduction arrangements, that in some cases no retransfer of U.S. weapons would be permitted, and that embassies and military representatives abroad would not be allowed to promote arms sales. Finally, future U.S. transfers were tied to the human rights records of would-be recipients.

As things have turned out, the Carter administration has been severely criticized for the uneven manner in which it has implemented these policies and the logical inconsistencies inherent in such guidelines. It has been argued on the one hand that the policy was too moralistic and too tied to human rights issues, thereby penalizing otherwise pro-Western countries and denying them arms and other military services that they would otherwise have received (i.e., Argentina, Chile, Brazil, Turkey, Taiwan). On the other hand, the policy has been criticized for hypocrisy; namely, that although it initially noted some of the procedures that were flawed in the policy it inherited (e.g., the excesses and mismanagement of the Nixon-Kissinger arms transfer policies to countries in the Persian Gulf), when faced with the reality of day-to-day politics the Carter administration continued to sell sophisticated arms to important clients such as Iran and Saudi Arabia. Logical flaws in the initial Carter policy were most apparent in the context of the ban on development or modification of advanced weapons solely for export. What this policy meant was that the only U.S. arms that could be requested by would-be recipients were those already ordered for the U.S. armed forces or in service with them. Since U.S. forces tend to adopt extremely sophisticated and expensive weapons, the Carter policy thus ensured that "acceptable" recipients (which turned out to include many Middle Eastern countries) would purchase the most advanced weapons in the world, which was hardly the original objective of the Carter policy. Furthermore, by forbidding manufacturers to design or modify weapons for local use, the United States prevented the transfer of weapons that might well have been much more suitable for friendly clients who faced serious infrastructure and logistical problems and were therefore not well adapted to receive the most advanced U.S. arms.

Perhaps the most serious problem with U.S. arms transfer policies has been that they were never fully integrated into the framework of U.S. defense policy. While it is understandable that some arms transfers should be made for nonmilitary reasons, in many cases the relationship has been out of kilter between our own defense planning and the arms sold and support systems provided to local countries. The classic case was U.S. arms sales to Iran under the shah. In retrospect, we had more power and leverage in Iran than we thought at the time and could probably have influenced the shah in building an armed force more suitable for his country's security requirements rather than in assisting him with the more flamboyant projects that he advocated over the years.

One remedy to the current problem would be *closer cooperation within the Department of Defense (DOD) on the issue of defense planning and arms transfer policies.* In many cases, arms transfer decisions have been based upon political judgments by the State Department concerning the merits of particular requests. Since there is a tendency in that department to focus upon immediate political relations, the frequent temptation is to support arms requests unless there are compelling reasons not to do so. In the early days of the Carter administration, constraints on State Department approval or disapproval tended to come from the White House, where considerations of human rights were given high priority. What is needed, however, is more coordination from those within the Department of Defense who are responsible for U.S. defense planning for contingencies that may involve military cooperation between the United States and the recipient country. This is not to imply that the DOD has not played a major role in arms transfer decisions. It has. But all too often individual services have tried to market their own weapons with inadequate emphasis upon the impact that their often successful efforts would have on our defense posture.

At the time of writing (January 1980), it appears that the Carter administration is in the process of abandoning most of its early policies on arms transfers. American arms manufacturers can now design and reconfigure weapons specifically designed for export, and U.S. arms sales to Pakistan, Turkey, and Egypt have been increased.

A new administration should have no qualms about pursuing an active arms sales policy *provided* that careful analysis of the requirements of the recipient are made in the context of U.S. national security interests. While some would argue that this has always been the policy, one can only answer that it may have been so in theory, but in practice we have made some awful mistakes. For it is not suggested that we return to the lax period of the early 1970s when just about anything was sold, but rather that *military* criteria and concern for infrastructure and logistics support be taken more seriously in weighing the merits of particular cases. In configuring military assistance and sales agreements with Middle East and west Asian countries, for instance, much more attention should be paid to needs of U.S. armed forces in these countries in the event that the United States has to project force to the region in the future.

LONGER-TERM GEOPOLITICS: RESOURCES, THE OCEANS, AND OUTER SPACE

So far, this chapter has focused upon some near-term defense options that concern U.S. security in critical areas, such as the Persian Gulf. Obviously, our ability to survive during the coming decade is the number one priority of a new administration, and access to Persian Gulf oil will be a key strategic concern of national security policy within this time frame. But what of the more distant future? Assuming that we manage to get through the next ten years and to gradually reduce our dependency upon the Middle East, what longer-term geopolitical goals should a new administration be thinking about now?

On the assumption that our basic conflict with the Soviet Union will not go away even if the gulf crisis diminishes, there is scope and need for imaginative thinking about our long-term security as the United States approaches the twenty-first century. The year 2000 can be used as a milestone for thinking through long-term policies. Above all else, the twenty-first century brings with it the promise of new technologies, new frontiers, and new geopolitical horizons which can determine the relative balance of power in this period.

What follows are some geopolitical observations based on present trends in the economic, technological, and demographic arenas that, at this point in time, deserve careful scrutiny and should be taken into account by a new administration that wishes to think and plan beyond the immediate set of problems.

The Drive toward New Frontiers

During the next hundred years the remaining remote regions of the world will probably be developed and populated. These include the Amazon basin, the eastern Soviet Union, the polar regions, and the deep oceans. Although the levels of population settlement will vary greatly—the deep oceans and the polar regions will pose greater problems for habitation than the Amazon or Siberia—developments in technology and increases in demand for resources will make the extraction of natural resources from all remote regions more economic than is the case today. There is also a strong possibility that within this time frame the industrialization of space will begin in earnest and the first space colonies will be established, including those needed for mineral extraction operations on the lunar surface to obtain materials for building large structures in outer space.

Historically, the exploitation of new frontiers has had a major impact upon the geopolitical perspectives of states and has eventually had a significant and sometimes decisive impact upon national policies. The opening of the New World, the Cape route, and the American West are three classic examples of new frontiers which have changed the situations of millions of people. A review of the reasons why, at a particular point in history, individuals sought new frontiers suggests two sets of explanations: first, what might be termed small-group or "micro" explanations; second, systemic or "macro" explanations. Into the first category would go ideology and adventure, greed and price, luck and foresight, national interest and anarchy. Thus the Age of Discovery would be interpreted as the outgrowth of the renaissance spirit and the unique economic conditions of Europe in the fifteenth century. The second category of explanations would refer to the interaction of three basic variables: population dynamics, technology, and the demand for and supply of scarce resources. Using these variables, the discovery of the New World would be seen as the inevitable result of growing population and growing demand in Europe coupled with the development of new technologies—in this case, improved

maritime technologies—which were initially exploited by
the most imaginative and needy countries.

As with most historical events, both sets of explanations
need to be understood in order to appreciate why certain
things happened and when they happened. It is not enough
to use macro theories to explain the activities of Prince
Henry the Navigator or Marco Polo or Christopher Columbus. The macro approach may tell us why it was inevitable
that a European country would eventually disvocer and exploit the riches of the New World, but it will not tell us why
Columbus sailed across the Atlantic in the second-to-last
decade of the fifteenth century.

With this in mind, it can be speculated that the coming
decades will witness major expansion of activity in three
arenas which have great relevance for U.S.—Soviet geopolitical relations: outer space, the oceans—including the Arctic
basin—and the eastern Soviet Union. The technology, infrastructure, and logistics for exploiting these frontiers are
currently being developed. The Soviet Union intends to exploit its Siberian resources in a major way in the twenty-first
century and, given the vast potential wealth of that region,
this phenomenon has long-term implications for the United
States. The completion of the Baikal-Amur Mainline
Railroad (BAM) in the mid-1980s will radically change the
economy and political importance of eastern Siberia. BAM is
one of the most spectacular engineering feats of the twentieth century and will have a major impact upon Soviet
strategic relations with China and upon the Soviet role and
position as a Pacific power. BAM will permit access to the oil,
minerals, and timber of Siberia and will encourage the
development of the coastal area of the Far Eastern Soviet
Union. No resource base similar to Siberia is available to the
United States on its continental territory despite undoubted
riches in Alaska and the Rocky Mountain states.

The Oceans and Outer Space

In the arena of ocean technology and outer space, however, the United States has important advantages which, if it is prepared to exploit them fully in the decades ahead, could alter the geopolitical map by the early twenty-first century and extend American power into new dimensions. *It is argued, then, that the United States must develop the innovative technology to exploit the seas and space if it is eventually to compete with the phenomenal resource base that the Soviet Union has within its own territory.*

In the context of ocean engineering, the United States should accelerate its investments in oil, gas, and mineral exploration and retrieval, and should more fully exploit its extensive and potentially lucrative fishing areas. These pursuits should, of course, be carried out within the context of the emerging Law of the Seas which, although placing certain restrictions on unilateral U.S. activity in certain sea areas, guarantees the United States legal access to far-flung seaways and oceans which, combined, will be a vital national security interest to the United States and its maritime allies for decades to come.

Of even more importance is the potential U.S. role in outer space. When the space shuttle makes its first flight, perhaps in the late 1980s, it will—assuming the system works—usher in a new era in space transportation. The lower cost of certain categories of payload that will be possible with repetitive shuttle flights has far-reaching implications for both military and commercial activities in this medium. In the military sphere, the shuttle will permit the deployment and servicing of larger, more sophisticated, satellites which can perform a host of tasks including command, control and communications, navigation, reconnaissance, surveillance, electronic ferreting and eavesdropping, and antisatellite operations. The impact of new space technologies on bat-

tlefield management and strategic warfare, including anti-
ballistic missile defense, could have as significant an impact
as the introduction of the telegraph and the wireless had on
naval operations in earlier years. Real-time navigation and
real-time reconnaissance will be possible and, while
scenarios relating to U.S.−Soviet warfare suggest that the
satellites have problems due to their inherent vulnerability,
the possibilities are far reaching for outer space activities to
assist the United States in strategic nuclear deterrence and
to aid its allies in cases of regional and nonnuclear conflict.
*Thus new space technologies can most certainly help our mili-
tary capabilities and can provide some counter to the ter-
restrial constraints on access mentioned previously.*

Ultimately, the space shuttle will permit the construction
of large battle stations in outer space. Whether this will
result from breakthroughs in laser and particle-beam technology is still a matter of great debate. Nevertheless, the idea
that space will forever be a hostile environment for military
operations needs to be carefully examined. There is no inherent reason why the United States should not be able to
develop a superior military capability in space, especially if
the technology is closely tied to commercial activities in
outer space.

In the commercial arena, the shuttle will have an immediate economic effect. Even conservative analysts point to the
numerous advantages that will occur as large satellites in or-
bit permit smaller receivers on earth. This shift in the relative size and art of space-based and earth-based systems will
reduce the costs of a host of activities from instant communications to electronic mail. In sum, the information
revolution on earth as a result of improvements in outer
space technology should produce new economic benefits including resource management, environmental control, as
well as communications activity. More futuristic en-
treprencurs talk of the development of large structures in
space for production of pharmaceuticals, certain crystals,

and possibly, in the distant future, solar-power satellites which could help to end our dependency on foreign oil as a major energy source. Whatever perspective one takes, the horizons are limitless.

The reason for a reemphasis on the space program has to do with the inherent nature of competition between the United States and the Soviet Union, competition that transcends the nuts and bolts of the arms race. Despite structural weaknesses and gross inefficiencies which suggest to some that the Soviet Union is an insecure, backward state that cannot compete over the long run with Western capitalism, the reality is that the Soviet Union is large enough and complex enough and has enough human and natural resources to do just about anything it wants to do at a certain price (provided, of course, that its leadership survives the very real economic plight the Soviet Union may face in the 1980s). The military buildup, for instance, has been achieved at enormous sacrifice to the civilian sector. Yet it has succeeded in providing the Soviet forces with very modern weapons. Since the Soviet Union does not use the systems analysis approach to economic and social trade-offs, to talk of "waste" or "duplication" in the Soviet system is of little avail. Consider, for example, the investment in capital and labor that is going into the BAM Railroad. According to Western reports, there has been a stupendous waste of effort on this scheme and millions of rubles have been squandered, but—and this is the point—the railroad will be completed and it will open up the Soviet Far East. A hundred years from now will anyone really care about the initial capital costs? The Suez Canal and the Panama Canal were not built by cost accountants but by visionaries who saw the tremendous geopolitical importance that these engineering feats would have upon the course of world history.

A concerted U.S. space effort would fire the imagination of a new generation of Americans who were too young to have been influenced by Vietnam but who have been raised in the

Star Wars environment and who have the energy and scientific talents that need to be tapped. It would give the country a national goal at a time when the absence of such goals, beyond reducing the level of inflation, is very apparent and when there is great confusion about America's future place and role in the world. In short, the United States needs to regain its sense of destiny. If this sounds jingoistic and imperial so be it, for we live, whether we like it or not, in a highly competitive international environment in which the benefits of cooperation are obvious but in which cooperation alone is not enough to insure that the national security of the United States is maintained.

If we are seriously to pursue commercial and military activities that are not proscribed in outer space by current treaty obligations, it can be expected that the Soviet Union, too, will invest more in space activities. If space competition continues at an accelerated pace, the major advantages to the United States are in the commercial arena. What will eventually be needed is a "constabulary" capability to protect our growing investment in outer space. This, in turn, suggests that it is none too soon to begin thinking about new military doctrines that will be necessary for protracted operations in outer space and about patterns of logistical and basing infrastructure that will be necessary to project power and to maintain a presence in the fourth dimension.

CONCLUSION

In conclusion, then, the United States must think and plan for its long-term security beyond the current crisis over access to foreign oil. A new administration must establish innovative goals and articulate imaginative strategies to achieve these goals. Above all else, it will be essential to present to the American public a coherent and consistent national security policy that relates, in both the immediate and long-term time frames, to the never-ending relationship between technology, the economy, and national defense. If the opportunities of the next decade are missed because of poor leadership which lacks vision and confidence, we will have no one to blame but ourselves.

5

WILLIAM R. VAN CLEAVE

Quick Fixes to U.S. Strategic Nuclear Forces

Weaknesses in U.S. strategic force programs. The Strategic Alternatives Team. A perspective on quick fixes. Force vulnerabilities—ICBMs, bombers, SSBNs. Specific actions now available to improve the U.S. strategic posture.

Interest in "quick fixes" for U.S. strategic forces has arisen from a sense of urgency about the problems these forces face and from awareness that present programs are inadequate to deal with those problems in a timely manner. Soviet strategic force capabilities are rapidly outgaining or already surpassing those of the United States. Objective analyses clearly show a peak of relative Soviet superiority vis-à-vis the

United States within a couple of years, well before the United States can respond, given current programs. This loss of essential equivalence is particularly threatening because of its precise strategic nature. It will be characterized by dangerous vulnerabilities in major components of our deterrent forces and by a substantial disparity in favor of the Soviet Union in the ability to fight, win, and recover from strategic nuclear war. In short, the Soviet Union will be able, during this period, to expect advantages based upon the ability to threaten nuclear war much more credibly than the United States. This cannot help but reduce the effectiveness of all U.S. military forces and influence the determination to use those forces. The implications for American security interests are obvious.

Such a situation has developed as a result of a determined Soviet effort to achieve strategic superiority at the same time that U.S. strategic programs have been delayed, constrained by the Strategic Arms Limitation Talks (SALT), or canceled outright. The shortfall in defense spending, compared with the last five-year defense plan proposed by the Ford administration, is already in the tens of billions of dollars. No area of military capability has been unaffected, but our strategic force programs, receiving less than 10 percent of the defense budget, have particularly suffered. Yet current strategic force programs are not only incapable of keeping pace with the threat through the mid-1980s, but it is also most doubtful that they will produce the turnaround projected by the administration for the late 1980s.

Clearly, immediate attention must be given to identifying and fixing the weaknesses in our strategic posture as rapidly as possible. We have slipped to the point that minor percentage increases in defense spending, even if real rather than fictional, will not retrieve the situation. We must concern ourselves now with what needs to be done and how we can do it rather than with arbitrary percentage increases in the defense budget.

For the past two years a voluntary group, the "Strategic Alternatives Team," has explored quick fixes for our strategic forces. Part of its work was presented earlier this year in a book, *Strategic Options for the Early Eighties: What Can Be Done?* (Van Cleave and Thompson 1979). Whatever one's preference for any of the specific options presented in the book, its general conclusion remains untarnished. That is, that there exists a variety of actions that could significantly improve our strategic posture within some thousand days.

The book has apparently had some success in arousing or reinforcing interest outside of the U.S. government. Within the government, however, there is little evidence that the book or its message have met with much interest or have had any impact on policies or programs. When officials have been moved to articulate some reaction, it has generally been to dismiss quick fixes as unnecessary, unreliable, or simply uninteresting.

Does this mean that the threat and the need for quick fixes are officially denied? The answer is one of confused ambivalence: the need is both cited and denied. Officials now acknowledge, thanks to the political situation, that we must do more in defense and that some increase in defense spending is necessary. Suggested minor increases are for the most part applied to the general purpose forces. Strategic force programs, we are told, are proceeding nicely, in the right direction, and at a satisfactory pace.

At the same time, however, the chairman of the joint chiefs of staff warns in his annual report to Congress (Brown 1979) that we have slipped "another year closer to a potentially unstable and acutely dangerous imbalance," and that *"regardless of U.S. actions,* Soviet strategic capability will continue to increase relative to that of the United States through the mid-1980s." Secretary Brown devoted a good deal of the fiscal year (FY) 1980 report of the Department of Defense (DOD) to carefully tailored analyses that purport to show that everything will be all right—eventually. Yet at the same time he admits that "our most serious concerns — *which we need to act now to meet*—are about the period of the early-to-mid 1980s."

How are these inconsistencies reconciled? They are not. They are papered over by ignoring the immediate problems of the next several years while basing our effort on programs that would putatively turn around the trends by the late 1980s; that is, if they are allowed to proceed as planned. Comparison curves are made to look better by understating problems in our own forces, overstating the ability of current programs, ignoring the requirement of timeliness, and implicitly reducing retaliatory requirements and strategic stability to assured destruction criteria. In my own view, the long-term programs set forth in the FY 1980 report and repeated in the more recent FY 1981 report are uncertain and will not, by any stretch of inventive graphing, accomplish what is promised. One cogent analysis by a former Department of Defense official concluded that "the acceptance of prolonged strategic inferiority is probably the real message behind the FY80 defense budget."[1] I am inclined to agree. The FY 1981 budget does not change that.

The matter is compounded by the fact that this year's DOD report articulates an ambitious declaratory policy. "Essential equivalence" is confirmed as a minimum essential and a new "countervailing strategy" is proudly announced which sets forth major-warfighting and even damage-limiting force requirements. Our strategic forces cannot meet those standards; in the next few years they may not even assure strategic or crisis stability unless a major program of quick fixes is funded and undertaken *now*. Over a year ago the Strategic Alternatives Team warned that "time is short and rapidly growing shorter for adjusting our strategic nuclear forces to the threats they face." The need for quick fixes has grown even more urgent since then.

QUICK FIXES

Before turning to strategic nuclear force (SNF) problems and possible timely fixes, I would like to remind us of the nature and purposes of quick fixes. Simply, they are worthwhile improvements that can be rapidly achieved, compared to what we are now accustomed to regarding as "normal" lead times. Such quick fixes are not necessarily easy, cheap, or short lived, so the term should not be reduced to derogatory references to "Band-Aid" approaches. The emphasis, of course, is on what can be accomplished rapidly to meet urgent problems rather than on what may seem optimal in the long run. That does not, however, mean that there will always be incompatibility between quick fixes and long-range considerations. Nor does it mean that strategic force requirements can be met and sustained by quick fixes alone. Quick fixes are not alternatives to sensible but more time-consuming modernization programs; they would supplement, not supplant, less hasty approaches. Their purpose is to enable a safer pursuit of long-range solutions by helping us cross the dangerous period between now and their culmination.

Having said this, however, let me suggest a somewhat different perspective on quick fixes in comparison with major force programs. Our recent record of accomplishment based upon major long-term programs is not good. The larger and more expensive the program, it seems, and the more drawn out it is, the higher the risk that it will not be successfully carried through. Equally important is the consideration that "small" force problems tend to be ignored, to grow and accumulate, while the services focus their attention on favored major programs. The problems with the B–52 force have multiplied, for example, while the U.S. Air Force has focused first on the B–1 and now on the MX (missile experimental). To protect major programs, the services are parsimonious of their funding and attention when it comes to problems and fixes that might "compete" with the major programs.[2] It is as if they believe that $30 billion programs are intrinsically more effective and justifiable than many $2 billion programs. That may not be the case, especially if major programs turn out to be as vulnerable as they have been recently. Instead of one costly major service program, perhaps more consideration should be given to a larger number of less costly and less time-consuming improvements or fixes, both to meet urgent threats and because these may turn out to be the most likely to survive budgetary, environmental, and other political pressures.

QUICK FIXES AND DOCTRINAL OBJECTIVES

Some have erroneously interpreted the sole objective of quick fixes to be that of securing an assured destruction capability. This is because most of the options discussed do address the problem of force survivability, and because doctrinal issues have thus far not been emphasized in the debate over quick fixes.

As a matter of necessity, the first priority for quick fixes must be to heal or to prevent force vulnerabilities, both because these pose the most severe near-term problems and because it is essential to strategic stability that none of our forces have major vulnerabilities that might be exploited. Moreover, the vulnerability test must be stringent; it must not be based upon the assumption of strategic warning. Secretary Brown uses the criterion of a "well-executed surprise attack" in his FY 1980 report. I agree: all of our forces must survive such a test sufficiently to assure that they will never be put to that test. In addition, I also agree with Secretary Brown that they should be survivable "over an extended period of time," and thereby usable with "whatever timing, and degree of deliberateness and control, proves desirable." If Secretary Brown wants that, I can require no less.

This does not address the question of what we want our forces to do once they are made survivable, nor does it establish the levels of capability we want. In this regard, I suggest we take seriously the criteria and objectives that have been enunciated in official documents and in statements by responsible officials over the past half-dozen years. Despite vestiges of mutual assured destruction (MAD) rhetoric that have recently crept into such statements, these objectives do not boil down to such a minimal posture, however measured. They stipulate the need for effective, flexible, and selective targeting capability against the full range of relevant targets, including hardened military targets, over an extended period of war with warfighting, escalation control, and damage-limiting objectives. Essential equivalence means not only equality (a minimum requirement, in my view) with the Soviets in major peacetime measures of capability, but in the ability to attack military targets, to limit damage to ourselves, and to disallow the Soviet Union a more favorable postwar outcome; in short, the ability to deny the Soviets any warfighting advantage over the United States.

Technology, I believe, offers the possibility of basing strategic deterrence more on selective military targeting, damage limiting, escalation control, and defense than on massive destruction. I believe we should move in that direction, and I see no reason why quick fixes cannot be so oriented.

Unfortunately, our vulnerability problems have grown so severe that most of our energies for some time will probably be absorbed by addressing those problems.

Let me turn to a summary of major force problems before addressing specific quick fixes.

URGENT STRATEGIC FORCE PROBLEMS

The extreme vulnerability of our ICBM (intercontinental ballistic missile) force in the immediate future is officially acknowledged. It is so bad, in fact, that Secretary Brown has argued that it would not be helped if the Soviets were to dismantle their entire SS–18 force, over 5 million pounds of throw weight. There is no program to meet the threat as it arises or for several years thereafter; unfortunately, even the program designed to relieve the problem by the end of the decade is a dubious one. It is entirely likely that the "racetrack" scheme, a basing mode for ICBM launchers, will not survive the operational, cost, and environmental tests it must stand. In fact, one must suspect that the administration expects the plan to self-destruct after the fate of SALT II has been determined. We seem to be set on the road to launch of ICBMs on warning,* a reckless and uncertain course of action to which no nation with our resources should have to resort in desperation.

Focusing on the ICBM vulnerability problem tends to divert attention from other force problems which are perhaps equally severe and urgent. Despite the DOD's understatement of its problems, the bomber force has serious deficiencies that require quick fixes. The same analysis referred to earlier ("Galen" 1979) reported that:

No one in DoD is honestly allowed to examine and analyze B–52 vulnerability, alert rates, and penetration capability. This aspect of U.S. capability has been so politicized by the Air Force that no one really knows what the facts are.

The facts are not all that unclear, however. The force is maldeployed for prelaunch survivability; real alert rates may

---

*Launch of ICBMs on first warning of an impending Soviet attack, despite uncertainties as to the truth of the information, the magnitude of the attack, or the possibility that doing so—as opposed to being able to ride out the attack—will worsen the outcome.

be as low as 20 percent in peacetime; reaction and escape times are inadequate; warning and communications systems are fragile; and the prospects of penetrating Soviet air defenses without major fixes may be somewhere between very low and nil. (Penetration probabilities in the mid-1980s are impossible to evaluate accurately on the basis of tailored DOD and air force studies. It is instructive that in recent Senate testimony [Committee on the Armed Services 1979, pp. 1387-1482], General Ellis, Commander of the Strategic Air Command [SAC], admitted that the majority of programs necessary to meet expected penetration rates in 1985 are not even funded in the five-year defense plan.) Bombers that would escape base are not hardened against nuclear effects, are dependent upon tankers for refueling, and lack retainability over time. In addition, the bombers are suffering from aging. The ALCMs (air-launched cruise missiles) now planned for the force cannot correct these problems.

The problems described have long been recognized and pointed out to the DOD and the U.S. Air Force, but there has been resistance to their resolution. For example, over a decade of effort has failed to get the air force seriously interested in inland rebasing where bombers would gain critical warning and reaction time in the event of attack.

In the past we have tended to regard the bomber force as something of a bonus. This is reflected not only in McNamara's Posture Statements (see, e.g., those for FY 1966 and FY 1967), but in Carter's decision to cancel the B–1. That was because we did not foresee that our ICBMs would become so vulnerable so fast and because a successful B–1 program was anticipated. It is now imperative that we give more attention to shoring up the bomber force.

As for the other leg of the triad of strategic offensive forces (ICBMs, bombers, SSBNs), the fleet ballistic missile (FBM) force, the problems seem less pressing, except for shortcomings in command, control, and communications (C^3). That may be, however, because information pertinent to nuclear ballistic missile submarine (SSBN) vulnerability is too closely held and tightly compartmentalized to permit alternative analyses and our knowledge of Soviet antisubmarine warfare (ASW) is not complete. It may also be because we tend to evaluate threats in terms of near simultaneous destruction rather than attrition over time, despite the fact that we regard the SSBNs as a retainable reserve. Like the bombers, the peacetime alert rate is low; common also with the bombers, C^3 improvements are urgently needed. The force in addition requires more flexible targeting capability, now being restricted essentially to soft-point targets.

Perhaps a major problem with the SSBN force lies in the costs and uncertainties of current modernization programs, especially the Trident boat (class of submarine) whose cost has increased, whose deployment rate has slipped, and whose value compared to other alternatives has been increasingly questioned. The fate of the postponed D−5 (Trident II) submarine-launched ballistic missile (SLBM) has also become uncertain.

There are other examples of areas with major vulnerabilities and deficiencies requiring immediate attention: the national warning, information, and communications systems, C^3 I, continental air defense, and civil defense. Classification considerations prevent specific discussion of the first, but it has become increasingly open knowledge that severe vulnerabilities do exist. Air defense acquires increased importance due to the Backfire bomber. Civil defense, in my view, is a serious national weakness meriting priority attention in any consideration of quick fixes. It is important both for its intrinsic value and in view of the enormous disparity between the Soviet Union and the United States in this capability. It magnifies other disparities and could take on critical dimensions in crisis decision-making and ultimately in deterrence.

SOME SUGGESTED SNF FIXES

Since the theme of this book is weakness to strength in the 1980s, I have included for our discussion actions that are truly quick fixes (i.e., measures that could be significantly effective in about three years), and programs that should be undertaken immediately but which would not have significant payoffs until sometime after three years. Some of these suggestions involve accelerating or redirecting existing programs; others advocate different approaches than those currently planned. For example, I recommend that we scrap the "racetrack" basing mode for ICBM launchers and return to square one, multiple vertical shelters (MAPS/MPS). I also depart from air force preferences in not linking this rebasing to MX. It should proceed with existing Minuteman III (MM-III) ICBMs and in present deployment areas rather than new ones, instead of awaiting the production of an MX. (The MX, however, could be phased in as it became available.)

Existing forces and programs are inadequate to meet the Soviet threat of the early to mid-1980s. We must move quickly to improve our strategic deterrent forces in order to deny the Soviets the advantages now looming and to assure safe deterrence. It is possible to do so.

The specific suggestions in the following summary are examples of feasible and worthwhile actions that we have available. In the summary I have also included comments on the likely effect of SALT on the particular options.

Summary

Some Fixes to U.S. Strategic Nuclear Capability that Could Be Undertaken with Immediate Increases in the Strategic Nuclear Force Program Budget
(Strategic Alternatives Team)

ICBM FORCE

[Summary discussion: First priority should go to rebasing the Minuteman III force in MAPS/MPS configuration; second, to upgrading the Minuteman III and reopening its production lines; and third, to development of a follow-on ICBM, presumptively the MX, but also a smaller ICBM option for air or land mobility future alternatives. SALT drives us toward larger ICBMs, as the MX, to obtain the necessary throw weight and countermilitary potential whereas, without SALT, strategic logic would weigh heavily toward a larger number of smaller (possibly single reentry vehicle [RV]) ICBMs. The latter would ease survivability problems and promote strategic stability far more than the larger ICBMs in relatively few numbers.]

Significant Operating Capability (SOC) in Short Term:

Redeploy MMIII (and possibly MMII) in the multiple vertical silo protective shelter mode (MAPS/MPS).

SALT COMMENTS

The administration, facing Soviet objections, has apparently decided that SALT II, in fact, rules out this option. If so, SALT is driving us toward less timely, less effective, and more expensive options for ICBM survivability; in essence, it prohibits us from solving this problem in time to meet the maximum threat in the early to mid-1980s. On this account alone SALT II should be rejected unless it is renegotiated or clearly amended to permit this option; or unless the administration explicitly claims, under SALT II, the right to this deployment and then proceeds with it.

Upgrade MMIII and reopen production; deploy more (in MAPS).	Major upgrading possible (e.g, for better accuracy and adaptability). Can produce all wished under SALT II (e.g., for breakout) but can deploy only 270 more on existing launchers, and that would force us to limit MIRVed (multiple independently targeted reentry vehicle) SLBMs to 380 and ALCM cruise missile carriers (CMCs) to 120.
Accelerate and increase Mark (MK) 12A (or improved RV) production and deployment plans.	No SALT constraint. Now plan to refit 300 MM or less with MK12A.
Improve flight test program.	Qualitative and quantitative upgrade necessary to any realistic expectation of improved accuracies. Ranges and range facilities also need improvement.

Summary (continued)

ICBM FORCE	SALT COMMENTS
*Significant Capability in Mid-Term:**	
Continue MX development; accelerate pace.	See prefatory summary comment. A major SALT II constraint is that it prohibits both the deployment of a larger number of smaller ICBMs and the development and testing of a small new ICBM or other alternative to the MX while the MX is being developed. Without SALT II we would undoubtedly be pursuing such development; to do so under SALT II would require test-development of a derivative of an air-launched, submarine-launched, or intermediate-range ballistic missile (ALBM, SLBM, or IRBM) *if* the U.S. would do that as a SALT failure hedge. C–4 and D–5 recommendation constitutes such a hedge but is not as desirable as test-development of a new small ICBM.
Concurrent development of new ICBM; e.g., smaller ICBM for land or air mobility options.	
Develop more accurate Trident I (C–4) and/or accelerate Trident II (D–5) development as possible ICBM options.	
Larger number of smaller ICBMs in MAPS.	Prohibited by SALT.
Increase funding for antiballistic missile (ABM) development as supplement to ICBM rebasing.	
Deploy ABM defense as necessary to ICBM survivability.	Prohibited by SALT I.
Develop long-range alternatives or supplements to MAPS/MPS.	

BOMBER/AIR-BREATHING FORCE	SALT COMMENTS
SOC in Short Term:	
Accelerate and increase planned ALCM production and deployment.	We now plan only 12 externally carried ALCMs on 120 B-52Gs. SALT II prohibits deployment on more CMCs without drawing down numbers of MIRVed ballistic missiles. Could still keep within SALT II and place 20 ALCMs on 120 Gs, or—without SALT—equip all 170 Gs with 20 or more ALCMs.** Program acceleration could produce such a force in three years, while accelerated development of a new CMC could be timed to absorb ALCM production thereafter (if no SALT).
Go into production with both competitive ALCMs.	The purpose would be to increase ALCM production over time for more rapid and increased deployment, which would be severely constrained by SALT II. A variation would be to convert the second-place ALCM competitor into a stretched version for interim longer range while a new ALCM is being developed.
Rebase B-52s inland.	An essential requirement: 20–40 new main operating bases (MOBs) located beyond 700 nautical miles of coast needed.
Re-engine 50 to 100 percent of B-52G and H.	Would greatly improve performance as CMC, enable more and better utilization runways/bases, and make planes tanker independent in CMC role. Boeing-Wichita will do so at fixed price, guaranteed performance.
Increase B-52 alert rate and further decrease reaction time.	Extent may depend upon degree and success of rebasing, which should have higher priority for funding, but particularly those B-52s with ALCMs during the years before full operating capability should be placed on the highest practical alert rate. An increased ability to go more rapidly to higher alert rates and to sustain those rates would be part of the improvement.

Summary (continued)

BOMBER/AIR-BREATHING FORCE	SALT COMMENTS
Harden B–52G and H.	Extent, again, may depend upon success of above and of any follow-on bomber/CMC program, as well as consideration of priority given the level of funding available.
	The last four suggestions face no apparent SALT II constraints.

SOC in Mid-Term:

[Summary discussion: A major issue is the question of trade-offs and funding priorities between such improvements to the B–52 force as suggested above and development of a follow-on penetrating bomber or CMC. With the improvements noted above, the B–52 would be an excellent ALCM-carrier, but many feel that a penetrating bomber is needed as well, and with good reason. On the other hand, many problems of penetrating Soviet air defenses in the future remain to be solved, if they can be so satisfactorily. The optimum solution seems to be to proceed simultaneously with B–52 improvements oriented toward a CMC and with a B–1/B–1A program oriented toward a penetrating bomber; if the penetration problem, meanwhile, cannot be satisfactorily solved—or can be—later decisions can be taken accordingly. Clearly, this approach will require substantial additional funding.]

| Restart B–1 (or B–1A) program, along with major research and development (R&D) program to improve penetration. | B–1 specified in SALT II as heavy bomber and therefore subject to aggregate limits and, as ALCM carrier, to MIRVed vehicle limits. SALT II constraints would not apply until production. Program should proceed as if production is the goal. |
| Development of new CMC: advanced medium short takeoff transport (AMST), or possibly B–1, derivative. | |

Tanker force improvements.

Issue of tanker dependence rests upon resolution of some of foregoing points. Re-engining B-52s frees from, or reduces, tanker dependence. Better to be able to regard tanker capability as bonus than to have to rely upon it; but to the extent the tankers are needed, the need must modernize along same lines suggested for B-52 force. Re-engined B-52G could be converted into more capable tanker if B-52G turns out to be transition to better CMC.

Advanced, longer-range ALCM.

Development and early production a high priority as Soviets extend air defense perimeter. Threat of Backfire bomber in interceptor role, e.g., requires much longer-range ALCM capability.

SEA-BASED FORCE

SOC in Short Term:

SALT COMMENTS

Improve communications; e.g., proceed with extremely low frequency system (ELF).

Expedite and increase planned C-4 deployment; simultaneously develop more accurate C-4.

Produce sea-launched cruise missile (SLCM) and deploy on available platforms.

Protocol governs only through 1981, after which, presumably, free to deploy SLCM without constraint. As an early deployment mode, e.g., might deploy on 10 old Polaris boats at 6 to 8 per tube (and give to Supreme Allied Command/Europe [SACEUR]?) or externally on subs.

Summary (continued)

SEA-BASED FORCE	SALT COMMENTS
SOC in Mid-Term:	
Accelerate D–5 with improved accuracy.	
Develop advanced, longer-range SLCM.	
Accelerate prototype R&D follow-on, or alternative, SSBN.	
Accelerate prototype R&D on strategic nuclear-powered cruise missile submarine (SSCN).	
Work on extending life of Poseidon boats so no dip in numbers of SLBMs around 1985.	With SALT II MIRV limits depend upon MIRVed ICBM and ALCM choices (e.g., see note **).

OTHER FIXES: DEFENSE, C³	SALT COMMENTS
[Note: Significant improvements in all of below could be accomplished in the short term, but full impact would probably be mid-term.]	
Increase funding and research, development, testing, and evaluation (RDT&E) for ABM: ICBM defense (e.g., supplement to MAPS) and defense of other critical targets.	SALT I treaty prohibits deployment beyond one site and prohibits development of sea-, air-, space-, or mobile land-based ABM. On the other hand, 1972 U.S. statement appended to the treaty stipulates the right to withdraw from the treaty if supreme interests are jeopardized. Should at least develop rapid (six-month) deployment capability.
Deploy as needed.	

Revitalize air defense.

Important not to allow Backfire a free ride. Options available for both short and mid-term resting on combinations of available and future surface-to-air missiles (SAMs), airborne warning and control systems (AWACs), interceptors; e.g., multiply AWACs and phase in F–14 with Phoenix; deploy Patriot in strategic air defense mode.

Civil defense.

Major improvements possible, beginning with suggestions in *Strategic Options* book and the administration's initially announced but now defunct program; more advanced plans and options already exist.

C^3.

Major improvements for wartime durability as well as early warning and initial exchanges have been an established, high DOD priority for some time. Despite that, little has been done. Should not wait for a master plan, but should proceed with obvious improvements to pieces of the problem.

(FY 1980 DOD report acknowledges that secure and reliable C^3 for at least the SLBM and bomber/ALCM force is lacking.)

---

*Three to four years is used as the dividing time between short and mid-term SOC.

**More variations are possible depending upon the numbers of MIRVed ICBM/SLBMs deployed; e.g., by limiting those to 1020 could deploy 150 B–52G with 20 ALCM and 150 new CMC with 36 ALCM (8400 ALCM) and remain within SALT II constraints.

6

RICHARD R. BURT

Washington and the Atlantic Alliance: The Hidden Crisis

Political bases for Atlantic security problems. Détente and the prospect of another Cold War. NATO's needs and strategy. Carter and the neutron bomb fiasco. Soviet nuclear forces. The balance between conventional and nuclear options.

Shortly after entering the White House in 1977, Jimmy Carter proclaimed that a top priority of his new administration was to bolster the political cohesion and the military strength of the Atlantic alliance. Yet three years later the North Atlantic Treaty Organization (NATO) faces some of the most troubling problems of its thirty-year existence. This chapter will make a brief effort to describe how some of the problems came about and how they might be remedied in the years ahead.

Simply stated, the basic problem confronting the alliance is that Western governments no longer possess a common view of the security predicament confronting NATO. Outside of Europe, allied governments disagree over whether such non-NATO regions as the Persian Gulf should be treated as alliance responsibilities. Within Europe, governments also disagree over whether Soviet military power actually constitutes a "threat" and whether the West should risk détente with Moscow by matching its conventional and nuclear buildup.

Intra-alliance disagreements over policy toward the Soviet Union and over NATO's relevance to conflicts in the Third World are, of course, not new. The reticence of West European governments to follow the Carter administration's lead in reacting to the Soviet invasion of Afghanistan was similar in some respects to the reluctance of Europeans seven years ago to support American policy during the Yom Kippur war in the Middle East. But while perceptions and definitions of security problems have long differed on both sides of the Atlantic, the divergence is sharpening. If allowed to continue, the alliance itself will be placed at risk.

Many of the contemporary problems that now divide the alliance have political roots. To begin with, although we associate détente as a political strategy with Henry Kissinger and Richard Nixon, it is the Europeans who have profited most—in psychological, economic, and human terms—by closer ties with the East. Thus, while it has been relatively easy for the United States—even prior to Afghanistan—to shift to a more militant strategy toward Moscow, in Europe this has proven to be more difficult. The disinclination, moreover, of some European governments to adopt a tougher line toward Moscow not only reflects fears of possibly entering a new Cold War. It also reveals the new caution of Europeans in following American policy initiatives. The caution, obviously, is not difficult to understand: for three years America's allies in Europe have been almost continuously surprised and irritated by Carter administration policies that they neither expected nor understood.

The confusion and inconsistency of Carter administration policy toward the Soviet Union is a case in point. While highly critical of Moscow's human rights performance at home, the administration only gradually grew concerned with the projection of Soviet power abroad. Rapid reversals in policies toward Moscow led some European governments to conclude that Washington's strong initial reaction to Afghanistan would probably soon be replaced with a more conciliatory line. But European confusion over Washington's policy toward Moscow is only part of the problem. Other aspects of American foreign policy over the last three years, particularly efforts to stop the proliferation of nuclear weapons, technology, and conventional arms, have also irritated Europeans and contributed to the fundamental divergence of perspective that now threatens NATO.

But political differences over détente with the Soviet Union or over how to react to developments in the Third World are only the most visible problems that confront the alliance. Behind these problems is a hidden agenda of military and strategic problems that have yet to receive adequate attention. Given the Carter administration's early emphasis on bolstering the capabilities of the alliance, it may appear strange to argue that NATO's basic problems remain military in nature. But in retrospect it is now clear that the administration's stress on upgrading the defense of Central Europe came in the absence of any integrated, overall concept of what an improvement in NATO forces was supposed to accomplish. Thus the administration's policy of emphasizing NATO defenses has essentially been an *ad hoc*, incremental strategy, designed to throw money at problems.

THE CARTER PLAN FOR IMPROVING NATO'S CONVENTIONAL DEFENSES

The core of the administration's defense policy toward Europe has been the long-term defense program (LTDP) which was approved by the allies at a NATO summit meeting in Washington early in 1978. Divided into ten categories (nine for conventional force improvements, one for nuclear), the program is meant to set objectives for each of the member governments. Some of the areas emphasized in the LTDP, such as air defense and anti-armor forces, have long been ignored by the alliance and it is important that they at last receive some attention. At the same time, the administration's program suffers from some important deficiencies, such as the following:

• Understanding the impact of new technology. Rather than utilizing new technology to maintain existing military roles and missions, developments in such areas as command and control, target acquisition, and conventional munitions could be exploited in several lucrative ways. For example, nonnuclear cruise missiles and remotely piloted vehicles could take over many of the strike roles now assigned to manned aircraft in heavily defended areas in Eastern Europe. The trick, however, is not simply to use new technology to do old tasks better, but to recognize that new technology allows new tasks to be performed.

• Adjusting tactics. Just as important as understanding the implications of new technologies is appreciating the need for changes in tactics. In this area, two suggestions seem worth making. First, while NATO, because of inferior numbers of men and equipment, cannot avoid being on the defensive in any major conflict in the Center Region, this does not rule out the possibility of using selected NATO forces for offensive operations that could throw the attacker off balance. Second, as Steven Canby (1974/75) has long argued, NATO in general needs to get away from basing its planning on the notion that the West could win a firepower-dominated war of attrition with the Warsaw Pact nations. Lacking very little defensive depth in the Center Region, NATO—to hold its own in any future conflict—will have to fight a war of maneuver in Europe. Canby and others have pointed out that this will require a new set of tactics and European reserve forces.

• Defending the flanks.   Although the problem of defending Central Europe offers the most demanding military challenge, the ability of NATO to deter possible Soviet thrusts into northern Europe or southern Europe or to defend against them is not guaranteed by maintaining the balance in the center. A military equilibrium in Central Europe does make any Soviet move against Norway or Turkey less likely, but local defenses are still necessary to protect NATO's flanks. In the north, Norway in recent years has made good progress in bolstering its own "trip wire" defenses and in working with the United States and others on a reinforcement program in the event of attack. In the south, however, the picture is much gloomier, with Turkey's massive economic problems hindering Ankara from modernizing its armed forces. Ironically, as Turkey's military problems have grown worse, its strategic importance to Western interests in the Middle East and the Persian Gulf has become all the more important.

THE NUCLEAR LINK

Perhaps the biggest fault with the administration's NATO strategy has been a failure to relate its conventional force improvement program to a doctrine for nuclear weapons. The administration has pursued the long-term defense improvement program for bolstering the alliance's conventional defenses under the increasingly questionable assumption that this would enable NATO to raise the so-called "nuclear threshold"; that is, improvements to NATO's conventional posture would ease the pressure on the alliance to respond with nuclear weapons to an attack by Moscow. The maintenance of deterrence in Europe obviously does depend on the sequential threat of escalation—the notion that a small conflict could break out but that it could then spread to engage the territories of the two superpowers. But given the growth of Moscow's strategic and theater nuclear forces, it is by no means clear that the United States—as it once hoped to do—could control the escalation process.

In other words, the challenge confronting the United States and its allies in the 1980s is not simply that of raising the nuclear threshold. Moscow possesses both the forces and the doctrine to use nuclear and conventional weapons in a militarily effective manner. Under these circumstances, NATO strategy must undergo a revolution in the 1980s of the sort it underwent in the 1960s. At that time the notion that the West needed to improve its conventional forces worried many Europeans because it was viewed as beginning the process of American nuclear disengagement from Europe. But the push for greater conventional forces was understandable. Moscow had demonstrated the capacity, for the first time, to target the United States with intercontinental-range missiles and U.S. leaders recognized that war in Europe could no longer be credibly deterred through the simple threat of massive nuclear retaliation.

Although the Kennedy administration's concept of flexible response was debated for years within the alliance, most Europeans gradually came to recognize that an improved conventional posture did not mean that Washington was unwilling to use nuclear weapons in the defense of the alliance. Indeed, improved conventional defenses enhanced the credibility of American nuclear escalation by providing

Washington with much greater flexibility in deciding when and how the nuclear weapons would be used.

But the military balance has changed since the 1960s and the West's strategy of flexible response now requires nuclear as well as conventional force improvements. Moscow's attainment of strategic parity in intercontinental forces and its existing advantage in longer-range theater nuclear systems means that the alliance, to deter war, must now possess the capacity to undertake discrete and effective nuclear strikes in a European conflict. Clearly, the adoption by NATO of a nuclear war-fighting strategy is likely to be resisted by observers on both sides of the Atlantic who believe that the threat of nuclear use is sufficient by itself to stop the outbreak of war. But the growth of Soviet conventional and nuclear capabilities no longer gives NATO a choice between deterrence and defense: to build a credible defense in the 1980s will require both conventional and nuclear force modernization. The alliance faces an adversary that has acquired a full spectrum of capabilities across the board. For NATO, there seems to be no alternative but to match Moscow in each of these areas, including a theater nuclear capability that can meet the kinds of Soviet threats that will emerge during the coming decade.

MAKING NUCLEAR DECISIONS: THE NEUTRON BOMB FIASCO

This said, it is important to ask whether the alliance will be able to make sensitive nuclear deployment decisions in the years ahead. In attempting to answer this question, it may be useful to examine two recent case studies of alliance nuclear decision-making. The first, of course, was the neutron bomb episode in April 1978 when, after months of uncertainty, President Carter decided against modernizing nuclear bat-

tlefield support forces with munitions that would produce
less collateral damage. Although a great deal has been written about how the neutron bomb decision raised serious
doubts concerning American coherence and leadership, in-
sufficient attention has been focused on how the decision
also represented an implicit choice by Jimmy Carter and his
advisers to shift the responsibility for NATO nuclear policy
from Washington to the alliance as a whole. Prior to the
neutron bomb debate, nuclear weapons issues had been
defined and disposed by the United States. While sometimes
controversial, Washington then clearly possessed greater
flexibility in taking nuclear decisions than the European
allies. But for reasons that are still unclear, the Carter administration decided to abdicate its responsibility for nuclear
policy in NATO and, with the neutron bomb case, to promote
a pluralistic model of handling delicate weapons decisions.
As a result, the administration declined to take a position on
deploying the neutron weapon until after allied governments
also demonstrated their support for the concept.

There are two problems with the pluralistic model of
nuclear decision-making within NATO. The first is theoretical. If and when West Germany and other major allies begin
to formulate their own approach to nuclear affairs, they are
quite likely (as the experience of France showed more than a
decade ago) to adopt positions that will be viewed in Washington as untenable. But it is really not a question of whether
nuclear decision-making should be pluralistic or
U.S.–dominated. As the neutron bomb episode demonstrated
in convincing fashion, most allied countries have yet to
create the political and societal underpinnings to make
difficult nuclear decisions. Asking them to stand up to be
counted on nuclear deployment decisions, as the Carter administration did on the neutron bomb in 1978, is a prescription for alliance immobilism.

LONG-RANGE THEATER FORCES

The deep strains created within NATO by the neutron bomb fiasco did result in a far more coherent approach to the NATO decision of December 1979 to deploy a new generation of long-range theater systems capable of reaching the Soviet homeland. This decision, which could result in the deployment of 464 ground-launched cruise missiles and 108 Pershing II ballistic missiles in five different allied countries in the early 1980s, was clearly one of the most important decisions the alliance has ever taken. And in distinct contrast to the neutron bomb affair, it was a decision very much shaped by the United States. Although the administration insisted that the alliance approach the long-range theater nuclear force issue as a collective decision, there was never any doubt that the United States strongly supported the deployment and was prepared to take political responsibility for promoting a program to modernize NATO's nuclear posture. As a result, while Belgium and the Netherlands had some last-minute doubts about proceeding with nuclear modernization, the program was approved by the alliance as a whole.

But this second case study of alliance decision-making also contained some potentially dangerous aspects. In order to give European governments the political leeway to approve the 572 new missiles, the alliance was forced to develop and unveil an arms control proposal for American and Soviet theater nuclear systems which, in the end, could pose major obstacles for further efforts to modernize NATO's nuclear posture. To begin with, the administration and other Western governments failed to identify any convincing military rationale for the new missiles. Rather than making a case for the new systems in terms of a new strategy of nuclear flexibility (required by Soviet nuclear modernization in numerous categories of forces), the new systems were merely justified by the growth of the Soviet SS–20 intermediate-range ballistic missile force.

The tendency to justify NATO nuclear modernization in terms of the SS–20 and possible negotiating outcomes has had the effect of making the program vulnerable to its critics, both East and West. As stated above, Moscow's nuclear modernization program is not centered around a single system but consists of several new weapons, including the SS–21, SS–22, and the SS–23 battlefield nuclear support missiles, the Backfire medium-range bomber, and the Su–19 Fencer attack aircraft. The problem, of course, is that having linked NATO's nuclear plans to the SS–20, Moscow, in future talks, could agree to limit its options for this system in order to gain leverage over the alliance's Pershing II and cruise missile program. While such a process might result in limitations on the SS–20, it would do little or nothing about the other Soviet nuclear developments alluded to above.

But a more basic problem with NATO's decision last December concerns the notion, strong on both sides of the Atlantic, that arms control offers a substitute for a coherent defense policy. Gradually, but almost inevitably, the alliance seems to be slipping into a stance in which it cannot make a difficult military decision without a corresponding arms control initiative. Of course, there are occasions in which arms control should accompany new military decisions. But in the case of NATO's declining nuclear deterrent, it is difficult to see how any potential negotiating initiative acceptable to Moscow would serve Western interests. Before any negotiations get underway, it seems clear that the West will have to take several steps to bolster the credibility of both its nuclear deterrent and its arms control proposals.

TOWARD A NEW POLICY AGENDA

Most of the problems confronting the alliance are deep-seated in character, reflecting divergent perspectives toward the Soviet Union and toward domestic constraints on both sides of the Atlantic. Nevertheless, it is possible to outline a few steps that could be taken in the next few years to revitalize NATO:

The first step is conceptual. As appealing as it sounds to argue that the United States can respond to the growth of Soviet military power by emphasizing either nuclear forces or conventional defenses, it is probably true that the era in which the alliance had the luxury of making such a choice is ended. The Soviet Union, outspending the United States by as much as 15 percent of its gross national product on defense over the last decade, has acquired well-balanced military forces across the board. While emphasizing conventional forces will tend to raise the threshold in local conflicts for the use of nuclear weapons, robust conventional defenses, when combined with deteriorating nuclear responses, will actually provide the Soviet Union with incentives to escalate in time of war. The alliance thus needs to adopt a strategy which stresses the mutually reinforcing character of balanced conventional and nuclear options. Such a strategy would allow the alliance to get away from the self-defeating dichotomy between deterrence and defense. Strong nuclear capabilities, when combined with conventional forces, will act to bolster deterrence. Likewise, deterrence does not end with the initiation of conflict, and nuclear capabilities together with conventional forces will provide the Soviet Union with incentives for exercising restraint even after a conflict gets under way.

Second, despite good intentions, the alliance's long-term defense improvement program, which has focused mainly on

conventional forces, is bogged down in bureaucratic detail.
As important as are such steps as greater standardization
and interoperability between differing weapon systems and
national forces, such technical subjects should not be allowed
to obscure more pressing military needs. These needs include
such politically controversial steps as strengthening reserve
forces in Europe. In addition, the alliance must take a hard
look at its existing means of carrying out its "forward
defense strategy." At present, NATO intends to defend
Central Europe by emphasizing the role of infantry supported by firepower. Steven Canby (1974/75) has argued,
however, that a strategy stressing the role of maneuver in
modern ground warfare is probably more appropriate for defending Europe in the 1980s.

Third, a comprehensive approach to theater nuclear
modernization must be taken in replacing the alliance's increasingly obsolete nuclear posture rather than taking the
piecemeal and *ad hoc* steps now underway. A comprehensive
approach, which by its very nature emphasizes the relationship between nuclear and conventional forces, will surely be
a controversial issue in some segments of European opinion.
But, as was stressed above, the Soviet Union is in the process
of deploying a whole new family of nuclear forces directed
against the alliance. Only a modernization program that
links long-range forces with battlefield support systems can
offer a suitable response to this impressive Soviet effort. To
gain political support for such a program, the alliance will
have to go beyond simply arguing that NATO should match
new Soviet weapon systems such as the SS–20 or the Backfire bomber. Instead, political leaders will have to make a
case for theater nuclear weapons on their own ground. This
means that the ability of nuclear forces to perform
meaningful military roles will have to be stressed along with
the simple escalatory character of these forces.

Finally, the role of arms control in Western Europe will
have to be deemphasized in the decade ahead. As almost ten

years of experience at the Strategic Arms Limitation Talks has shown, arms agreements tend to ratify complex military problems rather than to resolve them. Moreover, the momentum of Soviet conventional and nuclear programs within and outside the European theater makes it highly unlikely that Western negotiators will possess much leverage in future arms talks. There will be occasions when carefully crafted arms control initiatives can be used to accompany new weapon systems, new weapon deployment decisions. But it is a major mistake to make arms control a prerequisite to NATO force improvements.

If the West can face up to these problems and can make necessary improvements in both conventional and nuclear forces, then NATO in the 1980s will continue to provide the central solution to the security challenges posed by the Soviet Union. On the other hand, proceeding on the present path, given the continuing momentum of the Soviet buildup, could expose the alliance to a security threat of unprecedented gravity.

7

ALBERT WOHLSTETTER

Half-Wars and Half-Policies in the Persian Gulf

Alliance interests in the Persian Gulf. Large wars and small wars. The security of oil supplies. The Soviet sphere of interest. Radical Middle East states. Iraq and Saddam Husayn. The West and the Indian Ocean. Alternative proposals to reduce the threat.

A persistent objective of American policy has been to be able to deter or fight a big war in the center of Europe and also to handle a smaller war occurring at the same time or shortly before it. In the early 1960s, in fact, American policy aimed

* This chapter expands on material presented in a series of five articles published in the *New York Times* (January/March 1979).

at being able to deal with such a "half-war" without compromising our ability to fight *two* large wars at the same time
or immediately afterward. By the end of the 1970s American
policymakers had lowered their sights. They aimed at a
capability for dealing with "one and a half" rather than "two
and a half" wars. It is not clear that the reduction from two
to one big war represented a decrease in our estimates of the
probability that we might have to fight two rather than one.
It may simply have represented our decreasing willingness to
maintain a prudent defense. There was quite a bit of fuzzi-
ness in the early policy as in the more recent one. Nonetheless, whatever can be said about the "whole" or big wars, we
continue to recognize the need to deal adequately with a half-
war. Its importance has become more rather than less obvious with time, and in particular with the deterioration of
the position of the West in the Persian Gulf. The disasters to
alliance policy there and the critical dangers they imply for
the American alliance system are now too visible to require
extended comment.

For a "small" war in the Persian Gulf might be small compared to a big war in the center of Europe only in the sense
that it *would engage fewer forces in battle*. The stakes in such
a small war could be very large—no less than the cohesion of
the Western alliance itself. Our major allies in Western
Europe and in northeast Asia vary in their dependence on oil
from the gulf, but their dependency is very great. It is so
great that it makes little sense to ask whether an attack on
the gulf is less important than an attack on the European
center. An attack on the gulf would amount to an indirect attack on the center.

In the recent past it was common to feel that the protection of alliance interests in the Persian Gulf would not call
for any exercise of American or ailliance power: the Russians
would not risk intervention in so vital a spot for the Western
alliance and the contending regional forces would balance
out. If the Russians did risk it, or if regional powers didn't

balance out, it wouldn't much matter. Whatever countries were in control of gulf oil would have to sell it. They couldn't drink it. And they had no better place to sell it than to Western Europe, Japan, and the United States.

However, the experience of the last few years reminds us that whoever controls the swing production of oil can interrupt production not only for economic ends, as did the Iranians and Saudis in 1974, but for political ends, as did the Saudis in 1973. Control of a larger fraction of the oil by a radical state in the area could be considerably worse. And Soviet political control could be deadly. Members of the alliance have tended to neglect potential small wars in the gulf—apparently just because they would be comparatively small in the *size of forces engaged.*

Because a war in the Persian Gulf would be small compared to the big war in Europe, it was also tempting to think that we could handle it easily if we could handle the big war—that the capacity to fight a large war *implied* the ability to deal with a small one. The notion that a small war is simply a "lesser included case" of a large one proceeds from the notion, so to speak, that the dog that can handle the cat can easily deal with the kitten. Plausible enough, but not necessarily so. The circumstances governing the use of power in the Persian Gulf today, the meagerness of alliance infrastructure there, the instabilities within and among the regional powers may call for the application of quite different kinds of power and impose political constraints, time urgencies, and other demands more stringent than those in the center of Europe. We have, in short, to consider some small wars which are lesser *ex*cluded cases. In any event, the goal of our policy has been and must be to be able to handle a small conflict critical for the alliance without compromising the alliance capability to handle a large conflict in the center. The demand for a capability in the gulf is in *addition* to—not simply part of—the large capability needed in the European center.

In the aftermath of the revolution in Iran and the Soviet invasion of Afghanistan, the inadequacies of past alliance policy for the Persian Gulf have become very visible. There is a serious divergence among the allies, but both American and other allied responses to the crisis so far seem largely improvisations. Both here and abroad, political elites have yet to meet the challenge of developing a serious and sustained policy capable of correcting the obvious deficiencies of their policies of the preceding decade. Yet the goals that were defined before the crisis by American policymakers for dealing with a half-war—in the Persian Gulf or elsewhere—seem quite reasonable.

American policymakers have said in the past that:

(1) we want to be able to protect critical alliance interests that are endangered by a nonnuclear attack on the periphery by meeting such an attack at its own level—that is, without resort to nuclear weapons or to the bluff that we would use nuclear weapons (U.S. Department of Defense 1978, p. 80; 1979, p. 75);

(2) we want our response to be rapid and decisive enough to frustrate a quick takeover which would present us with a *fait accompli* (U.S. Department of Defense 1978, p. 225);

(3) we want to have such a capability steadily without sacrificing our capability to fight or to deter a larger war happening at the same time or shortly thereafter (U.S. Department of Defense 1978, p. 80);

(4) we want a reliable capability—one that will "meet a high standard of confidence" (U.S. Department of Defense 1978, p. 80)—rather than only to create some small uncertainty for the other side; we want more than a long shot for our side.

These four objectives seem eminently reasonable given the massive size of the stakes in a war for control of oil in the Persian Gulf. They define the criterion set down by the Secretary of Defense in his *Annual Reports* for FY 1979 and

FY 1980 for determining the adequacy of our power projection capability.

It is clear, however, that the steps so far taken and those announced by the U.S. government make up only a small part of such an adequate power projection policy for the gulf. The two carrier task groups stationed in the gulf in the spring of 1980 comprise essentially all the firepower that can be brought quickly to bear in response to an invasion endangering alliance interests there. Yet in the event of a Soviet invasion, Soviet medium bombers based on land in the Soviet Union and Afghanistan and staging in Yemen could attack the carriers in the Arabian Sea along many axes. They could thus impose severe problems on the carriers simply to defend themselves, not to say to project power on shore as well. It is questionable how much firepower two carrier task groups could then bring to bear in the critical upper gulf area.

Moreover, these carriers were drawn from the Sixth Fleet in the Mediterranean and from the Seventh Fleet in the western Pacific; the move cuts in half the number of our carriers deployed in those fleets. Yet the fleets were already stretched thin. The North Korean buildup, the assassination of Park, and the attendant uncertainties have not lessened the dangers in the western Pacific. Threats of a Vietnam invasion of Thailand further increased the dangers in the future. Nor have the imminent demise of Tito, the uncertainties in his succession, and the likely Soviet pressures in the Balkans reduced the dangers in the Mediterranean. The current American buildup in the Persian Gulf, then, does compromise our ability to fight a big war elsewhere—or even a second half-war. It therefore violates one of the requirements stipulated by the Secretary of Defense for achieving an adequate capability to project power.

We might, of course, respond to a Soviet incursion by escalation; that is, by starting a war elsewhere or by using or threatening to use nuclear weapons. That, however, would indicate another inadequacy in the capability we have developed so far, if we take seriously the secretary's criterion for testing adequacy: we want to be able to meet a conventional incursion in its own terms. It is one more indication that we have not yet fielded—nor have we yet projected—a serious sustained program for defending alliance interests in the gulf.

This does not, of course, mean certain disaster. The Secretary of Defense has been quoted as saying that we could not be certain of the outcome of conflict there, but then neither could the Soviet Union. This is plainly the case. (Neither side in a war can be certain of the outcome.) However, it is not entirely reassuring. As the secretary has stated in the past, we want a capability that "will meet a high standard of confidence" (U.S. Department of Defense 1978, p. 80). We want, in short, to do more than create some uncertainty—perhaps only a little—for an adversary. We want the odds on such critical matters to be on our side.

As for the future moves that we have so far projected and are beginning to get under way, they appear also to fall short of what the secretary requires of an adequate capability. The performance characteristics of a future CX transport aircraft are as yet undefined. It can increase the flexibility of deployments and shorten somewhat the time to reinforce an allied presence in or near the gulf, but it will not substitute for such a presence.

The rapid deployment force of marines being organized at present, which we expect eventually to supply with equipment kept on station somewhere in the Indian Ocean in some sixteen roll-on/roll-off ships, is almost sure to be very useful. However, no provision so far has been made for defending these ships while on station; it appears that the landings that the marines might make with equipment carried on these ships would have to take place a week or so rather than hours after a supposed Soviet incursion; and on the basis of the arrangements and forces planned to be available so far, such landings would have to be uncontested "administrative" landings to be feasible. (There is no assurance of local air cover or provision for it.)

Kenya, Somalia, and Oman, the countries with which the United States is negotiating for base facilities in or near the region, are not in a position to provide arrangements for an American presence close to the head of the gulf, steadily and in time of peace. Kenya is, of course, very remote, useful for such purposes as bunkering ships and as a liberty port for sailors. Somalia is not quite as far away, but is still quite distant and involves many political uncertainties. Oman, the closest and with a leadership that is most forthcoming, nevertheless is subject to many local radical as well as Soviet pressures and has made it clear that it cannot accommodate a steady-state American combat presence.

In sum, the U.S. program so far falls far short of "adequacy" as defined by U.S. standards enunciated before the crisis.

Nonetheless, if American programs to develop a serious long-term capability to deal with a half-war in the critical gulf are are still only half-formed—or less than that—such progress puts the United States ahead of its allies. It appears that our major allies have yet to face candidly the dangers made visible by the recent crises in the gulf region. Yet they have a larger and even more direct stake in the area.

THE NEED FOR NONMILITARY AS WELL AS MILITARY MEASURES FOR THE SECURITY OF OIL

About 20 million of the 50 million barrels of oil consumed every day by the non-Communist world come from the Persian Gulf. As other essays in this volume can attest (see Rowen, Chapter 11), a well-designed program of *non*military measures could significantly reduce our dependency and that of our allies on Persian Gulf oil, and such a program is urgent. However, unless Western economic policies are much more farsighted than seems plausible, and unless policymakers are much more willing to risk popular disapproval and transient domestic political difficulties, allied dependency is likely to persist for a long time to come. An improved military capability to protect Persian Gulf oil is therefore essential. But in the past decade, while allied military capability to affect events there has been weakening, allied dependency on the gulf has been on the increase.

The British, who had been the dominant power in the Persian Gulf for a hundred and fifty years, began the debate leading to their withdrawal not long after the return of the Labor Party in October 1964—with only a modest interest displayed by their major allies in Europe. Yet from 1964 to 1977 Western Europe's imports of oil from the Persian Gulf grew from 58.9 percent of its total oil consumption to 64.8 percent. Moreover, since oil consumption was increasing as a percentage of primary energy consumed, Western Europe was increasing its dependency on the Persian Gulf even more than is indicated by figures on gulf oil as a percent of total oil consumed. In percent of primary energy consumed, European oil imported from the gulf between 1964 and 1977 grew from 24.5 percent to 35.0 percent. In Japan, Persian Gulf imports as a percentage of primary energy consumed increased from 44.0 percent in 1964 to 59.2 percent in 1977. Some of our major European allies increased dependency even more rapidly than did Japan. French imports from the Persian Gulf as a percent of primary energy consumed increased very rapidly from 21.1 percent in 1964 to 51.6 percent in 1976, making France almost as vulnerable as the Japanese. They declined to 46.3 percent in 1977, which is still more than double their 1964 dependency. France consumes much more energy in the form of oil than countries such as the Federal Republic of Germany, which has substantial amounts of coal. American imports from the Persian Gulf in the same period grew very rapidly in percent of primary energy consumed. However, since the United States produces much of the oil it consumes and has extensive domestic sources of energy besides oil, its dependency is much smaller than that of Europe or Japan. In percent of primary energy consumed in the United States, American imports from the Persian Gulf for oil grew from 1.4 percent in 1964 to 8.4 percent in 1977. The trends over time are indicated in Figures 1 and 2 and in Table 1.

ADVERSARY STRATEGIES FOR EXPLOITING POTENTIAL ALLIED DIVERGENCE

One point that emerges, then, from even a rudimentary economic analysis of alliance dependency on oil from the Persian Gulf is that the direct dependency of our allies not only exceeds our own, but varies greatly among themselves. This does not mean, as is sometimes suggested, that Persian Gulf oil is "vital" for our allies but only "important" and not "vital" for us (see Collins 1979). Simple dichotomies between "vital" and "nonvital" or "important" and "not important," of course, approximate only crudely differences within the continuously varying and interdependent interests of our allies and ourselves. In the long run, if the alliance itself is essential for us, as we have frequently affirmed, oil which is essential for our allies is also essential for us. However, it does mean that our allies will have different short-run vulnerabilities.

The short-term interests of our allies, therefore, may frequently diverge from each other's and particularly from our own. This has implications for an understanding of the potential aims and strategies of an adversary in the gulf. The

Figure 1
Persian Gulf Oil Imports as a Percentage of Oil Consumption*

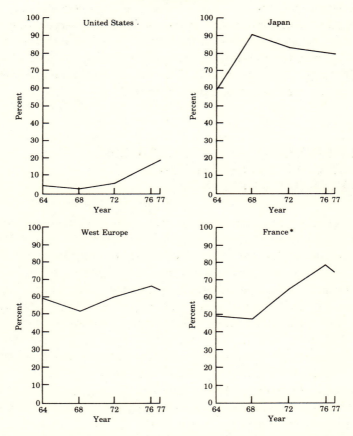

Sources and methods of preparation: Derived from tables on apparent supply of crude petroleum and world movement of crude petroleum in United Nations, *World Energy Supplies*, various volumes: no. 15, 1961–70; no. 21, 1972–76; no. 22, 1973–78. The oil component of total energy consumption was increased by 5 percent to account for non-energy oil uses. Hydro and nuclear electricity have been converted to primary energy by dividing by 0.373. Crude oil consumption and imports were adjusted to account for trade in refined petroleum products.

Figure 2
Persian Gulf Oil Imports as a Percentage of
Primary Energy Consumption*

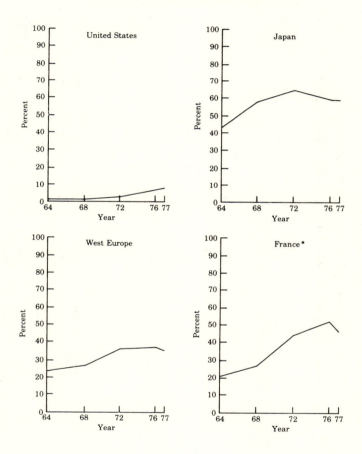

*It is important to note that France imports approximately an additional 10 percent of crude oil to be refined into finished products for export. We have excluded this 10 percent of crude oil imports in our calculations, though the refining activity produces revenue and would be interrupted if the oil imports were not available.

Table 1
Persian Gulf Oil Imports as Percentages of Total Oil Imports and Total Energy Consumption

Year	(1)[1] MTOE*	(2)[2] MTOE*	(3)[3] MTOE*	(4)[4] MTOE*	(5)[5] %	(6)[6] %	(7)[7] %	(8)[8] %	(9)[9] %
United States									
1964	1,207	466	72	17	39	6	1	4	24
1968	1,465	562	90	13	38	6	1	2	14
1972	1,728	692	224	43	40	13	3	6	19
1976	1,789	745	346	130	42	19	7	17	38
1977	1,816	788	394	152	43	22	8	19	39
Japan									
1964	123	93	63	54	75	51	44	59	85
1968	193	123	124	112	64	64	58	91	91
1972	280	215	217	178	77	77	64	83	82
1976	318	233	233	186	73	73	59	80	80
1977	321	241	242	190	75	75	59	79	79

Western Europe

Year	¹	²	³	⁴	⁵	⁶	⁷	⁸	⁹
1964	743	309	293	182	42	39	24	59	62
1968	875	466	443	240	53	51	27	52	54
1972	1,084	638	621	391	59	57	36	61	63
1976	1,154	641	624	432	56	54	37	67	69
1977	1,160	627	592	406	54	51	35	65	69

France*

Year	¹	²	³	⁴	⁵	⁶	⁷	⁸	⁹
1964	106	45	43	22	43	41	21	49	52
1968	127	72	69	34	57	55	27	47	49
1972	163	111	109	71	68	67	44	64	65
1976	171	113	112	88	66	66	52	78	79
1977	176	110	109	82	63	62	46	74	75

Sources and methods of preparation: Derived from tables on apparent supply of crude petroleum and world movement of crude petroleum, in the United Nations, *World Energy Supplies*, various volumes: no. 15, 1961–70; no. 21, 1972–76; no. 22, 1973–78. The oil component of total energy consumption was increased by 5 percent to account for nonenergy oil uses. Hydro and nuclear electricity have been converted to primary energy by dividing by 0.373. Crude oil consumption and imports were adjusted to account for trade in refined petroleum products.

*Million metric tons oil equivalent.

¹Total primary energy consumption.
²Total crude oil consumption.
³Total crude oil imports.
⁴Total Persian Gulf crude oil imports.

⁵Oil consumption divided by energy consumption.
⁶Oil imports divided by energy consumption.
⁷Persian Gulf oil imports divided by energy consumption.
⁸Persian Gulf oil imports divided by oil consumption.
⁹Persian Gulf oil imports divided by oil import.

¹⁰It is important to note that France imports approximately an additional 10 percent of crude oil to be refined into finished products for export. We have excluded this 10 percent of crude oil imports in our calculations, though the refining activity produces revenue and would be interrupted if the oil imports were not available.

persistent and critical dependency of the Western alliance on Persian Gulf oil and the potential divergence among our allies make clear that hostile political control over the flow of oil from the gulf—the ability of an adversary either to deny or to offer an assured supply to Europe and Japan—is a lever capable of prying the alliance apart. An attack in this region outside the North Atlantic Treaty Organization (NATO) treaty area (and many thousands of miles from our major ally in northeast Asia) would plainly involve smaller risks to the Soviet Union than a direct assault on the NATO center. Yet it would strike at the heart of NATO—and at the American alliance with Japan.

HOSTILE CONTROL OF OIL FROM THE UPPER GULF AREA

What should merit study, therefore, are contingencies in the upper Persian Gulf in which the objective of Soviet strategy would be not to destroy or even to interrupt the flow of oil, but to gain political control over the flow in order to be able either to assure a supply of oil at a tolerable economic price to Europe and Japan—or to cut it off. Some government studies have examined contingencies in which Soviet objectives or those of regional powers have included the destruction of the wells or of the means of shipping the oil, or blocking its passage. These are important cases worth studying, especially in connection with a conflict in the gulf occurring at the same time or shortly before an extended conventional war in the center of Europe. Our plans, at least since World War II, have always recognized the crucial wartime importance of gulf oil.[1] However, we have centered less attention on the damage the West would incur from hostile political control of the oil it requires during peacetime, whether that control is exercised by the Soviet Union or a radical state in the region and no matter how obtained—by subversion or external pressure or the actual use of military force.

SOVIET INTEREST IN THE PERSIAN GULF

The Soviet interest in the Persian Gulf sometimes is said, perhaps by way of reassurance, to be much less than that of the West: it is not in their case a "vital interest"; therefore they are hardly likely to challenge the West there. Such a judgment appears to be based on the fact that at present the Soviets produce more oil than they consume. The well-known study by the CIA in 1977, indicating that the Soviet Union will *become* a net importer of oil in the 1980s, seems then to qualify but does not eliminate the implicit optimism of this evaluation. That time is not yet here, and even then the Soviet Union will not "need" the oil as much as the West does.

However, the Soviet Union could derive much wider-ranging benefits from controlling gulf oil than the opportunity merely to consume it. Reserves in the Persian Gulf in the first place represent an enormous economic asset worth at current prices perhaps $25 trillion. More important, the income stream from the use of these assets would represent a very large increment in their gross resources and in the potential for exercising political and military influence. After all, the present Persian Gulf oil producers consume only a tiny fraction of the oil they produce. This is part of the reason that they—and not the United States nor the Soviet Union, which are the largest producers—have controlled the marginal production of oil. They can raise or lower their production by large amounts, and so have been able to affect the world price. Third, and more relevant for our purposes, Soviet control of the marginal or "swing" production would— insofar as Soviet interests are opposed to those of the NATO alliance and to the Japanese alliance with the United States—be of enormous benefit to them precisely because the oil is critical in peacetime as well as wartime for our major allies. And evidence abounds that the Soviets have directed their efforts for years at weakening or breaking up the American alliance system, whatever other ambitions may be driving them.

In fact, the Soviets have usually deprecated the notion that they were going to become importers of oil and denied that they had any interest either in oil from the gulf or in a warm-water port there. Very recently they have indicated that they may become consumers of Middle Eastern oil, and they made this the occasion to propose an all-European conference of their own on the security of oil routes from the Persian Gulf—as an alternative to the selfish American policies which threaten to turn the region into a powder keg (Fisher 1980). The prospect of the Russians as protectors of the flow of oil to Europe—against American selfish interests and also possibly against interruption by chaos in regional states—should give us pause. It holds out the possibility of some immediate confusion and pressures on regional producers as well as on the industrial consumers of oil allied with the United States. It also suggests the sort of pretext and cover that might be used for a future Soviet intervention.

Such a declaration of Soviet interest in the uninterrupted flow of Middle East oil fits well with their denial of President Carter's assertion in his 1980 State of the Union address that there is a Soviet threat to that flow, and with several other themes which the Soviets have been loudly sounding in recent times:[2] First, that it is absurd and even "brainless" for the United States to say that it has " 'the right' to regard the Persian Gulf which is thousands of miles from the American shores as a sphere of 'vital interests' and even to use military force to preserve the American monopolies' 'hold on the area.' " Second, that such an assertion is part of the U.S. "claim to the role of 'world policeman,' " and third, that the

Soviet Union does have the right to ensure its security interests in "neighboring" areas—that, in short, areas near the Soviet Union are part of its sphere of interest, not ours.

The notion that the interests of a state diminish steadily with distance has some base in traditional geopolitical theories. It was never rigorously true, and it makes a particularly bad fit for the current realities of world markets and interdependencies and for today's technologies of military as well as civilian transport and communications, and of weapons delivery. However, it has a certain resonance in the Third World, and specifically in the Persian Gulf. It underlay much of the regionalism propounded in the 1960s in Europe and in the United States, and formed part of the background for the withdrawal of the British from the gulf and the failure of the French and West Germans to recognize the value of the British or other alliance presence there as a contribution to NATO—and for the American failure to work out a joint alliance contribution for the protection of NATO and Japanese interests there, to fill the vacuum left by the British. The confusions and dangers of a revival of this old sphere-of-influence notion have a wider direct relevance than their application to the Persian Gulf. Our major allies are all much closer to the Soviet Union than they are to the United States. Norway and Turkey border the Soviet Union and the Federal Republic of Germany is only a few hundred miles away—about as far as the head of the gulf.

SOVIET (AND RUSSIAN) INTERESTS IN THE NORTHERN TIER

The Soviet Union has had an interest in extending its influence and control in Afghanistan, and in Iran, Pakistan, and Turkey—the "northern tier" of the Middle East— almost since the creation of the Soviet Union near the end of

World War I. One of the first violations of Soviet avowals at the time of the Brest-Litovsk Treaty (1918) had to do with its sponsorship of a separatist movement in Iranian Gilan and Azerbaijan. In fact, Soviet interests in some respects continue the long-term tsarist ambitions there, but with pertinent differences. In the Great Game between tsarist Russia and England, the northern tier figured as barrier or gateway to India. The Persian Gulf countries themselves, including those in the lower gulf, were also regarded as gateways to India. Since India's independence, and in particular since the critical growth in importance of oil for industrial society, the Persian Gulf has itself become the major regional stake in the game between the West and the Soviet Union—a very serious game. The foreign offices of the West have sometimes been confused by the change in the stakes. Our own Department of State at the beginning of the 1950s misunderstood the importance of Afghanistan for this reason, among others. It turned Afghanistan away when it requested aid and military protection.

After World War II, Turkey, Iran, and Pakistan formed a critical part of a barrier in the air and on the ground separating the Soviet Union from the Persian Gulf and the Indian Ocean. In the early 1950s that barrier extended without a break from the North Cape of Norway to Southeast Asia and beyond. Coming from the West, a Russian transport plane would have had to fly about 13,000 nautical miles (nm) nonstop to reach the gulf. Figure 3 illustrates this. The thick black line marks the land barrier. The long, mostly dashed, line starting from Russia's Kola Peninsula in the north to the upper gulf marks the air route. Its short unbroken segment covers the maximum length a Russian transport plane could fly without a refueling stop. The situation was not much better for the Russians coming from the east. Starting from Vladivostok, they would have had to travel for 7,000 nm. In short, they had no way of reaching the gulf by air.

Figure 3

Air Access in Early 1950s

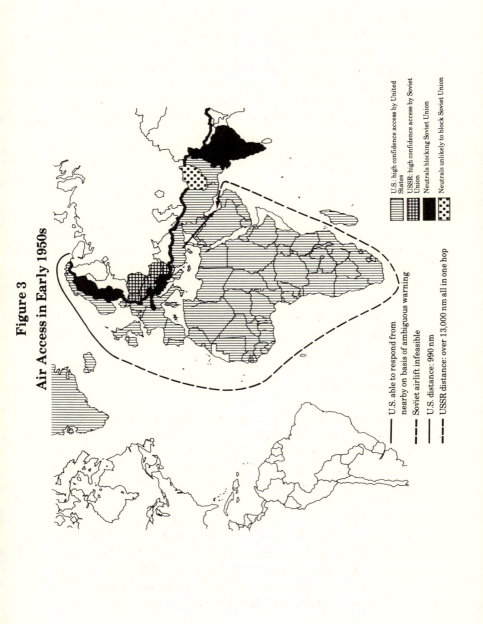

U.S.: high confidence access by United States

USSR: high confidence access by Soviet Union

Neutrals blocking Soviet Union

Neutrals unlikely to block Soviet Union

——— U.S. able to respond from nearby on basis of ambiguous warning

– – – Soviet airlift infeasible

——— U.S. distance: 990 nm

– · – USSR distance: over 13,000 nm all in one hop

The United States and its allies, on the other hand, had access in 1950 to base facilities and airspace along the northern and southern littoral of the Mediterranean and its major islands, and access to major bases in the gulf. The distance from Incirlik in Turkey to some key points in the gulf was a little over 1,000 nm. In Figure 3 the arrow shows one such route from Incirlik to the upper Persian Gulf, a distance of 990 nm.

Since the 1950s the relative position of the Soviet Union and the United States and its allies has been almost reversed. It is now the United States which has major difficulties with airspace and base facilities. The Soviet Union is now some 500 to 1,000 nm from the upper gulf along politically and militarily feasible routes. The United States, on the other hand, at the end of the 1970s would have had to travel nearly 7,300 nm from Fort Riley, Kansas, in order to lift heavy ground forces to Dhahran in Saudi Arabia and would have had to make three stops on the way. Figure 4 presents this change. The air barrier has been penetrated in many places, but most pertinently in Iran. The short arrows show the Soviets taking off from bases in southern Russia and Afghanistan, while the long arrow indicates the lift from the United States, starting from the interior of the American continent.

The change came gradually and almost without notice by the West. In the 1960s the Soviet Union breached the air barrier in Yugoslavia with permission to fly reconnaissance and antisubmarine warfare flights, and then continued to probe for at least intermittent openings elsewhere, and specifically in the northern tier, during the 1970s. The crumbling of the ability of the Iranians to offer any convincing defense of their airspace marks the culmination of a long period of increasing Soviet overflights with or without permission of the barrier countries. The access the Soviets had obtained by 1980 by air alone represents a vast increase in their ability to project power rapidly into the gulf region. Since they started

Figure 4
Air Access 1979

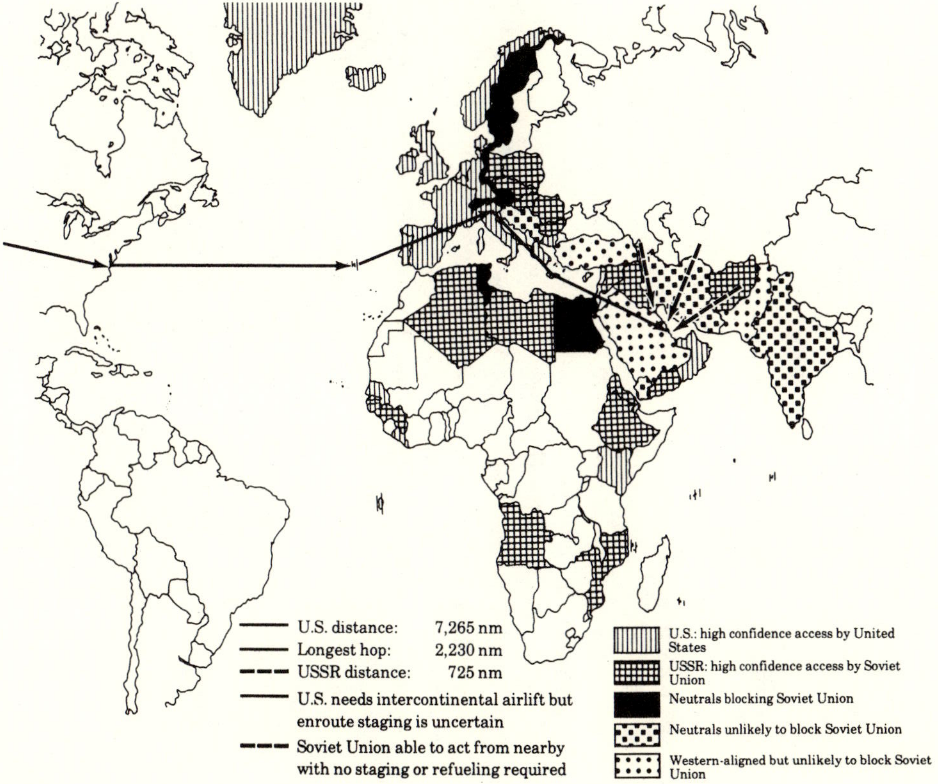

U.S. distance: 7,265 nm
Longest hop: 2,230 nm
USSR distance: 725 nm

U.S. needs intercontinental airlift but enroute staging is uncertain

Soviet Union able to act from nearby with no staging or refueling required

U.S.: high confidence access by United States

USSR: high confidence access by Soviet Union

Neutrals blocking Soviet Union

Neutrals unlikely to block Soviet Union

Western-aligned but unlikely to block Soviet Union

with a negligible capability in this area so critical for the alliance, we must count this change as one of the most important alterations in the strategic situation of the West since World War II—or indeed since World War I.

A parallel change has taken place in the availability of naval facilities for the alliance. Figures 5 and 6 present this change.

DEFENSIVE EXPANSION

The northern tier of the Middle East is also part of the southern border of the Soviet Union. The Soviets (and Russians before them) have been interested in extending their power beyond their borders to the south and also, naturally, in protecting their borders from invaders. The northern tier is both a gateway for the Soviets to the gulf and a back door into the Soviet Union. This obvious truth is capable of generating a great deal of apologetic and wishful justification for Soviet military moves against the northern tier.

Was the Soviet invasion of Afghanistan purely "defensive"? Or was it purely "offensive"? One may doubt that it was purely anything. For it is not possible conceptually to separate the two motivations. Control of the territory beyond its current borders will help defend those borders. On the other hand, inevitably it is a further extension of the border. The Islamic revival and chaos in Afghanistan, it is said, threaten trouble among ethnic minorities inside Soviet borders. So could chaos in Iran. A "defense" of the Soviet Union—under some circumstances—might therefore include an invasion of Iran. If successful, however, it would mean a great increment in Soviet power over regional powers of the gulf as well as over the West.

It is hardly credible that the Soviets are unaware of this. The kind of gateway they would like is undoubtedly a one-way turnstile, one that would let them exit but let no one else enter. There is no evidence that they have sought earnestly to block traffic in both directions.

Figure 5

Naval Facilities Available to United States and Soviet Union 1950

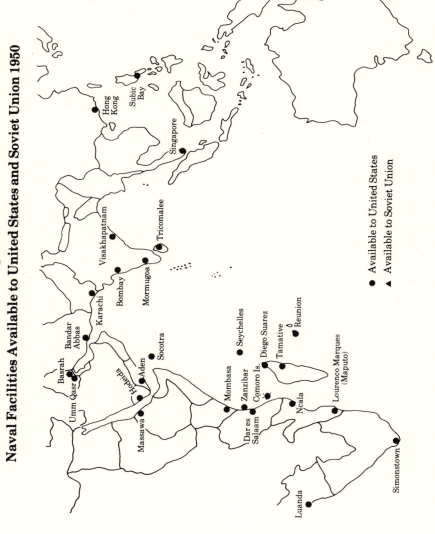

● Available to United States

▲ Available to Soviet Union

Figure 6
Naval Facilities Available to United States and Soviet Union 1979

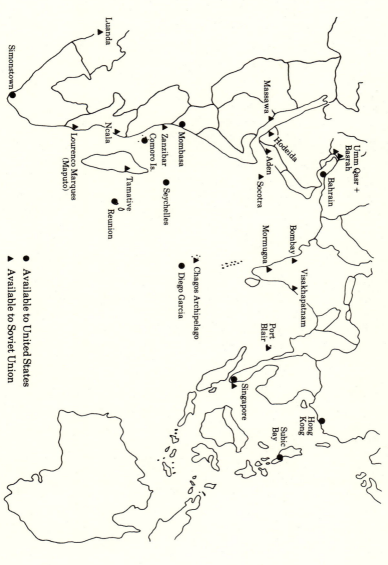

Luanda

Simonstown

Lourenco Marques
(Maputo)

Ncala

Mombasa

Zanzibar

Comoro Is.

Massawa

Hodeida

Aden

Socotra

Tamative

Reunion

Seychelles

Umm Qasr +
Basrah

Bahrain

Bombay

Mormugoa

Visakhapatnam

Port
Blair

Chagos Archipelago

Diego Garcia

Singapore

Hong
Kong

Subic
Bay

● Available to United States

▲ Available to Soviet Union

As far as the West is concerned, scholastic discussions in Western Europe and in the United States of "defensive aggression" as distinct from "offensive aggression" could hardly be more footless. The Soviets claim that their invasion of Poland and then of Finland early in World War II was "defensive." Arguably, that was true. Their takeover in Eastern Europe after World War II also undoubtedly improved the defense of their western borders against attack. There was a good deal of apologetic literature in the West, even by such an eminent scientist and operational research man as the British Nobel laureat P. M. S. Blackett, which argued that the takeover in Czechoslovakia was motivated and was made necessary in order to increase Soviet defense in depth against possible American attack. To East Europeans after World War II, however, a defensive occupation felt much the same as an offensive one; to the Poles and Finns at the start of the war, the consequences of a defensive invasion were operationally identical with the other kind.

The problem is a historic one. Mother Russia has always been concerned about defending her borders, and the problems only increased as Russia expanded and had more borders to defend. From the few thousand square miles of the duchy of Muscovy to the nine million square mile extent of the Soviet Union, the problem of defense has simply grown. Even if Soviet fears were groundless, as is sometimes said when analysts talk of Russian paranoia, this should not comfort us and does not mean we could adequately reassure them. Paranoids—it is familiar—can be very dangerous.

U.S. POWER AND THE SHORT– AND LONG–RUN INTERESTS OF OUR ALLIES

With few exceptions, our allies have been much more reserved than the U.S. government about the dangers to the security of the Persian Gulf, and therefore to themselves, which are implicit in the Iranian revolution and the Soviet invasion of Afghanistan.

French statements for example, after the Afghan invasion have said little about the interests of the alliance in this region outside the NATO treaty area. And little or nothing about the need for NATO jointly to increase its power to defend its interests there. And nothing in public about facilitating the application of American military power to help protect French and other European interests. (This does not necessarily mean that the French are unwilling to provide some help—like the regional powers—in less public form.)

In public they have been concerned, rather, to stress the importance of not increasing tensions excessively—of saving détente. Giscard d'Estaing has issued a joint communiqué with Indira Gandhi saying that the invasion of Afghanistan was "unacceptable," but without any mention of the identity of the invader. The communiqué fits the fluctuating, inconsistent stance that Mrs. Gandhi had adopted after the invasion. That stance varied between explicit support of the Soviet invasion of Afghanistan (like her support of the Soviet invasion of Czechoslovakia in 1968 and her father's support of the Soviet suppression of the Hungarian revolt in 1956) and the view that the invasion was unfortunate but only a response to prior American interference— and unfortunate in particular because it gave the Americans a pretext for continuing or increasing their presence in the Indian Ocean. The emphasis in the joint communiqué on the need as soon as possible to lessen tensions in the area, as Raymond Aron (1980, p. 68) has suggested, really means an acceptance of the invasion as a *fait accompli* in spite of the nominal declaration that it is unacceptable.[3]

West German reaction has been somewhat more forthcoming, but still rather cautious and concerned about the pressures that a forward German stance might invite. Chancellor Schmidt has taken the lead in the important matter of bolstering Turkey, a NATO country whose strategic position for the defense of the Persian Gulf is of maximum importance. But the joint communiqué which Chancellor

Schmidt issued together with Giscard d'Estaing (Fitchett 1980)[4] was only a partial advance over the communiqué issued by Giscard with Indira. The communiqué strongly condemned the invasion of Afghanistan and indicated that détente could not sustain *another* shock of the same order. Détente, this implies, has absorbed the shock of the Soviet invasion of Afghanistan.

There have been encouraging German statements expressing "solidarity" with the United States in its positions on the gulf, but such expressions seem to offer moral support to protection of American interests there rather than a recognition that the alliance interests that are most directly affected are those of Germany and other European countries. In fact, there has been recent discussion in Germany of a rather scholastic sort on the question of "the divisibility of détente" (Sommer 1980), with much influential opinion coming down on the side of those who feel that "détente must remain divisible." To an American, this appears to mean a division in which Europeans would continue to carry out détente in Europe while the Americans carried on a confrontation in the Persian Gulf, and in which the chief interest for the Europeans would seem to be to make certain that the Americans manage the crisis there soberly and with restraint. For there is much evidence that our major allies strongly doubt the idea expressed in President Carter's State of the Union message that "the implications" of the invasion of Afghanistan "could pose the most serious threat to world peace since the second World War" (*New York Times*, 24 January 1980, p. A12). Some of those implications have to do with the long-term growth in Soviet power that preceded the invasion and the willingness of the Soviets to use that power in the area so critical for the alliance. This may indeed present latent dangers more serious than any since World War II. Nonetheless, many Europeans think that the president's State of the Union message exaggerates the threat.

It is not only our major allies in Europe and in Japan who seem to be lukewarm about perils in the Persian Gulf region that affect them more directly than they do us. It is also true of the conservative and centrist states in the region which, in the past, have leaned toward the West. They are reluctant to offer facilities for an American presence in their countries, even though a continuing presence in or very near the gulf seems essential to match the massive Soviet presence not only in Afghanistan but in the Transcaucasus and the Transcaspian. Oman, which has been the most forthright and eager to help, has made it clear that it wants no permanent American presence nor much expansion of the modest but useful employment of Omani facilities which we have been making and that its major interest is in having us supply the means for Omani forces themselves to defend the Strait of Hormuz.

Saudi Arabia, whose fear of Soviet aggression is manifest obviously has a huge stake in protection from outside. Nonetheless, the Saudis have no intention of allowing American forces to be stationed on Saudi bases and believe that such a presence would make it impossible to rid the gulf of the Soviet presence (*Wall Street Journal*, 4 March 1980).[5]

Like ourselves, the Saudis sometimes want incompatible things. They do want protection against Soviet aggression which the regional powers are palpably unable to repel themselves. But keeping American or other alliance forces out of the gulf regions would not rid the gulf of the Soviet presence, even if the Russians acquired no further bases near the gulf, gave up their use of facilities in South Yemen and Ethiopia, accepted the "neutralization" of Afghanistan, and kept their ships out of the Indian Ocean. They can now have quite direct access to the Persian Gulf from south Russia. Protecting Saudi interests against Soviet attack may require help from other Western powers also. Some of the false premises of past American and NATO policy (as well as that of Saudi Arabia and of Iran under the shah) had to do with neglect of this requirement. Nonetheless, in reaction to the Iranian revolution and the invasion of Afghanistan, at least one high Saudi official has announced a three-point program for maintaining stability in the Middle East which involves the dictum that the United States as well as other "big" powers should keep out of the region (see *Wall Street Journal,* 11 March 1980).

Sheik Ahmed Zaki Yamani, the Saudis' oil minister, has recently said, "We do not want to see the superpowers present in our area. We must try to bring back a quiet atmosphere" (*Reuters* [London], 7 February 1980). Like other Saudi officials, Yamani is opposed to bases for the United States in Saudi Arabia or, indeed, elsewhere in the area. On the other hand, Yamani believes that "if the Soviet Union marched into Saudi Arabian oilfields there would be a third world war because they would be met there by armies of the United States, Europe and Japan." Sheik Yamani is a hard-headed realist on tactics of negotiating terms for the sale; but not, apparently, when it comes to military logistics.

All of these reactions from our allies and friends to the evidently increasing dangers in the Persian Gulf have puzzled many Americans, since our allies are much more vulnerable than we to any shift which would bring a major increment in Persian Gulf oil under Soviet control or under the control of a radical state. After all, as we have already emphasized, by comparison with the United States, Western Europe derives four times the proportion of the primary energy it consumes, France, nearly six, and Japan, seven. Aren't their interests plainly on the side of joining us in the defense of the Persian Gulf? Isn't it even more in the interests of the centrist and conservative states in the region to help us prevent a Soviet or radical takeover of their own countries?

Probably so, in the long run. But in the near future what concerns each of these states is that joining us in an increased defense of the area is likely to expose them to threats and pressures from the Soviet Union, from forces of the left inside their own country and, in the case of the regional powers, from their radical neighbors. In the short run, therefore, they worry about the extra risks to which they would be exposed by association with us.

This short-run fear is compounded by a frequently explicit worry about whether the United States will be there in the long run to help them—whether we will have the will and the power, and specifically the staying power, essential to do so. In brief, then, just what their net interests are and how much they overlap with ours depends on our will and ability to contribute to the protection of our and their interests in the region. It depends, in short, on the future of U.S. power there.

The Saudis were clearly unsettled in January 1979 when we responded to a Soviet warning not to interfere in the internal affairs of our ally, Iran, by declaring that we had neither the desire nor the ability to do so. We warned the Soviets not to interfere, but since we had said that we could not do so, it was not clear precisely how we would enforce that warning. The loss of American access to airspace and facilities en route and in the region has been related to our hosts' fear of pressures by the Soviet Union or by local powers who see their interests as opposed to ours—pressures that we might not be able to counter. On the other hand, countries in the northern tier and some on the gulf, including Saudi Arabia, have increasingly permitted the Soviet Union to use their airspace, even when it seems obviously to be directed against their own and allied interests. The Saudis, for example, who have worried about the threat against them presented by the Marxist regime of South Yemen, disclosed recently that Moscow had requested and received permission to send military planes over Saudi territory on the way to South Yemen (*New York Times*, 27 February 1980). This illustrates once again the point that weakness in our ability to affect events in the region has a cumulative effect. Allies who might facilitate our projection of power there have hesitated to do so, and in fact have greatly restricted our access in recent years. This in turn has weakened our ability to protect them, and so on. It has seemed recently as if "we can't win for losing."

On the other hand, as the example of Russian power in the region will suggest, a reversal of the trend toward decreasing power is also likely to be self-reinforcing; and even more so since our long-run interests are closer to those of our allies than are the interests of the Russians.

CONFLICTING INTERESTS OF RADICAL STATES AND THREATS FROM INSIDE THE REGION

The Soviet Union is not the only potential source of harm to alliance interests in the Persian Gulf. Some radical states inside the region threaten their neighbors either overtly or indirectly by supporting subversion or revolutionary forces. Even more or less spontaneously generated internal changes can be adverse. The radical Islamic transformation of Iran, for example, has done substantial direct damage already and has introduced further instabilities that could lead to something worse: the disintegration of Iran into several separate states (Azerbaijan, Arabistan, Turkmenistan, etc.), threats against Iran's neighbors, the stirring up of Shi'ite minorities within nearby countries led by Sunni governments, disruptive local wars which the chaotic government in Iran might provoke or for which it might merely provide a tempting opportunity, and, in the end, the extension of radical hostile control over a larger proportion of gulf oil. The collapse of the shah's regime in any case removed a considerable counterweight to the long-standing ambitions of Iraq against Kuwait and of South Yemen against Oman, North Yemen, Saudi Arabia, and so on.

The multiplicity of active and latent rivalries within and among these regional states, then, can be deadly. They belie the conventional belief that multipolarity is somehow inherently much more benign than a bipolar world. The Soviet Union did not invent these explosive instabilities, though it might stir them up or benefit from them no matter how they arise.

Alliance policy in the last decade relied on these rival shaky governments to compose their differences and to construct formal or informal regional security arrangements— arrangements that were supposed to be able both to control regional antagonisms and (implicitly) to defend regional and Western interests against any likely threat from the Soviet Union. While such past anticipations of a stable regional equilibrium supported by the twin pillars of Iran and Saudi Arabia now appear to have been extremely unrealistic, this has not prevented the revival in 1980 of new Western hopes—especially in Europe—for regional security arrangements that would make a Western presence nearby unnecessary.

Some of these hopes, implausibly enough, are centered on Iraq,[6] which has had a Treaty of Friendship with the Soviet Union since 1971 and which has until recently been regarded as the most radical state in the region. Anticipations of the realignment of Iraq are the latest Paris fashion which bids fair to sweep the West. For this reason, and because past government studies of the security of the gulf have in general taken Iraq to be a potential troublemaker rather than a cop, it is worth looking carefully at the source of this new optimism and worth weighing in some detail the evidence for and against taking Iraq seriously as a possible threat. First, the evidence for:

The evidence of Iraqi designs on Kuwait is very substantial (see Fukuyoma 1980). Iraq's claim to part or all of Kuwait goes back over a half-century. The Turks had had suzerainty over Kuwait since the nineteenth century, and as a successor state to the Turks in Mesopotamia, the Iraqi government assumed the Turkish claim. It posed its most serious threat in June 1961, only six days after Britain granted Kuwait its independence. At that time Iraqi leader General Kassem announced that he regarded Kuwait as an integral part of Iraqi territory. The following day Iraqi troop movements were reported near the Kuwaiti border. A decisive factor in restraining Iraq was the prompt and forceful British military response as well as an unusual joint effort by Egypt, Saudi Arabia, and Jordan to defend Kuwaiti sovereignty.

In the early 1970s the Iraqis renewed their military pressure. Iraqi forces massed on the Kuwaiti border in December 1972 and began building a road from Um Qasar into Kuwaiti territory. Limited Iraqi military intrusion into Kuwaiti territory continued in 1973 and 1974. A combination of factors, especially the shah's determination to prevent Iraqi takeover of significant parts of Kuwait, Iraq's preoccupation with the Kurdish separatist movement in northern Iraq, and an increased Iraqi involvement in the aftermath of the October war with Israel constrained Iraqi designs on Kuwait.

The shah now is no longer an obstacle and the disintegration of military power in the present Iranian government makes it an unimpressive substitute in that role. Moreover, the Iraqi government has used its greatly increased oil income since the early 1970s for a massive buildup of the Iraqi armed forces. It is now, as it never was before, clearly the dominant regional military power. There is no plausible regional counterweight that could impose limits on the Iraqis' long-standing ambitions in Kuwait if an opportune occasion were to arise for an attempt at fulfilling these ambitions. Kuwait is a very rich prize. Though it is tiny, weak, meagerly armed, and generally unstable, its proven oil reserves are second only to Saudi Arabia's. In the past its reserves have been estimated at almost double those of Iraq.

Iraq has also disputed territory with Iran and has engaged in a series of skirmishes on the Iranian border beginning as early as the 1960s and continuing until the present day (see Tuohy 1979), with a brief pause after 1975. The chaos of Khomeini's revolution offers scope for larger Iraqi ambitions, and Iraq's greatly increased armaments may provide the instrument for wider-ranging interests that Iraq has voiced in oil-producing "Arabistan," its name for Khuzistan. The local obstacles to such larger ambitions, at any rate, have been drastically lowered.

Finally, it is hard to set precise and confident limits to Iraqi ambitions. Iraq clearly would like to be the leading Arab political force. And it cannot be excluded that, if they were not seriously and effectively opposed, Iraqi appetites might increase with what they feed on. Control of Saudi oil would be a powrful political asset, and analysis will suggest that the Saudi armed forces themselves could not stop an Iraqi advance from continuing after it reached the Kuwait–Saudi Arabia border. How plausible each of these contingencies is—in Kuwait, in Iran, or in Saudi Arabia— can only be evaluated in terms of the risks and gains they might bring. And this depends on the opposition from inside or outside the region. However, even the most limited and best evidenced Iraqi ambitions—those directed at Kuwait— if realized, would substantially damage Western interests.

There are a number of more hopeful signs. One that has less weight than the others is that Iraq has recently boosted its estimates of its own proven reserves. It has been said, therefore, that it has less "need" for the oil. However, this is not a very impressive point. For the Iraqis, as for the Soviet Union, control of an even more substantial fraction of Persian Gulf oil would give it a powerful instrument for extending its political influence and control. And the larger the fraction, the better.

Another item of evidence given in support of new hopes is the fact that Iraq, which has in the past gotten its military equipment predominantly from the Soviet Union, broadened its purchases to include the procurement of a considerable number of arms from the West as well—from France, Italy, and West Germany. In particular, it has bought an advanced fighter, the F–1, from the French. And it has increased its purchases of nonmilitary goods as well.[7]

Such purchases clearly are likely to enhance Iraq's independent military capability, but it is doubtful that they tie Iraq to the West. (Kuwait and other traditional monarchies in the region are diversifying *their* sources of supply to include the Soviet Union.) They do increase Iraq's dominance as a regional power.

The most substantial evidence for the optimistic view has to do with the Soviet Union and the relationship of Iraq's ruling Ba'athist Socialist Renaissance party to the local Communist party. The Ba'ath rulers of Iraq have always been a suspicious lot, and there has been evidence that they are increasingly wary of their Soviet partners (Borchgrave 1978, pp. 50–55). There is much to be wary about. The Russians have assisted Marxist coups in South Yemen, in Ethiopia, in Afghanistan, and elsewhere. In some cases they overturned governments that were already aligned with the Soviet Union in order to install ones still more closely aligned with it. Some evidence suggests that the Russians may have been associated with such an attempt in Iraq which failed in April 1978.

The most frequently cited evidence for a reversal of alliances or something close to it is based on that rumored attempt at a coup and on statements by Saddam Husayn, the Iraqi leader, afterward. In an interview with Arnaud de Borchgrave in July 1978, shortly after that attempted coup, Husayn has been cited as issuing "his first public warning against Soviet machinations in Africa and the Persian Gulf. 'They won't be satisfied until the whole world becomes Communist.' " However, Husayn followed his statement about the Soviet Union seeing "its own security in spreading Communism" with the statement that "the U.S. believes its own security lies in having the world with a bourgeois system."

Like Mrs. Gandhi, he suggests that the *fons et origo malorum* is prior Western, not Soviet, intervention.

Moreover, the degree of independence that he was insisting on from the Soviet Union was greatly exaggerated. Asked whether he hadn't compromised his independence by allowing Soviet military cargo planes to use Iraqi bases on their way to Ethiopia, Husayn answered,

No, we didn't allow Soviet planes to go to Ethiopia via Iraq. We objected and got a formal understanding from the Soviets that these planes would go to South Yemen instead. We deduced, of course, that some of these shipments were going on to Ethiopia by other transport, but there was nothing we could do about that.

Finally, when asked whether Iraq was trying to lessen its dependency on the Soviet Union by diversifying its sources of arms supply and specifically by buying arms from France, Husayn indicated that when he deals with an enemy "it does not mean the beginning of comprehensive changes in our stand." And that "when Iraq criticizes the policies of a friendly country"—namely, the Soviet Union—"it should not be judged that this is the beginning of a change in relations." So much for the reversal of alliances.

Viewed soberly, then, Husayn's statements are a long way from suggesting the realignment that has been hoped for in various Western capitals. In fact, the position taken in that interview, like more recent statements by Saddam Husayn after the Soviet invasion of Afghanistan, amounts in effect to an exclusion of the West from the Persian Gulf and a continuation of the present configuration of power there—with Iraq dominant among the regional powers and with the Soviet Union maintaining its present overwhelming preponderance.

As for the Iraqi reaction to Afghanistan, the hopes that have been floated on that basis recently in France and in the United States and elsewhere in the West for a westward-leaning Iraq on which we might count seem quite dubious. Doubts are raised if one notes in particular that Iraq's condemnation of the Russian invasion of Afghanistan was made in the context of repeated Iraqi calls for *both* superpowers to keep out of the gulf. Such a call is only superficially evenhanded, for the Soviets are there on the ground—very nearby. It continues Iraq's opposition to any U.S. presence in the Indian Ocean or to any military use of the facilities offered by Oman and other conservative states. And it does not alter the fact that the Russian bases in the Transcaucasus and east of the Caspian Sea are only five hundred to a thousand miles away from the largest oil-producing regions of the gulf.

In fact, the first press reports[8] of President Husayn's condemnation of the Soviet move in Afghanistan were misleading. A reading of the actual text of the speech, however, shows he nowhere explicitly mentions the Soviet Union. There is a great deal on U.S. imperialism, on aggressive Zionists, on the Egyptian regime's capitulatory policy, and on the hostility of some Iranian leaders towards Iraq. In fact, he identifies "the events in Iran and what has recently happened in Afghanistan" as serious because they have "provided the *United States*, whose policy has been condemned and whose plots have been defeated, with new opportunities to enter the area, tamper with it and realize its colonialist designs" (italics added). There are some vague references to imperialist forces, to covetous superpowers (in the plural), and to foreign intervention having to be opposed in all its forms. But he named no big power other than the United States.

The upshot of the January 1980 speech is simply, then, to reaffirm the long-standing Iraqi call for non-gulf powers to stay out of the Persian Gulf region. That would prevent the United States from affecting events there, but not the Soviet Union, which has direct and close access to the gulf from the Transcaucasus and the Transcaspian.

A hypothesis of possible Soviet-Iraqi cooperation need not and should not assume that Iraq is a Soviet puppet, that the

Ba'ath Socialist Renaissance government has no interests independent of those of the Soviet Union and different from them. (Pure puppet states are rather rare: Cuba, for example, is far from being a Soviet puppet. Castro moved against the local Soviet-supported Cuban Communists. Nonetheless, he has found no better partner in realizing his own ambitions than the Soviet Union.) It need assume only that there is a considerable intersection of interests between the two states. There has been such an intersection embodied in the past in the Treaty of Friendship and in massive Soviet support in armaments. Currently it appears that Iraq's long-standing territorial ambitions are realizable only with Soviet acquiescence if not with Soviet support. Iraq cannot, at any rate, expect to receive support from the United States and its allies in extending its borders. The prizes to be gained in the Persian Gulf are large enough to permit both Iraq and the Soviet Union to have their share.

Finally, the problem of affecting the behavior of a radical state such as Iraq—even more than in the case of the centrist or conservative states which have been aligned with the West—will have something to do with how that radical state assesses prospective, rich, short-run gains compared to the long-run value of the uncertain safety it might obtain by coming under the Western umbrella. It will depend on American and other alliance power. The development of an adequate and durable alliance ability o project strength into the gulf can deter actions hostile to the alliance. It can inhibit. That is on the negative side. However, the protection it would provide would also offer positive incentives to move towards the West. Improved Western power in the gulf would help to shape decisions inside the region. How nations assess their net short-run and long-run interests then will depend on the power we will be able to muster for Persian Gulf contingencies.

WESTERN PRESENCE AND INDIAN OCEAN ARMS CONTROL

The idea that peace in the region and the legitimate interests of all parties could be preserved if the superpowers would only keep their combat ships out of the Indian Ocean and if they would abandon base facilities on the littoral of that ocean runs as a common thread through the arguments advanced by quite diverse countries in the region. It continues to be propounded by Iraq and India, which have Treaties of Friendship with the Soviet Union. And, with modifications, it appears in the views of the traditional monarchies such as Saudi Arabia and Kuwait, which have been aligned with the West. In their case the difference is that, while they oppose a continuous U.S. presence, they premise some of their hopes for security on the possibility of the United States being able quickly to deploy power into the region in a crisis, and especially in the event of a Soviet attack. But they, too, declare themselves against a Western—and specifically against a U.S.—presence.

The policies of the United States and the West Europeans themselves were premised in the previous decade on the same assumption: that the regional powers could maintain stability and in fact preserve Western interests without a Western presence. Western proposals for Indian Ocean arms control embodied the idea in its most explicit form.

Proposals for arms agreements, much more than unilateral decisions on national defense, are plagued by the need to compare simple ratios of forces on the two sides without any clear criterion of what forces to compare; or of how to make the comparison so as to show that the stability aimed at in the arms control agreement would be achieved if the opposing sides had forces in that ratio. Questions of "stability" are much too complicated to be captured by a simple ratio.

Defense planners usually understand that, and the process of making decisions among alternatives in national defense, however flawed, usually involves much less rudimentary considerations. However, negotiations with adversaries on force levels and deployments on the two sides have to deal with simple observables if they are to reach conclusion at all.

In general, they rely on precisely such rudimentary and — it is to be hoped — verifiable relationships as force ratios. This frequently has very perverse effects, and nowhere more obviously than in the case of Indian Ocean arms controls. Western proposals for an Indian Ocean arms control agreement in essence have proceeded on the assumption that one need only compare Western bases on the shores of that ocean and Western naval presence there with Soviet bases and Soviet naval presence in the Indian Ocean. However, the vastly increased Soviet ability to project power in the Persian Gulf region was achieved, as we have suggested, mainly by the buildup of Soviet combat and military lift forces on Soviet territory, and by a greatly increased ability to penetrate the air and land barriers surrounding them. This capability would not be altered by the withdrawal of both Soviet and American ships from the Indian Ocean, nor by the removal of all foreign bases from the littoral of the Indian Ocean.

One of the U.S. Navy's essential missions is the projection of power ashore. For the foreseeable future, it is clear that this mission will be especially important in the Persian Gulf. The only power the United States has in the gulf at the present time is embodied in the two carrier task groups which it diverted from the Sixth Fleet in the Mediterranean and from the Seventh Fleet in the Pacific.

The Soviet Union, on the other hand, has no need for a navy in order to project power to the shores of the Persian Gulf. It can do so from the Transcaucasus or the Transcaspian (and now also from Afghanistan). The mission of the Soviet Navy in the gulf has been largely "sea denial" — that is, to deny the use of that sea to the United States. The Soviet Union could most handily and inexpensively accomplish the mission of sea denial by an Indian Ocean arms-control agreement. And such an agreement would have very little effect on its own ability to project power on shore in that region. The agreement could have such an effect only if it extended overland in the Soviet Union very far indeed to the north, perhaps to the Barents and Kara seas. But in any case it would call for an implausibly extensive demilitarization of large areas of the Soviet Union itself.

It is worth noting that if the Soviet Union had accepted the last American proposal for Indian Ocean arms control, the United States would not have been able to respond to the crisis in Iran nor to the Soviet invasion of Afghanistan by moving carrier task groups into the Indian Ocean.

The gist of the trends described earlier in Soviet and Western ability to project power into the gulf region is that by the end of the 1970s the Soviets had accumulated the military combat and transport forces, the facilities and the access needed to project massive power very rapidly into key parts of the upper gulf area. The Western presence, on the other hand, (the forces, the infrastructure, and the access both en route and in the gulf) had dwindled drastically. Moreover, contrary to some of the stereotypes about the growth of multipolarity, this was by no means a case of the strength of both superpowers decreasing relative to that of a multiplicity of local powers. The military equipment available to local powers had indeed increased in quality and quantity. However, the power of the Soviet Union in the area, which was very modest at the start of the period, had become quite overwhelming by the end of the period. The West had diminished in its power relative to some of the hostile or unstable states in the region. The Soviet Union had not. No plausible regional security arrangement can counterbalance Soviet power. And no American rapid deployment force based in the United States is likely to be rapid enough.

What is needed is an American and other Western presence able to bring firepower to bear in hours rather than in days or weeks so as to disrupt the complex—and vulnerable—initial elements of an invasion force. Things can be done to bolster regional defense, but it is inherently implausible to suppose that the small, unstable, and antagonistic rival states in the region are likely to be able to compose their differences, and still less likely that they will be able to defend themselves and Western interests against the Soviet threat. It is remarkable that wan hopes for this have been revived once more since the invasion of Afghanistan. Western Europeans who do not feel able to manage a defense of Western Europe without a large American military presence should hardly expect the gulf states to be able to do so.

MEETING THE THREAT

For our allies inside and outside the Persian Gulf region to expose themselves to the short-term risks entailed in helping us to help them, they must believe, first of all, that there is a serious and persistent threat to their interests in the gulf; second, that it is possible to do something about it by improving alliance strength; and third, that the leaders of the alliance, and in particular the United States, have a serious program that will be sustained over the long term and not simply announced in an election year—that the United States will be there to meet the long-term threat.

However, it is possible to argue that there really is not much of a threat, that talk of dangers in the gulf "more serious than any since World War II" is so much empty rhetoric. The growing preponderance of Soviet strength in this vital area and the weakness of the West may, by a curious inversion, be seized on as a kind of reassurance: the

Soviets would never strike at the West in so vital a spot where the West is patently at a disadvantage. That, it is suggested, would mean World War III. This sunny view of the matter can easily be extended in the manner of Pangloss. If the Soviets will not strike the West at a vital point where the West is weak, they are even less likely to strike at a vital point where it is strong. As for nonvital spots, the Soviets would be plainly foolish to risk striking for marginal gains.

The world envisaged in such an argument may not be the best of all possible worlds, but it does seem more satisfactory than the one in which we find ourselves. Reasoning of this kind is a way of cheering oneself up. It fails to take the possibility of war seriously, and it fails to understand that some possible wars which never occur can have an important actual effect.

In the event, for example, of a takeover of swing oil production by a radical local state, or in the event of an internal or ostensibly internal takeover by a hostile faction inside a swing oil-producing state, or in the event of some mixture of these two circumstances or possibly a combination of the two stirred up or aided by the Soviet Union, it is the West that might have the burden of initiating military action. And one may be reasonably sure that the Soviet Union would be in a position of warning us to stay out, and one may be sure that it would use regional or internal troubles for cover, if not as opportunity, for intervention or for threats to intervene. In such a circumstance a continuing preponderance of Soviet power would have its effect in deterring American or Western "interference." Such a preponderance and the outcome of possible conflict which it foreshadows can shape the behavior of internal factions or of other regional powers. Also the behavior of our major allies. It can make potential hosts reluctant to provide facilities or airspace in the region or en route. Nobody likes to be on the losing side. "Virtual" or shadow wars have many actual effects.

I believe there is a threat, and that the threat is obvious. Attempts to wish it away are whistling in the dark. Moreover, I believe there is nothing intrinsic or permanent in the disadvantage the West has allowed to develop in the gulf area. The disadvantage is *not* simply a matter of physical geography. The continents have not perceptibly drifted apart or shifted much in position in the last twenty years. It is a matter of the political-military use of geography, and its remedy is a matter of Western will to undertake a long-term effort to improve the position of the alliance. The most urgent immediate interim measure is the development of a serious and sustained program.

The debate in the wake of the Soviet invasion of Afghanistan has suggested four broad alternatives for reducing the danger to American interests in oil from the Persian Gulf.[9] The first three implicitly or explicitly assume that there is no way of redressing the conventional military balance. The first has been espoused, for example, by George F. Kennan (1962, p. 261), in line with his familiar view that military strength declines steeply and in a straight line with distance, that the "power radiated from any national center diminishes in proportion to the distance involved." The advantage to the Soviets in the gulf, he believes, is intrinsic. He holds, therefore, that the United States should substitute for an increase in military capability a program for reducing American dependence on foreign oil.

A second alternative advanced by those who oppose any effort to increase American military power in the gulf would rely on regional powers. Paul Warnke and John Gilligan, for example, have recently proposed regional security agreements "in which both Moscow and Washington would guarantee the neutrality and security of countries in the area" (Burt 1980). Such guarantees, of course, only reintroduce inexplicitly the military power of Washington as well as of Moscow as backup for the guarantees. There would be no reason to expect an American guarantee to be persuasive in the gulf if our military disadvantage were intrinsic. In any case, extra regional guarantees are a fillip in a more general revival of interest here and abroad in regional security arrangements to which we have already referred.

The third alternative proposed, or more usually hinted at, by those who think it inherently impossible to overcome the advantage in conventional strength which the Russians are supposed to achieve simply by having their homeland nearby would rely implicitly or explicitly on a threat to escalate — that is, to start a war outside the region or to use nuclear weapons.

Finally, there is the alternative of advancing a serious program to increase the alliance's military capability for meeting the threat at its own level. Here there are many variants — in the current administration and among its critics.

The first alternative, that suggested by Mr. Kennan and others, of undertaking a program to reduce American dependence on foreign oil, is fine as far as it goes. It cannot, however, go far enough. It cannot entirely replace an alliance effort to redress the balance in the gulf by expanding its military power to affect events there. It is important to reduce American dependency on Persian Gulf oil, if not on oil imports in general. (Harry Rowen's chapter in this volume presents one economic program for that purpose.) It is unlikely, however, that any politically feasible program will reduce the dependence of our major allies on the gulf drastically and soon enough to make the protection of their interests in the gulf unnecessary.

As for the second alternative — to rely on defenses put up by regional powers and to rely on any likely regional security arrangement — this simply revives the fantasies of the late 1960s and the 1970s, fantasies one might have hoped would have crumbled with the crumbling of the twin pillars on which we had previously founded our hopes for a security of the gulf involving little effort on our part beyond the profit-

able sale of expensive military hardware. The intense instabilities in the area are now too obvious to ignore, as is the
obvious vulnerability to Soviet power. Little needs to be said
about the idea of meeting a possible threat from the Soviet
Union by securing a guarantee from the Soviet Union. The
issuance and acceptance of such a guarantee would invite
the Soviets to insert military forces to restore stability in the
event of some future turbulence. Even the turbulence might
be preferable.

As for the threat of escalation (the third alternative), some
such possibility is always there. However, the actual execution of a threat by the United States as leader of the alliance
to start a war elsewhere—for example, on the Northern
Flank of NATO—might only worsen matters for us and for
our allies. It is not likely to be welcome "elsewhere." For example, it seems improbable that the Norwegians would
welcome opening up a front in the Northern Flank, in particular since it may seem to have no direct connection with aggression in the gulf. The threat of using nuclear weapons in
response to a conventional incursion—of introducing a tripwire or plate-glass defense of the Persian Gulf—is likely to
frighten allies, especially those in the region, more than it
will the Russians. A nuclear tripwire defense in the European center becomes progressively less persuasive as Soviet
nuclear strength increases at short, medium, and intercontinental range. A tripwire in the Persian Gulf is likely to be
even less persuasive. In general, a tripwire policy does not
register a determination to use nuclear weapons in time of
crisis; rather, it registers a lack of will before the crisis to
prepare to meet a nonnuclear threat on its own terms.

We are left with the broad alternative of meeting a conventional threat on its own terms. To do that will require not
merely a force rapidly deployed from the United States on
the basis of signals of an attack. It will also require a continuous and politically tolerable allied combat presence in
the region. Such a force must be able to defend itself against

land-based air attack and yet project enough firepower ashore to deter, delay, or disrupt an initial adversary surprise attack aimed at seizing key points on the gulf. The delay must be long enough to bring in reinforcements by air, and the allied combat force has to be able to protect the points at which the reinforcements would land. Signals of an attack are likely to be extremely ambiguous if they occur days before the attack —too subject to error to permit a costly response by the United States, by its major allies, or by its local hosts. We must measure the costs in terms of the political risks imposed on hosts, as well as in economic terms. The amount of warning time—where warning is shorn of ambiguities enough to permit the insertion of firepower or massive movements to the theater—is likely to be measured in hours rather than in weeks or even days.

On the other hand, the firepower and the presence required can be more modest if it is available very early. Soviet power-projection forces in the process of moving to the theater and initiating attack would have many vulnerabilities. They involve complex, highly coordinated movements of airlift vehicles, airborne regiments, motorized rifle regiments, and combat aircraft. A cat set among these pigeons while they are continuing to take off, are on the way, or as they arrive, could disrupt the attack and give time for a rapid deployment force to bring in reinforcements. The presence of such a force could so increase the risks to an aggressor as to discourage him from attacking.

This is not the place to present a detailed net assessment of potential allied and adversary movements to and within the theater and the potential outcome of combat there. Still less to detail an optimal or at least adequate program. I believe that an essential part of it would be a greatly increased naval combat presence, able to defend itself and to project power ashore. A naval presence can keep to a minimum the political risks to which local powers are exposed by help from outside the region. If we had a serious ongoing program to build and station a naval combat force that we could keep in or near the gulf without drawing on the forces we need to deter or to fight a large war elsewhere, such a program would offer some evidence to states in the area that we could protect them in case of attack. This might make them more willing to offer land facilities for alliance use. They could then feel better able to resist pressures from the Soviet Union, from radical neighbors, or from radical factions. A continuous naval presence, then, would make it more likely that the alliance would be able to get a land presence as well, or at least an increased use of land bases in a crisis.

A substantial net increase in the alliance capabilities to keep conventional forces in the region and to deploy reinforcements there rapidly is essential for meeting the conventional threat on its own terms. This will involve changes in alliance armies and air forces as well as in navies. It is the fear that such an event might be very costly if not infeasible that drives some of the participants in the debate to advocate one or the other of the first three broad alternatives I have listed:

(1) the futile hope that the alliance dependency on the Persian Gulf can be eliminated;

(2) the wan and discredited hope that regional powers will be willing and able to protect the persistent critical alliance interests there;

(3) the reliance on desperate and unconvincing threats of escalation, possibly to nuclear war.

An adequate and less reckless defense cannot be secured on the cheap, and it will not be undertaken without strong political leadership. The effort required is far from being so extensive that it means "The Militarisation of Western Society," "Life Underground," or any of the other bogies which we sometimes conjure up to avoid sober thought or action. The United States is spending about 5 percent of its gross national product on national defense. Its major allies are for the most part spending very much less. A program to redress the imbalance in conventional arms which we and our allies have allowed to grow in the Persian Gulf might involve annual increments in defense budgets of 10 to 15 percent. That would mean an increase for the purpose of projecting power there of less than one percentage point of the GNP devoted to defense in the United States and considerably less than that for our allies — over and above whatever increases are needed for other essential defense purposes such as increased readiness, nuclear force modernization, etc. This is substantial, but it would hardly impose intolerable hardships.

The United States managed in the 1950s to increase consumer outlays, to continue increasing productivity in industry, and to keep inflation within bounds while it was spending 9 or 10 percent of its GNP on defense. We should be able to manage 6 percent today. And Western Europe and Japan can hardly excuse a failure to increase their smaller efforts on the ground that they cannot afford to do so. The Soviets have obtained their advantage in conventional power through a steady expenditure of national resources to build their capability for projecting strength, and by a persistent political and military effort to secure direct and close access to the gulf. It would be absurd to regard the need for a corresponding increment in allied effort as a demonstration of a supposed strategic fact that it is "inherently impossible" to overcome the present Soviet strategic advantage. Rather, it would be a demonstration of wishfulness or lack of political will.

8

ROBERT F. ELLSWORTH

Quick Fixes
in Intelligence

Major problem areas in the U.S. intelligence system. The National Security Act of 1947. Functions of the DCI and the political action agent. Conflicting analyses of information. The use of satellites. Crisis management systems. Data distribution. Electronic and tactical intelligence.

For over five years now Americans have debated the role of secret intelligence in an open society. For the most part this debate in the Congress and the media has been concerned with issues from the past, most of them turning on questions of abuse, impropriety, and excess, while many important substantive issues have gained relatively little attention.

173

As for the future, scant attention has been given to what U.S. intelligence needs will be in the 1980s and beyond. What kind of world will we live in? What kinds of threats and challenges are we likely to face? More precisely, what can intelligence do to help us successfully defend our open society? Given the state of freedom in the world, it may now be timely to reissue Shakespeare's "warnings and portents of evils imminent" as well as to help in dealing with them. Such will be the task, it seems, for American intelligence in the 1980s.

At a quick glance, nine major problem areas come to mind when one thinks, in an organized and comprehensive way, about the future of the American government's intelligence community and its roles. It certainly will not be possible to correct all the problems which exist overnight or even over the course of a year or two. Given a sense of urgency and commitment from the White House, the American intelligence community could be built to a high level of capacity—better than before—within five years. But it is possible to undertake "fixes" (some of which will be quicker than others) in all these areas of concern.

CONFORMITY TO PREVAILING FASHION

It is first necessary to free our government intelligence community from the broad, shifting cultural preconceptions which tend to govern our global outlook. Intelligence must be completely dedicated to following the evidence regarding foreign threats whatever its direction, even if it leads to a refutation of currently fashionable doctrine. For example, for at least two decades America's foreign policy establishment view was that the biggest game in town was a mix of competition, collaboration, and maybe some condominium, with Russia. Among other things, this implied a convergence of strategic nuclear doctrine (and force sizing) in the direction of minimum deterrence. Without arguing the validity of these concepts, the point is that they so captured the imagination of the intelligence community itself that broad strategic assessments of Soviet military developments became warped. For example, beginning in the 1960s the Central Intelligence Agency (CIA) embarked upon a consistent underestimation of the Soviet intercontinental ballistic missile (ICBM) buildup, missing the mark by wide margins; its estimates became progressively worse, on the low side. Then in the mid-1970s the intelligence community underestimated the scale and effectiveness of the Soviets' multiple independently targetable reentry vehicle (MIRV) programs. Even more important, Soviet warhead accuracies that have already been achieved—and that have equaled U.S. accuracies—had been estimated by American intelligence to be unattainable by Moscow before the mid–1980s. Many of these errors stemmed from a set of very human preconceptions: that the Soviets were basically copying us—creating a force that would simply mirror image our own.

Governed by the same preconceptions, U.S. intelligence also grossly underestimated overall Soviet military effort. In 1976 the CIA (which had figured the Soviets were devoting to defense between 5 and 7 percent of gross national product [GNP], only slightly higher than the U.S. level) announced that Moscow was spending on defense between 11 and 13 percent of GNP (up to nearly three times the U.S. level).

Such flawed intelligence estimates helped to form American national security policy for the past twenty years. In the mid–1960s the United States began its decadelong strategic stall, basically abjuring new strategic initiatives. It was then that Secretary of Defense Robert McNamara (1966) informed the public that "the Soviets have decided that they have lost the quantitative" strategic arms race and "are not seeking to engage us in that context." Lest the point be missed, he added: "There is no indication that the Soviets are seeking to develop a strategic nuclear force as large as ours."

Part of the problem is that American intelligence was centralized by the National Security Act of 1947. A single director of central intelligence, it was argued, would make it easier on policymakers such as presidents and their staffs to get a straightforward story on foreign intelligence. The reality is that intelligence is made up of many bits and pieces; this makes it easy for bright people to compose different stories from the same set of data. The new U.S. system became different from that of Great Britain which has at least five separate organizations responsible for intelligence, France which has four, and West Germany with three. (Intelligence sharing with these and other services is an extremely low-cost, high-benefit fix which should be expanded immediately.) The American structure, in contrast, headed by a director of intelligence (DCI), has lumped a veritable array of responsibilities—for paramilitary operations, technological collection, military order of battle estimates, and political and economic analysis—into one institutional framework. This consolidation has opened the intelligence community to similar political and cultural pressures and has reinforced the tendency of most elements to sway together with shifting moods. It has tended to discount competitiveness and to stultify speculative thought and imagination.

This problem could be eased by loosening the 1947 act, thereby promoting independent, competitive centers of intelligence collection and analysis and legally separating the nation's top intelligence officer from his dual responsibilities as CIA director. The bureaucratic argument against this arrangement is that it would deprive the DCI of his power base (e.g., personnel, budgets, etc.). This is wrong. The fact is that the DCI's power base is in all cases the confidence of the president.

President Jimmy Carter's Executive Order of 24 January 1978 moved in the opposite direction. Responsibilities laid on the DCI were specified to include (a) acting as chief of the

CIA itself, (b) exercising full and exclusive authority for approving the budget of *all* intelligence arms (i.e., agencies in the departments of Defense, State, Treasury, and Energy, in the Federal Bureau of Investigation [FBI] and the Drug Enforcement Administration in addition to the CIA), plus (c) shouldering responsibility for the accuracy and value of *all* intelligence appraisals. This 1978 Executive Order has assigned dual roles not only to the DCI but also to the CIA's own National Foreign Assessment Center and Directorate for Administration.

The two functions—head of national intelligence in terms of both budget and estimates and operating chief of the CIA—should be separated. Such a move, which can only be completed by Congress, would eliminate considerable confusion. Far more important, it would improve the caliber of reporting by divorcing the United States' main intelligence chief from concerns for the immediate agency and its activities. The new, liberated director of national intelligence could coordinate all intelligence programs without special responsibility for any one segment. In case of a conflict between the director's sense of national intelligence needs and the desires of one agency, the presumption would be in favor of the national perspective. Moreover, such an official could sharpen the president's understanding of foreign threats by pointing out the ways in which U.S. defenses do or do not deal with such threats: a "net assessment." This is not done by our intelligence community today.

Nonetheless, the new national director should stay clear of the traditional sand trap and not take it upon himself to impose "coordination" upon intelligence estimates or analysis. He should present the president with the conflicting evidence and opposing views which well up from the newly dispersed intelligence network and avoid placing his distinctive stamp on the product. The president himself must grapple with alternative interpretations of events and with the risks and costs of adopting one view of policy rather than another.

Admittedly, this would immerse the president ever more deeply into foreign affairs. Most presidential hopefuls promise just the contrary, that they would devote nearly all time and energy to domestic affairs, but this does not mesh with current reality. A president is first and foremost the nation's foreign policy and security manager. When he is not, the nation suffers.

INTERMEDIATE ACTION CAPABILITIES

As for other quick fixes, one of the most urgent should be addressed to the roles of the traditional political action agent. Such capabilities have never been more in demand and that demand is sure to grow as the intentions of our adversaries—or of subgroups—in important areas like the Middle East and southwest Asia become every bit as important as major military threats. For deep-seated reasons whose origins lie in history, now made more incendiary by oil, it is unlikely that the political environment in that part of the world—so important to us and to our allies and friends—will improve in the near future. Years from now the United States will still be attempting to deal with a large set of unstable situations. I suggest the need for capabilities which would range across the whole spectrum between diplomatic actions and military force. Such capabilities could be both overt and covert, and need not necessarily be under the charge of the intelligence community. Moreover, it is necessary to distinguish clearly between clandestine collection personnel and political action agents. The former have to be secret; the latter need not be entirely covert.

Those who hold to the belief that a resolution of the Israeli issues would bring stability to the Middle East and Persian Gulf region underestimate the reach of historical events and attitudes which embitter Arab and Muslim relationships:

Sunnis against Shi'as; Egypt against other Arabs; Iraq (50 percent Shi'a) and Syria contending for paramountcy in the Fertile Crescent; Iran against the lot; Soviet agents, terrorists, and freebooters operating throughout in situations of opportunity.

Yet our intermediate action capabilities (actions which are neither strictly diplomatic nor strictly military) have been severely hurt in recent years, partly because of their misuse in domestic affairs, partly because of media and congressional attacks, and partly due to defectors who have turned against their former colleagues and identified them.

These programs desperately need repair. They need a clear statement of missions, firm direction, and support from the executive and legislative branches to include a sensible, effective means of ensuring that intelligence officers serving in operations abroad are provided with good cover if needed, and that overt operations are provided with good, responsible policy direction. Above all, it is necessary that the president feel and express the need for such capabilities.

ANALYTIC PROWESS

Good human intelligence of course must be backed up by good analysis. In the past, the National Foreign Assessment Center has focused too much on current intelligence and has been content with a lack of professionalism on the part of country and regional specialists. This became clear in the early 1970s after the National Security Council ordered the CIA to address an age-old topic: Yugoslavia after Tito. The report was more superficial than those written in the German and Swiss daily newspapers. It turned out that the agency analysts who wrote it averaged less than two years' experience with the country and had not tapped outside expertise.

Three years ago the leadership of the analytic branch of the CIA realized that it could not achieve from within the needed upgrading in breadth of expertise and perspective on world affairs. They sought to find a way to gain access to the best minds in the nation for help in analyzing intelligence information. A strategy was developed to find and focus the talents of people from academia, business, private research groups, and others to assist the agency and to be available as a resource for selected agency analysts on momentous matters. But the effort was sabotaged from within. It should be revived.

The need for a net assessment—comparing foreign threats with U.S. defense capabilities—has been mentioned as an appropriate function for a new director of national intelligence. Quite apart from the question of who might do net assessment, however, the need is pressing. The CIA has considered such assessments to be outside its jurisdiction, on the entirely reasonable ground that its job is to report and analyze the foreign side only. The military, for their part, have resisted anyone outside the military analyzing U.S. forces. True, the secretary of defense does net assessments, and they have been powerful and indispensable tools in recent years for understanding the meaning of intelligence reports. But there remains a clear and present need to integrate net assessment more fully into the warp and woof of intelligence and to bring the prowess of net assessment directly into the ken of the president himself.

However, even the best human espionage is of limited value in trying to penetrate a closed, compartmented society like that of the Soviet Union. It can occasionally confirm data from other sources but can rarely furnish reliable original information. In the end we must depend on penetrating analysis of scant facts for our understanding of the Soviets.

SATELLITE VULNERABILITY

We need to know not just what the Soviets have done or are doing, but what they will be doing years from now. For most weapons systems take somewhere between two and twelve years to research and develop, and have a lifespan (on top of this) of between five and twenty years. Hence today's defense planning must be based on estimates of a far tomorrow's adversary capabilities. Even if future agreements hold down or reduce weapons more effectively than the Strategic Arms Limitation Talks (SALT), the United States will nonetheless have to anticipate trends in weapons development allowed under their terms. Without SALT the case is even clearer and more demanding. Without unlimited funds for defense we simply cannot hedge against every possible threat. Thus we need to know as best we can where to put our money as far as future systems are concerned.

The deficiencies of HUMINT (collection of intelligence by agents) must be compensated by signals intelligence, which can best help us to learn what others are up to—especially the Soviets—in terms of weapons research and development, and to surmise what they are likely to have in the field three to five years out. President Carter has confirmed in public for the first time that the United States relies to some extent on satellites to monitor Soviet compliance with strategic arms treaties. It takes no great imagination to realize that such monitors may be able to perform other intelligence functions as well, such as guarding against surprise military moves by foreign nations. It is no exaggeration to describe our reconnaissance sensors as the eyes and ears of the nation, a fourth leg of our strategic deterrent.

Maintaining adequate satellite capability is one of the most important responsibilities of any American government. Given the slippage in the American military posture compared with that of the Soviet Union, which seems likely to persist through most of the 1980s, and given the increasingly bold and ruthless Soviet activity around the world, we must take every step to ensure that we will continue to have a vigorous reconnaissance satellite program.

That means we must provide for redundant capability. Despite the great care that goes into building government satellite systems, some have been lost on launch. Others do not perform as well or for as long as anticipated. All are vulnerable to attack by the impressive and threatening Soviet antisatellite capability.

Backup or redundant U.S. satellite capability must be bought now in order to reduce the chance that in the 1980s we will be faced with a period of many months without our strategic eyes and ears due to the loss of a satellite with no available substitute. Moreover, we must make the commitments now to fund new generations of these satellites if we are to have an adequate capability in the mid–1980s.

INDICATIONS AND WARNING

The nation's indications and warning and crisis management systems—i.e., the means whereby our political and military decision-makers will be informed of the kind of attack, where it is going to come from, and what is happening in key areas—are today unnecessarily thin and vulnerable to disruption. Essential communications links in general lack redundancy and survivability. Ground stations for our satellite communications are limited in number and vulnerable to attack. Multiple land lines should be created and additional ground stations constructed without delay to give our command authorities alternate lines of communication.

Only within the past year, and after great prodding from Capitol Hill, did the director of central intelligence establish a focal point for warning within the intelligence community. Few steps have been taken, however, to breathe life into what could and should be a number one priority for the Central Intelligence Agency; namely, providing the National Security Council with sophisticated analysis of the strategic threat facing our country. With virtually no expenditure of money, that situation could be improved. All it takes is the attention of management.

The foregoing should not be taken as relevant to development of a launch-under-attack capability or doctrine. That is another question entirely, involving order of magnitude differences with what is required at present.

RIGID COMPARTMENTATION

Another impediment to better use of intelligence which could easily be removed is that of unnecessary compartmentation. Intelligence collectors tend to try to keep to themselves the information they collect rather than to seek out who in the government needs that information and get it to them. It is quite possible that, out of an understandable but counterproductive zeal to protect sources, vital pieces of information are being collected but are not being disseminated to the right people. A way around this roadblock can be found and the situation remedied quickly. At the same time—and with equal dedication—measures must be pursued to protect the integrity, the secrecy, of our nation's intelligence.

ELECTRONIC INTELLIGENCE (ELINT) EXPLOITATION

Much has been written about the modern electronic battlefield where literally thousands of electronic emitters will be operating at once. A major effort has been underway for years on the part of U.S. intelligence components to gather and analyze electronic emissions from Warsaw Pact military units at sea, on the ground, and in the air.

Yet there is so far no central management in the intelligence community for electronic intelligence (ELINT) exploitation. The lack of such centralized control is ineffective and costly in peacetime, but it could prove to be a disaster in wartime when the rapidly changing electronic environment will require full application of all of our integrated electronic intelligence and combat support elements.

CIA/DOD COOPERATION

In recent years several efforts have been made in the Nixon, Ford, and Carter administrations to improve the management of our intelligence assets. Unfortunately, one effect of those changes has been to disrupt the close relationship that used to exist between the director of central intelligence on the one hand and the deputy secretary of defense on the other. Between them, those two officials control virtually all the intelligence collection assets of the country.

In the past those two (at times together with the president's advisor for scientific affairs) joined in what was called the Executive Committee (EXCOM) to determine which new—and very expensive—technical collection systems ought to be researched and developed. It was a cooperative endeavor that drew upon the technical expertise of both the CIA and the Department of Defense (DOD).

Today the DCI has instead been given sole responsibility for deciding which new systems should be funded. One result has been to lessen incentives for the DOD to cooperate as fully as in the past. A further result has been to draw the DCI—and his staff and his time and his energy—too deeply into the issues surrounding tactical intelligence. This is time which he can ill afford to take from his more important responsibilities for truly national intelligence for the president's ears. Immediate steps should be taken to resurrect the spirit of cooperation, and that probably will require the reinstitution of some formal bureaucratic structure such as the EXCOM.

TACTICAL INTELLIGENCE

This is an inherently difficult problem which must be worked at constantly, but several immediate steps can be taken to improve tactical intelligence support to combat forces. For example, there is available an advanced tactical intelligence collection package called GUARDRAIL V which is carried on the RU–21 aircraft. GUARDRAIL provides corps level communications intelligence support to battlefield commanders. Procurement and deployment of this important combat support system could be speeded up if additional funds were included in the administration's budget request.

Another key battlefield support system which could more quickly be put in the hands of our military forces is TEREC (tactical electronic reconnaissance). This system allows battlefield commanders to locate and identify enemy electronic emissions which are so essential to modern, high-technology weapons systems. Moreover, by insisting that the U.S. Navy use the TEREC system instead of trying to develop its own distinct program, the navy could be deploying this capability now rather than years from now.

The U.S. Air Force has decided to reopen the U–2 line, calling the newer model the TR–1. Procurement of this high-altitude, multi-intelligence mission aircraft is currently scheduled at a rate of four to six aircraft per year. They could be produced at a rate of two per month, getting the total buy

of twenty-five to the air force in one year and at a lower overall cost than the current, dragged-out schedule. Again—as
with TEREC—the TR–1 program can support the time-
sensitive information needs of ground and naval forces: in
Europe, in the Middle East, in the Persian Gulf, in the Caribbean, and so forth.

These and a number of other newly developed systems are
ready to be procured and deployed. If we act quickly, the net
effect will be to dramatically improve our battlefield
capability in a relatively short time. Much more needs to be
done over the longer term to ensure that our rapid deployment of combat support systems already available will start
us on the right path and at the right speed.

CONCLUSION

The most important "fix" to be undertaken is to provide the
conceptual and institutional basis for our national intelligence to free it from pressures to conform to doctrinal or
political fashion.

Never again can we narrow our scope to the Soviet Union
or even to the Eurasian land mass. We must collect and
analyze data on all parts of the world, with primary emphasis
on points where the Soviets or their surrogates may intervene in unstable countries. And we must sharpen our focus
on the growing economic problems which arise out of competition for natural resources.

It is also necessary to keep firmly in mind that advanced,
sophisticated intelligence hardware—coupled to the most
professional and powerful minds available in the nation—is
absolutely essential to help us know how and where to hedge,
in our defense programs, against future threats from Soviet
weapons developments. If our defense funds are not
unlimited, and they are not, we must concentrate them

where we think they will be needed. We must be sure we are concentrating on the right things.

What the nation requires, then, is national intelligence that is so tough, shrewd, and ruthless that no trend or fashion will ever again screen data or warp perception. What is required is such realistic and icily penetrating national intelligence that no degree of conformity—with the press or with academia or with political fashion—will force such blunders in the future as those we have suffered in the recent past. It is a tall order.

9

MILES M. COSTICK

Soviet Military Posture and Strategic Trade*

Soviet priorities in economic and industrial development. Technological developments in the past decade. R&D manpower expansion. Technology transfer, overt and covert. Military use of commercial and educational developments. Congressional investigation of U.S. international trade policy. Détente and the threat to U.S. security.

The rapid quantitative and qualitative enhancement of Soviet overall military capabilities raises the question of how

*This paper is based on *The Soviet Military Power and Western Technology* to be published in spring 1980 by The Institute on Strategic Trade.

Table 1

The Technological Balance*

General	Specific
U.S. clearly superior:	
"Black box" electronics	Aircraft
Computers	Air-to-air missiles
Integrated circuits	Artillery amunition
Microtechnology	Electronic countermeasures (ECM), counter-
	countermeasures (ECCM)
Night vision	Look-down shoot-down systems
Small turbofan engines	Precision-guided munitions
Space technology	Remotely piloted vehicles
Submarine noise suppressants	Strategic cruise missiles
Terrain-following radar	Survivable submarines
USSR closing gap:	MIRVs
Aerodynamics	Missile accuracy
Composite materials	Satellite sensors
Inertial instrumentation	Tactical nuclear systems

USSR clearly superior:
Cast components
Commonality of components
Ease of maintenance
High-pressure physics
Magnetohydrodynamic power
Rockets and ramjets
Simple systems for common use
Titanium fabrication
Welding
ABM battle management
ICBM "cold launch" capability

Air defense missiles
Antiship missiles
Armored fighting vehicles
Artillery/rocket launchers
Chemical/biological warfare
Cold weather equipment
Gas turbines for ships
ICBM payloads, yields
Mobile ballistic missiles
Ship size v. firepower
Tactical bridging

Status uncertain:
Acoustics
Adaptive optics
High explosive chemistry
Inductive storage and switching systems
  for pulsed power control
Reduced drag for submarines

Antiballistic missiles
Antisubmarine warfare
High energy lasers
Charge particle beams
Satellite-borne radars
Extremely low frequency (ELF)
  communication systems

*Basic data from Collins (1978, p. 65), DIA briefing by Jack Vorona, Assistant Vice Director for Scientific and Technical Intelligence DIA, and research by author.

it came about. How was it possible for a country with a gross national product (GNP) less than half that of the United States, with a poor indigenous technology and with general inefficiency in its productive sector, to outproduce the United States in practically every category of conventional, tactical, and strategic arms? Table 1 makes it clear that the USSR has seized a technological lead from the United States in some critical military weapon systems. How was it possible?

Last year, while testing prototypes of two new intercontinental ballistic missile (ICBM) systems, the Soviets demonstrated the capability of delivering nuclear warheads within 600 feet of a designated target. Until recently, U.S. intelligence estimated that the Soviets would not achieve such accuracy with their ICBMs until the mid-1980s or later. Secretary of Defense Harold Brown subsequently had to admit before the Senate Armed Services Committee that by the early 1980s (1982–1983) the U.S. Minuteman III ICBM force could, as a result of greater Soviet accuracy, fall prey to their first-strike capability.

In December 1978 the Soviet Union successfully tested its huge SS–18 ICBM (Soviet designation RS–20) with twelve nuclear independently targetable reentry warheads (MIRVs); on 26 April 1979 an SS–18 ICBM was fired from the Baikonur Complex at Tyuratam on a flight to the Kamchatka Peninsula, demonstrating Soviet capability to deploy twenty objects or vehicles on an SS–18 missile independently. Analysts believe the Soviets were experimenting with targeting variations and deployment options in the flight test, which provided U.S. monitors with ten clearly definable reentry vehicles and ten extra objects, all of which were separately launched from the SS–18's post-boost vehicle and directed on different targets (*Defense/Space Daily*, 13 November 1979, p. 51). The U.S. Minuteman III ICBM carries no more than three such warheads.

The MiG–25 and MiG–27 combat aircraft have recently been equipped with a look-down radar which had been judged by many U.S. intelligence analysts as beyond what was thought to be the Soviet state of the art in radars.

Just how was all this possible? What has brought about the rapid advance in Soviet technological capabilities? How did the Soviets raise the efficiency of their industry?

In examining these Soviet technological and industrial successes, I have interviewed about fifty former Soviet scientists, researchers, industrial managers, military officers, and KGB—affiliated individuals. I have also discussed these questions with a number of North Atlantic Treaty Organization (NATO) intelligence officials and representatives of the Israeli intelligence service.

The January 1980 decision by the Carter administration to suspend sales to the Soviet Union of critical technology and industrial equipment amounts to an admission that U.S. technology has contributed to Soviet military capabilities. Soviet aggression in Afghanistan was facilitated by deployment of military hardware manufactured with U.S. equipment. For example, trucks and tank trailers produced in the Kama River truck complex, built with U.S. assistance, provided the principal means of ground transportation for Soviet troops and armor; heavy rocket launchers Frog 4 and Frog 7 as well as 122—millimeter BM—21 rocket launchers were produced at the ZIL plant which widely utilizes American equipment and technology; the T—54 and T—62 battle tanks were produced in plants built and equipped with Western technology; MiG—21 Fishbeds, MiG—23 Floggers, and the Su—17s have engines derived from Rolls-Royce engines and are manufactured with Western equipment.

The most crucial question is whether the suspension of strategic sales to the USSR by the Carter administration represents a temporary or permanent policy change. It is not only an American problem. Our NATO allies must also decide which way to go—to join the United States in temporary curtailment of strategic exports or to disregard our move.

SOVIET PRIORITIES

Lenin's dictum that "electrification plus industrialization equals socialism" was translated into the Five-Year Plans that formed the basis of Soviet economic policy. The policy stressed development of heavy industry. The Bolsheviks' obsession with heavy industry was in fact a conscious policy geared toward arming the Red Army.

The choice facing the Communist leadership was that between raising the economic and social welfare of its citizens and the fulfillment of politico-strategic objectives. In the early stages of economic development, consumer satisfaction would have called for the development of agriculture and light industry relevant to orderly economic growth. The Bolsheviks, however, opted for the second choice, which involved development of heavy industry relevant to a buildup of military power. The economic development and industrialization of the USSR—as indicated unanimously by Soviet expatriates—had a single purpose: to facilitate and maintain political and military power. Science, research and development (R&D), as well as most of the educational effort were all harnessed in this direction.

This point is perhaps most evident in the fact that it is virtually impossible to identify a single industry in the USSR which manufactures only civilian goods. Every scientific institute, every research and development facility, every educational institution, every factory, has its "First Section" staffed by military and KGB representatives. All identified Soviet scientific and research institutions devote between 70 and 80 percent of their time and resources to work requested by the party/military/industrial complex and supervised by the First Section. And all these enterprises utilize Western scientific and technological discoveries as well as advanced scientific instruments, testing and control devices, computers and manufacturing equipment.

Soviet commitments are stated quite explicitly by high intellectuals and officials. To quote a senior Soviet political officer in the late 1960s (Korniyenko 1969, pp. 2–3):

Strengthening of its defenses is now the foremost political function of the Soviet State. . . . Never before has the internal life of the country been subordinated to a war so deeply and thoroughly as at the present time.

Roy Medvedev, Soviet historian and intellectual, recently told an American living in Moscow (Herr 1979, p. 15):

We are going to overtake the United States, and that is inevitable. . . . Our country is a military machine . . . our system allowed the spending of colossal resources for one purpose alone—military might. We may be primitive, but we will take over. . . . We put everything into rocketry. . . . The government does not care whether or not anything is left over for the population.

In the famous treatise on Soviet military strategy, Soviet Marshal V. D. Sokolovskiy (1963, p. 421) commented:

In the present epoch, the struggle for peace and the fight to gain time depends above all on an unremitting increase in Soviet military power and that of the entire socialist camp based on development of productive forces and the continuous growth of its material and technological base.

SOVIET TECHNOLOGICAL CHALLENGE

In evaluating the current Soviet scientific and technological effort and its dynamics, experts agree that the USSR has been making an enormous and determined effort. According to Defense Secretary Brown (U.S. Department of Defense 1979), the Soviet military R&D expenditures are 75 percent greater than those of the United States.

The present and near-term Soviet military capability reflects a technological base that has grown steadily during the last decade. Military R&D, a high priority sector, received regular large infusions of capital investment leading to significant growth in those research, design, and test facilities so critical to weapons development. For example, there has been roughly a 30 percent growth in aerospace facilities. A concurrent increase in the size of the R&D manpower force has also been significant; in sheer numbers, the Soviets passed the United States in the mid-1960s.[1] This force was estimated in 1979 at 800,000 scientists and engineers—the world's largest—and at least 270,000 new engineers graduate each year, a rather phenomenal number by U.S. standards. The best qualified members of this important R&D manpower resource are earmarked for the military sector. The Soviet Union, as a closed society, enjoys a few advantages not duplicated in the United States.

Leadership, starting with Lenin, has stressed science and technology. Command emphasis and a coherent strategy ensure an increasingly skilled cadre, continued heavy investments, and continuity. The focus remains on military research and development, with scant fear of repercussions caused by domestic demands.[2]

Extreme secrecy shrouds Soviet efforts, often concealing courses of action and intent until the start of field testing. Shortcuts are possible, because published reports of U.S. plans and progress point them out. The Kremlin consequently can concentrate on carefully chosen goals that simplify the search for superiority in a selected sector (Currie 1976, pp. I–6, II–2).

TECHNOLOGY TRANSFER

This discussion would be incomplete without examining the relationship of technology transfer to the Soviet military posture. The industrialized free world during this decade, in addition to being the source of much of the Soviet Union's electronic and computer technology and manufacturing know-how, has supplied the Soviet industrial sector with over $50 billion worth of efficient machine tools, transfer lines, chemical plants, precision instrumentation, and associated technologies which have unquestionably played a major role in the modernization and expansion of Soviet industry. Although much of the technology embodied in the Western equipment is known and understood by Soviet technicians, its purchase via long-term low-interest loans has enabled the Soviet Union and other Warsaw Pact countries to achieve industrial expansion at a substantially faster rate than would have been possible with indigenous resources.

The Soviets follow Western developments avidly through acquisition of scientific and technical journals, attendance at conferences and symposia, scientific exchange visits, and the purchase of at least one copy of each of the 80,000 U.S. government documents and government contractor reports deposited each year with the National Technical Information Service of the Department of Commerce (Vorona 1979, p. 21).

Many technologies of greatest interest to the Soviet government have important military as well as commercial applications. In recent years the leading edge of these technologies has increasingly been developed by the private sector for commercial application and only later for military application. Actual improvements in Soviet military capabilities owing to the acquisition of Western technology are often difficult to quantify—such as truck tires suffering one-third greater wear because of superior carbon black from a Western-built plant, or long-range transport aircraft that suffer less down time because of the use of engine components produced on Western manufacturing equipment. Yet increased U.S. commercial contracts with the USSR and its COMECON (Council for Mutal Economic Assistance) partners may result in the outflow of significant technologies before they are applied to advance weapon systems in the United States.

Sometimes, from the point of view of foreign countries, the sole or principal purpose of the transaction may be to procure information. Soviet intelligence agencies have a long tradition of seeking to acquire industrial expertise. The Soviets have made major covert efforts to obtain key components of high technology, particularly in the computer field. They often focus on very small firms which can supply particular critical components or facilities, and not infrequently they seek out firms in free industrialized nations other than the United States in the belief that the controls there may be less strict (Iklé 1977, p. 6).

The Soviet agency which actually uses a product may be different from the agency that purchases it. End use controls are therefore often ineffective, particularly with sales to a completely state-owned economy of the Soviet bloc. This problem of multiple end uses is, if anything, more acute with the most modern technology. Reprocessing plants may produce plutonium for bombs as well as for fuel; technology for the production of wide-bodied aircraft can contribute to military airlift capabilities as easily as to civilian transportation; the equipment for production circuits used in pocket calculators may also be used in making guidance computers for missiles. New medical technology may have highly important military or intelligence applications. Computers for processing seismic signals in geological exploration may also process sonar signals in antisubmarine warfare (ASW). Capabilities for launching communications satellites may launch military missiles. The technology for high-bypass turbofan engines and high inlet temperature turbines can be used in military as well as civilian aircraft. And NASA's joint ventures in space exploration will inevitably help Soviet experts to run their military space program.

In addition to the acquisition of Western industrial plants and equipment, the decade of the 1970s has witnessed greatly expanded contact between the free world and Soviet scientists and engineers. The scope and depth of Soviet interest in advanced and emerging technologies is shown by the exchange agreements the Soviets have negotiated with the United States since 1972. There are ten bilateral U.S.–Soviet agreements in existence comprising about 240 or so working groups in which Soviet and U.S. personnel are working jointly. They include such subtopics as computer science, metallurgy, microbiology, chemical catalysis, physics, science policy, meteorology, earthquake prediction, fast breeder reactors, controlled thermonuclear research, and magnetohydrodynamic (MHD) power generation. One provision common to many of these bilateral agreements encourages the establishment of separate agreements between individual U.S. companies and such entities of the Soviet government as the State Committee for Science and Technology. The Soviet Union has negotiated such agreements with a large number of U.S. companies—significantly, I believe, with companies which are front runners in areas in which the Soviets are deficient. There is no formal U.S. government oversight of these agreements unless the accord results in the sale or transfer of an item or of technical data requiring a validated export license. I view these agreements as still another mechanism for the potential transfer of advanced technology.

For example, a team of about forty Soviet specialists has visited and studied production processes at Boeing, Lockheed, and McDonnel-Douglas plants. As a result, the Soviets gained the necessary knowledge for production of wide-bodied jet aircraft. Swindell-Dress Company, a division of Pullman, Inc., has trained about four hundred Soviet engineers in Pittsburgh (Stengel 1974, p. 277); they are the key personnel at the Kama River truck complex which produces military vehicles and engines for Soviet armor. Gould

Laboratories Materials Technology, a division of Gould Incorporated, has trained thirty-six Soviet experts in Cleveland for a period of one year in areas of metallurgy, polymetric chemistry, electrochemistry, mechanical engineering, and fluid-flow physics.

Soviet acquisitions are not limited to the purchase and diversion of equipment and goods. Soviet scientists and engineers study Western scientific developments and acquire technological know-how. One specific example with direct military application is that of a Soviet exchange student who came to the United States in the academic year 1976–1977 to study at a leading university, his subject the science involved in fuel-air explosives. It appears that this Soviet "student" is himself involved in research directly related to fuel-air explosives (Vorona 1979, p. 25).

In addition to these examples, I see the Soviets making a concerted effort to gain as much information, technical knowledge, and equipment as possible on new and emerging technologies which may not have reached the military application phase in the United States but which certainly have the potential for such use. These include magnetic bubble memory technology for computers, genetic engineering (specifically, the recombinant DNA [deoxyribonucleic acid]), fracture mechanics, and superplasticity. Under the auspices of an agreement between the U.S. and Hungarian academies of science, one Gyorgy Zimmer, who heads the Hungarian effort in magnetic bubble research, has been coming periodically to the United States to conduct research at a leading universities, to attend conferences, and to visit other facilities in order to observe and discuss American findings. As in all such fields, we believe the Soviets have access to most if not all Hungarian and other Warsaw Pact research and information including that which Zimmer gains in the United States. I would be surprised if this were not the case; indeed, foreign visitors tend to confirm this fact (Vorona 1979, p. 26).

Other bilateral agreements that we believe to be effective transfer mechanisms are those that provide for the student exchange program between the United States and the USSR/Warsaw Pact/China. Soviet exchange students who come to the United States for an academic year usually already possess the equivalent of a U.S. doctoral degree, are on average about thirty-five years old, and probably have had about eight years of practical experience. (For topics studied by Soviet and U.S. exchange students, see Table 2.)

What the Soviet Union needs to improve its strategic tactical and conventional forces is not purely military in character. The Soviets lack certain key applied technology that is now available in commercial application from the United States, France, Germany, Japan, and the United Kingdom, technology that will improve Soviet guidance systems, avionics, missile technology, and key bomb components. The acquisition of such "nonmilitary" technical information should enable the Soviet Union to upgrade its bomber forces quickly and allow it to make almost instant improvements in its targeting and warning systems.

Because of the lack of coherent national policy to control the transfer of technology to Communist-dominated countries, critical information has been transferred to the Soviets either directly or through the back door. Here are some of the major transfers that have taken place:

• The Soviets succeeded in obtaining American wide-bodied jet aircraft technology critical in the deployment of air-launched cruise missiles and for long-distance transport of troops and war materials.

• Another such example is in the production of Soviet KAMAZ trucks. The Kama River truck plant located near the city of Naberzhnyye Chelny in the USSR was built almost exclusively with Western technology. Among other things, the United States supplied the automated foundry for making the engines, the production line, and the computer that

Table 2

Subjects Studied by IREX Students

Students	Subjects Studied
Americans in USSR	Language and style in the Chet'i Minei of Dmitri Rostovsky
	Socioeconomic development of formal organizations in Vilnius in the period 1860–1914
	The professionalization of Russian psychiatry 1860–1911
	Marriage patterns in Russia and USSR 1897–1975
	The state and the economy in Catherinian Russia
	Soviet criminal law and codification
	The development of medical sciences in 19th-century Russia
Soviets in U.S.	Research in digital automatic control and diagnosis
	Ferroelectric ceramics
	Technological possibilities and efficiency of computer application for control of machine-tool systems with digital set control
	Passage of shock waves through inert and combustible heterogeneous mixtures
	Conversion of hydraulic signals into electrical signals
	Photoelectric phenomena in semi-conductors
	Solid-state electrochemical thermodynamics

controls the plant. When it reaches full production, the plant will produce 150,000 trucks and an additional 100,000 engines per year. These trucks are more efficient and reliable than those they are replacing and have a 60 percent greater haul capability on a one-for-one basis. Some of these trucks are indeed going into the civil economy (where they are always subject to call by the military); others are actually being used by the military. One continues to receive reports that some of the engines are destined for tanks and armored vehicles (Vorona 1979, p. 23).

• An entire series of Soviet computers is based on IBM 360 and 370 models that were illegally diverted via a free world firm into the USSR in 1971 and 1972. These diversions may have been the basis for the Soviet/Warsaw Pact development of the RYAD I and II computers. The number of known cases of computers embargoed by COCOM[3] that have been diverted into the Soviet Union may be just the tip of the iceberg (Costick 1978, pp. 16–22; Vorona 1979, p. 23).

• The Soviets obtained RB–211 high-bypass ratio turbofan jet engine technology developed on $300 million in U.S. government R&D grants to the Lockheed Corporation. The engine powers wide-bodied jet aircraft and is suitable for a long-range bomber.

• The Soviets succeeded in obtaining U.S. semiconductor technology of critical importance in guidance systems for ICBMs and other missiles as well as in miniaturized military computers.

• The Soviet Union obtained from the United States numerous space technologies also relevant to military effort in space (space capsule-coupling technology, astronaut's space-suit technology, relevant computer technology, etc.).

• The most modern and the only effective air traffic control centers in the USSR—Moscow's Vnukovo Airport is one of the examples—are being constructed with integrated circuits from the United States (the contract is valued at $74 million). These computerized air traffic control systems have a direct military spillover.

• Soviet dissident Anatoly Sharansky was sentenced to a long term for informing Western reporters that the Soviets have violated agreements signed with the U.S. Department of Commerce regarding the use of U.S.–purchased computers. In his capacity as computer expert within the Soviet military establishment, according to Sharansky, he worked on American computers sold to the USSR for civilian purposes only.

• The Soviet Union is making every attempt to obtain a critical military technology from the United States: the small, high-efficiency, aircraft gas turbine engine of the type currently used in the U.S. Air Force/Boeing ALCM–B and the U.S. Navy/General Dynamics Tomahawk cruise missiles. The manufacturer in the United States is Detroit Diesel Allison. The engine, ironically, is classified as "commercial" and consequently is easy to obtain by any Communist government. The application is pending to permit the export of engines and manufacturing technology to Poland and Rumania. The amazing aspect of the potential sale is, in fact that the Carter administration denied this technology to U.S. NATO allies and is considering its sale to the Soviets' Warsaw Pact allies.

While the United States is at the forefront of electronics manufacturing, we are but one of about eleven free world suppliers of metalworking and fabrication equipment. An Austrian firm—Gesellschaft für Gertigungs Technik und Maschinenbau (GFM Corporation) of Steyr—is the world's principal builder of precision rotary-forging equipment, an exceptionally efficient machine for producing high-quality gun tubes. No other type of machine in the world is competitive with these machines. The Soviets have been one of the firm's principal customers for almost two decades, purchasing probably hundreds of millions of dollars worth of this equipment. These machines can radically increase production rates while simultaneously producing the higher-quality barrel required for the greater rates of fire and higher muzzle velocity of today's weapons. In addition, with today's higher-quality steel, the overall life of artillery weapon systems is increased. As a result, the Soviets probably have the greatest gun-barrel manufacturing capability in the world (Vorona 1979, p. 24).

The U.S. heat-seeking, shoulder-launched Redeye missile was acquired by the Soviet Union through one of the Scandinavian countries. In the USSR it served for development of the Soviet SA−7 Strella missile which destroyed numerous U.S. aircraft in Vietnam and during the Middle East war and which is today a weapon dear to terrorists of all shades and colors.

Soviet air-to-air missile AA−2 Atoll is a copy of an American original, the early AIM−9B Sidewinder. When first seen on 9 June 1961, carried by various Soviet fighters in an air display, it was almost identical to the U.S. weapon, and it has since followed the development of the more advanced Sidewinder models. AA−2 Atoll is the standard weapon on MiG−21s and MiG−23s. The Soviets obtained the first prototype from Chinese Communists who collected several which had been fired by Chinese Nationalists in October 1958, had missed their targets and had fallen to the ground undamaged. In 1968, however, Soviet intelligence agents stole from the German Air Force and NATO Zell Air Base in Bavaria the latest Sidewinder model with a new seeker head known as FGW Mod 2.[4] This Sidewinder enabled the Soviets to upgrade their AA−2 Atoll and two other air-to-air missiles.

A recent defector from the USSR, still under security wraps, has produced new evidence of the way that export of American technology for peaceful purposes can come back to bite us. He claims that equipment sold to the Soviets to modernize their weather forecasting has been secretly diverted to improve the efficiency of their spy satellites (Meyer 1979, p. A−9).

In the SALT I treaty, the United States accepted Soviet quantitative superiority in throw weight and number of launchers on the grounds of a U.S. qualitative lead in accuracy and MIRV technology. The Soviets have rapidly pressed ahead, however, to close the quality gap, with a great deal of unwitting assistance from the United States. In 1972 the State Department was instrumental in approving the sale by a U.S. firm of 164 Centalign−B machines with accompanying technology that produce precision miniature ball bearings milled to extreme tolerances (a twenty-fifth millionth of an inch). This allows the Soviets to close the critical MIRV gap. The precision miniature ball bearings may be used to reduce the friction of the moving parts in the guidance mechanism of a MIRV warhead, enabling the missile rapidly to change direction in flight in order to get sharper on-target accuracy (Costick 1976, p. 7; Graham 1976). The Soviet Union today has some 7,100 operational MIRVs available for deployment against the United States (Middleton 1977, p. 10). The $20 million sale approved in 1972, at the peak of détente euphoria, is thus to some extent responsible for the $30−40 billion MX missile system program. Edwin E. Speaker, a weapons expert for the Defense Intelligence Agency (DIA), testified before a congressional subcommittee in 1976 (Costick 1980, p. 87):

It is a certainty that the products of these grinders could and will be found in a wide variety of current and future ground, air, sea, and space military hardware that require precision guidance equipment, optical recording devices as well as associated scientific test equipment.

In October 1969 the United States bowed to French pressure and COCOM approved the first phase of a transfer of semiconductor manufacturing technology from the French firm Sescosem to Unitra, a Polish government-operated enterprise. This first phase involved silicon planar transistor technology; the second phase was approved in 1972 and involved the transfer of bipolar integrated circuit (IC) technology.

The specific technologies were digital or logic circuits, the principal logic IC technology used in both industrial and military applications at that time, and linear IC technology. The devices in question are complex electronic circuits that are reduced photographically and etched on tiny silicon chips. They can be used, for example, in the fire control systems of missile guidance systems and fighter aircraft, giving computer-like control with minuscule weight, bulk, and electrical drain. They are typical dual-purpose technology end products also used in such nonmilitary items as pocket calculators, digital wristwatches, microwave oven controls, and television and high-fidelity sound systems.

This program provided Poland with an initial facility capable of producing twelve million integrated circuits per year. A U.S. Defense Department (DOD) employee who visited the Unitra plant within the first year after the agreement noted that it was already in partial operation at the time. The plant was fully operational in June 1974. The Soviet Union has also acquired integrated circuits technology and manufacturing capabilities from Japan in one of the most daring clandestine undertakings of its industrial espionage.

Soviet acquisition of sophisticated U.S. ICBM technology goes beyond integrated circuits and precision ball-bearing technologies essential to build the guidance systems and gyroscopes for ICBMs and other types of missiles as well as MIRVing mechanisms. Major General George J. Keegan, Jr., U.S. Air Force (Ret.), former head of Air Force Intelligence, recently observed to me: "The Soviet Union has acquired through bilateral scientific exchanges all of our inertial guidance technology." Pursuing the lead he provided, I spoke to a number of former members of the Soviet scientific community and to several faculty members at the Massachusetts

Institute of Technology (MIT), and found that a number of
Soviet scientists—full professors—spent sabbaticals at MIT
teaching and conducting research during the early 1970s.
While there, these Soviet citizens established and cultivated
contacts in the Greater Boston area with smaller U.S. companies known for their work in the inertial guidance field.
We were told—by both the former Soviet scientists and MIT
faculty members—that Soviet academicians were able to obtain the latest in U.S. inertial guidance from these firms and
through association with some American scientists involved
in such work at MIT.

In August 1967 Anatoliy K. Kochev, a scientific member of
the Leningrad Polytechnical Institute Imeni M. I. Kalinina,
arrived at the Catholic University in Washington, DC, to
work on "construction methods of equipment to measure
small accelerations and displacements"—that is, the
manufacture of accelerometers. Kochev arrived under the
auspices of the State Department Academic Exchange Program and stayed at the Catholic University throughout June
1968. The accelerometer is an intricate device which
measures the pull of gravity on any vehicle such as a missile
or a space-orbiting device. It happens that the Leningrad
Polytechnical Institute was the principal Soviet R&D institution conducting research in accelerometer technology and
Kochev was one of the principal researchers involved in that
project. The Leningrad Institute was also producing under
laboratory conditions the first Soviet accelerometers for
missiles, space-orbiting devices, and military aircraft.

In the course of interviewing Soviet expatriates, I also
spoke to several individuals who had worked until relatively
recently on Soviet guidance and autopilot systems. They told
me that in building gimbaled gyroscopes for a variety of
Soviet missiles they have used precision miniature ball bearings milled on U.S. Centalign-B machines in the Moscow Ball
Bearing Plant. A DIA official told the United States Congress on 8 November 1979 that the Soviet acquisition of 164

precision miniature ball-bearing grinding machines from the United States made "a distinct contribution to the Soviet military procurement effort." Dr. Jack Vorona, Assistant Vice Director for Scientific and Technical Intelligence of the DIA, stated in sworn testimony before the Subcommittee on Procurement of the Senate Committee on Armed Services chaired by Senator Harry Byrd, Jr., of Virginia, that "these machines are making a distinctive contribution to the Soviet military effort and could very well be producing the precision miniature ball bearings used in current and follow-on high quality MIRV guidance systems" (Vorona 1979, p. 22). Under questioning by Senators Byrd and Warner, Dr. Vorona acknowledged that the Centalign-B machines acquired by the USSR in 1973 and 1974 are being used to provide the latest versions of the SS−18 (RS−20) ICBM with its highly accurate MIRV guidance systems.

Many other technologies which protect the current U.S. military lead in certain areas are also little-known dual-purpose items. Small array transform processors (ATPs) are used, for instance, in seismic oil exploration equipment. ATPs are electronic devices which enhance computer speed so that computers can interpret millions of tiny variations in the sounds of geologic formations below the earth. Attached to shipboard computers, ATPs perform a central function of antisubmarine warfare: they assist the computer in digital signal processing and signal analysis which enables the computer to identify tiny differences in the sounds under the ocean's surface—a process that yields the location of enemy submarines.

Geospace Corporation of Houston, Texas, has sold thirty-six ATP systems, critical to the submarine detection process, to the Soviet Union and the People's Republic of China. Litton Industries is another business enterprise involved in the sale of similar ASW devices to the USSR. For two days I interviewed a former Soviet intelligence specialist, a geologist by profession, who revealed that he and some Soviet navy

personnel—trained in Houston by Geospace Corporation—
had carried Geospace Corporation's ATPs (1703 and 1704)
on board Soviet submarines with ASW mission and Soviet
ASW surface ships and installed them next to the shipboard
computers. The Soviet expatriate told me that the small computers (1703 and 1704) were purchased for the All Union
Research Institute of Geophysics in Moscow via Geospace's
French subsidiary and directly from its headquarters in
Houston. The All Union Institute acted on behalf of the
Soviet navy, and my informant was the control officer for the
operation.

In summary, the Soviets are seeking Western technology
and equipment by any and all means. In the past, due to a
limited technological base for specialized components, Soviet
weapon designers appeared to be somewhat constrained in
the effectiveness of the products they could develop. Technology transfer affords them the opportunity to rectify such
deficiencies. Much of what they acquire is slated for the industrial sector, but it is axiomatic that this equipment and
technology has been and is important to the Soviet military.

THE CAUSE OF THE PROBLEM

U.S. policy on international trade consists of two elements
that are often not reconcilable: (1) to promote trade and commerce with other nations, and (2) to control the export of
goods and technology which could make a significant contribution to the military potential of any other government
or governments when this would prove detrimental to the
national security of the United States.

The given empirical evidence proves that since the onset of
economic détente, resulting in the liberalization of trade legislation pertaining to commerce with the Communist governments, export control efforts have failed. In addition, politi-

cal détente with the USSR and its satellites has brought a flood of Communist agents into the United States. Numerous government-to-government scientific, technological, and cultural exchanges have created tremendous opportunities for stealing U.S. scientific and technological secrets. All these, as we have demonstrated, have had a serious impact on U.S. national security and are continuing to do so.

CONCLUSION

The U.S. government's objective in controlling exports of U.S. technology should be to protect U.S. lead time in the application of technology to military capabilities relative to the nation's principal adversaries. In addition, it is in the national interest not to make it easy for any country to advance its own technology in ways which could damage U.S. interests.

Effective export controls need *new definitions* and *new administrative procedures.* The first point is to define "critical technology," the classified and unclassified nuclear and non-nuclear unpublished technical data of any kind that can be used or adapted for use in the design, production, manufacture, utilization, testing, maintenance, or reconstruction of articles or materials. Such data may take the tangible form of a model, prototype, blueprint, or operational manual, or they may take the intangible forms of technical services or of scientific and technological exchanges. Control of this critical technology also requires control of certain associated critical end products defined as "keystone" that can contribute significantly in and of themselves to the transfer of critical technology because they (1) embody extractable technology and/or (2) are equipment that completes a process line and allows it to be fully utilized.

Acquisition of such technology by Warsaw Pact members or by any other potential adversary, whether obtained directly from the United States or indirectly through another recipient or whether the declared intended end use by the recipient is military or nonmilitary, could contribute to the military potential of such a country and could endanger U.S. national security.

As a second point, we conclude that the U.S. Department of Defense should be assigned responsibility for defining what constitutes critical technology. The Defense Department should also designate those items to be considered as defense articles and defense services so that they can be properly placed on the U.S. Munitions List administered by the State Department. The Security Assistance Act and Arms Export Control Act of 1976 in its present form does not require this procedure. Under none of the individual classifications of this act is there specific provision for the identification of any design, production, or test data as *significant combat equipment*. The criteria used to select such categories do not necessarily involve judgment as to strategic or advanced technology. For example, while *significant combat equipment* includes M1 rifles and bayonets, it excludes CDC's Cyber−76 computer and certain technologies and equipment necessary for the production of nuclear warheads.

To protect and strengthen U.S. defense production capabilities, procedures need to be established which separate the military articles required by most foreign countries from the design and manufacturing know-how essential to the production of those articles. Under existing agreements with our NATO allies, a number of projects involving coproduction and standardization specify the transfer of such information in both directions, but this flow of technology with other friendly countries requires more control than is possible at present. Similarly, while the export of some commercial technological products could be more readily available to even the Soviet Union, it is essential to restrict the export of associated data concerning the design and manufacture of those products which are also on the U.S. Munitions List.

The present Commodity Control List of the U.S. Commerce Department is derived from the U.S. Munitions List by way of the Battle Act and the Mutual Security Assistance Act, which are administered by the State Department. Because the role of the DOD has not yet been specified in any legislation as the basic source for the definition of "defense articles" or "strategic technology," there continue to be uncertainty and delay in the processing of Commerce Department and Munitions Department license applications. The present reports required by the Arms Export Control Act and the studies to be required when the Export Administration Act comes up for deliberation before the U.S. Congress would now provide the administration with the unique opportunity to restructure the entire arms and export control process.

Events in recent months have made even more serious the problem of transferring to the Soviets technology with military uses. The initial reaction of the Carter administration in the wake of the Soviet invasion of Afghanistan moves in the right direction, but there is much more that we can and should do. In light of difficulties discussed elsewhere in this book, the transfer problem becomes particularly critical.

Discussion:
Part II

Discussions at the Belmont House conference (December 1979) included, in addition to the authors of this book, the following participants: Richard Allen (Potomac International Corporation), Angelo Codevilla (Senate Select Committee on Intelligence, Office of Senator Malcolm Wallop), Fleming Fuller (Documentary Department, KRON–TV), Eric Hemel (economist, Office of Senator Patrick Moynihan), Charles Kupperman (Research Director, Committee on the Present Danger), Robert Osgood (Professor of International Relations, School of Advanced International Studies, Johns Hopkins University), Dale Tahtinen (Reagan for President campaign), and Victor Utgoff (representative of Zbigniew Brzezinski, National Security Council). These excerpts pertain to subjects discussed in Part II.

ON QUICK FIXES

ROWEN: What would you like to see spent on these programs in the next year or several years?

VAN CLEAVE: Well, for each of these fixes I have a ballpark, but reasonable, figure. They are not just plucked out of the air—they are based upon some kind of research. I could add them up, but I don't like that approach. I would really prefer to decide on the true status of our strategic forces, the real problems with them, where they do not meet the tests, and then correct the faults.

Now, having said that, the costs are nowhere near prohibitive, I feel certain.

I think we could do the fixes for between $6 and $10 billion in the next few years. To redeploy the ICBM force in the type of mode we are talking about, including the types of modifications necessary to the Minuteman III, you are talking somewhere near $7 to $9 billion. Some of these things probably pay off for four or five years or so down the line, but they must be initiated right now and will cost money now as well. I have advocated here, for example, acceleration of the plans to develop a follow-on bomber.

ROWEN: That wouldn't be costly until later on.

VAN CLEAVE: It depends. But these are things that are going to have to be done. I mentioned the figure for the bomber force. That includes the armaments. The cruise missile program will cost more.

But I should like to see FY 1980 and what we spend on the strategic nuclear force programs under $11 billion.

Priorities, of course, have to be established. Admiral Zumwalt mentioned 7 percent of GNP, and some have said 6 percent. Within those kinds of increases all of these things, of course, can be accomplished; but not along with everything else that needs to be done, and this is why decisions have to be made.

UTGOFF: As you might guess, I differ with your conclusions in a number of places. On the other hand, I have to agree that we have a lot of problems in the strategic area. And it does seem clear that we are going to fall behind to some degree in the early 1980s.

I don't think, however, that it is the disaster that you make it out to be. It is something we cannot live with for any length of time—and I think the longer-term programs that we have set in place to fix it are going to fix it. I think the main consequence is that we are not going to be as well hedged as we would like to be in this period. We did look at the question of short-term fixes, however. And we went to the point of pressing people to come up with their most reasonable options. We have costs for some of these things, like running higher alert rates for bombers. A 10 percent increase in our bomber alert rate would be perhaps $250 million per year.

But there was enormous reluctance within the Department of Defense [DOD] to adopt such measures—and it was not just from Harold Brown, but also from the Joint Chiefs of Staff. Their judgment is that if they had the amounts of money that are involved in pursuing these kinds of things, they have other things that they would much prefer to spend it on. And they have made that point again and again.

ZUMWALT: I think it is important for civilian authority not to be overly persuaded by that kind of an opinion from the Joint Chiefs. It gets back to the point I made earlier—by and large, the senior military feel that you must err in favor of conventional forces. Most senior military just feel in their gut that the other side is never going to escalate. They have not, by and large, come to understand the fact that civilians just will not move and make decisions in the face of Soviet strategic superiority. If civilian authorities want to be free to threaten or to use conventional forces, they must move to regain strategic parity as well as certain conventional advantages.

BURT: The MX, particularly the racetrack system, is in danger of becoming a dollar sink for the entire U.S. strategic force budget for the 1980s—to the extent to which any administration is going to be able to focus on other problems in the strategic force area—because of both the bureaucratic interest in saving this system as well as the financial implications.

UTGOFF: It is clear the system is expensive, and it is clear it is going to compete for resources with other things that we all think are very important. I think there are two points to keep in mind, though. One is that the way the cost estimating was done for this is rather promising. There was no attempt by the administration to come riding in at the last minute and drive the estimates way down in hopes that the system would sell better. I think the cost estimates are more realistic.

Second, we are trying to keep pretty good tabs on how cost estimates are evolving. I had a report yesterday that DOD thinks that it has found some ways to actually reduce those costs.

Another point that has been made is that we ought to get back to the vertical silo system. And I would like you to understand that the primary reason for moving away from that system was that by doing so it would be possible to hedge against the losing of location security by moving the missiles around rapidly. So the horizontal shelter system was adopted more to facilitate rapid movement, or the reshuffling of the location of the missiles, than anything else.

NITZE: I honestly believe that to be contrary to fact.

UTGOFF: Those are the arguments as I heard them.

NITZE: I know that is the rationale that the executive branch gives, but it just is not so. The question at issue is whether this particular racetrack mode was decided upon because of doubt as to the risk of the Russians knowing where the missile was, at which silo it was, prior to the attack—in other words, the question of location security. Was that the reason why they went to the racetrack mode as opposed to the vertical silo mode? I believe that this is not the case. I believe it is the case that it was considered that the vertical silo mode was not consistent with the treaty as the Russians interpreted the treaty and, as I believe, as the language clearly indicates the treaty should be read. Now I know that it has been asserted that we could just bully it through and interpret the treaty to permit the vertical silo mode. But it is an awfully hard argument to sustain; the decision was made not to try to sustain that argument.

As a consequence, the White House decided they had to have a mobile system in order to be in a better position to argue consistency with the treaty. The most unambiguous way to define a mobile system is as one that has a transporter/erector/launcher as an integral device—enabling the missile to be launched directly from the transporter/erector/launcher. Having decided that you had to have a transporter/erector/launcher, it was decided to capitalize on its potential and get what benefits you could from its capability for relatively rapid motion from one protective shelter to another.

This capability, however, runs into difficulty. In the event the Russians threaten our system with short-warning submarine-launch missiles you don't have enough time to get from where the transporter/erector/launcher is to any large number of silos in time to button up that silo. So I think the decision now is that rather than to try to get into a silo at all, what we would try to do is to have that transporter/erector/launcher leave its shield and run as fast as it can to the end of the valley and hope that it survives.

So the complexity of the racetrack system springs from the treaty itself and I can see very well why the executive branch does not want to say so.

ROWEN: If we had not been so constrained in our thinking about nuclear forces in the past ten years, I suspect we might have evolved a really different posture and somewhat different doctrines. MX is a product, I am certain, of the whole arms control process.

For example, at this stage we might have come to the view that the pressure on our resources, together with the range of contingencies that could emerge, should lead us to give emphasis to forces that have some diversity in use, forces which could do more than one thing.

The MX, whatever it can do, can't do very much. And that is also a problem for the Trident submarine-launched missile. Suppose we decided that it was an important objective to be able to deliver nuclear weapons with high confidence against a variety of targets of the Soviet Union, and also to have a good reserve capability, high accuracy, and good command control, and so on. And to be able to meet contingencies of several kinds—for example, in the Persian Gulf, and nonnuclear as well as nuclear contingencies. What would we be buying? Well, I suspect we would be buying —or giving a lot more emphasis to—long-range aircraft.

Van Cleave mentioned the importance of going ahead with the bomber program. Well, the bomber program, if it is the right kind of program, might turn out to be really useful in a variety of different applications. B–52s, after all, whatever one assesses their effectiveness to be, were used in Vietnam rather extensively.

And in the future we are likely to want to have long-range bombers for many contingencies.

Cruise missiles, or unmanned aerodynamic vehicles more generally, have a variety of important applications, I think, and not all of them involve carrying nuclear warheads. Again, if we had somehow managed to break loose from the shackles of thinking about the strategic nuclear business in the way we have been locked into, we would perhaps by now have decided that unmanned aerodynamic vehicles had a very large range of potential applications, one set of which could be usefully met by having nuclear warheads in them.

CODEVILLA: I think it is very important to begin a discussion regarding these matters with clear understanding of strategic objectives. We have not seen our objectives clearly, and have not decided well on weapons because we have put ourselves in an intellectual straightjacket, called SALT, over the past decade. Common sense suggests that the main question to be answered is: what do we want to do concerning our enemies' armed forces?

I suggest that we are not going to get terribly far unless we agree that the first thing we want to do is to keep those forces from hurting us in case of war. This means we have to target our strategic forces against Soviet strategic forces, not against cities, and it means we have to build active defense against Soviet missiles and aircraft.

The decisions against counterforce targeting and against active defense have not been made for technological reasons. The Soviets have faced technological problems worse than ours for many, many years. And yet for many, many years they have concentrated doggedly on counterforce targeting and active defense. The Soviets are working hard in both fields and we are not. We have seen the Soviets' achievements in the field of counterforce—the SS−17s, −18s, and −19s. Technology in the field of active defense has been growing by leaps and bounds. There are developments which render the discussions of ten years ago on ABM quite obsolete. Soviet forces reflect a certain single-mindedness. Our forces reflect a certain confusion. The time schedule in which a nation achieves a certain kind of force is less limited by technology than it is by strategy, and most certainly by politics.

KUPPERMAN: Isn't it somewhat artificial to say we are trading conventional force improvements for strategic force improvements? The timing is different, the priorities and objectives are different. And you are not going to get the conventional program fixes. You may do some things differently in operations, but programs are not there for the short term.

UTGOFF: Well, I think the conventional force improvements are not quite so long-term as you think. There are more useful things that can be done mid-term in conventional forces.

KUPPERMAN: Programs or operational fixes? It takes time to equip and train divisions, as much as it does the things at the strategic level. In some cases we can do things quicker at the strategic nuclear level than at the conventional level.

SULLIVAN: But you can have an equivalent quick fix program for your conventional forces. The administration does not see a sense of urgency to justify them. If they wanted an FSDL/FDL force in the next three years, they could get it. And they would get it from the commercial sector. You can get it within eighteen months if you really want it.

You know, Boeing is going to make more airplanes next year commercially than the Defense Department is going to buy for its own purposes. And if you want them, you can get them if you are willing to mobilize and if you believe the issue is important. As a matter of fact, you can quick fix either side of our forces if you believe that the threat is there. And I think clearly you have to surmise from what is going on here that the administration does not see a threat of that magnitude on either side. And they are proceeding accordingly.

UTGOFF: I think that you are overstating your case. Look at the concrete decisions that have been made—such as the spending increase of the 1981 defense budget and the five-year (1981–1985) defense program that goes with it. The attitudes reflected by this decision—the MX decision and so on—are all fairly concrete admissions of the fact that our defenses have to be improved.

ZUMWALT: The central issue is that well over a majority of the people in this country will not believe we are in trouble until the president says it. And he has not said it publicly. He continues to say that we are now number one and always will be. You can find a phrase or two or a clause or two which suggest concern. But he is not admitting the central fact, which is that we are in deep trouble in the military balance.

ON EUROPE

OSGOOD: The importance of strategic cohesion for NATO, prior to weapons decisions, has properly been emphasized. A coherent and unambiguous strategy is, however, difficult to devise. I fear some ambiguity—in fact, a lot—is unavoidable. I guess the principal reason is simply that whatever strategy we have in Western Europe has to serve a number of different objectives, some of which inevitably conflict with each other.

Thus, we want a better deterrent and at the same time we want one that is usable and that is susceptible to limitation. We want coupling in order to reassure our allies, and yet we want what they call some option for de-coupling in order to bolster our own courage. Of course, the politics of different allies alter strategic logic as well. It seems to me there is just an inherent difficulty of getting everything that we want out of a strategy in Western Europe that will serve the political purposes of keeping an alliance together in addition.

And added to this is the overriding difficulty that the Soviet Union doesn't seem in its doctrine to have much intention of playing our game with limited nuclear options, perhaps not even limited conventional options.

So to test the proposition of a more coherent strategy, what kind of theater strategy would you have us pursue and, for example, how would it apply to what we used to call tactical nuclear weapons? Which kinds of weapons would be used? When? Where? Against what kind of targets and that sort of thing?

I have great difficulty in resolving such ambiguities, simply because we have never had a test case. And in its absence, we are speculating about quite unpredictable things. I suppose that you, as I do, look forward to several kinds of limited warfare options in the European theater. But are those realistic? And what is your slightly more coherent strategy?

BURT: We have a lot of elbow room with the notion of flexible response. What I said was that we have never really pursued the notion of flexible response to its logical conclusion, in particular in the area of theater nuclear forces.

That issue has been a microcosm of what you described accurately as a kind of inherent, insoluble tension within the alliance. My argument is that that tension is in some ways passé; it reflected the kind of luxurious period that we lived in in the 1950s ond 1960s when we could decide whether or not we were going to have the bulk of the deterrence rest on our strategic, retaliatory capability, or whether or not we wanted local forces to raise the threshold of any kind of strategic response.

In a perverse way, the Soviets have allowed us—or should force us—now to be a lot more clear-minded about what we need to do. We no longer need to debate with the Europeans over whether or not, in the event that a drunken tank driver crashes Checkpoint Charlie, we are going to have an American tank right there or whether or not we are going to launch a Minuteman.

The point is that Moscow has a full spectrum, a panoply, of options—conventional, chemical, nuclear, limited in the theater, a highly stylized counterforce—in other words, a wide range of military operations both in the center region and on the front that make it essential for us to try to match those capabilities from the conventional on up through the strategic nuclear.

Now that means, by and large, that we have to in some way adjust our strategies to the kind of game that Moscow wants to play, and that doesn't mean that we need to mirror Soviet forces literally. My understanding of what the Soviets are doing and what they are saying is that they take the possibility of war in Europe very, very seriously.

They have a very credible threat. That means that we have to be able to respond to that on a variety of levels. We need the ability to carry out certain military operations against them that would force them to escalate.

In the theater nuclear area, you need more than simply a spastic nuclear response—namely, the ability either to obliterate Central Europe with short-range systems or to strike a target on his homeland to duplicate the functions of some of our strategic forces.

What it means is that we must be able to carry out real military operations. It means that there should be a theater nuclear stockpile away from some of the shorter-range systems. We should go beyond the notion that we have to fight a nuclear war on our own territory, and develop targets in Eastern Europe and in the lesser military districts. This would have an immediate impact on the Soviet capacity to wage a full-scale offensive in Europe.

It means going after that whole set of targets in the second and third echelon of armies: command controls and capabilities, bunkers, air fields, logistic areas. The notion of a threshold goes back to this notion of the era of luxury. We want to be able to fine-tune the threshold. We want nuclear capabilities that before a war breaks out appear to the adversary to be a low threshold, but capabilities that in the event of a conflict do not force us to go nuclear. We want conventional and nuclear capabilities that can act concurrently or sequentially and that pose real military penalty.

And that calls for a pretty far-reaching change in the existing stockpile. Clearly the 572 system that we just put in there is only the beginning. There really should be a thorough reappraisal.

MARSHALL: Admiral, those Pershing IIs are going to be distributed among fifteen airfields. They have got to be an easy target. They have no reach. This isn't adequate, it seems to me, to compete with what is being proliferated against them. Hoping to make use of them in a trade-off seems to me the equivalent of a high school football coach hoping to make a player deal with the Dallas Cowboys.

ZUMWALT: But it's a comparative question. In comparison to what we have there, it is an improvement, though it hardly in itself restores the balance.

VAN CLEAVE: It just doesn't equate with the type of theater nuclear modernization the Soviet Union has engaged in. You know, there are few ground-launched cruise missiles going in between now and the end of 1985—less than two hundred. Cruise missiles are worthless unless they are deployed in large enough numbers and a large enough variety of purposes to saturate defenses, because they are easily defended against. And less than two hundred cruise missiles between now and the end of 1985 is no threat whatsoever.

Pershing IIs merely replace a very old system in small numbers with a new system with very old technology and the same small numbers, but without our ever thinking through their purpose, their strategic implications, or the way they meet with other priorities. I don't regard these moves as modernization in any way whatsoever.

But I am worried about comparative judgment. I want to know what the price is going to be. Will the price be *real* theater nuclear weapon modernization? We are going to use these as the symbols of modernization, and they will prevent us from taking the measures to provide (a) real survivability for the capabilities we have in the system today, and (b) enhanced radiation (neutron bombs) and real modernization where it is needed—in the battlefield nuclear weapons.

ZUMWALT: What would your advice be as to what should be done?

VAN CLEAVE: There are about three things that need to be done. First of all, of course, is thinking through what kind of strategy of defense we really want. I don't think we have thought that through in deciding to deploy a Pershing II or something like that. These are being introduced without ever facing the major doctrinal problems that we have always had to face in the theater. Those have been neglected, and they are still neglected. I think these are placebos.

Secondly, the major problem of the theater is the same problem we face with our strategic forces, and that is survivability. Pershing II isn't mobile enough to be survivable. I don't even know how a cruise missile is going to be configured. We expect by 1990 we will have four hundred and some in hardened sites, but that is ill-defined. But through 1985 there is nothing.

And thirdly, even if you can solve the survivability problem and the doctrinal problem, you will not have as important an addition as the enhanced radiation weapon would have made. I am afraid that these types of things will probably be substitutes for the enhanced radiation weapon.

The last of the three is probably a little more parochial on my part. I think that probably the doctrine or the survivability problems are by far the more important. This enhanced radiation weapon is worthless unless you solve those.

KEMP: I can agree with you on the military analysis, but what about politics?

VAN CLEAVE: That is, of course, a difficult question. It would be easier to go ahead with the third one—which, I think, is the least important of the three—than with the first two. And it may well be that the reason we are going ahead with ground-launched cruise missiles and Pershing IIs, without going through the whole doctrinal implications of them, is because going through the doctrinal implications is too difficult politically.

CODEVILLA: I just finished with two meetings with French authorities in these matters, and the feeling I came away with is that we have been far too timid. The French are talking precisely about the problems of survivability and of operational doctrine. That is to say, they are talking about how to fight a war. We have seen that in some articles published in this country by Frenchmen.

They are thinking in terms of how to use weapons in war. They want deterrence, yes, but General Beaufre taught them a long time ago that the only kind of deterrence which means anything proceeds from the conviction in the adversary's mind that you can win a war if it comes to having a war.

Regarding survivability, they have but one answer — mobility. They are under no illusions regarding the political difficulty of moving strategic systems around. But you fish or cut bait on something like this. You never know the limits of the politically possible until you try. And certainly, in the case of the enhanced radiation weapon, we did not try, politically. We submitted to a Soviet offensive and did not answer it.

The other half of the concern so much expressed by the French is counterforce. They felt quite comfortable with the original conception of the *force de frappe* when nuclear war looked kind of irrational. But as nuclear yields come down and as weapon accuracies go up, nuclear war looks more and more rational. So why not adopt a counterforce strategy, they say. Deterrence is still the objective, but the way to achieve it must change.

It all comes down to a basic point: do we want to be prepared to fight a war in case war comes?

KEMP: Are you raising a straw man by bringing up French attitudes on tactical nuclear warfare in Europe? The French have not been particularly involved in these current discussions. What you really have to answer is, could we have twisted the arms of the Belgians, the Dutch, the Germans?

CODEVILLA: The Belgians go with the wind and they tell you that they go with the wind. The Italians were quite ready, from the very beginning—or at least this particular government was quite willing to go along with any modernization of the theater nuclear force, especially with anything that could hit the Soviet Union. This is due to certain internal political conditions liable to change.

To predicate everything on the attitude of the Dutch is, I think, self-defeating. That is how we handled the enhanced radiation weapon. We put ourselves in the position to be vetoed by the weakest sisters in the alliance, with predictable results.

ZUMWALT: I would hope that the reservations that we all have about the tremendous tactical nuclear superiority that remains to the Soviet Union in Europe—twice the number of weapons, six times the area of destructive capability, ten times the throw-weight, and twenty-five times the megatonnage—I would hope that we would all seek to have our candidates hammer away at those things in the presidential race and in all other forms of debate so we can go on from this very limited step to something that is much more meaningful.

TAHTINEN: What about the proposal for building small submarines as an alternative, in a sense, to an MX-type system? Is it very practical?

ZUMWALT: We have examined, a number of times, different ways of putting the missiles to sea in diesel submarines and on small nuclear submarines. The more I have examined the MX proposal, the more I have to believe that there are a number of sea-going variants that would be a lot likelier to work than the MX. It seems to me that the MX is a monstrosity born out of SALT II—that would never have even been put forward if it was not for the fact that SALT II prohibits the multiple aim point systems [MAPS] of vertical silos. Anything from more of the present Trident submarines—and they are far from optimal—to smaller submarines of very modest size with a few missiles, it seems to me, makes better sense.

ADELMAN: I am wondering about McGeorge Bundy's [former assistant for national security affairs to President Kennedy] recent claim on the Cuban missile crisis in which he says that the question of the strategic balance was not an issue, that the ten-to-one kill ratios didn't count—that during the whole crisis and his whole time in the White House no one ever thought in these terms.

ZUMWALT: I think McGeorge Bundy has just simply forgotten what happened. Mr. Kennedy not only asked at great length about relative kill, but he also, you remember, went to the extent of risking getting Penkovsky shot to get a story from inside as to what preparations the Russians were making. He was very much aware of the fact that the relationship of power looked as though we had the superiority, but he, even so, wanted to assure himself that the Russians thought that way too. He was very reassured to go ahead and deliver the ultimatum when he heard back from Penkovsky. So in that crisis, and in the Berlin crisis, it was very much on the minds of all working on it as to who would win and who would lose. And at the time of the Yom Kippur war it was very much on our minds. The only difference was that it was a different side that would win and a different side that would lose. We did the backing down.

IKLÉ: I have two remarks, one pessimistic and one optimistic. In a crisis, your prescription could be quite nice. But in a period that is considered to be détente, or even a mild Cold War, when push comes to shove and you have convinced yourself that you are convincing the other side that the nuclear threshold is low, then people on our side and on the other side may also fear that the nuclear threshold is low. They may then find that the better course to take is to avoid a conventional war which risks that low nuclear threshold and to make concessions.

In other words, that focus on nuclear escalation as being an option that NATO may initiate would discourage the alliance from taking advantage of the quite substantial conventional capability it has for fear of being driven into that nuclear war, a fear which was much less prominent in the past crises (while not absent in them) because of the more favorable strategic balance.

I don't think there is an easy way out of this, but I think the way out has to go much more in the direction of emphasizing the use of NATO's theater tactical nuclear capability as a deterrent to Soviet first use, so that in a real crisis there might be the courage to use the conventional capability, which is a substantial deterrent to attack.

Now the optimistic comment, which is the area of arms control. You expressed your fear that NATO would be boxed into this new arms control scheme and get to an impasse.

The present arms control position in NATO could lead to an impasse. I think there is a 60 percent chance of that, but there is at least a 40 percent chance—if not higher—that it will develop as much as the MBFR/"Mansfield" interaction developed in this country (when majority-leader Senator Mansfield annually *demanded* cuts in our European forces).

But we got out of it. Nothing untoward happened in MBFR I, and Mansfield is singing a different song and everything is changed. So we didn't really get hurt. Likewise I could see, a few years down the road, the political scene changing somewhat in Europe and what is now being started as MBFR II and SALT III will peel away, sort of like MBFR I dribbled away, and the arms control impasse and inhibitions will disappear.

BURT: First of all, about the only issue that I do disagree with you on is on the question of theater nuclear forces. What I meant by being able to adjust the threshold and in some circumstances have it low and in others have it high and let NATO manipulate the threshold was meant to say that we don't simply announce where the threshold is. There is a reality about where the threshold is. The reality of the threshold is what kind of capabilities we have.

If we have very weak conventional forces, then the threshold is low, even if we announce that it is high.

IKLÉ: Well, it is an alternative to surrender.

BURT: Yes. Now what I am saying is that maintaining a robust theater nuclear capability would not necessarily create divisions, the sorts of divisions within the alliance that you describe, if we could complement that with a robust conventional capability.

I am not arguing—and certainly my remarks should not be interpreted to mean—that we need now to de-emphasize conventional force improvement so we can build up a nuclear dominant defense. I think what I said was that we need a balanced capability, a continuum of capabilities from the conventional through the theater nuclear up through the strategic.

If we have that balanced capability, then in the event of conflict or in the event of a crisis in Europe the Europeans need not be concerned that we are going to have a nuclear escalation or a nuclear war in the theater, because we have robust conventional capability. You can say, "We are going to deter this conflict," because the Soviets view our nuclear capabilities as threatening and we might use them; but at the same time our conventional capacities have given us some leeway in when we are going to make that decision, and that politically, by the way, I think is the only way you can justify these forces. You can't go to the Europeans and say, "We want you to build up your conventional capabilities because we don't want to use nuclear forces." In fact, the only incentives that have ever worked with the Europeans in getting them to go along with conventional force improvement is that it was a means to keep us involved in the nuclear business in Europe.

We told the Europeans that if the nuclear threshold got too low because we ignored conventional forces, we couldn't continue to threaten the use of nuclear weapons in the event of a conflict.

What I was suggesting is that we have to go to the Europeans and explain the changes in the balance and the new strategic situation which requires us not only to have a credible conventional capability but, for the first time, a credible theater nuclear capability.

Last on this point, I don't understand the argument that all we need to be able to do with our theater nuclear forces is to deter a first strike, or Soviet first use, because that is an incredible threat. If all we have got is a symbolic capability there to destroy some Soviet targets, then the Europeans know and certainly the Soviets know that they can respond with a truly effective military strike and then we are forced to escalate to a level that is unpalatable.

IKLÉ: To deter a limited first strike requires a very credible capability.

BURT: My feeling is that if we are unable in the next decade to shore up our theater nuclear deterrent and our forces there, then we need to think about getting those forces out of Europe altogether. We are in a situation now where we have a nuclear posture that is positively self-deterring.

I agree to some extent that we might get out of the window dressing we put on nuclear decisions. But you know, it is a real problem that we cannot take defense decisions without justifying them in terms of arms control. You very correctly pointed out that one of the major factors behind the MBFR decision was the Mansfield amendment that has faded. But you know, there are a lot of Europeans and a lot of Germans that take MBFR very seriously. That may not be a problem now, but it could very well be a problem. In fact, it is continually a problem in a lot of European countries. We saw what the Dutch did with their nuclear pressures there.

What is really dangerous is the precedent, I think, of not being able to take a decision without linking it to arms control.

IKLÉ: No, I am suggesting that they may be behind us. They may be moving in the same direction.

NITZE: My question goes to the point of whether or not this 572 missile deployment in fact constitutes a robust capability. As I understand it, the number of nuclear storage depots we have in Europe is extremely limited. I understand we would need tactical warnings in order to be able to get these theater nuclear missiles and their launchers scattered to positions in which they are not sitting ducks.

Even if we did get them dispersed in time, the Soviet superiority in theater nuclear weapons would be at least of the order of two to one, so is this really robust or is it not? It could be destabilizing. I find it disturbing to find myself making the same arguments as Paul Warnke and Adam Yarmolinsky, but in a way I am.

MARSHALL: Even a stopped clock is right twice a day.

BURT: Could I respond to this? I agree 100 percent. That is why I was so distressed over the amount of political capital that went into getting the alliance to take this decision because it should be viewed as only part of a long-range effort to reconfigure the posture completely.

I think it is still viewed within the administration in many quarters as really a political response to concerns raised by Helmut Schmidt two years ago and not because of a true military threat.

If enough work is not going into thinking about basing, into command and control, and into targeting and into follow-on complementary conventional and nuclear systems, then it could very well turn out to be a destabilizing thing.

THOMPSON: Let me just ask a further question on the nexus of internal/external European relations, namely, the effect of the SALT debate on internal European attitudes and the summoning forth of leftwing views in Europe by the Carter administration to prove that alliance cohesion would be fractured in the absence of a SALT agreement.

BURT: I don't think anybody has really understood what has been happening in Europe over the last six months, and in particular in some of the smaller countries. There is no debate in Holland, in Belgium, in Denmark, or Norway about SALT or, for that matter, on theater nuclear forces. What has happened is that the domestic political situations in these countries have become brittle, whether it is in Belgium with the Flemish-speaking disputes or the role of religious parties in the Netherlands.

These issues, SALT and theater nuclear forces, have truly become surrogates for internal political debates. They have become symbolic issues; they are not debated seriously. In fact, the amount of real emotion behind these issues is much less than people really understand. You don't have people marching in the streets for SALT II and you don't have people debating in the little coffee shops at night about the Pershing II. The real problem is, what are we going to do with some of these small countries that have really opted out of international security issues altogether? This is a problem that we have to address, along with the British, along with the Germans, and along with the Italians.

One of the really positive things, by the way, about the theater nuclear force—from a political standpoint—is that once the Germans were convinced we were prepared to support this deployment they played an unprecedented role in working with the governments of these smaller countries to bring them along. That is true burden sharing.

ON THE PERSIAN GULF

ROWEN: Let me begin with the power projection changes that have taken place in the Persian Gulf, which have been dramatic. If we go back to the situation in the 1960s with regard to the Persian Gulf area, the British still had a presence east of Suez. They had some presence in the gulf area itself, in Oman and the Trucial States. The United States had a substantial airlift capability, and most importantly, it had a good set of bases giving access to the region—en route bases in the Azores through southern Europe, Turkey (and, if necessary, Israel) into the region.

We still had a major base in Libya, not very far away. We had good relations with the northern tier countries. "The northern tier" had some meaning. These were countries— Turkey, Iran, Pakistan—which looked in varying degrees to the United States for security.

There were, of course, political instabilities within the region. Iraq, for example, and Egypt had undergone revolutions, but several important countries looked reasonably stable, two of the most important of which were Iran and Saudi Arabia.

The Soviet Union at that time had very little lift capability, very limited short-range tactical air, a very modest naval capability largely oriented to defense of the sea approaches to the Soviet Union, little by way of overseas bases, and as far as ground access to the Persian Gulf area is concerned, the ground logistics were miserable. There were few roads.

Now the United Kingdom has left east of Suez. The U.S. access to the area has greatly eroded, as we have found out on more than one occasion. Our ability to use bases en route has rapidly shrunk. The Europeans are really not very keen on having us use their bases in contingencies—certainly Arab-Israeli contingencies. We might be able to use them in contingencies in which their oil is at stake. But the circumstances in which we can use en route bases is an uncertain matter.

The northern tier has fallen apart altogether. Turkey is very much disaffected with us. Iran we know about. Pakistan is in bad shape. There is a substantial improvement in the Soviet airlift capability, which has not only increased in capacity but is now being used. We observe substantial operations as far as Angola and more recently on a sizable scale in Ethiopia.

Their tactical air is much improved. It is much longer range. The Backfire is a very important system. Naval capacity is also now much more a blue-water one, not so much a coastal defense one. They have bases and presence in the area—in Afghanistan with regular military units, Aden, Ethiopia, naval forces in the Indian Ocean. Their ability to get into the region from the southern USSR and to move within the region is improved because of road improvements.

The instabilities within the region have grown substantially. We have seen the first really major piece of evidence that the stability of the regime in Saudi Arabia may be not so enormously great. Oman is vulnerable. There is uncertainty about Egypt. Kuwait is uncertain; Iraq made a move against it in the early 1960s and we may see Iraq move against Kuwait sometime soon. This is not an exhaustive list.

This has some implications which are fairly obvious. We are seven thousand miles from the Persian Gulf. That hasn't changed. And the Soviet Union is about a tenth that distance away. That hasn't changed. What is new is that the Russians are closing in on the area. They are surrounding it. They have improved their ability to project power, forces, into it very quickly, getting there fastest with the mostest.

That is a threat that will have a political impact just because of its existence, but the actual events may unfold in a somewhat different way, not taking the form that it is now taking in Afghanistan, but with arms and support in various other forms for friendly regimes that will need the Soviet support to stay in power. They will get it.

An analogy that is useful to ponder is what differences it would make geopolitically if the Soviet Union and its allies got 40 percent of their oil from the Caribbean. That is roughly the situation that we and our allies have in the Middle East. It has to be an enormously important geopolitical fact, and shift in the balance, which has not been perceived adequately. The events in Iran are bringing it to the fore, but what it all means has not sunk in yet.

Let me come back a little bit later to what to do about it, and turn now to the more strictly energy aspects of this, because on the one hand there is a resource which is arguably vital—40 percent of the non-Communist world's oil—and on the other hand it is threatened. It is only rational to go back and inquire how vital is that oil really. Is it absolutely vital?

There is some evidence on this. We have had two oil shocks in the last six years, one in late 1973 and early 1974 and, of course in 1979. In the 1973–1974 episode there was about a 5 percent reduction on the average in the available oil supply to the Western world for a period of about six months. It was deeper than that at one point, but it was not a really huge gap.

A recent estimate of its impact is that this cut depressed real economic output in the United States by 2 percent in 1974 and by 5 percent in 1975, plus heightened inflation and other impacts.

The worst case considered in my paper—not the worst case, by any means, but a very bad case—is the loss of all Persian Gulf oil for a year, which results in an estimated loss of about 30 percent of the gross national products of the OECD countries. That is worse than the Great Depression in terms of loss of output.

There are several optimistic assumptions. This particular calculation assumes that somehow the price of the remaining oil that is imported—for example, from Venezuela or Indonesia—does not go up in price at all; how that could happen isn't clear.

Now, these estimates assume that there do not exist large stocks of oil in the consuming countries. That is a good assumption for the United States because we have about eleven days' worth of imports of oil in our strategic petroleum reserve. That is effectively zero. The Japanese and the Europeans have done rather better, but even they do not have very large stocks.

This situation, as it now exists, reflects a failure of American national security policy of very large proportions. It has the happy property that it is bipartisan, for the failure began with a Republican administration and it has continued in a Democratic administration and certainly involved the Congress as well as the executive branch. So everybody is implicated in the plot. And you can throw in academia as well.

We are in a real mess. We haven't stockpiled oil. We have only 92 million barrels of oil in our strategic petroleum reserve, and it is a scandal. The basic assumption has been for the last several years that this is not the time to add oil to the stockpile because next year will be better. In my view, the odds are that next year will be worse.

Now, during this period of stringency and tightness, the Japanese and the Europeans have been buying oil feverishly. In view of the situation, they get better marks than we do. They do not expect that next year is going to be better. I think their behavior can be regarded as prudent.

Meanwhile we have expended our energies, as you know, on the system of price controls, the infamous entitlement system which subsidizes imports, the wrangling about a windfall profits tax: a collection of policies of which at best one can say that they are irrelevant. But actually most of them are really harmful in terms of this external threat.

Now that isn't to say that nothing has been done. We have gradually moved to decontrol oil and gas, although very, very slowly. One can explain why we have done so badly, but that doesn't really justify it.

In assessing this vulnerability and how to limit the damage, it is important to understand certain fundamental properties of the oil market. The first important property is that it is a world market, and oil is a relatively fungible commodity once it gets to sea. It can go almost anywhere.

We have had a magnificent system for distributing that oil through the major companies. They have acted as a buffer between the buyers and the sellers and they have been able to redistribute the shortages. They have had customers to satisfy and they have tried to spread around the remaining oil; their business interests and the larger political interests have more or less coincided.

Their role is now being substantially reduced as both the exporting countries and the importing countries go more to bilateral dealings which reduce flexibility in the market. One of the reasons why the Japanese have been scrambling for Iranian oil is that they are getting much less oil from the majors than they used to, so their trading companies have been trying to make up for what is lost. Besides, they want some of the business. In any case, they can't be served as adequately by the majors.

So that buffer is being eroded, and perhaps in five more years the major oil companies will be unable to perform this buffering function very well.

What should we do? I frankly do not believe that the present situation is, in the ordinary sense of the word, "tolerable." I think it will before long be perceived as being really intolerable. There are things we can do, both with regard to energy policy and with regard to military policy. On the military side, some of the contingencies may be very hard or impossible to effect—for example, internal political chaos—but some, especially those involving the Soviet Union, we can influence. We have to simply reverse the trend which has put the Soviet Union in the dominant position in the area. We need a military capacity in the area and also rapidly deployable to it which gives us a fighting chance of being able to cope with any potential Soviet moves. After all, that is our oil and we'd better protect it. We also need to recognize that the very high dependence of Japan and Western Europe on gulf oil means that, if the Soviets have it, they will have a very powerful wedge to create large splits in the Western alliance system.

This suggests permanent deployments in the area. Not too many folks there want to have us on land. That means a substantial part of what we do is going to have to be at sea. We do need some bases in the area or nearby it. We can leave for the discussion where they might be. There was a suggestion about Egypt, Israel, Oman, East Africa. We need to improve airlift. We need to do this on a much more rapid scale than the administration has proposed. We just don't have the time. We face a danger now, and we can't wait until the mid- or late-1980s to correct it. There may be political or military developments, perhaps soon, which will be very adverse. We do not have much time.

Under the heading of the longer-term measures, we should implement the Tokyo Summit's announced goal of reducing to 4 or 5 million barrels a day of oil imports by 1990. The best way to help do this is with a tariff and not with a physical quota system or a gasoline tax. There are many more things to be done on energy which I haven't touched on here.

THOMPSON: Recently the head of a friendly—and highly competent—military intelligence agency said that he did not really expect the Saudi regime to last more than a short time further, just to begin this discussion on a high note. When I pressed him to be more specific, he said, "Well, one to 300 days [he thought] would be the range." I can't imagine a person of his competence and skills to have said something like this without a fairly firm base of projection, even if it turns out to be too dismal.

One of the things that impresses me in looking at the work going on, particularly in the administration, is the really Pollyanna-ish character of it—that all is best in the best of all possible worlds.

One group is arguing that the Strait of Hormuz is not very vulnerable to closure, for example. Bottom mines are no good over 200 feet, and most of the strait is around 300 feet deep;

and anyway, it is a lot wider than most people realize. It is twenty-five miles wide, and it would take a lot of carriers spread across that distance to block it up.

If you wanted to close down the oil facilities and you wanted to know how many air strikes it would take by Backfires based in the southern Soviet Union to do so by not taking into account the real world, you can come up with the calculation that it would take literally hundreds of strikes to knock out enough oil facilities to decrease American oil purchases from the Persian Gulf even marginally. But in the real world those calculations are worthless. If Backfires are bombing the oil fields, the threat to us and to the West as a whole will be frontal, not marginal.

You can go on and on like this looking at Soviet weaknesses—for example, in the fact that its carrier task forces are vastly smaller than our carrier task forces, although, of course, the goal of theirs is mainly to neutralize ours, which takes a much smaller force. You can make assumptions about what you can overfly—and you can improve the scenario for us in the Persian Gulf enormously—just by assuming that Soviet overflights of Turkey will not be possible, even though they have been steadily on the increase by the Soviet Union.

In the Melian dialogue of Thucydides the Athenians say that your strongest arguments depend upon hope and the future, and your actual resources are too scanty as compared to those arrayed against you for you to come out victorious. Now it seems to me that that sums up the present situation very appropriately.

One calculation is that if we were really to have a chance in case of a Soviet invasion of the Persian Gulf oil fields, we would have to increase the effectiveness of our forces by a factor of eight to get to first base, as it were.

I recall looking at a map of the Persian Gulf in the executive branch office recently after a briefing which was purporting to demonstrate that the Soviets would have grave

difficulty mounting an invasion of Iran or really doing anything on any scale in the region. The optimism was based on
the assumption that they would use only two of their seven
airborne divisions because they simply wouldn't want to
remove any of the airborne divisions from the north around
Moscow, as if they couldn't move in heavy replacements to
those and fly the airborne south. (In the Afghan invasion
they did in fact use airborne divisions from northern Russia.)
It was assumed that they wouldn't use any of their
capabilities in the Caspian Sea—a rail barge, for example, or
the hundreds of tugs that are capable of bringing in tanks or
whatever, if the Soviets were really serious.

The whole thing had a surrealistic character. Most of the
work that I have seen has the surrealistic character of projections in which you fantasize what the real case is going to
be and you assume there is a best case, which is much too
good, and a middle case that really comes out fairly advantageously. And then there is a worst case on the other side
which, of course, as if by definition, is the one that is least
likely to occur.

But of course our worst case is, for the Soviet Union, often
the best case. One hasn't seen them go into military situations without an adequate amount of capability to do the job
which they had set out to do. And I cannot imagine their
going into the Persian Gulf or any kind of military operation
without, in fact, having figured exactly what it was going to
take.

The point is that our worst case/best case analyses have to
be seen as Soviet best cases and worst cases.

KEMP: I'd like to discuss two issues: the Iran crisis and
the emerging Arab-Israeli military balance. There are two
points we need to draw out of the Iran case. First, a military
operation to punish the ayatollah would be a unique operation. We should look instead at a much broader case where
there might be some allied cooperation. Second, Iran's armed
forces are now in a shambles. This, in part, is because we

overloaded them with exremely sophisticated equipment to which they were not suited at the time.

Some of the Arab countries fall into a similar category — Saudi Arabia, for example. They are having great problems absorbing their equipment; it is unlikely that they will be able to do very much with their F−15s and other sophisticated weapons in the near term.

In terms of the regional military, we must also look at what is happening in Iraq and Syria and their very, very impressive build-up since 1973. The introduction of new weapons has been paralleled by the development of an infrastructure — both for commercial and military reasons — which has improved the land communications between Syria, Iraq, and the Mediterranean and the gulf way beyond what they have had in the past.

If you add to this Iraq's investment in tank transporters and the modernization of their overall mobility forces, then it seems to me that we are adding a new variable to the Arab-Israeli equation. If you carefully examine the Arab-Israeli military balance during the 1980s, the Israelis look very good up until about 1983 or 1984. Certainly the peace with Egypt has in the short run added a great deal of stability to the military factors in that conflict. This is because of the demilitarization clause, and the fact that even if Egypt wished to come back into the conflict it faces a problem of getting across the Sinai Desert. But we must not lose sight of what has been happening on the northern front. By the mid-1980s, given the current trends, Syria, Iraq, Jordan, and possibly Saudi Arabia could bring up between nineteen and twenty-one divisions along the northern front — well-equipped, reasonably well-trained. This would be against an Israeli capability of between eleven and twelve divisions, and the Israelis would, of course, always have to ensure that something was left for the Sinai Desert just in case Egypt joined it.

I am not suggesting that the balance is shifting to the point where Israel is going to be seriously threatened in the mid-1980s. I am suggesting, though, that the balance could shift more in favor of the Arabs. This trend adds another factor to the overall deteriorating situation in the Middle East.

How does this trend tie into the issues of the Persian Gulf and the scenarios that have been discussed? There are dozens of scenarios for gulf conflict. Certainly, the basic facts we have heard about the growth of Soviet power projections are correct, and often there is an implicit assumption about Soviet-Iraq cooperation.

Now it is not at all clear that the Soviet Union and Iraq are going to maintain the close relationship which will permit them to engage in mutual planning for an attack on Saudi Arabia or Kuwait. Iraq is its own actor and may decide to opt for a more independent role in the Middle East in the years ahead.

In any event, there are problems in moving Soviet forces from the southern Soviet Union to the gulf unless there are really secure lines of communication. And if you do have secure lines of communication, it is still a long way and there are vulnerabilities en route.

The sealift is improving, but there are chokepoints. It is a long way to the Persian Gulf from the Black Sea if you cannot use the Suez Canal, and if you do use the Suez Canal it is very vulnerable. This is, of course, why Iran and Afghanistan are so critical, because if the Soviets had access to these countries then their sealift problem would be so much easier. Their airlift capacity is certainly growing, but you can't rely just on that.

With respect to some of the lesser gulf contingencies, the military balance is not all bad. In terms of power projections to areas like the Yemens or even Ethiopia, there is more symmetry in U.S.–Soviet capabilities, provided there are some agreements with allies for overflight and basing access.

What it all comes down to is that both the Soviet Union and the United States, in anything short of general war, have to count very much on the cooperation of local countries for their respective scenarios, best case or worst case. And since the political stability of the region is so volatile, it is perhaps the critical variable in many of these calculations.

THOMPSON: On the Iraqi case, I agree. Now it seems to me that the critical variable with respect to Iraq in any conflict scenario in the early 1980s or mid-1980s is: how does it perceive the will on our side, especially given the asymmetries which we have discussed? If they see that we are not going to persevere, they are going to come out on the Soviet side, however independent-minded they are.

In other words, I think the variable of their Communist affiliation is much less potent than the variable of their perception of who has staying power. I am not sure that that is very good news.

KEMP: I do think there are things we can do in the short run between now and the mid-1980s to make it very unpleasant for Iraq if it does want to attack Saudi Arabia. They are not a superstate. If the Saudis were prepared to provide us with facilities, then the combination of U.S. land-based and sea-based air and the types of antitank or antiarmor capabilities we could develop in that region between now and the mid-1980s is something no Iraq government is going to be relaxed about.

THOMPSON: But you have got to consider the strategic balance. In a conflict between Iraq and Saudi Arabia in which the Soviet Union is seen as a beneficiary, then the fact that we could, for example, destroy the Iraq Air Force with a couple of quick strikes with little difficulty has to be weighed against the unlikelihood that the Soviets are going to permit that to happen. In other words, they escalate the crisis up the nuclear ladder or they move against Berlin or another indefensible Western position. The world is, strategically, a unified theater.

WEST: Harry Rowen made the case why the Persian Gulf is vital. We can't create forces for the Indian Ocean if there are no land bases there. We are not welcome to the several nations there because of our past history. And the proposed program of the administration for a rapid deployment force will take between three and seven years to take hold. If we want to do something now, we have to use the forces we have today. Without land bases, the only forces you have today to move in there that would be credible are our carrier forces and marines.

But where would they come from? They can either be from East Asia or the Mediterranean. So my first question is, what area of the world do we pull out of in order to go into the Persian Gulf, because there are no other options?

The second question is whether overt aggression, Iraqi or Soviet, isn't the cleanest analytical case because it is overt and we thus feel free to move; but isn't it the least likely of what may really occur in the area? Isn't there a higher probability that what we may be faced with, in the forthcoming decade, is equivalent to the Iranian model of gradual disintegration? If you look at the moves of the Saudi extremists who occupied the mosque in Mecca, at first they appeared to be very stupid. Then we realized that they had set out to kidnap the king of Saudi Arabia and to seize control of the public broadcasting, at which point they didn't appear to be so stupid in what they were doing. My question is: since gulf oil is vital, do you see a consensus to use covert action, in case of a muddled situation?

ROWEN: The other model is the Libyan or Iraqi model — a coup, a radical regime takes over, and then we find out the true character of the regime and its foreign connections.

If a new Saudi regime is willing to sell oil to all countries and is really just interested in the money, that is one thing. If it also has a political interest and is closely associated with the Soviet Union, that is something else again.

WEST: Would you be willing to let that happen and then find out later?

ROWEN: No, I would take steps. The range of possibilities is very rich.

On the forces side, I doubt that we have exhausted the possibilities. There has been mention of the possibility of having some forces in Israel and Egypt. But the importance of having naval forces deployed to the Indian Ocean is of such high priority that they will have to come from elsewhere, at least in the short term. And the elsewhere is going to have to be mainly the Pacific.

WEST: In the case of Soviet moves in Saudi Arabia, you might blockade Aden.

SULLIVAN: That is an act of war. You just don't stick blockades wherever you want to.

THOMPSON: The trouble is that it took almost half of what we now have in our navy to orchestrate the Cuban missile crisis blockade in 1962 and that was in—to put it mildly—preferable ground to Aden.

ZUMWALT: There is one tiny bit of stretch left in our naval forces. It is possible to increase the availability of forces in the western Pacific and the Indian Ocean—by the home porting of an additional carrier task force at Cockburn Sound in Australia.

And if one also completed the facilities at Diego Garcia and Oman/Masirah you would have a line of bases that a carrier could support. Also, aircraft from the carrier could get into action rather quickly even if the carrier happened to be in home port by staging forward to Diego Garcia.

SULLIVAN: Shouldn't the energy question pull the allies together if we really work at it? The question is whether we are willing to take whatever happens or what might happen if we really address ourselves to it.

ROWEN: I really am optimistic. I won't call it a blessing because we don't need blessings like this, but it could turn out all right.

SULLIVAN: Only if people work at it.

BURT: Why would it draw the allies together?

SULLIVAN: I don't think there is any larger common problem, other than nuclear warfare, perceived by the entire West.

BURT: The solutions to that problem, particularly in terms of strategy in the Persian Gulf, are extremely diverse. You have a situation where the Europeans and the Japanese, with the exception of the French, do not have to think about using military power to influence events. They by and large are practicing the policy of economic appeasement.

And their policies are designed to accommodate to changes in the local situation. We have already seen the examples of that. In just over the last year the Europeans have begun dealing with—even recognizing—the PLO, which this administration views as undercutting its policy.

The Japanese, who feel particularly frustrated on the issue of nuclear energy because of domestic backlash over their own efforts to become more self-sufficient, may come to the conclusion that it is much more productive and profitable simply to accommodate political changes in that area so they can continue to get access to oil, rather than to bring any military force to bear.

I think the kind of situation the West is likely to face in the gulf is not going to be a black and white military threat of seven Soviet airborne divisions. It is going to be a problem that some people define in military terms and other people define in political terms. When Iraq threatens a neighbor, some people are going to beat a door to Iraq. And I think that the alliance-splitting possibilities are really profound.

NITZE: If we are going to do something, we have to be clear and we have to be right on the choice that we make on this important question.

We have to be right that there is sense in trying to use a military presence of some kind to affect the situation, as opposed to concentrating on the political aspects of it.

And if what Scott Thompson said about the difficulties of doing something militarily is correct, then we ought to recognize that a military option is not a feasible option. I am not sure that one carrier is going to do anything for you in the area against the kind of opposition we are likely to face.

And if you can't do more than one carrier, all you are going to do is make a gesture and then pull away from what you proposed to be doing, then the Europeans who say that you ought to address this politically will turn out to be right.

We therefore should go to the Europeans and say, "We believe that the prerequisite to doing anything there is to improve political relations in the area and we want your help to do that, because we don't believe there is any military thing we can effectively do short of that."

KEMP: I think if we follow the line that we can't do anything, that political accommodation is the only alternative the Western world has, we might as well divide up the area; the Soviets would get Iran and Iraq and we the rest.

I am being slightly facetious there, because it seems to me that there are things that we can do. Don't forget each European country in the alliance has a different dependency on the Persian Gulf and those curves are changing.

The British and Norwegian dependency is going down. The Norwegians have gone down completely. The British are falling way off. Each country, therefore, is going to have a very different sort of perspective on its own vital interests in the event of shortfalls in oil, with Japan being the most pressed and France and Germany probably being next.

To expect any sort of Western consensus on a neat menu of things to do in the Persian Gulf is unrealistic. But bilateral negotiations with each of these countries for specific purposes, like base rights in cooperation at the military level and resharing of the burden, might work—rather than some sort of high caucus where we all get together and forge out a Persian Gulf policy.

SULLIVAN: I agree that there are a few options left, but not many. Very shortly I think the country is going to have to draw a line somewhere and get forces in there.

If you can still get a toehold in Saudi Arabia, you can move forces in and keep them there, and put together a combined force of Israelis, Egyptians, Americans, and whoever wants to play which could stabilize that region for a while.

I have trouble figuring out any solution if Saudi Arabia has gone down the drain and you can't land there. Saudi Arabia is really very key.

ZUMWALT: I realize Geoffrey Kemp was being facetious, but my view is that if we offered the Russians a deal today—"You take Iran and we'll take Saudi Arabia"—they would reject it.

I believe they think they can do better than that.

Now the military situation, within which a political judgment ought to be made, is that we do have the military capability to handle any situation until the Soviets get into it. At that point is when I think we lack the capability.

And I believe the Soviets can get into it not only by taking a stand militarily in the Middle East, but also by doing something to NATO. So that we get right back to the point that we were talking about earlier—we are talking about the best way to lose. Or the president can make the risky decision that the Russians are going to be cautious enough so that we can get away with, essentially, a bluff.

NITZE: What would you do in a serious crisis? Make the bluff or not?

ZUMWALT: If I were the president I would buy what Leonard Sullivan has said. We have reached a point beyond which free men cannot go; I would make the bluff.

SULLIVAN: It isn't clear to me that it is a bluff—if you are really trying to give the impression that you are trying to do it.

ZUMWALT: Well, that is a bluff. [Laughter.]

ON INTELLIGENCE

THOMPSON: The problem of fashion—everyone conforming to the same intelligence methods—comes from on high, from the president and the head of the National Security Council. That is where the drive to ignore the facts comes from; at the lower levels there is much more concentration upon the facts.

Secondly, we did inadequate justice to the intermediate type of action, between military and diplomatic, that was touched on. The point is that the president has to come to the conclusion that such a capability is important to him and then be potent enough to get it done.

And there are real risks. If you look at the past record, it wasn't all beer and skittles when we did have that intermediate capability.

The next point is to improve the analytical prowess within the intelligence community. My experience is that the difficulty there has been that, in order to make good analytical judgments, you have to get into the field of *net assessment*, that is, comparisons; any real analytical judgment depends upon comparing somebody else's capabilities to your own. If the CIA considers it to be not within its charter to evaluate our own and allied capabilities and thus to be able to compare enemy capabilities with our own, then it really is in nobody's charter.

The Joint Chiefs of Staff try to do net assessments and the Defense Intelligence Agency tries to help them. But they are a little bit unhappy about doing it, and are not willing to let the CIA in on it. I would agree that competition is the best thing—to have some net assessments done in the Pentagon and others in the CIA and in other communities, and then have the Director of Intelligence compare them.

MARSHALL: The First Continental Congress established the Committee on Secret Correspondence. The Second Continental Congress continued it. It asked for a report from the committee on what it had been doing. The committee refused and said it was none of their business. Actually, it had been setting up dummy trading companies, importing all kinds of things under false bills of lading, bribing like mad, and getting commercial agents to spy in the House of Commons and the Court of St. James.

So we are talking about an activity that is older than the republic, antecedent to the Declaration of Independence and the Constitution. But then there was a great gap.

Lincoln handled the gap in the Civil War by making a contract with the Pinkerton Detective Agency. He farmed it out. And incidentally, you might consider farming it out to a corporation and have them do it. They might do it much better than regular servants.

But then in World War I and World War II, intelligence was handled by an agency set up by the executive under a war powers act. Then we had Congress take it over. And Congress has to supervise its creatures; we are the only country in the world, except for West Germany, in which legislature has such a role.

IKLÉ: Two points on the "intermediate action," which I think is an apt word, better than "covert action" because it need not all be covert—covertness is not central to it. Covertness is necessary for parts of it, but when there are *overt* actions which beg to be done and are not being done now, that is important.

A second point is the protection of secrets that are important to be kept secret. The integrity of the intelligence community has gone downhill because of the legislative action taken in the last four years. That would argue against knocking down the compartmentalization—of which you otherwise rightly complain—too rapidly, before we have fixed that. Some compartmentalization is needed.

ALLEN: I have a complaint: there exists a huge intelligence lobby in this country comprised of former intelligence
officers and people who have spent most of their lives as
dedicated professionals in the intelligence business from the
OSS days or even perhaps prior to that. That they should exist as a lobby I have nothing against. However, my experience in trying to navigate the shoals of that intelligence
lobby is that the moment you try to touch anything in that
sacrosanct community's organizational structure, screams of
pain and anguish go up and epithets begin rolling.

I don't know how you get over that. These people react
very adversely and quickly and shrilly to notions of intelligence failure. Trying to locate the responsibility for an
intelligence failure or a policy failure is a very difficult task.

Nitze comments that good analysis depends on net assessment. We know that is true, but I am not sure it is something
that we want the intelligence community to do. You know,
some of the problems we have had is that the intelligence
community has produced key judgments or findings which
are implicitly net assessment, but we really haven't had the
basis for them, and I think these have gotten us into trouble
at times.

ELLSWORTH: Just as an historical footnote, we went
through all of the argument on the congressional role with
the great constitutional lawyers that existed in the White
House in 1975 and 1976 and we lost, and I don't know if we
can revive the issue. I will be glad to join in a revival movement of the issue, but I think it is futile. There was a judge by
the name of Adams on the Second Circuit Court of Appeals
sitting in Philadelphia who wrote a dissenting opinion in one
of the cases around that time that develops it in its full
historical and legal flower, and it is a fascinating opinion.
But in any case, so far we are in the minority along with
Judge Adams.

BROWNE: Yes.

NITZE: Should the CIA be in the net assessment business at all? Shouldn't they just look at what we know about other people's capabilities? It turns out that when you write a National Intelligence Estimate [NIE] you can't write anything intelligent that will answer anybody's need if you just describe the system. You've got to describe it in terms of what *U.S. capabilities* are and what the U.S. requirements are and what would happen in the event it does engage with somebody else. If you just describe Soviet ships without any description of what they might be able to do against opposition here, there, or the other place, you are not really contributing much.

Because of that fact, the CIA does in fact deal in net assessment. All true, they are reports; but they don't acknowledge the fact that they are making net assessments and therefore they do it incompetently, irresponsibly, and without pointing out what they are doing, and I think that is one of the greatest defects in the NIE—which is the fact that there are hidden in the NIEs all kinds of improper, inaccurate, net assessments. If you challenge them, they say, "Sure, it isn't our business to know what U.S. capabilities are or what allied capabilities are, and therefore you've got to forgive us for having made these errors"—but the errors are in there.

ELLSWORTH: I don't think we are going to get Congress out of the business. Congress is deeply into the business. It can be managed. The arguments that were going on in the White House were highly technical and detailed, but had to do with the proposition that under the constitution the Congress had to have such and such a constitutional role; and as a matter of fundamental constitutional law my position was that the intelligence function of the president transcended the constitution, and that such role as Congress had was a matter of negotiation between the president and Congress.

III

The Politics of Strength

10

EDWARD N. LUTTWAK

On the Meaning of Strategy . . . for the United States in the 1980s

The need for strategy in U.S. policy. Past effects of British power, U.S. economic strength, and "containment." NATO and SALT. The systems' analyst. Civil efficiency v. military effectiveness. Substrategical perspectives. The rules of strategy.

As a nation, Americans are pragmatic problem-solvers rather than systematic or long-range thinkers. Our whole experience tells us that it is best to narrow down complicated matters so as to isolate the practical problem at hand, and then to get on with finding a solution. Strategy by contrast is the one practical pursuit that requires a contrary method: to connect the diverse issues into a systematic pattern of things; then to craft plans—often long range—for dealing with the whole. In the life of this nation it has not been strategy but rather pragmatic problem-solving that has created a society wealthier than most—and now also more just than virtually all others—and it has not been long-range planning but rather the impatient dynamism of a hard-working people that has allowed so many to pursue happiness as well.

That is why it is now so very difficult for Americans to accept the ineluctable fact that to achieve even moderate success the nation's external policy must be guided by the alien rules of strategy.

BASES OF PAST U.S. POLICY

It was not always so. Until the beginning of this century, the United States enjoyed the classic prerogatives of the great sea powers of history: it could take as much or as little of the world's affairs as it wanted. Neither a powerful navy nor broad oceanic borders assured this fortunate state. Rather was it the power of Great Britain, a nation then itself exquisitely strategical, that secured for the Americans all they really needed of the outside world. Even in intermittent discord there was shared interest in all the fundamentals. To keep others busy with large land armies and thus themselves supreme at sea, the British used both diplomacy and force to maintain the warlike equilibrium called the "Balance of

Power"; hence the Americans had the Great Powers balanced for them and kept from their door.

The British kept trade open for all in order to keep trade open for their own industry. The Americans thus had their trade as free as they desired and still as protected as they chose. Above all, to maintain their own moral economy the British pursued idealism too; hence the suppression of slavery, the punishments of the czars for their pogroms, and the pervasive teaching of decent practices in international life, sometimes by Mr. Gladstone's sermons and sometimes by Lord Palmerston's cannonades. Thus the Americans could look out on a world steadily advancing in the manners of civilization and in the legalities of international transactions.

Since the British made their greater decisions in the privacy of country houses and London clubs and since they were in the habit of using pragmatic and reticent language, the fact that their affairs of state were guided by a coherent strategy relentlessly pursued was not at all evident. The discretion is understandable. Maintenance of the Balance of Power was a harsh business not at all confined to the beating down of bullies; it required also favoring the Turk against Christian powers—and a Greece that Byron chose to die for—and it meant opposing the unification of Europe, no matter how progressive the union might have been. Until 1945 the Americans were merely called to war, and that briefly. It was the British who set the strategy and who chose our enemies for us.

Even after 1945 the Americans needed no strategy merely to keep on an even keel. There was an economy so powerful that others could scarcely keep their own, resources so abundant that the world's oil price was set by "Gulf plus freight"—that being the Texan shore and not the Persian. Then there were war industries so amply productive that any enemy would ignore the dissolution of the armies after the victory over Japan, seeing in prospect those thousands and thousands of aircraft and tanks ready to pour from the production lines. On top of all, there was the nuclear weapon—first the fission bomb and then the thermonuclear—that others could perhaps emulate in sample numbers but which only the United States could really use on a large scale, and scale still counted in the days when the total number of weapons was still small.

And so it was that the simplest of strategies, "containment," could be triumphantly successful. Europe, Japan, and their appendages duly recovered from the ravages of war safe behind the shield of American power. The task was made easier—and perhaps even made possible—by the great weakness of the Soviet Union. Behind Stalin's six million men in arms there was a desert of war destruction in all the Russias west of Moscow, with cities in ruins and agriculture beaten down to a level medieval; even east of Moscow, in the lands that had remained beyond the reach of the Germans, the population was exhausted and greatly lacking in men. Stalin and then his first heirs desperately tried to keep the only true secret of those most secretive times: that behind those six million men in arms there was not the capacity to sustain their fighting. And they were successful. By any calculus of power that cold-blooded men might have made, Stalin did not have the strength to keep the large part of Europe that Russian arms had won. After all, the czar had danced in Paris after Waterloo, yet the British had their Russians driven back all the way to eastern Poland very soon after the music stopped.

With "containment" the Americans pursued what the British had once pursued for them—until Vietnam. Then it was not only the wisdom of policy that broke down in the enervation of an elite; it was not only the competent pursuit of war that collapsed under the weight of a luxuriant military bureaucracy indifferent to the earnest study of the true phenomena of warfare. It was the very notion of strategy that waned, even that largely passive strategy of containment which required merely that we react.

But still, even after the final defeat—which brought with it not merely a totalitarian rule but also one far bloodier than even war at its worst, even after we had consigned millions who had pledged trust with us to Hanoi's brutalities and Pol Pot's autogenocide—even after that defeat, Americans could nevertheless think that the discipline of strategy remained unnecessary. There was still a slim margin in our favor in the "strategic-nuclear" balance (the very term a reminder of the degraded meaning of "strategic" in our discourse), and even if all who desired could very easily project the advent of unambiguous inferiority in the 1980s, most could still imagine that all was well, since few desired to project. And by then we had the Strategic Arms Limitation Talks (SALT) whereby, as we are even now reminded, the great strength accumulated by the steady effort of the Russians would be negated, at low cost and at no risk, through the drafting of legal documents. In that atmosphere it was an easy matter for the instrument—arms control—to displace the purpose, for only a national strategy could define the purpose and we had no national strategy. Hence the pursuit of SALT as an end in itself, the only real test of each proposal being its negotiability and the only test of that being the Russians' acceptance.

SALT, NATO, AND THE MILITARY

Aside from SALT, most of our defense policy was defined by the North Atlantic Treaty Organization's (NATO's) real or fancied needs. That was not at all a strategic choice, but rather a political compromise. Those who had wanted America "to come home" and those who were still residually internationalist could find a compromise in an all-for-NATO defense policy. Thus two acronyms substituted between them for the difficult business of constructing a national strategy responsive to our needs at home and cognizant of the dangers abroad—SALT and NATO, NATO and SALT. Too bad that a defense policy that made NATO its only real focus under the slogan "No more Vietnams" would mean that we would only be enhancing stability in the one segment of the perimeter of our interests that was already rather stable; too bad that we would only be adding strength where our weakness is least—these being procedures that no self-respecting junior officer would use in defending a company perimeter. But NATO and SALT, SALT and NATO had to do duty for the thought, the plan, the consensual strategy that was absent.

It was perhaps inevitable that sooner or later some ineffable figure innocent of strategy but taught in the arts of public relations should think of mating the acronyms; and so we had the experience, in its own way memorable, of being told insistently that NATO would not survive without SALT. The moment in which Cyrus Vance, Secretary of State, chose to hesitate theatrically in open hearings before saying "I don't know" to a senatorial query on whether NATO could withstand a rejection of SALT II shall undoubtedly be recorded as the nadir of America's unstrategical decade. Such a gross defection from the duties of statecraft demonstrated how far policy could stray without the anchor of strategical priorities. To Mr. Vance, the SALT II accords were merely his brief; the hearing, his court; and the White House, his client. Our allies had much reason to be shocked. It is not that SALT is incompatible with strategy. It could and indeed should be: in the context of a coherent strategy, SALT could be a most powerful instrument of policy. But the good ingredient unbalanced makes bad medicine—in this case, of the narcotic variety.

In the absence of strategy, it is substrategical impulses that govern what we do. Thus the weapons we design,

develop, and eventually build reflect the technical ambitions
of the engineers as well as the ideal forms of our bureaucrats
in uniform. Only tactical logic is absent from the process.
The army, having failed for two decades to obtain a new battle tank, insists nevertheless on having its new XM-1 tank
propelled by a gas turbine—at high cost and greater risk of
failure. Such propulsion adds nothing whatever of combat
value to the XM-1 but it satisfies the technological urge, and
there is no tactical logic to satisfy anyway. After all, tactics
must be derived from the operational method of warfare—be
it *Blitzkrieg* or defense-in-depth, the hold-and-counterpunch
or the agile defense. There can be no operational method of
warfare unless it is derived from *theater strategy*, and that in
turn cannot be framed except within a national strategy. No
wonder that an unguided technical ambition dominates the
scene. Nor is it surprising that in the War Colleges our officers study much about management but not at all about the
Art of War. Far better to muster those techniques so useful
in civilian life than to study war—a painful process since the
"data base" is merely the library of military history and
some books are even in languages other than English.

What the army has done in trying to develop armored
fighting vehicles is a subject already notorious: the ten-year
program that failed to yield an infantry combat carrier (a
thing already achieved even by the Yugoslavs), the billion-
dollar program that could not produce a scout car (as even
the Brazilians have). The story is always the same. Without
the discipline of strategy and of its tactical needs, luxuriant
technicity yielded machines of legendary technical attain-
ments and of unattainable cost. And so also it has been,
though perhaps in less bloated form, with the other armed
services. Technicity is a wonderful servant and a disastrous
master.

In the absence of strategy, it is substrategical choices that
govern the form of the armed forces we deploy. In war, two
great phenomena contend: maneuver, made of circumvent-

ing action, to bypass the barrier, to outflank the thrust, and to evade the main strength of the enemy in all things from weapon design to grand strategy. Such maneuver is the product of surprise, deception, and above all agility in thought, planning, and action. And then there is the other great phenomenon: firepower, assayed by volume, by accuracy, by lethality, and made of industrial strength, transportation, and efficient logistic distribution. Throughout the history of war, blends of maneuver and firepower have contended in a thousand forms. Maneuver has generally been less costly in blood and treasure, but firepower was always the safer course and demanded merely an outright superiority in means. But even in the face of superior firepower and superior resources, maneuver in all its forms—tactical, operational, theater-strategic, and developmental, as well as the higher maneuver of grand strategy—has always held its own and often has elegantly prevailed.

THE IMPACT OF TECHNOLOGY

But that was before maneuver finally met its match in the figure of the American "systems' analyst." When this new apparition came to take its place alongside the Great Captains of history, the long line of men from Mauricius the Emperor to Manstein of the Donetz, from Marius of the legions to the colonel who planned the Entebbe raid, then and only then was maneuver finally undone. Its fatal defect was that no numerical index can be attached to surprise, deception, or the outmaneuvering action. Thus no criterion of effectiveness stated in numbers can be defined for the purposes of systems' analytical computation. Firepower, by contrast, is very easily measurable, volume being tonnage, accuracy being hit probability, and lethality being a known factor. In countless mathematical models the "combat value" of forces is thus measured exclusively by their firepower. The "simulations" now widely used to define what weapon characteristics are needed, what type and size of forces are to be deployed, and even to assess what passes by the name of tactics, are all in fact firepower-exchange computations.

All this may seem excessively recondite. But it is of the essence. For many years now, the weapons we build and the forces we deploy have been heavily influenced by mathematical criteria of choice that do not capture a most important dimension of warfare. That is one reason why our army, half as large in numbers as the Soviets', has only 16 divisions to their 168—ours being heavy in logistics to sustain firepower, producing it by methods of industrial style. That is a main reason why our aircraft must be so large and costly, since there is apparent efficiency in the economies-to-scale of the large vehicle. One pilot produces more firepower with the larger aircraft—and never mind that numbers give flexibility for action, and never mind also that the large fighter is seen by the smaller one before the smaller one is seen by the larger one. And that is why our navy is shaped by the logic of bigness on one side—as if ballistic-missile submarines were firepower factories—and by prejudice against "offensive" warships on the other, as if the nation that has no effective navy is thereby made more moral by the impotence that results.

Yet the logic of strategy in such things begins precisely with the rejection of the logic of civil efficiency. The large thing is often more efficient in producing the unit of firepower. But in war the very objective must be to mingle in the fight, and then the large thing is often almost as vulnerable as the small thing of which more can be had. In civil life one builds the bridge over the river using trusted formulae to construct the safely engineered solution; but in strategy there is perpetual contention and the fixed solution is merely outmaneuvered. No natural river will deliberately set out to evade the span that would bridge its banks, but that is quite the normal thing in the realm of strategy.

There is thus a fundamental opposition between (civil) efficiency and (military) effectiveness, almost entirely ignored because instead of strategists we have only book-keepers of cost and effectiveness. And where are our generals and admirals who will rise to protest such methods, who will expose their falsehoods, and, if needs be, resign? They are busy supervising their own "systems' analysts" who make their own suitably rigged calculations with the same misleading criteria of choice. Already themselves far too removed from the true study of war to uphold its endless unquantifiable complexities, these are not the men who will remind us that the force with the greater firepower has lost more often than not in the record of war. They are not the ones who will insist that maneuver as well as civil efficiency be the criteria of choice. It is so much easier to bend to the fashion of the day and to fill endless rolls of computer print-out with "simulations" that will serve to advocate what their bureaucracies want. Thus a nation which spends much too little for its armed strength anyway receives even less than it pays for.

THE CURRENT SITUATION

In the absence of strategy, it is substrategical perspectives that govern our understanding of what confronts us. Over a period of several months in the years 1978–1979 Americans debated, first, the meaning of the supply of Russian submarines to Cuba; then the meaning of the arrival of new high-performance MiG–23s with Russian pilots; then the discovery in Cuba of modern air-defense weapons for battlefield use; and finally the revelation that a Soviet armored brigade was stationed on the island. Each episode was separated from the next by a few weeks or months, and that interval proved long enough to ensure that each episode would be viewed in isolation.

Of the submarines, it could be said—by those eager for inaction—that they were nonnuclear and thus harmless. Of the MiG−23s, the question was merely asked if they were fitted with provisions for nuclear bombs. Of the air-defense weapons, nothing was said at all, the questions of why and where being too recondite to answer. Cubans in Africa had no need for such weapons; Cubans to be sent to Arabia might well need them, but Arabia is far from Cuba and to connect the two distant places would require a strategic mind. Of the brigade, it was asked only—and foolishly enough—whether it might invade the United States of America. The president eventually proclaimed, as the Russians had claimed all along, that the brigade was only in Cuba to train and not to fight. With that revelation the matter was then simply dropped, and the question of why the Cubans needed armored-warfare training—useless in Black Africa but essential in Arabia—was not asked at all. Since it is only within the framework of strategical understanding that diverse things may be connected to form a view of the whole, the genuine profile of the danger—that is to say, not the submarines as such, not the MiG−23s on their own, not just the air defense, not merely the brigade but rather the entire transformation of Cuba into a first-class military power—never emerged at all. That indeed was the one issue not debated, even while hawks and doves spoke and wrote millions of words on each fragment of the whole that was never even recognized as such.

Until the later years of the 1970s there were still residues of power, or at least residual delusions that the United States could prosper even in weakness. Only now, as of this writing, is the long holiday finally over—at long last and so late, so very late. The agencies of our education were several: the relentless exposure of the most intricate details of our "strategic-nuclear" weakness engendered by the Senate hearings on the SALT II accords, the growing realization that a NATO-only defense policy meant a fatal passivity in the face of a Soviet strategy that creates bases of power between us and some of our most vital interests, and then finally—at the hands of the mobs of Iran—a belated education in the all-too concrete value of the intangibles of prestige and authority. Of course, deep emotional resistance is not so easily overcome. As of this writing at the end of the year 1979, the United States was still refusing to behave as a Great Power must in its dealings with Iran. But at least the mood of the people has changed, and profoundly, and the need to enhance the nation's armed strength has been very widely accepted.

The time has finally come when the acknowledgment of weakness and the understanding of its unacceptable price has educated us all in the need for strength and for a national strategy that can use it wisely. Its shape must be dictated in many lesser decisions made over time by executive and legislature, but the broad rules are the same for all nations, and we too must frame our desires within them:

• Never deal with the single crisis, or the single matter of any kind, in isolation. When, for example, Soviet power intervenes to decide the outcome of war in Ethiopia, do not look at Ethiopia alone but rather at the consequences of action or inaction for the whole of East Africa, for the Middle East, for the world.

• Do not seek partial solutions without considering their effect on the general equilibrium of power. If SALT offers a "parity" of strategic-nuclear weapons, ask if there is also "parity" in theater-nuclear weapons, in nonnuclear weapons and forces, and in other means too—clandestine-military and cover-political action, and then also in the constructive instruments of aid and trade, in that order. Otherwise a guaranteed parity in one class of weapons alone may seal inferiority overall. The partial solution may still be desirable, and practical solutions will almost always be partial solutions but they cannot be framed in a partial view. If there is a national strategy, there may well be need of SALT negotiating tactics also, but let not those tactics usurp the place of strategy.

• Do not confront strength but maneuver around it; do not allow the enemy to exploit every area of weakness without acting to do likewise, for otherwise there is no hope of success. If it is the Soviet policy to separate the alliance, active measures of alliance solidarity are essential but they must be complemented by a relentless campaign to embarrass the Soviet Union in Eastern Europe: it is neither useful nor moral to incite Hungarian children to confront Russian tanks, but it is merely appeasement to have our officials speak of "socialist" countries when we should speak only of Russia and of captive nations. More substantially, if it is the Soviet policy to conspire against us in Iran, let us reciprocate in Afghanistan where, as of this writing, Russian armed helicopters are decimating—for want of a few portable anti-aircraft missiles—the warriors ranged against them.

• Do not confuse ethics and aesthetics. Ethics must reflect the moral calculus of least human suffering. Aesthetics merely reflect the superficial appearance of things. If the Organization of Petroleum Exporting Countries uses the market strength of a cartel to inflict inconvenience upon us, poverty increases in such countries as Turkey and Brazil. When the marginal countries suffer impoverishment, Asian peasants actually starve for want of crops—that is to say, for want of water for their crops; that is to say, for want of diesel oil for their tube wells. And so let armed power be brought in to balance market power, for our own good and for that of many others.

• Do not make of others what they refuse to be. The Soviet Union is the vehicle for the aggrandizement of the Russians, the one truly imperial nation left on this earth. The Russians have a strategy, and it is an imperial strategy of classic form: to protect Muscovy, the Ukraine and Byelorussia must be held; to protect the latter, a further cordon of non-Russian lands from Estonia to Moldavia must be annexed to the Soviet Union; to protect the latter, the states of Eastern Europe too must come under Russian power lest their freedom inspire revolt in the non-Russian fringe. But Eastern Europe will remain restless so long as the countries of Western Europe parade their liberties and prosperity before its peoples—thus Western Europe must be tamed if Eastern Europe is to become permanently obedient so that the non-Russian fringe lands will be obedient also, so that the cordon will be safe, so that Moscow will remain powerful over all.

But Western Europe will never be tamed so long as American protection intervenes to allow its elected leaders to defy Moscow's demands for obedience. And so the Soviet Union's imperial strategy relentlessly pursues the struggle to diminish American power and to separate Europeans and Americans. Now the new prospect of achieving both great objectives by acting against a third, the Persian Gulf, has opened vast new possibilities for Moscow. Let us defend the perimeters directly under threat, but that cannot possibly suffice. Hence the need to maneuver and articulate power where opportunity offers scope and in East Asia in particular. The best defense for Europe is most probably located somewhere between Outer Mongolia and the banks of the Ussuri. Thus the folly of a "Eurocentric" strategy, precisely because Europe is justifiably held to be most important for us.

• And then finally, and above all, we need tenacity. That is not a quality as easily admirable as creativity or compassion. But it is the one quality that strategy unalterably requires. That is not quite the same thing as calling for more virtue or preaching "motherhood," as the saying goes. No doubt we shall find that many of our elite institutions will have to be rebuilt with new people who do not share the paralyzing enervation that nowadays passes for sober restraint, who do not fundamentally believe that the United States should be weak, for if strong it must be recklessly destructive or at least the upholder of an unjust order of things. After all, just as strength without strategy yields very little, strategy and strength combined will not avail if both are in the hands of an elite that prefers retreat over the advancement of power and which, in its worst moments, has a positive longing for the humiliations of defeat, think that . . .

Οἱ ἄνθρωποι αὐτοὶ ἡσαν μιὰ κάποια λύσις. *

* ". . . the Barbarians, after all, were some sort of solution"

11

HENRY S. ROWEN

The Threatened Jugular: Oil Supply of the West

The threat to supplies of oil from the Persian Gulf. Possible means of disruption. Power positions in the Middle East. Inadequacies in the U.S. energy policy. Characteristics of the world oil market. A tariff or a tax? Steps toward reduced vulnerability.

Two recent events have suddenly illuminated the looming threat to the West's oil: one is the sharp decline in Iran's oil production over the past several months; the other is the Soviet invasion of Afghanistan. That these shocks have come as a surprise to most Americans is powerful testimony to the prior failures of U.S. administrations and members of Congress to alert the American people to the dangers of dependency on Persian Gulf oil and to the urgent need to limit our dependency.

The simple fact is that the West is highly dependent on oil from the Middle East—and the Persian Gulf in particular—whose continued flow is threatened. This dependency implies risks of grave economic damage, political divisiveness and perhaps even collapse in the Western alliance systems, and the possibility of conflict which could escalate into major war.

It should not be surprising that the international flow of oil could be the occasion for conflict. The Japanese decision to attack the United States in 1941 had been influenced to no small degree by the U.S. embargo on oil shipments to that country in 1940, and in Europe access to Rumanian oil was important in Germany's prewar and wartime actions.

The main fact bearing on the West's oil supply is this: The non-Communist world obtains almost one-half of its oil from the Middle East, about 40 percent from the Persian Gulf producers. The importance to the United States of oil from this source does not derive principally from our direct usage of Middle Eastern oil but from the exceptionally high dependence of our major allies. Table 1 shows the present pattern of oil flows in the non-Communist world. It shows that Japan gets about 70 percent of its oil from the Persian Gulf, Europe about 50 percent, and the United States (counting oil refined in the Caribbean and shipped on) about 25 percent. In the aggregate, the United States and its allies get about 40 percent of their oil from this region (about the same percent of Persian Gulf usage as the non-Communist world as a whole).

How should we interpret this pattern of production and consumption? The outcome of the Arab oil embargo in 1973, directed against the United States and the Netherlands during the Arab-Israeli War, suggests that the oil market has great flexibility and that attempts to limit supplies to any single country or small set of countries will be offset by the

Table 1
WOCA* Oil Consumption by Source

Consumption (MMBD)	Production (MMBD)				
	OECD	Non-OPEC LDCs	Persian Gulf	Other OPEC	Total
OECD	14	1	15	8	38.0
United States			(4)		(18.5)
Japan			(4)		(5.5)
Western Europe			(6)		(12.0)
Other			(1)		(4.0)
Non-OPEC LDCs	–	3	3	2	8.0
Persian Gulf	–	–	1	–	1.0
Other OPEC	–	–	–	1	1.0
Total	14	4	19	11	48.0

*World outside Communist area.

working of market forces. In that instance, the major international oil companies rerouted their shipments of oil so as largely to offset the effects of the embargo. Moreover, the shortages resulting from the Arab production cuts—a much more serious matter—were more or less evenly allocated among their international customers. (Much of the immediate economic damage seems to have been caused by the governments of importing countries which amplified the disturbance.)

But what about the future, which may see much deeper cuts, perhaps of longer duration? For instance, if oil from the Persian Gulf were to be wholly interrupted, Japan would lose 70 percent of its oil supply—about one-half of its *total* energy consumption. Would the United States be willing to ship oil from Alaska to Japan instead of to the U.S. west coast and also to divert imports of Indonesian oil to Japan? The International Energy Agency (IEA) Sharing Agreement implies diversions of this kind, but how confident are the governments of the most vulnerable countries that they will occur?[1] In my judgment, we would do so because preventing the collapse of the Japanese economy, and the political consequences of such grave economic damage, is a vital American interest. More broadly, it is in the interest of all members of the Western alliance system to avoid the collapse of any single member. But to predict that, in the event, we would all hang together does not necessarily imply that this perception is universally held among the allies of the United States.

ACTUAL AND POTENTIAL ECONOMIC DAMAGE

Moreover, the prospect of a collegial "hanging" is not a happy one. Even small reductions in Middle East oil supplies inflict large losses on consumers. A recent estimate of the energy shock in late 1973 and early 1974 concludes that it depressed real output in the United States by 2 percent in 1974 and 5 percent in 1975 in addition to adding substantially to inflation (Mork and Hall 1979*b*). An estimate of the recent shock, beginning in late 1978 with the interruption of Iranian oil supply, is that without offsetting macroeconomic policy actions it will depress U.S. real output by 1.1 percent in 1979 and 2.8 percent in 1980 (Mork and Hall 1979*a*).

Estimates of losses from deeper cuts of longer duration than these have been made by John Weyant of Stanford University (see Rowen and Weyant 1980). For example, a reduction of 6 million barrels per day in Persian Gulf production (about one-third of the production from that area) lasting for a year, in the absence of offsetting actions such as drawing on strategic oil reserves that might exist, would cost the Organization for Economic Cooperation and Development (OECD) countries about 7 percent of their aggregate gross national product (GNP). A loss of all Persian Gulf oil for a year results in an estimated loss of about 30 percent of the GNP of the OECD countries, even if somehow the price of the remaining oil imported is prevented from rising at all. (These estimates by Weyant are *lower bound* estimates; unlike those of Mork and Hall, they assume a smooth response of the economies of the importers to the shortfall of oil supplies.)

In short, even if the major importing countries cooperate closely, in the absence of protective measures they face the risk of catastrophic economic damage.

MECHANISMS OF DISRUPTION

Four mechanisms of supply disruption can be identified: (1) deliberate manipulation of oil supplies by producers for politics or profit (e.g., as in 1973–1974); (2) reduction in sup-

ply as a consequence of loss of governmental control and internal chaos (e.g., Iran in 1979); (3) conflict among governments in the region which interferes with oil production or
shipments (e.g., a conflict between Iraq and Saudi Arabia);
and potentially most serious, (4) Soviet interference with or
influence over oil supplies from the region. We have not yet
experienced the consequences of the workings of the third
and fourth mechanisms, but we may do so during the
1980s—as well as repetitions of numbers one and two.

Two bad experiences and the threat of worse have had a
substantial political impact on the industrialized countries.
Several governments, with that of France perhaps in the
van, have tried to carve out special relations with the oil producers. Much has been offered in technology and arms (most
ominously in "sensitive" nuclear facilities and materials).
There is little evidence that it has bought them much in price
or supply security. But this unseemly scramble bodes ill for
the more serious crises which very likely lie ahead.

THE SOVIET THREAT

The most dangerous threat is that resulting from the growth
in the capacity of the Soviet Union to project military power
into the Persian Gulf area. Fifteen years ago the United
States, together with Great Britain, had a capacity to move
military forces to the area superior to that of any other
power including the Soviet Union which, after all, does not
have to move its military forces very far in order to reach the
oil fields of the Persian Gulf, especially now that its forces in
Afghanistan are only six hundred miles from the Strait of
Hormuz. Nonetheless, the Soviets then had little capacity to
move forces by air to the region, a modest naval capability,
and a formidable problem of movement over land given the
poor ground transportation facilities. All of these impedi-

ments are now eased: They have a substantial naval presence in the Indian Ocean, bases in Ethiopia and South Yemen, troops in Afghanistan, a greatly expanded airlift capacity, and can take advantage of much improved ground communications in the region. Meanwhile the British have left and U.S. access to the area has been greatly reduced. No longer can we count on *en route* bases in southern Europe and access through Turkey, nor do we have bases in Thailand which were helpful in gaining access to the region from the east.

In short, the Soviet Union, in a reversal of power positions, now has an advantage in power projection into the region. This may not be irreversible, but while it lasts it means that in any confrontation or conflict with the Soviet Union the Soviets will have the potential to threaten the oil supply of the West. That power would not have to be applied in the most direct way in order to cause us trouble. Because they have the potential of using it to produce grave economic damage to the West, the prospect of their doing so might be used to create divisions among the Western allies. If the price of noncooperation with the Soviets could be the loss of a large part of one's oil supplies, rationalizations for cooperation might be found.

There are other uses of superior power in the region that we should think about. For instance, in confrontations or conflicts with the Soviet Union that might take place elsewhere in the world in the 1980s, the Soviets will have available the option, at a price, of cutting the supply of much of its adversaries' oil. At least they will have this option if we do not deny it to them. And we need also to consider the effect on the North Atlantic Treaty Organization (NATO) of the interruption of oil supplies at a time when we are engaged in a major wartime mobilization effort, a contingency which cannot be ruled out for the 1980s.

There are political costs even now from our dependency. Our foreign policy aims in the Middle East face the threat of the use of the "oil weapon" by producers. The Arab producers have done this before, in 1973, and they have been trying to force changes in our policies toward Israel and the Palestine Liberation Organization (PLO); Libya (and also Nigeria) have made similar threats regarding our policies toward southern Africa.

The argument has been made that the Soviet Union may have a growing incentive to gain control over Persian Gulf oil because of the predicted shortage of oil in that country. This view was given a good deal of support from a Central Intelligence Agency (CIA) analysis published in 1977 which suggested that trouble with oil production could lead it to becoming a significant oil importer in the 1980s.

That view has since been modified. The Soviet energy situation does not appear to be as bleak as then portrayed. For one thing, economic growth, and therefore energy demand, is expected to be low—for reasons largely independent of higher energy costs. For another, the Soviet Union is developing its large natural gas resources at an impressive rate. In recent years it has been adding to supply about one trillion cubic feet per year of natural gas (equivalent to 500,000 barrels per day of oil). This gas increment alone is adding about 2 percent annually to the total Soviet energy supply. The additional gas supply will help substantially to offset problems with oil production.

Given the high world price of oil and the difficulty the Soviet Union faces in earning hard currencies, the Soviets have a strong incentive to continue to export oil to the West, diverting it from their current Eastern European customers—who will increasingly have to look to the non-Communist world for their oil—and replacing oil domestically with natural gas.

They are having energy supply problems, perhaps growing ones; but the Soviet interest in Persian Gulf oil is probably dominated more by geopolitical interests than by prospective import needs.

FAILURES OF U.S. ENERGY POLICY

The principal short-term protective measure that has been adopted by governments to limit the damage from supply interruptions is the stockpiling of oil. As of September 1979, Japan was reported as having a supply of 421 million barrels, amounting to seventy-six days of consumption, including both private and government-held stocks. If these figures include amounts in working inventory, they are not all available for use in a crisis; perhaps forty days of this supply would be available for use in a crisis. Germany's stockpile was reported at 237 million barrels in June 1979, and France's as 199 million barrels. Again, if these were the totals in the systems, allowing for necessary "pipeline" amounts leaves probably around thirty days of excess supply in each country.

The United States, in contrast, had as of October 1979 only 94 million barrels of oil in its Strategic Petroleum Reserve (SPR), an amount equivalent to about five days of consumption or twelve days of imports. (In addition, unknown amounts of oil—above working inventory—are in private stocks, but these are probably not large.) In contrast, our stated target SPR level is 1 billion barrels. This meager level, six years after the 1973 oil shock, is clear evidence of a failure of American energy policy. It is a multipartisan failure, one shared by Republican and Democratic administrations and by Congress as well as the executive branch.

The failure of the United States to build an oil stock, especially during the period of relative market slackness from 1975 to 1978, together with our increased oil consumption and imports after 1973, has generated strong resentment on the part of our allies. They have done more both to limit growth in consumption and to provide insurance against interruption than we have done.

Indeed, our behavior has been bizarre, viewed in the light of the external dangers visible since at least 1973. We have expended our governmental energies on price controls, including the infamous "entitlements" system which subsidizes oil imports; adopted environmental legislation which, however worthy the aims, has impeded shifts away from vulnerable oil; maintained a system of utility rate regulation which encourages excessive energy consumption; allowed the real value of gasoline taxes to fall through inflation; moved slowly to bring natural gas from Mexico and Alaska; failed in the attempt to move Alaskan oil east from Los Angeles; been slow in converting electricity-generating plants from oil to coal; and we are about to adopt a "windfall" profits tax on domestic oil production which, in part, will be an excise tax on oil production. (It will be such a tax because a "windfall profit" is defined to include profit from oil sold at above today's real oil price. Future real oil prices are expected to increase. The tax therefore will discourage future investments that are keyed to the expectation that the real price of oil will rise.)

This portrayal is perhaps a bit one-sided. For instance, we have—belatedly—moved toward oil and natural gas price decontrol, and various supply initiatives are being taken. But these measures warrant the description "too little and too late." Our behavior has been so much at variance with what the objective situation seems to require that an explanation is needed. Several come to mind.

• One source of failure was our overestimation of the political stability of the states bordering on the Persian Gulf. When the British removed themselves from east of Suez in 1970 (despite American objections), the next best supplier of stability in the gulf was seen as the Shah of Iran. Iran itself was not seen as a source of instability, nor implicitly did security problems in the area seem very formidable.[2]

• The Soviet Union was not seen as a serious threat, partly because of our failure to recognize adequately the adverse trends in power projection that were taking place and partly because of a belief that the oil was so important to the West that a Soviet move against it would mean war. This happy assumption not only ignored changes in the overall East-West military balance but the considerable variety of ways short of direct attack that countries allied to the Soviet Union, or the latter itself, might be able to affect the West's supplies.

• American diplomacy from 1974 on, as before, was focused more on the Arab-Israeli dispute than on oil. No doubt it has seemed difficult or impossible for Henry Kissinger or Jimmy Carter to play the role of peacemaker between Arabs and Israelis while at the same time giving high public prominence to what the former were doing to the West's economies through their wealth transfer *vis à vis* a five-fold increase in the price of oil and while ringing the alarm on the dangers in continuing to rely on Persian Gulf oil. To be sure, Gerald Ford's administration launched Project Independence, but that project lacked persuasiveness and force. It was all too evident that there was not an inherent problem in oil imports, say, from Canada or Mexico. A policy of oil autarky was not plausible and Project Independence soon faded from sight.

• Among the major consuming countries, the United States is the only one with a large, established domestic oil industry (Britain has large domestic oil output, but its industry is new). This has meant that, if the market were allowed to work, the large increase in the world oil price would imply large transfers of money from consumers to producers within the United States. This internal income distribution issue has dominated much of the public debate, at high cost to our welfare. It perhaps would only have been overcome by a clear focus on the external dangers.

• The fact that our own direct oil imports from the Persian Gulf, although growing, were arguably not at a "critical" level has induced complacency. This perspective of course omits the vulnerability we derive indirectly through the high exposure of our key allies.

In short, bad politics has been joined to bad economics to place us in a precarious position.

SALIENT CHARACTERISTICS OF THE WORLD OIL MARKET

Understanding how to limit the damage we suffer in our present position, and in time to reduce vulnerable dependency to a tolerable level, requires a look at some key features of the world oil system.

First, as observed, this is a world market and oil is a relatively fungible commodity. Although differences in grade of oil matter for many uses, there is a high degree of substitutability possible in its flows among uses and among countries.

Second, the oil exporting countries can only raise the real price by restricting production (or by holding it constant while rising income levels cause demand to grow). Announcements that, for instance, the Organization of Petroleum Exporting Countries (OPEC) has decided to raise the price of oil by $X per barrel, if they mean anything, mean that one or more of its members have decided to restrict production by an amount sufficient to produce that price increase.

Third, OPEC is not a proper cartel with a production-sharing formula. Instead, the price maintainers of the system are a subset of countries—up to now dominantly Persian Gulf producers—who act as the "swing" producers. Saudi Arabia, of course, is the lead "swing" country, although Iran has, largely inadvertently, acted in this capacity this year. Specifically, increases in the real oil price imply a reduction in Persian Gulf production.

Fourth, the costs of *slowly* rising real oil prices to consuming countries is low, very much lower than the cost estimates reported above for sharp cuts. This is because the long-term elasticity of substitution between oil and other factors of production (other fuels, capital, labor) is high. For instance, as machinery is replaced, the cost of substituting low-fuel efficient machinery with more efficient machinery is modest. Conversely, as we have seen, the costs of trying to make such substitutions in the short run are enormously high.

Fifth, slower economic growth in the developed countries (and probably also in the industrializing ones such as Brazil and South Korea), together with reduced demand for oil as its real price rises, means that the overall demand for oil in the non-Communist world will grow very little in the 1980s. For a particular case examined by John Weyant (Rowen and Weyant 1980), that of the price of oil going from $20 per barrel in 1979 to $32 per barrel in 1990 (in 1978 dollars), the oil demand in seven large industrialized countries will be almost unchanged from now to 1990. (This result is, of course, sensitive to assumptions about price elasticities of demand and to the speed of adjustment to higher prices. But for the values of these parameters most consistent with the available evidence, demand will be nearly flat.) During this period there will become available some additional oil production, e.g., from Mexico, the North Sea, and some of the developing countries. It seems unlikely that the oil consumption of the less-developed countries will grow rapidly enough to absorb the increasing non-OPEC output (probably an additional 5 to 7 million barrels per day by 1990—almost 60 percent of the total oil consumption today of the developing countries). In short, the Persian Gulf "swing" producers are likely to face again a period of glut in oil markets similar to that in the

1975–1978 period. In order to keep the oil price increasing, and perhaps even to keep it from falling (in real terms), they may have to trim their production substantially. To the extent that this happens, the consuming countries would be less vulnerable to sudden interruptions of supply. This assumes, of course, that chaos—or the Soviet Union—has not overtaken the Persian Gulf in the meantime.

THE TRADE-OFF BETWEEN LONG-TERM PRICE AND VULNERABLE DEPENDENCY

The trade-off between long-term cost of paying a probably higher price of oil and reduced exposure to interruptions is shown in Figure 1. The curve d_1 represents the long-term demand schedule for oil in the United States. The curve d_s shows the short-term schedule; d_s is steeper (has a lower elasticity) than d_1 because of the difficulty of adjustment to rapid cuts in oil supply. If a cut occurs from the present level of U.S. oil consumption, 18 million barrels per day, to 11 million barrels per day, representing a possible U.S. share in cuts if all Persian Gulf oil is interrupted, the gross national product loss is represented by the large area, triangle PST. (There would be an additional GNP loss from higher prices paid on the remaining oil imported.) However, if at the time of the sudden cut the United States—and, implicitly, its allies—is consuming at point Q, the maximum GNP loss (again neglecting higher import prices) is represented by the much smaller triangle, QRU.[3]

In short, there is a trade-off between paying a lower price for oil in noncrisis periods, consuming more of it and being more dependent on Persian Gulf oil, and paying more for oil while having less vulnerable exposure. To the extent that we give weight to the latter strategy, we should *not* be encourag-

Figure 1
Trade-Off between Long-Term Price
and Vulnerable Dependency

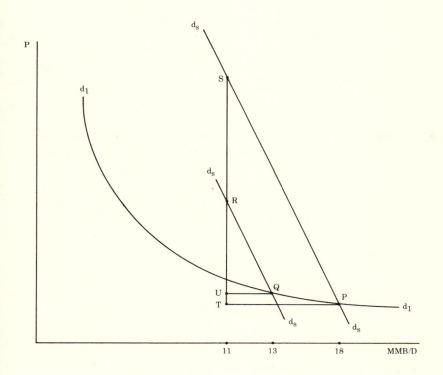

ing the Persian Gulf producers to increase production except in emergencies. On this view, repeated urgings by American officials to the Saudis to expand their production are somewhat off the mark. In contrast, urging that they expand their production *capacity* as a surge capability available for possible crises has much more merit.

This analysis implies that the world price of oil does not reflect its true cost because of the externality associated with vulnerable dependency. Such an externality can be internalized, at least partially, by imposing a tariff on imported oil. A tariff would of course raise the domestic price of oil above the world price and this would cause an economic loss domestically. But there would be two important benefits. Our reduced consumption would put downward pressure on the world oil price and therefore on the transfer of wealth from the United States and other importing countries to the oil exporters. And, secondly, it would reduce our exposure to sudden cuts. Although there is necessarily a good deal of subjectivity in assessing the second of these two benefits, it appears that an import tariff of at least $5 to $10 per barrel could be justified.[4]

The disadvantage of a tariff or, even more, of a higher gasoline tax is that once imposed they are likely to be permanent, even after the need has disappeared. The question, then, is one of balancing among evils.

WHAT SHOULD WE DO?

The needed actions are of two types: military and nonmilitary. Among the nonmilitary actions, an urgently needed one is that of building a substantial petroleum reserve. The payoff from such a stock can be very high. As an example, the economic saving to the United States from having a billion barrel SPR versus having none is about $100 billion if a cut occurs of 3.3 million barrels per day for a period of a year.[5] An SPR of that size would incur costs of around $3 to $4.25 billion annually. This implies that it pays to have a reserve of at least this size if, on the average, we estimate that there is at least a 30 to 50 percent probability of a cut of this seriousness at any point in the 1980s.

This estimate is independent of the institutional arrangements under which the stocks are held, public or private. Many other countries have relied heavily on private stocks (held especially by oil companies) for their strategic reserves. Private stocks are not subject to objections to spending federal budget dollars on the SPR, but the purchase of private stocks, as with public ones, in the current tight market would put upward price pressure on *all* oil that is imported. This makes an incremental barrel of oil bought today for storage—or consumption—cost more than its nominal price. Purchase for stocks is warranted under such conditions only if the insurance value for the contingency of disruption more than offsets the high cost. On balance, we have far too small a stockpile, and encouraging private stocks may be the only way we can obtain a strategic reserve of adequate size. A sizable reserve would help to deter deliberate coercive moves by foreign suppliers; it would strengthen U.S. diplomacy; it would reduce the likelihood of costly panic reactions by firms and industrial consumers in the United States if a crisis occurs. Given heightened danger of further Soviet action in the Persian Gulf, the case for adding to the SPR now has become compelling.

Other urgently needed steps to prepare for interruptions of this magnitude should include energy conservation plans and accelerated fuel-switching actions by industry and by state and local governments. They should also include consultations with other governments on cooperation in oil crises, including cooperative steps to deal with deep and prolonged as well as less traumatic cuts and steps involving a wartime crisis.

Steps to reduce our vulnerability that take effect in the longer term should include much more rapid energy decontrol in the United States, encouraging increased oil production in secure areas where there is an incentive to produce more oil, accelerated steps to enhance energy production in the United States including synfuel production, and additional conservation efforts.

We should adopt an oil tariff, one with exemptions for the most secure sources of oil—say, from the Western hemisphere. Failing a tariff, a substantial added gasoline tax (one more than $0.50 per gallon) should probably be imposed.

A tariff on imported oil would increase domestic oil prices. Much of this increase would be captured by the proposed "windfall" profits tax and all of it could be captured by an excise tax equal to the tariff. A $5 per barrel tariff would generate about $13 billion annually; an excise tax of that amount on domestic oil would generate an additional $18 billion. This $30 billion could be used to offset taxes which have been inhibiting capital formation and therefore economic growth.

All of these steps should be taken on the assumption that there is no basis for confidence that we can get through the 1980s—or even 1980—without a grave oil crisis centering on the Persian Gulf. The threat of imminent hanging should, finally, have the beneficial effect of clearing our minds.

CONCLUSION

A U.S. effort along these lines would help reduce our exposure to damaging interruptions and would substantially reduce the damage caused if they occur. But the basic problem remains: It is the exposure of our principal allies rather than ourselves that should be of greatest concern. This strategy would of course benefit them so long as they continue to take parallel actions to relieve their Persian Gulf dependency.

The international mutualities of interests, interdependencies, and externalities are evident. The contrast between this perception and most of the public discourse which has taken place in the past six years is so great that, if a strategy along the lines described here is to be implemented, a major effort appears to be needed to gain public recognition of these external dangers. The Soviet Union's invasion of Afghanistan should provide the necessary illumination. Greater clarity is needed on several essentials:

• The problem is *not* that the world is running out of energy; it is going through yet another period of transition among fuels.

• The American consumer is *not* a sinful energy hog; he has simply been responding to the prices faced in the marketplace.

• The major oil companies are *not* the source of the problem; the oil industry is competitive and the companies have been earning a barely competitive return on investment.

• We *can* protect the environment while increasing energy supplies; doing this means moving away from wasteful and inflexible regulatory standards and toward much more use of market-like mechanisms.

• The economy *can* flourish despite higher energy prices if they do not rise too sharply; our economic stagnation seems dominantly to be caused by low savings and investment and work disincentives and only modestly by energy price increases.

Correcting these and other confusions and adopting a more sensible strategy, one which focuses on our survival and that of our allies, is no small task. On form, it is likely to be imperfectly implemented at best. Although we all *may* become less dependent on Persian Gulf oil by 1990, there is no assurance of that outcome. At best, the West will remain highly vulnerable for years to come. To get through the 1980s, more than nonmilitary measures will be needed. Even more urgent than the energy measures described above is a military program intended to reduce the likelihood of inter- ference with oil supplies and to help assure their defense if an attempt is made by the Soviet Union or its allies to control them.

12

KENNETH L. ADELMAN

Revitalizing Alliances

Recent U.S. withdrawal from overseas alliances. The effect on Japan. The Soviet network. President Carter's NATO policy. The U.S. in Africa and the Persian Gulf. French and British strength in the Middle East. The situation with Asian nations. The U.S. needs allies.

With the coming of the dangerous 1980s—the first decade in history to witness a stretch of Soviet strategic superiority and of new Soviet reliance upon Persian Gulf oil—America must look to allies and friendly nations for the common security. The value of doing so is rather obvious to most people. The means of doing so is not, and hence is the consideration at hand.

BINGE OF DISENGAGEMENT

Since the shrill Vietnam days, the United States has been striving to tone down foreign commitments. The Southeast Asian Treaty Organization (SEATO) died in 1976 and the Central Treaty Organization (CENTO) passed away about the same time. Neither organization ever amounted to much, but their demise poignantly symbolized the binge of retrenchment that became America's trademark in the post-Vietnam period. Also apparent have been certain woes of the North Atlantic Treaty Organization (NATO), whose once-potent deterrent of U.S. strategic power, as Dr. Kissinger uttered in late 1979, has become a deterrent with few clothes on.

Likewise stripped was the Mutual Defense Pact with Taiwan. President Carter's recognition of Peking was a smart move, though the manner of de-recognizing Taiwan was not. The administration's confessed failure, for fear of being rebuked, even to *ask* Peking to pledge a peaceful settlement on the Taiwan issue was silly. Its initial refusal to own up to a major concession—the one-year moratorium on arms sales to Taiwan—was too sly by half. And the president's failure even to mention the Mutual Defense Pact in his televised nationwide announcement reinforced the impression that his government was cavalier, if not careless, on matters of national security—both America's and those of her allies.

It all adds up. The guru of the Vietnam-era consciousness, Eugene McCarthy (1978, p. 12), wrote that the "American government tends to treat its enemies as if they were allies. Meanwhile, American allies are treated as if they were enemies." This appraisal suggests an element of surprise. But Mr. Carter sounded the warning with clarity, campaigning often on how our foreign policy ought not to be based on military might nor political power nor economic pressure. It ought to be based on the fact that we are right and decent and honest and truthful and respectful, in other words, that our foreign policy itself accurately represents the character and ideals of the American people.*

Recently, and much to his credit, Mr. Carter has come to realize that emanating goodness and morality in the world is simply not enough.

BASIC VALUES OF ALLIANCES

But alliances can and do help. Sharpest is the help to self-preservation and self-defense—the we-all-hang-together-or-we'll-all-hang-separately idea which applies to the defense of the homeland as to that of the critical sea lines of communication (Japan's and Western Europe's very lifelines). Alliances also help advance the global goals so well highlighted by the Carter administration, which include halting the spread of nuclear weapons, dampening regional arms races, and furthering human rights. Such pursuits are best managed within a robust alliance apparatus.

Lastly, alliances are critical pep pills, invigorating the underlying common interests and common goals which caused their initial formation. Otherwise former friends may drift apart, with serious strategic repercussions. The brilliant Chinese strategist Sun Tzu recognized in 500 BC that the acme of military skill—an enemy's as well as one's own—is "to subdue the opponent without fighting" which is better "than a hundred victories in a hundred battles."

---

*The pitch was repeated daily during the 1976 campaign, but this particular quote was taken from his appearance before the National Democratic Issues Conference in Louisville, Kentucky, on 23 November 1975.

DRIFTING APART: THE CASE OF JAPAN

Regarded most crudely as the threat of "Finlandization," the phenomenon comes in degrees rather than in deluge. To take Japan as one of many possible examples. Tokyo has been rattled by a cascade of crises: the Nixon Doctrine and Nixon Shocks; U.S. withdrawal from Vietnam and later its fall; removal of U.S. bases from Thailand; announced withdrawal (without consulting Japan) of U.S. ground troops from Korea (since put off); declining relative strength of the U.S. Pacific fleet; and the withdrawal of troops and defense ties and diplomatic recognition from Taiwan. Total U.S. troop strength in Asia since the pre-Vietnam days (25,000 in 1964) has been sliced in half.

The Japanese need no weatherman to know which way the wind is blowing. One of Japan's sharpest international observers, Kei Wakaizumi, writes (1978–1979) that "Japan's long psychological attachment to the United States appears to have been severed almost as definitely as Commodore Perry's 'black ships' ended an era of diplomatic isolation in 1853."

With such psychological decoupling, in turn, comes an eminent Japanese economist who presents what he deems "a newer theory" on defense in one of the nation's foremost magazines: In the event of Soviet overzealousness, "the Japanese should receive the Soviet force coolly with both a white flag and red flag. So far as we stand firm"—he writes, innocent of detecting any contradiction—"we can build a socialist economy which will fit the conditions in Japan ... [in a] new life under Soviet dominance" (Morishima 1978).

The cost of erosion of U.S.-Japanese cooperation does not emerge as a clear blue-to-red phenomenon. No one expects the Japanese to cozy up to the Russians because of shocks coming from the Americans. Rather it emerges in nuances and lessened cooperation in various cases. This was seen most clearly during the Iranian crises. For ten days after the taking of American hostages on 4 November 1979 in Tehran, neither the Japanese government nor the press objected to the violation of international law or to the U.S. humiliation. When one Tokyo editorial finally appeared, it blamed both the Iranian revolutionaries for their current behavior and the United States for its past support of the shah.

Washington bristled as the Japanese bought up at least 20 million of the 30 million barrels of Iranian oil once destined for the United States, and did so at the spot market price of $40 per barrel rather than Iran's then-official price of $23.50. By yielding on price, Japan sought to gain on supply. It could count on Iran for some 20 percent of its oil needs or 14 percent of its total energy requirements, nearly double its past take from there. To add further salt to the wounds—infuriating both President Carter and Secretary Vance— Japanese banks were advising Iranian financiers on how best to skirt the U.S. freeze of Iranian assets, both in American banks and in their European branches. Such can be the costs of drifting apart by once-tight allies.

What can be done in a case like this? First and foremost is to heed the late Senator Hubert Humphrey's definition of consultation: "No surprises." Both nations have to build a record of honesty and a bond of trust that serves as a foundation for an alliance. This takes time and patience and energy; in alliance-building, there are simply no "quick fixes." Sadly, with Japan this has not been managed well. Under President Nixon were the Nixon economic shocks and the surprise opening to China (without any consultation with Tokyo), and under President Carter was the announcement of withdrawing American ground troops from Korea (likewise without any consultation). The "no surprises" dictum has clearly not been followed.

Second, in a crisis such as Iran, Washington must be crystal clear as to its expectations. The Japanese felt somewhat betrayed as the Department of Energy conveyed approval for Japan's purchasing of Iranian oil, given Japan's enormous reliance upon Persian Gulf crude, while the State Department publicly castigated Japan's actions.

Third, there must be consultations on alternative policies for a nation in Japan's bind. The United States can and should, in such a crisis, help Tokyo find alternative means of gaining its requirements rather than leaving it out in the cold.

SOVIET ALLIANCE TIGHTENING

Such parting of the ways, not dramatic but detectable nonetheless, contrasts with a discernible tightening of the Soviet security structure. The core element is of course the Warsaw Pact, which becomes mightier with each passing year as its members (especially East Germany) become more helpful to Soviet goals overseas (especially in Africa).

The Soviet's second team is also strengthening. This consists of those states with full-fledged twenty-year friendship treaties with Moscow, all adorned with provisions for military cooperation. One recent signatory, Afghanistan, learned discipline the hard way when up to 100,000 Soviet combat troops streamed into that country beginning Christmas week 1979.

This was truly a historic precedent, one without analogues. Soviet troops have never been actively and massively engaged outside Eastern Europe in peacetime since World War II. Afghanistan fell under the 1968 Brezhnev Doctrine which postulated the Soviet's right to intervene in any socialist state—*not*, in Brezhnev's words, confined to East Europe at all—for the sake of socialist solidarity. Virtually any state signing a Treaty of Friendship and Cooperation with the USSR could come under the doctrine, whether its leadership is tossed aside or not. Such states have doubled in number over the past year when South Yemen, Afghanistan, Ethiopia, and Vietnam joined Angola and Mozambique and, before them, Iraq and India.

The invasion showed also that when Moscow moves militarily it moves massively, leaving little to chance. This was made clear in 1968 when the amount of Russian materiel and personnel sent to Czechoslovakia far exceeded that needed to achieve the objective. It was also clear from Soviet and Cuban moves in Angola (1975) and Ethiopia (1977–1978). In short, Moscow has no patience for such gradually escalated responses as the United States practiced in Vietnam.

The third level of the Soviet alliance network consists of states who are neither members of a formal alliance nor treaty signatories but who nonetheless lend a little help to their friends. Among this crowd stand Algeria, Mali, Benin, Congo-Brazzaville, Guyana, and Barbados—all cooperating with the Soviets when in 1975 they vigorously transported Cuban soldiers by ship and by plane to Angola.

All three tiers of the Soviet alliance network seem to be strengthening—nothing dramatic, but something steady. The Soviet overseas military involvement is expanding—in contrast to that of the United States—while Western economic, political, and cultural interests abroad remain many times greater than those of the USSR. Since 1965 the number of U.S. bases overseas has declined by 40 percent. To compare the number of countries in which one of the superpowers has one hundred or more soldiers, since 1966 this total has declined by a sixth for the United States and has doubled for the Soviet Union. Since 1972, for the first time in modern history, the Soviet government stations a greater number of troops abroad than does the U.S. government.

EUROPEAN WOES AND TRIUMPHS

As the dates of these comparisons reveal, the decline of America's overseas military presence and the injuring of its alliance system did not begin with President Carter. Indeed, he entered in office to face a host of problems long afflicting NATO. These included:

a rising Western political consciousness that the Soviet military buildup has reached awesome proportions and shows no sign of slackening, regardless of Western policies;

a wave of technological breakthroughs on cruise missiles, neutron warheads, and guided antitank weaponry which fundamentally alter the nature of modern warfare and add new uncertainty to the already murky exercise of fashioning a military balance;

the absence of standardization, a lack which reached epidemic proportions with seven different main battle tanks in NATO, over one hundred types of tactical missile systems, guns of different caliber, and the rest of the now-familiar litany;

the economic stagnation and inflation gripping the West since 1973 and the related sense of extreme energy vulnerability;

a political malaise enveloping the Western world, where democratically elected governments seem incapable of meeting their citizens' expectations.

Such factors have been discussed and rehashed now for three decades. Mentioning these problems brings to mind the Walrus's question in *Alice in Wonderland*, " 'If seven maids with seven mops swept it for half a year, do you suppose that they could get it clean?' 'I doubt it,' said the Carpenter, and shed a bitter tear."

Mr. Carter lamented the untidiness and cleaned up some problems. In fact, Mr. Carter has done more for the military bolstering of NATO than any president since Dwight Eisenhower. Aside from augmentation in such dreary though critical areas as reserve mobilization, air defense, electronic warfare, rationalization, and logistics, Mr. Carter has set the course for alliance members to upgrade their defense allocations by at least 3 percent per year in real terms. Whether all members follow suit or not—now West Germany seems not, with a 2.9 percent increase scheduled for 1980, 2.1 percent for 1981, and 1.6 percent for the two successive years—the course has at least been set. And the U.S. government, at least, has adhered to it—neither any small accomplishment. Within NATO circles Mr. Carter has spread the gospel according to Adam Smith: "Defense is of more importance than opulence."

In addition, the president adroitly maneuvered the December 1979 NATO decision for the deployment of 572 Pershing IIs and cruise missiles in Europe beginning in 1983. The NATO decision was announced as unanimous. This is not exactly the case, but nearly so. Denmark and Norway were reluctant, but neither was asked to provide basing for the new missiles. The Netherlands (scheduled to take 48 ground-launched cruise missiles) and Belgium (also scheduled for 48) expressed reservations, but each is handling its domestic political problems with skill. The Italians were courageously supportive (scheduled to take 112), as were the British (160).

Most helpful of all, though, was West Germany (scheduled for 96 cruise missiles plus 108 Pershing IIs). Aside from Mr. Carter, Helmut Schmidt deserves most acclaim. He maneuvered for 85 percent of the delegates of his Social Democratic Party, meeting in Berlin in mid-December, to endorse the plan. Then his party stalwarts fanned out across Europe to drum up parliamentary support in Belgium and Holland and elsewhere.

Their arguments were sound and carried the day. It was explained that two-thirds of NATO's present tactical nuclear warheads have a range of under a hundred miles, most between ten to twenty miles. The new thousand-mile range weapons with good accuracy reduce the need for NATO's nuclear weapons to be fired on Western Europe's own territory. Also, existing systems (F—111s and Pershing Is) are vulnerable to a Soviet conventional or nuclear strike. Neither is a match for the SS—20 mobile missile or the Backfire bomber.

The arms control argument was stressed even more; without the NATO decision, any negotiations on European security would be doomed, as Moscow would lack incentive to limit its own forces. The U.S. pledge to withdraw 1,000 of its 7,000 short-range nuclear weapons and to dismantle 572 additional systems in Europe made it clear that the United States was not increasing the total size of its theater nuclear force.

AFRICA THROUGH EUROPE

Besides making progress in dealing with allies on strictly European affairs, Mr. Carter has been working closer with them on affairs outside the NATO confines, principally in Africa. This is a dramatic turnabout since the administration's first two years, when missionary zeal fashioned an African policy without much regard for local realities, U.S. national interests, or the tried and true experience of allies.

In the second half of 1978 and throughout 1979 the United States began to play second fiddle to the British on Rhodesian negotiations—previously UN Ambassador Andrew Young and the State Department's Anthony Lake had championed this cause—and to the French on Zaïre and on the handling of its former colonies such as the Central African

Republic. Befitting its frantic zeal in African diplomacy at the outset, the administration later fell back in exhaustion. President Carter and top advisors channeled their energy elsewhere, dipping back into African affairs only superficially when they could not afford to do otherwise. Budgetary constraints and perceived needs for greater military expenditures in Washington hushed up past rhetoric about extensive U.S. aid for African development. The domestic costs for the new and progressive African policy were seen as far outpacing international gains.

The new back-seat-to-allies approach on African diplomacy should be encouraged and expanded. For U.S. national interest is simply not as tied to Africa as to other areas of the world. The enormous cost in time and attention of the president and secretary of state was just not worth the price. Self-interest may be the driving consideration in America's future approach in Africa as it has long been in that of France (Adelman 1978, pp. 22–27).

ALLIED HELP IN THE PERSIAN GULF

U.S. national interest is strongly tied, of course, to the Persian Gulf. Indeed, President Carter's 1980 State of the Union address made it crystal clear that the Persian Gulf now falls within the U.S. defense parameter. This simply cannot be done without critical help from American allies. And this is perhaps the greatest area in which to expand allied cooperation and consultation over the coming years.

In a little-noted interview shortly after the State of the Union address Mr. Carter admitted forthrightly: "I don't think it would be accurate for me to claim that at this time, *or in the future*, we expect to have enough military strength and enough military presence there to defend the region unilaterally." This statement is quite accurate, but nonetheless it stands in stark contrast to the words and tone of the State of the Union address. Therein the president spoke exclusively of the American commitment and of the American protection of the region.

What precisely can our allies do there, and how can the United States encourage them? Actually, France and Britain can do a great deal and can use a great deal of encouragement and assistance.

France's security interest in the area has been growing apace. Today in Paris are detailed contingency plans for its own projection-of-power capabilities. And it has the means at its disposal: a modern division and a half (25,000 to 30,000 men) trained and equipped to move into the gulf region and prepositioned equipment, including more than 250 French-built AMX tanks in Saudi Arabia. Contingency plans call for these tanks and similar equipment to be manned by French soldiers in times of crisis.

And times of crisis have already arisen. It seems that on 23 November 1979 King Khalid contacted President Valéry Giscard d'Estaing to ask for French assistance. That was a few days after Saudi assault forces suffered severe casualties when vainly rushing the heavily armed and well-trained rebels holding the Grand Mosque. France quickly and silently dispatched a team of elite antiterrorist forces who took command of the 3,000 Saudi paratroopers and national guardsmen. French officers reorganized the assault plans and provided new equipment to enable the Saudis to triumph, before just as quietly departing.

Such a move is a small but critical demonstration of France's rapid deployment capability, which has been used on a larger scale in Africa to protect French interests. France could muster greater assistance in the Persian Gulf if the need arose. For a large portion of the French fleet, including one of its two aircraft carriers, stands on station in the Indian Ocean. The French have halted previous plans to evacuate the thousands of French troops stationed in its former colony of Djibouti, which is strategically located across from the southwest tip of the Arabian peninsula. As Paris recently realized, Djibouti would be key to any military operations in the region. And the region is, of course, vital to France, which takes more than two-thirds of its oil needs from the Persian Gulf.

Possible assistance from Britain is on a smaller scale, but is nevertheless important. London is cooperating fully with the United States to build up Diego Garcia as a major military base. Though Foreign Secretary Carrington recently said the Conservatives "did not see at the moment any need to reestablish any substantial permanent U.K. military presence in the area," that government has shelved the Labor government's previous plans to withdraw British presence from Oman in 1983 or 1984.

This is heartily welcomed since the British are playing a key role there. Some six hundred British officers command and train the small Omani armed forces at the behest of the Sultan of Oman, himself a graduate of Sandhurst who purchases mostly British equipment including Jaguar and Hunter jets. When Lord Carrington visited Oman last December, he assured the sultan that the British officers would serve in the Omani forces for as long as required. The British-Omani cooperation helped U.S. officials gain the sultan's acceptance of American use of those facilities on an as-needed basis.

Such French and British involvement in the Persian Gulf should be encouraged strongly by Washington. Whatever help can be rendered to their efforts should be given in a generous and far-sighted manner. It seems bizarre to recall that in the fall of 1977 the U.S. government refused to allot $300,000 for a continued British presence and operation of communications facilities on the Masira Island of Oman and denied the sultan his desire for closer security links with the United States to replace the then-departing British. Now, of course, U.S. officials are pleading with the same sultan for as much American-British presence and security links there as possible. This is a change in direction which is all to the good.

Besides such encouragement, Washington could take concrete steps to further collaboration and to better assure Persian Gulf security. First is the joint planning and joint contingency analysis which needs to be done by the Americans, the British, and the French—perhaps with involvement of friendly local authorities in the region. Second could be joint military exercises, the type done continually in Western Europe, to show a solidarity to potential adversaries and to show a competence and capability for concrete cooperation to ourselves. Third, intelligence on local political, economic, and military factors needs to be vastly expanded and better coordinated or shared by Paris, London, and Washington. Involvement of Israeli sources and tapping of Israeli intelligence might add to the overall capabilities.

Regardless, however, the intelligence exchanges should be vastly expanded. For the future threats in the area are unlikely to be bald and crude invasions, à la Afghanistan, but rather subtle and subterranean—Soviet aid to subvert the Saudi royal family or to help foster a coup in Oman or to push the Moscow-loving Tudeh Party in Iran. Future tests will demand better Western intelligence, since they will be far tougher to decipher—witness the ongoing confusion about the degree of Soviet involvement in the takeover of the Grand Mosque—but simpler to effect. Ambiguous situations are far more susceptible to remedy than unambiguous Afghanistan-type ones. With keener intelligence (shared widely among Western nations), less aversion to paramilitary delving abroad, and stauncher leadership, the possibilities of the West turning around the ghastly times are impressive.

ASIAN THREATS SEEN AS DIMINISHED

Asia took a back seat even to Africa from 1977 to 1979, to say nothing of being outshadowed by the focus on European NATO. This was no great surprise. Mr. Carter both inherited and reinforced a "Europe first" strategic outlook, due to six different factors.

Most potent is America's war-weariness with Asia in reaction to the Korean and Vietnam conflicts. This is felt and magnified by the composition of the Carter team, split between fervent Vietnam war-supporters or war-managers at the top level and opponents at the second echelon. Members of both groups shared the same trauma from different sides of the barricades. Both now wish, perhaps above all, to avoid any replay.

Second, threats in Europe are sharper, clearer, keener; there American troops and allies squarely face Soviet troops and allies. The neat bipolar cast does not apply in Asia where, even on the volatile Korean peninsula, U.S. troops and U.S. allies face no Soviet forces. Asia is more perplexing, subtle—a four-power region with the United States, the Soviet Union, the People's Republic of China (PRC), and Japan each having its own area of supremacy and influence and its own nuances in relations with the other three.

Third, the administration's human rights campaign dims the luster of Asian allies; overblown but real infringements exist in South Korea, the Philippines, Indonesia. In all friendly Asian states save Japan, in fact, Western Europe shines by comparison.

Fourth, the political, economic, and psychological malaise gripping Europe may demand a firm security undergirding as a foundation for rejuvenation. The blossoming of Asian economies and the absence of social or political pathology in Asia places no such demand.

Fifth, European allies are superb at working Washington. Asian allies are not. European leaders push their interests adroitly in the White House, in the bureaucracies, and on Capitol Hill. Members of the Asian crowd (with the half-exception of Taiwan) are either too deferential—Japanese Prime Minister Fukuda opposed the Korean troop withdrawal scheme, but in February 1977 was so subtle to Vice President Mondale as to be missed—or are simply ignorant on the means of influencing U.S. officialdom, as was evident in the heavy-handed Korean bribery case.

Last is the presumption that the Sino-Soviet dispute neutralizes dangers in Asia. The point has been made so well in the National Security Council and the Department of State that it has been picked up in Japan's Defense Agency (1978, p. 50) *White Paper.* "Because of the Sino-Soviet confrontation," it read, the "threat is directed toward the inland districts of the Asian continent, rather than toward the peripheral areas. This is an unignorable factor contributing to the military stability of the peripheral areas."

The analysis overlooks another "unignorable factor": that the Sino-Soviet dispute may also *upset* "the military stability of the peripheral areas." Soviet and Chinese assistance to North Vietnam in the past, as to North Korea in the present, has been reinforced (not mitigated) by their split. Neither can afford to deny an ally in need. The signing of the Sino-Japanese treaty in August 1978 may have prompted Moscow to sign its treaty with Vietnam three months later. With the guarantees thus offered, Vietnam launched its offensive against Cambodia the following month, spurring China to invade a strip of Vietnam two months later (February 1979). Such a chain reaction illustrates the error of being so consoled by the Sino-Soviet dispute, though it can and does occasionally work to our advantage.

The United States Playing the Japanese Card

But the Japanese enjoy being consoled. Having been jolted by perceived punctures in the U.S. commitment (as sketched above) and seeming unwilling as yet to provide for its own defense, Japan looks toward any ray of hope. One is now beaming from the emergence in Asian affairs of a friendly PRC.

Though Japan exports largely to the West and imports largely from the developing world—Persian Gulf oil constitutes a third of its total imports—its leaders widely believe that the nation's destiny will ultimately be shaped by the one billion Chinese. The attraction goes deeper than the economic level of potential markets to the psychological factors which simultaneously remind Japan of its cultural debt to the Chinese and yet highlight its existing economic, industrial, and technological superiority over them.

Such reawakened adoration, however, does not take the sting out of objectionable Soviet actions. These include the steaming of the Soviet Union's first aircraft carrier, the *Minsk*, off Tokyo Bay in June 1979, an event which stole banner headlines from the Western economic summit then in progress, and the Soviet military buildup on the four northern islands grabbed during World War II. Such moves raise doubts over whether Japan should continue as what ex-Prime Minister Sato dubbed a "completely new experiment in world history"—a weakly militarized major power (the second highest in gross national product [GNP] after the United States). Since the 1960s Japan has allocated less than 1 percent of its GNP to defense, less than any sizable nation on earth save Mexico and Chile.

Despite prodding from Peking and Washington—most recently when Defense Secretary Brown was there in January 1980—and provocations from Moscow, Tokyo is unlikely to undergo a defense "breakout" soon unless there were to be a volcanic action such as a second Korean conflict or a first Sino-Soviet one. For the Japanese government defines its role as carefully forging a wide consensus among key actors, not heroically leading them towards a clear objective. At present, a consensus is emerging that Japan's security is slipping, but there is none that Japan itself should do much about it.

Given this political reality does not mean the United States should give up prodding Japan. It should prod, but in ways which allow Japan to skirt the politically explosive breaking of the 1 percent barrier. This can and should be done in various ways.

First, the United States should deepen and widen U.S.¬Japanese defense cooperation on the operational level. Rhetoric on this score has shrouded the absence of any serious joint maneuvers and joint planning. Second, Japan should assume more than its current half of the $1.2 billion doled out annually for U.S. forces stationed on the islands. A year ago Tokyo made the first of what should become a series of steps by laying out some $100 million over the next two years to build new American bases there. Third, there should be an endorsement (or planting of the idea) of a Japanese "national security account" to fold in its military personnel and materiel costs—the current .9 percent—with those for oil and food stockpiles. This move would defuse the domestic political fallout inevitable with breaching the 1 percent barrier by obfuscating budgetary accounts.

Fourth, Japan should be pulled into the big leagues of global politics. It should become a subject, not an object of international affairs, a player pitching in for the industrialized democracies. Last summer the Tokyo Summit laid the foundation for this metamorphosis. It was the first international summit held there since the war. Then Japan, also for the first time in the postwar period, agreed to help bail out distant yet desperate Western friends. It allocated millions of dollars to aid Turkey and Egypt. Through financial aid to geostrategically vital allies, Japan can best help bolster Western security interests without sending fearful tremors throughout its own polity and throughout unforgetting smaller Asian states.

Japan Playing the U.S. Card

In turn, Japan should prod the United States to maintain its Pacific military presence at least at its present size. Clear voices from Tokyo should chime in with those of the incongruous twosome—U.S. Ambassador to Japan Mike Mansfield and Chinese Vice Premier Teng Hsiao-ping. Each launched his stellar career by clamoring for U.S. military retrenchment and each now clamors for U.S. military reinforcement. Recently Ambassador Mansfield publicly advocated that American forces in Asia "be beefed up and be given parity, at least, with those in the Atlantic and Western Europe." The ambassador pointed out the far way to go, since the United States has "213,000 troops in West Germany compared to 46,000 in Japan and probably 35,000 or so in Korea" (*Baltimore Sun*, 10 October 1979, p. 4).

Everyone Playing the China Card

A key strategic question facing Washington and Tokyo is whether to "play the China card"—whatever that means— or to tighten ties to the traditional friends of Taiwan and South Korea. These two are the primary—or the only— spots on earth where Japanese and American policies and goals diametrically oppose those of China.

Taiwan and South Korea have a population of more than 50 million—about half that of Japan—a sustained real growth rate over the past fifteen years of some 10 percent yearly, and enormous purchasing power. Together they buy three-fourths as much from Japan as the entire European

Community, which is the world's largest single market. The People's Republic of China has its staggering population, of course, but also has an impoverished economy and small purchasing power abroad. This Tokyo learned the hard way in 1978 when Peking reneged on hints of large contracts with Japanese firms.

Teng's modernization drive has already stalled because of an empty tank of foreign exchange and a lack of infrastructure. It is unlikely to get going for some time, thereby dashing plans and hopes for significant military modernization as well. The fact is, as Secretary of Defense Brown saw close up in January 1980, that China's military is fifteen to twenty years behind the times. Most equipment is remolded, tinkered, with weapons built from Russian blueprints of the 1950s. Its military weakness in everything but manpower — illustrated clearly in battle when the Chinese did not do well against the Vietnamese in February 1979—makes the "China card" more rhetoric than reality.

Besides, China is coming up against its "lost generation" of those now reaching adulthood who lack sufficient expertise because the country's schools and universities were long closed. Political turmoil may well emerge from an anticipated economic malaise or, more accurately, the lack of any economic structure. For modernization cannot easily endure as the leadership's guiding philosophy so long as the citizen's daily living conditions languish. Since ideology holds out no such promise for a more prosperous life—and hence cannot be disproved with hard facts—it can be used more prudently as the leadership's means of control over the masses and their allegiance.

This means that the 1980s may hold a dramatic move leftward in China, towards the philosophy of the Gang of Four. This can be facilitated by the generational shift in leadership from those walking alongside Mao in the Long March to their sons and daughters. So, in essence, Tokyo and Washington might not have much of a "China card" to play then if they have such to "play" now. The decade of euphoria over the mainland may have blinded both to more fruitful opportunities in countries opposed by the mainland, in South Korea and Taiwan.

LOOKING ELSEWHERE AROUND THE GLOBE

Though the "China card" may not provide all that the likes of National Security Advisor Brzezinski and others contend, it certainly does cause fits in the Kremlin. This may not prove to be "the answer" to grave Western security threats, but the process itself may be. This process involves reaching beyond traditional friends and allies in Europe and Japan to help provide for the common defense.

The Carter administration has identified the prime threat—the Russians—and the prime area of greatest U.S. national interest—Western Europe—yet it has, by too much highlighting, directed nearly all U.S. conventional firepower to the least likely theater of future conflict. By riveting such singular attention on Europe, the U.S. military has become less able to operate effectively where national interests appear less evident but where the threats are more evident and more likely to materialize in the 1980s.

Clearly, the Soviets have been most active in areas peripheral to Europe and Japan—in the Middle East–Persian Gulf region, Southwest and Southeast Asia, the Horn of Africa, and sub-Saharan Africa. Too much American preoccupation with the defense of European territory makes it handier for the Soviets to win high payoffs in efforts elsewhere; namely, around the flanks of NATO and Japan. This was seen most clearly in the Soviet invasion of Afghanistan.

So rather than to adopt a U.S. defense and deterrence posture of "NATO and Japan First," Washington might best prepare itself to defend "NATO and Japan Last," or more precisely, next to last before the U.S. homeland.

American efforts in such strategy would concentrate on defending against incursions in the rimlands which could go far to encircle Western Europe and Japan, or at least to crush them economically. The Arabian peninsula readily comes to mind in this regard, as do South Korea, Taiwan, sub-Saharan Africa, and sundry other spots.

The approach would also seek to foster security ties with regimes throughout the globe which, despite their other flaws, strive to counter Soviet expansionism. Such regimes would include not only China but such midlevel states as Brazil, Saudi Arabia, Israel and Egypt, Pakistan, Somalia, Kenya, South Africa, and others.

Not that such states will prove to be as appealing allies as the traditional European and Japanese friends. Indeed, most would not, since many do not share our practice of freedom nor do they extend human civil and political rights to all their people. Some practice domestic and international policies not to our liking.

Attention must be given to a government's internal legitimacy, however, in seeking its support. A dictator such as Somoza can never be a reliable ally because widespread opposition in his country will sustain instability and unreliability. In considering any potential alliance with a nondemocratic regime, therefore, we must insist on the fuller participation of the populace in the state's affairs as socioeconomic and security conditions permit; we must also require that the means used by the regime to elicit compliance will steadily become less harsh. These are conditions which manifestly do not exist in any Communist-controlled state. We should be prepared to encourage our allies in this direction, but only at times and under circumstances which would avoid strengthening the regional or even international support of our adversaries—as, for example, would clearly be the case today were the United States not to really behind Pakistan.

But in security affairs, as in so much of life, it is a choice not of black versus white but of the lesser evil. Edmund Burke once called political choices those "between the disagreeable and intolerable." Since Soviet-backed regimes most consistently and persistently violate human rights, since their international deportment is blatant, crude, and bold (as seen in Afghanistan), and since the Soviet Union itself is the sole power to endanger our nation and our way of life in the foreseeable future, this security approach of reaching beyond traditional friends to help provide peace and stability may be the shrewdest approach. Indeed, as time goes on it may become nigh unto unavoidable to U.S. security in the dangerous 1980s.

13

FRANCIS J. WEST, JR.

Conventional Forces
beyond NATO

Evolution of current U.S. strategy. Concentration on NATO's Central Front. The condition of U.S. military forces. Rapid Deployment Force. Fallacies in current assumptions. The need for conventional essential equivalence — submarines, bombers, missiles, TACAIR, infantry forces, space weapons.

A strategy devised in 1969 determines defense forces and budgets. That strategy is out of date for the 1980s, as explained in this chapter. A different strategy is suggested, leading to a different set of policy concepts and force priorities.

To be a superpower means—by definition—to possess overwhelming military force. There are only two super-powers, and one of these has no claim to that status other than military power. In contrast, the United States has for several years sincerely attempted to underplay the role of military force in the conduct of foreign policy. The American concessions in the Strategic Arms Limitation Talks, SALT I and SALT II, were not trivial; military aid was refused to Turkey, to Pakistan, and to the pro-Western side in the Angolan civil war; the B–1 bomber was cancelled and a nuclear carrier was vetoed; for months on end the U.S. responses to the Iranian hostage crisis were appeals to the United Nations and a pledge not to use force. However, when the Soviets invaded Afghanistan in early 1980 President Carter said: "My opinion of the Russians has changed more drastically in the last week than even the previous two-and-a-half years."

Presumably, as a result of this change in opinion, U.S. efforts to eschew military power will be reassessed. Part of that reassessment must include a review of our conventional military strategy.

HISTORY

U.S. general purpose forces in the 1960s were theoretically sized to fight simultaneously "two and a half wars" against Russia, China, and some lesser foe like North Korea. While defense resources did not match this ambitious theory, U.S. nuclear superiority compensated for our shortcomings. In 1968 the lack of resources for "two and a half wars" was manifest. The Vietnam war was consuming the energies of all four services. Our forces for the North Atlantic Treaty Organization (NATO) were in dreadful shape. We lacked the strength to respond when the North Koreans seized the

Pueblo. The request by the U.S. Joint Chiefs of Staff (JCS) for 200,000 additional troops during the Tet offensive was a disastrous political ploy to force President Johnson to place the nation on a wartime footing and to reconstitute our conventional forces worldwide.

By 1970, in recognition of the Chinese-Soviet hostility, the Nixon administration had reduced defense planning from "two and a half wars" to "one and a half wars." Either the United States and its allies might fight the Soviets or the Chinese, but not both simultaneously. With the celebrated opening to China and with our withdrawal from Vietnam, the strategy was further modified: U.S. forces would concentrate on NATO, while the Nixon Doctrine of some U.S. support but no U.S. land forces was applied toward Asia. Given congressional revulsion about Vietnam, defense budgets continued to fall and U.S. efforts to give military or covert assistance to nations as diverse as Turkey and Angola were curtailed. In fact, President Ford fired his secretary of defense—James Schlesinger—in part for arguing too hard for a larger defense budget. Détente, arms control agreements, and vague political and economic leverage points ("linkages") were the preferred tools for coping with Soviet military power.

CURRENT STRATEGY

President Carter took office promising to cut the defense budget, to drastically reduce Soviet and U.S. nuclear stockpiles, to curb the Central Intelligence Agency (CIA), and to lessen U.S. involvement in the affairs of other nations. The divergent trends in Soviet and U.S. military strength, however, were very troublesome to the Pentagon. The initial response of the new civilian Pentagon staff was to write a study—called PRM–10—which acknowledged the consequence of the trends: in a war with the Soviet Union, West Germany appeared no more defensible than anywhere else. The predictable outcry from NATO and from American foreign policy interest groups resulted in a small increase in the U.S. defense budget and a reaffirmation that the strategy of "one and a half wars" had not changed. While in the post-Vietnam climate U.S. military efforts outside Western Europe were suspect, none could object to a strengthening of NATO. The Central Front—West Germany—was the heart of NATO and a region of heavy Soviet buildup. Consequently from 1977 through 1979 the Pentagon set in motion plans to increase rapid reinforcement to that theater by 40 percent and to raise by 1985 U.S. Army procurement investment by 66 percent. These were remarkable achievements, especially on a defense budget which from 1977 through 1979 rose in real terms by only 1 percent a year.

U.S. increases for the Central Front were basically financed by reducing investment in U.S. forces for other theaters. For instance, the U.S. Navy/Marine Corps from 1977 through 1979 were substantially reduced in funding; the ship-building budget was essentially halved. As the magazine *Armed Forces Journal* explained it (October 1979, p. 34):

One way of looking at the Carter Administration's defense priorities and its view of the Navy's overall value is by a simple budget comparison. In the fall of 1976, when Jimmy Carter was elected, the Defense Department's five year plan gave the Navy 33% of the total defense budget; by FY85 the Navy will be down to 28% of DoD's total budget ... a net loss in real buying power of some $35 to $40 billion.

Since Soviet capabilities were growing across the board and not just relative to West Germany, this shift in U.S. resources meant that military balances outside the Central Front, which in large measure meant naval forces, were permitted to deteriorate. Yet U.S. naval power, in the overwhelming majority of crises where American forces have been deployed, has provided an unquestioned superiority at sea and an ability to project air strikes or marines ashore. This power has assured the bargaining strength of our policymakers. While we have been involved in several land wars in the past third of a century, no nation has dared to challenge us at sea.

So civilian Pentagon staff tried to sidestep the consequences of the deterioration outside the Central Front by defining a NATO war in which certain NATO nations (and associates) need not be defended; namely, Norway on the Northern Flank and Greece, Turkey, Israel, and Egypt on the Southern Flank. When this refined strategy was leaked to the press, there again was an uproar and Defense Secretary Brown in 1978 flew to Norway and to other concerned nations to reassure our allies that we could and would reinforce them. But unlike the case of the Central Front, the secretary's words were not backed by the allocation of resources. Instead, the resource focus remained the Central Front case.

In 1969 five conditions underlay the "one and a half war" strategy. First, no one paid it close attention, since the focus of resources and of policy was upon Vietnam. Second, the Soviets were a continental, not a global, power. So Soviet conventional forces were not seen as a threat beyond the NATO region. Third, U.S. naval power provided us undisputed global reach. So, for instance, we could blockade North Vietnam despite the presence of Soviet shipping. Fourth, the Persian Gulf was ignored. Fifth, where we were conventionally weak — in NATO's center as well as on NATO's flanks — we could deter aggression by extending the umbrella of our nuclear superiority.

ADEQUACY OF THE CURRENT STRATEGY

Not one of those conditions any longer applies. The "one and a half war" strategy is out of date for the 1980s. On the Central Front we cannot today credibly threaten escalation above the conventional level. The Soviets possess a chemical capability; we do not. For theater nuclear war, the Soviets have deployed an array of new systems while we are several years away from modernizing our systems. U.S. nuclear superiority is gone. In fact, we will not have satisfactory strategic "essential equivalence" until the first-strike vulnerability of our ICBM (intercontinental ballistic missile) force is corrected, presumably by 1990 with the deployment of the mobile MX (missile experimental) missile system.

How, then, do we "extend" deterrence in the 1980s from the Central Front to NATO's flanks or elsewhere? Only by assumption. It is currently assumed that the "one war" of the "one and a half war" strategy is limited to a battle on the Central Front and that the United States can prepare (allocate resources) for that war under the assumption that fighting will not spread to other theaters. NATO forces in the Center Region will be so strong that the Soviets will not have sufficient forces to divert to other theaters. Nor will the Soviets start a war except on the Central Front because, if they do, NATO has the escalation option of initiating conventional war in the Center Region. In such escalation, Soviet forces would be caught out of position and the resultant losses, including portions of Eastern Europe, would not, to the Soviets, be worth gains elsewhere. In other words, the essence of the "one and a half war" strategy for the 1980s is that, if the center is strong, that strength will extend the deterrence of conflict to other regions where the military balance is even less favorable.

As to the "half war," until late in 1979 that case was given short shrift in terms of resources. This reflected our Vietnam experience. In 1977 President Carter ordered the phased withdrawal of U.S. ground forces from South Korea as the United States continued its retreat toward a U.S./West European–only axis. The concerns of the JCS, of the Japanese, and of the military intelligence community eventually changed the president's mind. But the order did illustrate the seeming illegitimacy of U.S. military force as a foreign policy instrument, except in the case of Western Europe. In 1978, however, the Chief of Staff of the U.S. Army took public exception to the exclusive focus upon the Center Region and urged the creation of an army "Unilateral Corps" for operations outside NATO. Early in 1979 Dr. Brown did say that the United States might use force to stop a Soviet invasion of Iran. The example was intended as a measure of U.S. capabilities for the "half war," not as a prediction of events (Brown 1980, p. 107). Left unspecified were the size, composition, and resupply of the U.S. contingency force. The "half war" idea lay dormant until the summer of 1979, when the discovery of a Soviet brigade in Cuba prompted President Carter to declare that any Caribbean adventurism by the brigade would be checkmated by the movement of an American brigade. In effect, the president ordered that U.S. forces be planned and procured to combat, without NATO participation, Soviet troops far from Soviet borders.

At the same time, the SALT II hearings in the Senate highlighted the poor condition of U.S. forces. Senator Sam Nunn (D-GA) and others announced they would not vote to ratify SALT II unless the U.S. defense budget was increased. When President Carter agreed, money was available to the Pentagon for the "half war" force. Dr. Brown decided that, of the $11 billion initially set aside for the force, $8 billion would be spent on tankers and transport aircraft. These aircraft could move men and equipment in the event of a short-warning "one war" in NATO's Center Region. They also could move up to 110,000 soldiers or marines to the scene of a "half war." The "half war" force was aptly called the Rapid Deployment Force (RDF), since the conceptual and budgetary emphasis were upon swift movement at the expense of combat capability. The concept was to move into a trouble spot before the shooting began. American troops, once on the ground, would not have the equipment or the resupply to fight credibly until sea lines of communication were established. They could, of course, cope with guerrilla bands or "student" mobs. But more important, their presence would serve as a tripwire to deter external aggression, since an attack against U.S. troops would be an act of war against the United States. In essence, the RDF appeared to be a code word for protecting the Persian Gulf oilfield against Iraq and/or the Soviet Union, a task of central importance after the seizure of the American embassy in Iran and the Soviet invasion of Afghanistan.

In 1969 the "one and a half war" strategy referred to a full-scale war throughout NATO against the Soviet Union and Warsaw Pact as well as, simultaneously, a "half war" against a non-Soviet power such as North Korea. In 1979 the "one war" strategy referred to a land war only on the Central Front of NATO, while the simultaneous "half war" referred to a U.S.–Soviet land battle somewhere outside NATO.

Some directive is necessary for planning and budgeting forces, and the "one and a half war" concept provides that direction for the 1980s. Dr. Brown (1980, p. 100) has said the "one and a half war" concept "has been the case since 1969 and [is necessary so that we] can be quite clear about our objectives and . . . military capabilities." Much has changed since 1969, and Table 1 attempts to summarize those changes.

The concept has several serious flaws. To assume the "one war" will be mutually restricted (by the United States and by the Soviet Union) to the Central Front of Europe is poor

Table 1
U.S. Force Planning Assumptions

Basic Strategy	1969	1979
"One war"		
U.S. plans to fight PRC	yes	no
U.S. plans to fight USSR:		
in Center Region	yes	yes
in Northern Region	yes	no
in Southern Region	yes	no
"Half war"		
U.S. plans simultaneously to fight		
USSR outside NATO	no	yes
U.S. plans simultaneously to fight USSR		
outside NATO and to fight North Korea	no	yes
Contributing factors		
U.S. possesses an edge in:		
conventional land forces	no	no
TACAIR	yes	yes
naval	yes	yes
chemical	no	no
theater nuclear	yes	no
strategic	yes	no
U.S. GNP devoted to defense	8%	5%
Soviet military spending as a percentage		
of U.S. military spending	80%	150%

strategy and poorer history, given the course of prior world wars. The Central Front—only strategy is an assumption driven by undue budgetary pressures. To assume that NATO strength on the Central Front can extend deterrence to other theaters is to ignore a decade of trends. The United States, by 1979, had lost the credible threat of escalation dominance. So it was only proper and prudent to build NATO's conventional strength in the Center Region. It was not prudent to assume that this effort—which was, in 1980, still fledgling—spread an umbrella of deterrence over other areas. Soviet strength had grown too powerful for the United States to regain the 1969 balance of power. It has not been strategically sound to neglect NATO's flanks and to discount U.S. strengths outside NATO's land mass (e.g., U.S. submarines) as a means of offsetting some Soviet strengths and NATO weaknesses. In sum, the "one war" concept is restrictive in focus and outdated in its concept of extended deterrence.

As to the "half war," the concept of the RDF was put together piecemeal in reaction to external events; e.g., the fall of the shah, the war in Yemen, the Soviet brigade in Cuba, the seizure of the U.S. embassy in Iran, the attack upon Mecca, the Soviet invasion of Afghanistan, etc. The RDF has great merit. But it cannot stand alone as a deterrent force suddenly flown into a crisis-wracked nation. On the one hand, if the United States is willing to commit the RDF, it should be willing to take less drastic steps in the same region, such as intelligence surveillance, covert political and paramilitary action, military assistance and training, air defense and close air support by sea-based aircraft. On the other hand, if U.S. soldiers with loaded rifles (instead of unarmed F–15s) are flown into a country like Saudi Arabia, the emphasis should be upon a combat deployment force.

The difference is not trivial. It is not credible that the United States would go to war against a capable foe (such as Iraq, let alone the Soviet Union) without prepositioning large amounts of supplies on land and at sea and without secure resupply by sea. This means a larger U.S. Navy and U.S. land bases in the Middle East. Without these prerequisites the U.S. Joint Chiefs of Staff, in their enthusiasm for the RDF as something rather than nothing, run the danger of endorsing a placebo. In the early 1960s all four services came up with gimmicks for combating the Viet Cong, gimmicks which distracted from serious strategic planning and which held the false promise of success at a cheap cost. Current defense planning holds the same false glitter when "one war" is, by the assumption of extended deterrence, limited to the Center Region of Europe while the response to the "half war" will be the airlift of a few infantry divisions supplemented by a few tactical air wings and carriers.

The "one and a half war" concept simply won't suffice for the 1980s. As the Iranian seizure of the U.S. embassy too graphically illustrated to the world, Third World nations are not awed by American power and will be quite prepared and able to fight the RDF when it lands. No longer applicable are analogies to Lebanon and the Dominican Republic, where the presence of American force stifled resistance. The early Japanese successes in World War II contributed to later Asian rebellion against European colonialism. The North Vietnamese victory over Southeast Asia and the long, televised imprisonment of Americans in Iran have contributed to future challenges against U.S. interests which will have to be met with force, not with presence and promise.

To the extent that perceptions of American weakness have fueled global instabilities and threats to U.S. interests, a change in American rhetoric alone will not convey strength and restore stability. The change in the 1980 U.S. defense budget was intended not as a response to Soviet aggression but as a means of securing a treaty the Soviets desired. To improve chances of Senate ratification of SALT II, in November of 1979 President Carter agreed to increase the defense budget by slightly less than 5 percent a year. When the Ira-

nians seized our embassy and the Soviets subsequently
seized Afghanistan, Mr. Carter saw no reason to further increase the defense budget.

Military personnel pay—which accounts for half the
defense budget—is currently 5 percent below inflation. If
and when military pay is raised to the level of inflation, little
real budgetary increase will remain for procurement and
research and development (R&D), where the Soviets are outspending us by 70 percent and have over the past decade
deployed $100 billion more in weapon systems than we have.
As Dr. Iklé's article in this book explains, the enormity of
that gap in military systems is well-nigh overwhelming. It
most certainly will not be rectified by a 5 percent increase in
U.S. defense funds, at least half of which should in all decen-
cy go toward pay. Nor will it be rectified by clinging to a 1969
"one and a half war" strategy whose assumptions are trim-
med to fit the budget.

PROPOSED CHANGES TO THE
CURRENT STRATEGY

It is, of course, easier to criticize than to construct. But the
Defense Department's (DOD's) fixation with the Central
Front in 1977, in 1978, and in 1979 has not been helpful to
national interests. Our forces on the Central Front needed
modernization. That is true of all our forces. The focus,
however, on one region of the world distorted both policy and
fiscal priorities. The prime military challenges to U.S. interests lie outside West Germany. Given the allocation of the
1980 defense budget, only in rhetoric is the importance of
forces beyond NATO acknowledged. For instance, the size of
the U.S. Marine Corps in 1980 is reduced and a shipbuilding
budget is requested which is smaller than Congress
authorized in 1979. So a starting point for conventional force

planning in the 1980s must be an understanding of why the 1969 "one and a half war" strategy is out of date.

A second measure must be a substantial increase in the defense budget. We see the magnitude of the task by looking at what the navy needs. To modernize—but not enlarge— our navy would require an increase in the shipbuilding budget of at least 30 percent and in the aircraft procurement budget of about 100 percent. Each year's deferral of such investment simply increases the total amount eventually required. This raises the odds that, rather than pay a staggering bill several years from now, we will eventually rationalize that being second to one really means we are superior to most.

A third step is the allocation of that budget in accord with a different principle than that of "one and a half wars," which is a tit-for-tat strategy designed to match Soviet strength with U.S. strength, checker for checker, as it were. But the Soviets are willing to invest in more checkers. Instead, we should view the geopolitical contest as a chess game and maneuver our force pieces where we hold relative advantages. We should espouse a principle of conventional essential equivalence which reinforces U.S. points-of-force leverage. Several systems hold special promise.

• U.S. submarines hold "awesome" technological edge over Soviet submarines and surface vessels.* The SSN (nuclear submarine) is among our last clear warfighting advantages. We should increase our submarine fleet and incorporate it as a tool of conflict resolution in U.S.-Soviet crises. Inherent in the concept of the RDF is the possibility of a limited U.S.-Soviet war outside NATO. In such a war, there is a spectrum of uses for our submarines—from blockade through underwater warfare in several regions, including Soviet home waters.

---

*Speech by Secretary of the Navy W. Graham Claytor, Washington, DC, 24 May 1978.

• A long-range, penetrating bomber with heavy conventional as well as nuclear payload capacity offers substantial force flexibility. In a worldwide conventional war, the Soviets would have to be quickly denied the use of their developing overseas bases. In a limited war, there is a growing need for "smart bombs." But as any combat infantry officer knows, there still remain classes of targets, including dug-in troops, for which massive bombing is required.

• The cruise missile for land and sea attack is needed on board our submarines and surface combatants. For years the U.S. Navy has been criticized for placing all its offensive eggs in a dozen carrier baskets. To diversify naval offensive striking power, the sea-launched cruise missile is needed in large numbers. This need conflicts with the arms-control goals of SALT II, which forbids the deployment of long-range sea-launched cruise missiles. The Soviets are fearful of a U.S. Navy which could strike their shores with nuclear or conventional missiles launched from hundreds of submarines and surface combatants.

• TACAIR in the antiarmor mission needs improvement. Compared to any other nation, the United States dedicates a much higher percentage of its defense budget to conventional tactical air. Part of the reason is cultural. The aircraft is the American way of war: it combines high technology, physical dexterity, intelligence, adventure, and individuality. Part of the reason is logistics and geography. The United States must prepare for battles thousands of miles away. Consequently, fire support for the infantry must be mobile. We cannot stockpile tanks and artillery around the world. So our TACAIR must offset the trend in other nations toward armor and self-propelled artillery. In this antiarmor mission our TACAIR forces need better weapons and more training. Much more training.

• Likewise, our infantry forces are going to meet armor and they need a system and training to defeat it. Especially will the Rapid Deployment Force confront a severe problem. Armor is the greatest single threat to our ability to defend Western Europe and to our projection of land power ashore in the Mideast or the Persian Gulf. We are the most advanced technological nation on earth. As the armored knight after the Battle of Crécy was vulnerable to infantry longbowmen, why shouldn't armor be vulnerable to our infantry in the 1980s? The standard response is that infantry forces crumble under the fear engendered by armored shock power — the noise, the concussion, the dust and dirt, the confusion, the volume, strength, and suddenness of the onslaught. That may be correct throughout the 1980s. But on the one hand, DOD is creating an RDF and is placing $8 billion into additional airlift to fly the RDF quickly into combat. On the other hand, DOD is sitting on top of a lightweight, rapid-fire anti-tank gun it has chosen not to fund. Why?

• Finally, we should look toward weapons in space and against those in space. As with cruise missiles, we have, for reasons of concern about arms control, refrained from exploiting an area of strong technological advantage. We have done this despite knowledge that the Soviets are developing antisatellite weapons. By the end of the 1980s space will be less mystic. Arms control is not going to curb technology and it is not going to change the human condition. In a limited war, we and the Soviets are going to use space as we will the sea and the land: as each dimension accords to our advantage. So in designing a conventional force strategy for the 1980s, we should include rather than exclude space.

To conclude, a strategy of conventional essential equivalence must attend to several military balances in addition to the Central Front.

(1) Cuban mischief in the Caribbean, Africa, and the Mideast merits a response, most probably in terms of economic sanctions and CIA covert action.

(2) We have alienated our traditional and increasingly powerful allies in South America, such as Brazil and Argentina. We should repair those relations and at least invite those nations once again to receive military training in the United States. After all, through the beginning of 1980 we extended that privilege to Khomeini's Iran, scarcely a paradigm of human rights.

(3) Korea merits the continued presence of American forces.

(4) The pressure upon Japan to do more for the sake of her own security should be unremitting. We simply haven't the naval and marine forces to continue on a steady level our presence in the western Pacific and simultaneously to maintain a strong naval force in the Indian Ocean.

(5) Conversely, we should curb our tendency "to play the China card." It only points to American weakness. China is not powerful or stable and has its own designs on "playing the American card," leading to increased U.S.–Soviet tensions and possible war. It is poor strategy to antagonize the Soviet Union to no purposeful end. China has little more to offer in insuring global stability and a world conducive to American and Western interests and values.

(6) On the Northern Flank of NATO, what is needed in northern Norway is a credible reinforcement package of mobile land forces and TACAIR. The U.S. Marine Corps fills that bill. But the marine budget has been steadily reduced, while the RDF is now seen as a more pressing marine-related mission. In addition, Norway has not raised its defense budget to cope with its acknowledged shortcomings. Since the Northern Flank is as stable as the Central Front in terms of foreseeable causes for conflict, deficiencies in that region do not appear to merit U.S. budgetary priority at this time.

(7) We must simultaneously aid and shore up relations with Turkey, whose position is pivotal. Toward Turkey, Israel, and Egypt, we must do more in a series of publicly separate bilateral arrangements. Bases are bound to follow,

reconstructed in Turkey and negotiated in the Sinai or along the Mediterranean coast.

(8) While a flexible conventional force is necessary because the locale of crises is not precisely predictable, the odds are that for the next several years the cauldron of instability will be the Middle East/Persian Gulf area. Our efforts toward the Central Front will not aid us, by extended deterrence, in that region. Naval and marine forces will. But they were the forces that were reduced to increase forces on the Central Front. So for the next few years at least, while we search for and construct bases, we are going to have to stretch even more thinly our naval forces. For the longer term we must increase our shipbuilding program.

Bases are a mixed blessing. A base takes two or more years and several billions of dollars to build or develop. Additional bases in the Mideast are needed, among other reasons, to allow the U.S. Army and Air Force to share the burden of unaccompanied hardship tours with the U.S. Navy and Marine Corps. We are on the verge of running our naval forces into the ground as we try to meet commitments in three oceans with a two-ocean navy. Since bases serve as jumping-off points, they do deter foes and reassure allies. By its presence, a base also constitutes a U.S. endorsement of the host nation. For reasons of human rights policies and regional rivalries (e.g., Arab fears of being manipulated for Israeli interests), this often results in political pain to the United States. Conversely, many national leaders are concerned about American fidelity when the going gets tough. For these reasons the United States must tread gingerly in establishing land bases or home ports. But tread it must, for the stakes in the Mideast region are too high not to become physically involved.

In summary, the current defense strategy of conventional forces for "one war" on the Central Front and of airlift for the "half war" is simply inadequate. Unless we receive a shock equivalent to the Chinese attack across the Yalu, it would be unrealistic to expect sudden major increases in the defense budget. So, on a constrained budget, we must trade off further prepositioned stocks in West Germany in order to have adequate forces beyond NATO. We must exploit our points-of-force leverage. We must play chess instead of checkers. We should replace the 1969 "one and a half war" strategy with a broad concept of several military balances and a design of conventional essential equivalence which employs our relative warfighting advantages.

14

LEONARD SULLIVAN, JR.

Correlating
National Security
Strategy and
Defense Investment

The need for modernization of strategies and equipment. Costs of system replacement programs. Deficiencies in procurement, manpower, and readiness. Conventional warfare and strategic warfare. Defense outlays and the federal budget.

The United States seldom concerns itself with its national security. Presidential candidates make campaign pledges to

cut defense spending before they really understand the problems. The White House, the Congress, and their staffs fret
with budgetary details, extract their political cuts, and never
debate national security policy. No basic changes have been
made in national strategy in fifteen years despite vast international changes, increased dependencies, and a far more
outward-reaching Soviet Union.

There is an increasing sense at the current time that the
chips are down. At this writing, American hostages are still
held in Iran and Soviet forces have occupied Afghanistan.
The president has asked the Senate to defer further consideration of SALT II (Strategic Arms Limitation Talks II)
ratification—a treaty which would acknowledge and accept
some measure of Soviet nuclear superiority. The NATO
(North Atlantic Treaty Organization) nations have accepted,
at least in principle, the need to modernize theater nuclear
weapons. The United Nations has roundly condemned both
Iran and the Soviets for their recent actions. Economic sanctions are beginning to be applied against both.

All of these events, taken together, have at least partially
awakened the people of the United States and the Congress
to the fact that we have reached a milestone concerning
present and future U.S. posture, influence, and security—in
a world quite clearly devoid of stability, reliability, or com-
patibility with our peaceful and unambitious national objectives.

We have, then, a rare opportunity to debate the state of our
national security. At issue are our national strategies and objectives, our resolve, our priorities, our willingness to forego
current desires to invest in the future, our military power—
and our willpower. The purpose of this chapter is to contribute some rough analytic bases for this long-overdue
debate.

The sustaining of national military power is a long-term
issue. Existing forces do not atrophy overnight. It takes
twenty to forty years for existing military equipment to wear

out or become totally obsolete, and it takes ten to twenty years to develop a new or markedly different military posture. For instance, it could easily take twenty years to rebuild a 600-ship navy—or to totally reconfigure our strategic forces.

We must take the long view and plan ahead. It is the cumulative effort in capital investment over the past ten years that will dictate our capabilities ten years hence. Our cumulative efforts and investment over the next ten years will dictate our posture and capabilities twenty years hence. The currently recognized changes in the conventional and nuclear force balances between the Soviet Union and ourselves have resulted from a slow, deliberate, continuous effort on the part of the United States.

THE BASIC ISSUES

The basic issues are very simple and very important. The United States has not changed its basic strategies for preserving its national security for well over a decade—despite extraordinary changes in the international political and economic scene, and despite fundamental changes in both world and regional balances of power and in the total correlation of world forces.

U.S. strategy for the deterrence of conventional war still revolves around the "one-and-a-half war" strategies of the late 1960s, although the primary emphasis of this administration centers on containing Soviet aggression in the NATO area. Considerations for actually fighting such a world war are seriously incomplete. The strategy itself is probably no longer appropriate or adequate.

U.S. strategy for the deterrence of nuclear war still revolves around the Triad of nuclear forces (ICBMs, bombers, SSBNs), a strategy deriving from the early 1960s when the United States had a virtual monopoly on such forces. Considerations for actually fighting a nuclear war are not only nonexistent; they are contrary to current administration policy. The strategy itself is probably no longer appropriate or adequate.

For ten years, defense spending for capital equipment to modernize our conventional forces has been at best half of that required to offset capital stock depreciation, let alone obsolescence. Our conventional forces age approximately six months each year, and well over half of their useful life has already been consumed. We probably cannot avoid continued force level reductions, particularly in our naval forces.

For ten years, defense spending for capital investment in new weapon systems to modernize our strategic forces has been less than half that required to offset capital stock depreciation, let alone technical obsolescence. This is true regardless of the proposed SALT II force levels.

For ten years, defense spending for items of capital consumption and capital protection during wartime usage has been less than half that required to sustain an extended war—conventional or nuclear—or to assure a favorable outcome and permit rapid postwar recovery. For twenty years, our industrial mobilization base has been permitted to atrophy and disappear.

In short, our conventional and nuclear strategies are seriously outdated, and for many years we have not been investing enough in force modernization to even assure the continued realism of supporting *lesser* strategies.

Statements to the effect that we cannot afford nationally to keep our defenses strong appear to be self-fulfilling but are clearly misleading. Moreover, annual real defense spending growth rates of 3 to 5 percent will at best sustain—or very marginally improve—the current force status over the next ten years. Much more is needed.

Current Equipment Replacement Costs

The first fundamental question concerns how much we should be spending annually for equipment modernization. There is no single precise answer to this, since it depends on many different factors. Nonetheless, a good ballpark estimate can be derived by adding up all the equipment of each type we currently have in inventory, dividing the number of each type by its anticipated useful life (generally between twenty-five and forty years), and multiplying by the average current replacement unit cost. This provides an annual steady-state modernization funding requirement in today's dollars. Useful life estimates must include peacetime attrition. This is essentially the depreciation schedule for the current inventory at today's replacement costs.

The result of this calculation is shown in Table 1 in a highly aggregated fashion. It indicates that we should be spending $19 billion annually (in FY 1980 dollars) for our conventional force modernization: $9 billion for navy and air force TACAIR and army helicopters, $3 billion for armored vehicles and air defense systems, and $7 billion for general purpose ships and submarines. Current outlays are roughly half of that desired figure—with the navy's shipbuilding program lagging the most.

Another $11 billion should be spent annually for strategic force modernization, with or without SALT. Bombers and ICBMs (intercontinental ballistic missiles) require over $6 billion annually, while SSBNs (ballistic missile submarines, nuclear) and their missiles require roughly $3 billion annually. Another $1.5 billion appears to be needed to cover our various space programs. Currently, there is virtually no modernization procurement for the air force systems, and SSBN modernization rates will not offset approaching block obsolescence of the POSEIDON fleet—built in three to four years.

Table 1

Required Procurement Outlays for Steady-State Modernization at Current Sophistication Levels

	Billions of FY 1980 Dollars
Conventional forces	$19.0
Air force TACAIR	$4.8
Naval TACAIR	3.2
Army helicopters	1.0
Armored vehicles	1.5
SA missile systems	1.5
General purpose ships and submarines	7.0
Strategic forces	11.0
Bombers and ICBMs	6.5
SSBNs	3.0
Space	1.5
Spares, mods, and consumables	20.0
Army	6.2
Navy	7.0
Air force	6.5
Other	0.3
Annual total required	50.0

Finally, spares, modifications (mods), and consumables require roughly $20 billion annually, of which about $4 billion is in army ammunition alone to build up war reserve stocks. We are at present spending roughly half of what is needed in all of these miscellaneous categories.

To a first-order approximation, we are spending $25 billion annually where we should be spending $5 billion in FY 1980 dollars. Our modernization rates have not kept pace with modernization requirements, and they are not doing so now if we are to retain constant force levels and equipment levels and if we are to avoid having obsolete equipment in the inventory. We must either spend more, buy equipment half as expensive, or make substantial cuts in existing force levels. At our current spending rates and purchase costs, the whole U.S. military equipment inventory is aging at the rate of half a year annually, and well over half of its projected useful life is already gone.

Quality Growth in Unit Costs

The picture is really somewhat gloomier than is indicated in Table 1. Every year our weapon systems and equipment become somewhat more expensive—even in constant, no-inflation dollars. Again to a very crude approximation, our equipment is becoming more expensive at the rate of approximately 6 percent each year. This is roughly equivalent to the consumer quality index on commercial products, which increases at a rate of about 0.5 percent per year.

This is shown on Figure 1. Over a period of years we buy different models of a given type of system. Each successive model is more expensive than its predecessor by about 3 percent per year. Then we develop and produce a replacement type, and product improve it for several years. Each new system is far more expensive than its predecessor, so that the net rate of increase in weapon systems unit costs has been running close to 6 percent. To prevent even more rapid annual growth, the Defense Department has cancelled some high-cost programs and gone to a high-low mix of new weapon systems.

Thus it is not enough to try to achieve a constant $5 billion annual modernization spending rate in FY 1980 dollars. If we continue to increase the technological sophistication at the rates evidenced over the past twenty years, we should be spending $50 billion in FY 1980, $90 billion by 1990, and $160 billion by 2000—all in 1980 dollars. Even if there were no current spending shortfalls in military pay affecting military skill levels and retention, and even if there were no shortages in the operations and maintenance account affecting military readiness, 6 percent annual procurement growth could barely be achieved within a total budget that is increasing at 3 percent annually.

Overall procurement deficiencies, manpower deficiencies, and readiness deficiencies cannot be eliminated within President Carter's recently proposed 4.5 percent annual growth in defense spending in the outyears. Much larger supplemental appropriations in the nearyears are needed. Neither the Department of Defense, the Congress, nor the White House appears to understand the extent to which we are mortgaging our future defense capabilities. No one appears to be looking further ahead than the next budget cycle. No one has a long-range plan. No one is looking beyond near-term political expediency. No one, that is, except the Soviets.

By comparison, it is clear that the Soviets are spending somewhat more than is required to maintain steady-state modernization, even assuming a somewhat shorter lifetime for their equipment. In other words, their funding profiles would indicate that in certain areas they should be force-building. And they are. Clearly, they appear to have a long-range plan to maintain and augment current force levels.

Figure 1
Required Procurement Outlay Growth for
Steady-State Modernization at Current
Sophistication Growth Rates

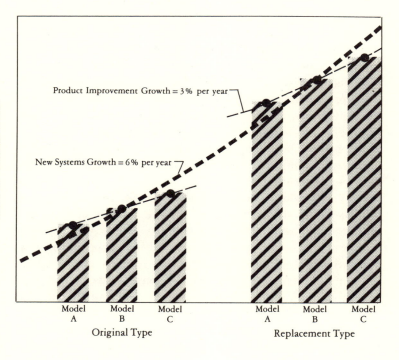

CONVENTIONAL WARFARE STRATEGIES

The foregoing discussion has attempted to demonstrate that current Department of Defense procurement funding is only about half of that required to modernize current force levels—force levels that are generally considered to be the minimum acceptable to carry out existing national strategy. It also suggests that as time goes on, and as technological sophistication continues to increase the cost of our weapon systems, the situation will most likely continue to get worse.

It appears absolutely essential that the White House and the Congress—and the nation as a whole—establish an appropriate, contemporary, composite national strategy and then provide the necessary legislation to achieve the forces to carry it out. Surely the American people should know what our overall strategy is and what it costs to achieve it. Conversely, it would appear unconscionable for the country—or its president—to assume that we are capable of following one strategy when in fact we are only spending enough money to support a lesser strategy. Yet that appears to be exactly what we are doing over the long run. We are claiming, for both our conventional and nuclear forces, substantial capabilities which we do not currently have and which will get further and further from our grasp as time goes on.

Alternative conventional force strategies are developed first. It would appear that our overall conventional forces and their capacity for mobility should be designed to deter or to fight one of three basic "worst case" wars. These are identified simply as a one-front war, a two-front war, or a three-front war.

This terminology is chosen to avoid use of the one-and-a-half war strategy currently in vogue but hopelessly outdated in the real world. The old concept of one war in one part of the world against the Soviets and another half-war somewhere else against someone else no longer seems appropriate. The Soviets now have global reach, and virtually all of our potential adversaries are Soviet-supported.

Our worst condition is a world war involving our allies and ourselves against the Soviets and their allies and clients. The basic question is how widespread this war might become. If it is limited to the NATO theater in Western Europe, this would constitute a one-front war requiring operations only across the Atlantic. If the war spreads to—or grows from— operations bordering *either* the Pacific or the Indian Ocean, then we would have a two-front war to cope with. If the war spreads to—or grows from—*both* the Pacific and the Indian Ocean areas, then we would need a three-front capability to cope. In the not too distant future we may even need to consider a fourth front—in the Caribbean and Central America.

If one believes that the Soviets plan direct aggression into Western Europe and are willing to take the consequences of its destruction in the process, then one might be willing to plan on a one-front war in the NATO theater. If, on the other hand, the Soviets wish the benefits of Western Europe without destroying it, then they might well try to force the United States to fight elsewhere in the hopes that Western Europe, by intimidation, would collapse without a fight. Given the increasing number of unstable regions in the world and given the continuing spread of Soviet client states, it would appear that they might entrap us in either the Pacific or the Indian Ocean—or both—in the hopes of reducing our deterrent in the NATO area. South Asia could serve that purpose.

With anything less than a three-front capability, we risk the loss of at least one front to save the other one or two. This does not appear to be a very reasonable bargain. Should we lose the Persian Gulf and Middle East to "save" Japan and Korea? Should we lose Japan and Korea—and then quite probably China—to "save" the Persian Gulf? Should we lose Western Europe to "save" the others—or vice versa? How should the question be phrased: can we afford to "save" all three, or can we afford not to "save" all three?

There is one additional consideration that should be included, and that is the possible duration of conventional combat in any or all of the three front regions. At present, we plan for very short conventional wars indeed—on the order of sixty to ninety days. The implication appears to be that either the conflict will terminate within that time period or it will escalate to the use of nuclear weapons. We have never fought a war as short as sixty days. We once escalated to the use of nuclear weapons—but only after four years of fighting. There seems to be little rationale for acceptance of the short war strategy other than as a means of saving money.

We have no indication whatsoever that the Soviets will exhaust their logistic support within sixty days. In fact, our professed strategy is to "be able to outlast the Soviets in conventional combat." At the same time, our actual procurement requests will only support sixty-day consumption rates of all but our simplest ammunition requirements. In any event, the Congress should be given the option of funding either a one-, two-, or three-front war capability for either a short duration (such as sixty to ninety days) or a long duration (something well in excess of one hundred eighty days). The latter option would allow more meaningful industrial mobilization and also permit greater support of allied needs.

One should note, of course, that if one has the capabilities for a longer three-front war and only a shorter one- or two-front war develops, all is not lost. The additional forces can be profitably used either to hasten the conclusion of the smaller war, to threaten the adversary with expansion of the war beyond his means to cope, or to permit a change to a more offensive strategy within any of the threatened areas.

Procurement Outlays for Conventional Strategies

To demonstrate the sensitivity of procurement outlay requirements to changes in national strategy for deterring or conducting conventional wars, the steady-state annualized procurements for the basic force elements of each strategy have been crudely estimated and summed up on Table 2. Force levels and annual procurement costs are shown for numbers of army/marine active divisions (including all their armor, surface-to-air missile [SAM], and helicopter requirements), numbers of ships and submarines in the general purpose navy, the number of active wings of tactical and support aircraft (including antisubmarine warfare [ASW] patrol and tactical airlift) for the air force, navy, and marines, and the number of large strategic airlift aircraft. Procurement values are shown for each of the three strategies for both short and long duration wars. Total annual procurement costs vary from $19 billion for a short one-front war capability to $44 billion for a long three-front war capability.

In response to recent proposals for increased defense spending, some critics have attempted to claim that such additional procurement funding could not wisely be spent in the near future. Such allegations are clearly preposterous. In order to demonstrate the available current procurement opportunities, Table 3 has been prepared to illustrate how the incremental expenditures proposed to meet the demands of a two- or three -front war could be satisfied with current acquisition programs.

Almost every item listed is currently in production at levels far below present production capacity. In cases where new production is not yet ready (e.g., AH–64 attack helicopter), then production of the current system (AH–1S) should be continued instead. Production of other systems is being stopped prematurely (M60A3 tank, M113 APC, HAWK, LHA, F–14, A6E, EA–6B) before inventory objectives are realized. In other cases, planned production is at minimal practical levels (KC–10, P–3, E–3A) due to lack of sufficient funds. In still other areas, U.S. military forces are also facing block obsolescence of their existing equipment with no firm

Table 2

Required Procurement Outlays for Steady-State Modernization
for Differing National Strategies: Conventional Forces
(billions of FY 1980 dollars)

Major Force Component	Conventional Strategies					
	1-Front War		2-Front War		3-Front War	
	Levels	Dollars	Levels	Dollars	Levels	Dollars
Active divisions (A, MC)	15	3.0	20	4.0	25	5.0
Active ships and subs (SSNs)	300	4.0	500	7.5	700	10.0
Active wings (N, MC, AF)	25	3.8	50	7.0	60	8.0
Airlift aircraft (strategic)	100	0.2	300	0.5	600	1.0
(spares, mods, cons) Short:	(8.0)	19.0	(12.0)	31.0	(15.0)	39.0
Total/war duration Long:	(11.0)	22.0	(16.0)	35.0	(20.0)	44.0

replacements in view or inadequate production rates to offset required retirements (attack submarines, destroyers, support ships, C–130s, etc.).

In the less glamorous areas of spares, modifications, and consumables, increased production is also readily available to meet obvious shortfalls in spare parts, ammunition, and expendable missiles. Moreover, there is virtually no funding applied to maintaining our industrial base or to make possible the rapid conversion of civil assets to military usage (such as arming merchant ships to defend themselves in convoys). In many instances, if a protracted crisis period developed we would currently be unable to significantly increase military output or conversions due to lack of planning or a firm production base.

STRATEGIC WARFARE STRATEGIES

It seems that we have chosen a defensive, short, one-front war strategy for NATO because it is cheaper, not because it accomplishes our overall national security objectives. Similarly, we appear to have accepted an offensive strategy in the use of our nuclear weapons, not because it best accomplishes national objectives but because it too is the cheaper alternative. This section deals with alternative strategies for our strategic nuclear forces. Three have been selected which appear to cover the gamut of realistic options.

The first strategic alternative is to relinquish the manned bomber leg of the Triad, essentially accepting a Diad (ICBMs, SSBNs) of land-based and sea-based intercontinental missiles. The second is to retain a Triad, including a manned bomber force (acknowledging its utility for both nuclear and conventional wars). For this case, it is crudely priced as a composite of penetrating and standoff bombers equipped as appropriate with cruise missiles and other air-to-surface

Table 3

Enhanced Conventional Force Modernization

(annualized incremental procurement in millions of FY 1980 dollars)

	2-Front War		3-Front War	
	Units/yr	Cost/yr	Units/yr	Cost/yr
Active divisions				
Increase production of tanks and APCs	+ 500	+ 500	+1,200	+1,000
Increase production of attack helicopters	+ 50	+ 150	+ 100	+ 300
Increase production of troop lift helicopters	+ 50	+ 150	+ 100	+ 300
Increase production of antiaircraft systems	+ 10	+ 200	+ 20	+ 400
Total increment		+1,000		+2,000
Active ships and submarines				
Increase attack submarine production	+ 1	+ 500	+ 2	+1,000
Increase VTOL carrier (LHA) production	+ 1	+ 800	+ 1	+ 800
Initiate amphibious ship procurement	+ 2	+ 300	+ 4	+ 500
Increase DDG–47 destroyer production	+ 1	+ 600	+ 1	+ 600
Increase destroyer (DD–963) production	+ 1	+ 400	+ 3	+1,200
Increase convoy defense frigate (FFG–7) production	+ 4	+ 600	+ 8	+1,200
Increase support ship (AOE, AOR, AS) production	+ 2	+ 300	+ 4	+ 500
Total increment		+3,500		+6,000
Airlift aircraft				
Increase tanker/transport (KC–10) production	+ 8	+ 300	+ 20	+ 800
Total increment		+ 300		+ 800

Active wings (navy, marine corps, air force)

	Short War Cost/yr	Long War Cost/yr	Short War Cost/yr	Long War Cost/yr
Increase F–15 production	+ 40	+ 600	+ 50	+ 750
Increase F–16 production	+ 20	+ 200	+ 30	+ 300
Continue A–10 production	+ 50	+ 300	+ 50	+ 300
Increase F–14 production until F–18 ready	+ 16	+ 400	+ 20	+ 500
Restore A–6E and EA–6B production until AV–8B ready	+ 20	+ 300	+ 30	+ 450
Increase P–3C production	+ 20	+ 600	+ 30	+ 900
Start C–130X production	+ 40	+ 400	+ 50	+ 500
Increase E–3A production	+ 4	+ 400	+ 5	+ 500
Total increment		+3,200		+4,200

Spares, mods, consumables

	Short War Cost/yr	Long War Cost/yr	Short War Cost/yr	Long War Cost/yr
Increase major systems spares procurement	+ 500	+1,500	+1,000	+ 2,000
Increase modifications to existing older systems	+1,000	+1,000	+1,000	+ 2,000*
Increase unguided munition reserve procurement	+2,000	+3,000	+3,000	+ 4,000
Increase guided munition reserve procurement	+ 500	+1,500	+1,000	+ 2,000
Regenerate industrial mobilization base	–	+1,000	–	+ 2,000
Total increment	+4,000	+8,000	+7,000	+12,000

*Includes kits for rapid conversion of civil assets.

weapons and defense suppressors. The third is to recognize the impending limits on offensive weapons and to undertake a more meaningful strategic defensive capability. This might include somewhat expanded ABM (antiballistic missile) capabilities, an improved air defense capability against second-echelon Soviet strikes with manned aircraft (using nuclear, chemical, or biological weapons), and a meaningful civil defense program to protect our population and enhance our capabilities for national survival and postwar recovery.

Procurement Outlays for Strategic Strategies

Strategic nuclear capabilities are broken down between ICBMs, bombers and cruise missile carriers, SSBNs, space equipment, and strategic defensive capabilities. The annual procurement requirements for steady-state maintenance of each of these components is indicated on Table 4 for each alternative (i.e., Diad, Triad, and Triad + Defense). Here the annual procurement costs vary from a low of $6 billion — assuming a much smaller total level of ICBMs and SSBNs — to a high of $18 billion for the current proclaimed nuclear force levels plus enhanced space and defense capabilities.

Just as there are clear opportunities for immediate increased investment in conventional force modernization, there are options available to bolster strategic nuclear force modernizations also, though not as many. Table 5, like Table 3, shows how the increments proposed on the preceding table could be funded in the near term.

The decision has recently been reached (but not yet funded in the outyears) to develop the MX replacement for the Minuteman III ICBM. Until MX production can be initiated, additional production and modernization of the MMII and MMIII could be reinstigated.

In the realm of manned bombers, the B–1 design is still undergoing test and evaluation and could be returned to production status. Although it may not be the optimum design,

Table 4

Required Procurement Outlays for Steady-State Modernization for Differing National Strategies: Strategic Forces
(billions of FY 1980 dollars)

Major Force Component	Strategic Strategies					
	Diad		Triad		Triad + Defense	
	Levels	Dollars	Levels	Dollars	Levels	Dollars
ICBMs	200	0.5	1,000	3.0	1,000	3.0
Bombers and tankers	0	0	500	3.5	500	3.5
SSBNs	20	1.5	40	3.0	40	3.0
Space	–	0.9	–	1.4	–	2.0
Strategic defense	–	0.1	–	.1	–	1.5
Total (spares, mods, cons)	(3.0)	6.0	(4.0)	15.0	(5.0)	18.0

Table 5

Enhanced Strategic Force Modernization
(annualized incremental procurement in
millions of FY 1980 dollars)

	Triad	Triad + Defense
	Cost/yr	Cost/yr
ICBMs		
Produce MX system as soon as possible	+2,500	+2,500
Total increment	+2,500	+2,500
Bombers and tankers		
Produce B–1A until B–1B design available (36/yr)	+3,500	+3,500
Total increment	+3,500	+3,500
SSBNs		
Increase TRIDENT SSBN/SLBM production to 2/yr	+1,500	+1,500
Total increment	+1,500	+1,500

Space		
Enhanced surveillance and verification space	+ 200	+ 400
More survivable and responsive command and control	+ 300	+ 700
Total increment	+ 500	+1,100
Strategic defense		
Undertake meaningful civil defense program	–	+1,000
Enhanced program for continuity of essential government	–	+ 400
Total increment	–	+1,400
Spares, mods, and consumables		
Additional major systems spares procurement	+ 200	+ 200
Accelerated B–52, FB–111, and tanker upgrading	+ 300	+ 300
Increased production/mobilization for cruise missiles	+ 300	+ 300
Enhanced modernization of MMII, MMIII, Poseidon missiles	+ 200	+ 200
Stockpiling equip/mtls to speed national recovery	–	+1,000
Total increment	+1,000	+2,000

production of the B–1A could be undertaken to satisfy penetrating bomber requirements for both conventional and strategic war scenarios, while an improved, cruise-missile-carrying B–1B version is taken through development. A mixed fleet of B–1A/Bs would be no more difficult to sustain than a mixed fleet of aging B–52s and FB–111s.

The current TRIDENT SSBN production rate is not adequate to offset impending obsolescence of the old POSEIDON submarines. Increased production of two per year was planned by the prior administration and could be reinstituted within a relatively short period of time.

There are also many opportunities to increase production of the various satellite and other systems which provide strategic intelligence, warning, and command and control functions.

Lastly, there have been many proposals for undertaking a meaningful civil defense program and for making adequate provisions to assure the continuity of essential government functions during and immediately following nuclear attack. Spending limitations in this area are clearly limited by national policy and not by the lack of resources or capabilities within the civil sector.

COMBINED CONVENTIONAL/STRATEGIC ALTERNATIVES

Table 6 sums the various conventional options with the various strategic options to show total annual procurement levels needed. As stated earlier, they vary from a low of $25 billion for a short one-front conventional force capability coupled with a minimal strategic Diad, up to $62 billion for a long three-front conventional capability backed up with a defense-augmented Triad. Two things are evident from this primitive exercise:

First, at least to a crude first approximation, it is possible to relate annual procurement spending requirements and the strategies which they support. The total range of strategies could produce differing total defense budget requirements of roughly $40 billion annually.

Second, current funding levels will simply not support our stated current strategy of a two-front conventional war backed up by a modernized Triad. In fact, if current funding levels are perpetuated—even with an annual growth which will offset increasing technological sophistication—our force levels will eventually obsolesce and decline until they can only support a one-front, short conventional war supported by a half-strength Diad. Apparently we are talking one line and buying another. The long-range impact of inadequate capital investment in force modernization does not appear to be understood.

To make matters worse, given the changes in the world balance of political and military forces over the past ten to twenty years, it seems highly unlikely that the currently espoused (but not funded) strategy is still appropriate. If the Western alliance is dependent on continued survival and independence of three regions of the world, it seems hardly adequate to be able to defend only one or two. Moreover, it appears incomplete to be able to defend those areas for a shorter period of time than the Soviets might be able to attack them. Finally, in an era of pending U.S. nuclear inferiority, it appears somewhat cavalier to plan the partial modernization of our offensive weapons but to disregard our nuclear defenses. In toto, we currently appear to be on the way to being militarily outnumbered, outreached, outlasted, and outlived.

Total Defense Budget Requirements

For different combined conventional/strategic strategies, changes would be required in other defense-appropriate ac-

Table 6

Required Defense Outlays for Steady-State Modernization with Different Combinations of National Strategies Added: Total Procurement

(billions of FY 1980 dollars)

Strategic Strategies	Conventional Strategies					
	1-Front War		2-Front War (claimed)		3-Front War	
	Short (funded)	Long	Short	Long	Short	Long (needed)
Diad	25.0	28.0	37.0	41.0	45.0	50.0
Triad	34.0	37.0	46.0	50.0	54.0	59.0
Triad + Defense	37.0	40.0	40.0	53.0	57.0	62.0

counts besides procurement. This is illustrated in Table 7, which lists all the major appropriation accounts associated with the budget of the Department of Defense. For simplicity, only three combined strategies are shown: a short one-front conventional war supported by a modern Diad, a long two-front conventional war supported by a modern Triad (Alternative A), and a long three-front conventional war backed by a Triad + Defense strategic posture (Alternative B). These three alternatives appear to cover the plausible extremes as well as the middle ground.

In addition to the major changes in the procurement account developed in the prior sections, some increases would be required in other appropriations for the most-capable case while no real reductions would be possible—at least, for many years—in the least-capable case. In Alternative B (most-capable case), a $1 billion annual increment would probably be justified in research and development (R&D) to cover the additional requirements of equipment developments needed to cover all three fronts. Moreover, higher manpower levels would be required to support the additional army divisions, the larger navy, and the larger air force. Higher manpower levels as well as higher equipment levels would then also require some increase in the normal levels of operations and maintenance (O&M) funding.

Reductions in the least capable case (FY 1980 projection) are not shown, although this may seem somewhat inconsistent. The rationale is essentially the same as for our current budget levels: We will continue to keep present force levels until they totally wear out, and this will require at least a constant level of manpower and O&M support. A case could surely be made for increasing O&M expenditures as operational equipment continues to age. For simplicity, however, it is here assumed that if O&M costs do rise, some cuts in military manpower will be made to offset them.

It should be clearly understood, however, that substantially larger manpower and O&M increases would be

needed—and immediately—if the United States wished to make a rapid improvement in defense posture to, say, change world perceptions of its national will and readiness.

Alternative Defense Budget Recovery Plans

All three budgets of Table 7 were developed in terms of their FY 1980 dollar costs. To maintain adequate capital investment in future years, these FY 1980 budget values must be scaled up at the rate of roughly 3 percent annually to account for the quality growth discussed in Figure 1. Figure 2 illustrates actual defense outlays since 1970 and suggests possible recovery plans to move towards more capable national combined strategies.

Alternative A adds roughly $25 billion to the defense budget in the course of the next two fiscal years and then follows the characteristic 3 percent growth thereafter. Alternative B adds roughly $50 billion over the next four fiscal years and then follows an equivalent 3 percent growth line. While it might be desirable to pursue more rapid recovery plans, they would appear politically and economically risky. As demonstrated in Tables 3 and 5, however, there is no shortage of existing defense programs on which these funds could be spent. Instead, it is a question of national will and priorities.

Responding to congressional pressure, the president recently proposed a 4.5 percent real defense growth rate for the next five years. The inadequacy of this proposal is also demonstrated in Figure 2: it would take an additional ten years to match the funding level of Alternative A, and roughly $130 billion less would have been spent on defense investment in the intervening years. It appears clear that the United States cannot recover from its presently preordained declining force posture with slight annual increases in real growth above the minimum 3 percent—which provides *no* growth in posture or in readiness.

Figure 2
Alternative Defense Budget Recovery Plans
(in constant FY 1980 dollar outlays)

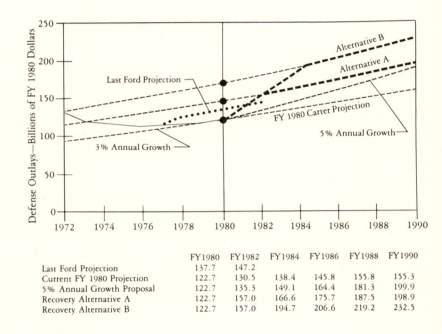

	FY1980	FY1982	FY1984	FY1986	FY1988	FY1990
Last Ford Projection	137.7	147.2				
Current FY 1980 Projection	122.7	130.5	138.4	145.8	155.8	155.3
5% Annual Growth Proposal	122.7	135.3	149.1	164.4	181.3	199.9
Recovery Alternative A	122.7	157.0	166.6	175.7	187.5	198.9
Recovery Alternative B	122.7	157.0	194.7	206.6	219.2	232.5

Finally, the last five-year projection of the prior administration is also shown. It too was clearly inadequate to sustain Alternative A over the long haul, even though in total it represents $60 billion more spending over ten years than does the latest Carter proposal. In short, considerably higher spending levels are required than are projected by either administration to support current strategy, and even more will be required if that strategy itself is to be modernized.

HISTORICAL PERSPECTIVE ON DEFENSE OUTLAYS

It is difficult to assess the ambitiousness of Alternatives A and B without seeking some historical perspective. This is done in Figure 3. Defense outlays since World War II are presented in terms of constant FY 1980 dollars. The peaks caused by fighting World War II, the Korean War, and the Vietnam War are clearly visible. Of possibly greater interest, however, are the relatively stable ten years of defense outlays between the Korean War and the Vietnam War. These years were essentially the Cold War years in which we developed our strategic forces and also made some effort to maintain the adequacy of our general purpose forces. In terms of constant dollars, the United States was spending more for its defense establishment at that time than it is now.

It is tempting, then, though possibly not very accurate, to regress along the 3 percent lines shown for the current FY 1980 projection as well as for Alternative A and Alternative B. These regression lines are also shown on Figure 3. The implication seems clear. If in 1971, when we returned to prewar spending levels, we had adopted a steady 3 percent growth in real terms, this analysis indicates that we would now be able to easily support Alternative B. Even if we had

Figure 3
History of Defense Outlays
(in constant FY 1980 dollars)

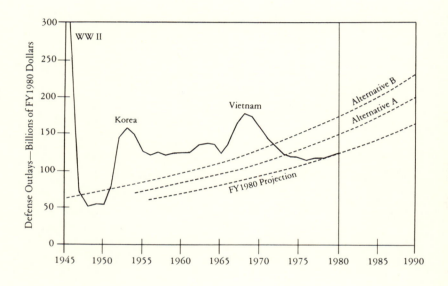

waited until 1973 to arrest the decline in defense spending, we could have supported Alternative A—our currently espoused strategy for national security—in relative confidence. By allowing the decline in real spending to continue through 1975, we appear faced with an inevitable decline in military posture well below that needed. The quest for a postwar bonus for tax relief and for nondefense spending appears to have created a problem from which we will not readily recover.

PROJECTED IMPACT ON FEDERAL BUDGET

The question must naturally arise as to the impact of increased defense outlays—as suggested in Alternatives A and B—on the overall federal budget. This subject is superficially explored here. Nothing could appear less wise than to project federal receipts and outlays for the next ten years of an uncertain economy with continuing high inflation. Nevertheless, it appears equally unwise to appear indifferent to the problems of overall national priorities and spending trends.

Defense has classically been funded with what's left over after other national priorities have been satisfied. First call on federal funds must be given to servicing the national debt and to supporting the entitlement programs for which annual appropriations are not required. These "open-ended programs and fixed costs" have grown from about 33 percent of federal expenditures in 1965 to roughly 60 percent in 1979, although the rate of growth now appears to have been arrested. It seems appropriate, then, to only concern ourselves with net federal receipts and outlays, after deducting the requirements for annual expenditures established by law. Figure 4, then, presents "net" receipts and outlays. It is within this remainder that all annual appropriations must fall. Broadly, the outlays in this category may be divided between defense and nondefense appropriations. It is within these categories that there is competition for defense resources.

Nondefense outlays grew rapidly during the 1970s, except for the last two years of tight fiscal constraint during which the current administration has attempted to decrease the endemic growth in the national debt. Clearly, nondefense appropriations will have to resume some rate of growth in the near future.

For the purposes of this superficial illustration, the following general assumptions have been made: Federal receipts will continue to grow at between 12 and 13 percent—a combination of inflation, real growth, and increasing tax receipts (due to the graduated payment schedule); the "relatively uncontrollable" federal expenditures will grow annually at a rate of 9 percent from FY 1980 levels—reflecting inflation and growth in the recipient population; and nondefense appropriations will return to an annual growth of 10 percent, combining inflation and new national programs.

Based on these assumptions, the impact of varying defense outlay levels can be determined. The display in Figure 4 perpetuates the myth that defense spending dictates the level of the federal deficit. Clearly this is not the case. One could as easily blame the deficit on the entitlement programs, on paying interest on the national debt, or on the nondefense annual appropriations. In any event, the sum total of the prior assumptions and the higher defense spending does produce a continuing deficit in federal spending through the middle 1980s, and it would appear unwise to claim the contrary. This means that continued fiscal constraint may be needed in tax relief, in the entitlement programs, and in nondefense appropriations, if a modest deficit is to be avoided.

Acceptability of modest further growth in the national debt must then be faced head-on. Even with current high interest rates, the cost of servicing the national debt is still

Figure 4
Projected Growth in
"Net" Federal Receipts and Outlays*

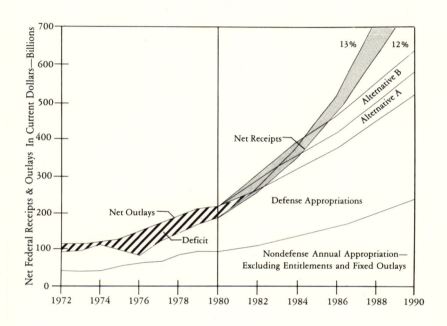

*"Net" R&O = gross R&O less the expected entitlement and fixed outlays.

declining as a fraction of the gross national product (GNP); it is lower now than in 1955. Moreover, the debt itself as a fraction of GNP is lower than it was in 1940. Reductions in interest rates would more than compensate for the costs of servicing a gradually increasing national debt. The popular concept of a balanced federal budget may be good politics; it is not good economics.

In fact, the national debt is only a small fraction of the total debt carried by the people of the United States. In part, at least, it has been the source of investment for the future. Further, the federal debt has been growing more slowly than the debt in most other sectors. For comparison, the current debt load in various sectors is shown in Table 8. Viewed in this light, it seems unwise to use avoidance of modest further increases in the federal debt as the primary justification for jeopardizing our future national security.

Table 8
Distribution of National Debt 1979–1980

Sector	Billions of FY 1980 Dollars
Mortgage debt	$1,100
Corporate debt	860
Federal debt (publicly held)	520
U.S.–held foreign stocks and bonds	430
Separate bank loans	350
State and local debt	295
Consumer installment debt	290

RECOMMENDATIONS

Based on the foregoing, five fundamental recommendations emerge that would amount to almost a total reversal of the way we currently conduct our national security business in the United States.

First and foremost, the U.S. government needs to update its national security strategies in the light of the substantial changes that have occurred in the world over the past decade. This update must correlate strategy objectives and the funding levels required to achieve them for both conventional and strategic forces. It must produce a consistent plan for the future.

Second, the Congress and the White House must stop playing expedient political games and recognize the continuing long-term demands for justifiable defense spending if we are to retain our national security. The White House should sponsor—and the Congress should endorse, in writing—a five- to ten-year topline projection of defense spending consistent with newly approved combined military strategies. Wherever possible the Congress should then provide multiyear entitlements for once-approved defense programs, demonstrating their intent to carry such programs through to completion.

Third, the Department of Defense must accept some congressionally decided long-range topline projection and then develop a sound ten-to-twenty year long-range plan composed of affordable force levels equipped with affordable weapons. These weapon systems should be acquired in accordance with a well-planned and well-phased acquisition program that can avoid block obsolescence as well as the boom-and-bust cycles within the defense industrial community. There must also be renewed efforts to balance the resources devoted to acquisition and those devoted to maintaining the operational readiness of equipments in inventory.

Fourth, if the Congress commits itself to a firm obligation to support national defense needs, then it will be incumbent on the Department of Defense to learn how to live within this projection. This will amount to nothing short of a "cultural change" in the way the Defense Department does its business. The department will have to discipline itself to avoid adding superfluous and expensive immature technology to its weapon systems. In the best of worlds, the decision to prefer quality over quantity is a dubious military choice. When that so-called quality is simply oversophistication with unproved and unreliable gadgetry, it becomes a formula for disaster.

Further, the defense community must accept commercial practices to constrain costs. Industry would not survive if all its decisions were driven by technologists who pride themselves on ignorance of the marketplace. While the Soviets may fret about their technological inferiority, it is time for us to begin to worry seriously about our own ill-advised technological superiority complex.

Moreover, the Defense Department could accomplish substantial cost savings by institutionalizing internal competition for their acquisition programs. Competition at present is frequently a farce, and is applied only when it is too late to make the fundamental savings required to bring defense modernization into line with fiscal realities.

In addition, the defense community—military, civil service, and industry member—appears peculiarly unaware of standard commercial management techniques. In that outside commercial world—the one that has built the world's strongest economy—people are actually hired for their competency and fired for their incompetency. Their pay is actually related to their individual performance and their job security related to their collective performance. Such concepts appear totally foreign to government agencies and to government-subsidized industries.

Lastly, the Defense Department will have to learn to use both foreign and commercial products and components. After all, our Western national security depends fundamentally on active collaboration between the members of our loosely knit alliance. Our national security, moreover, depends fundamentally on the basic and unchallenged economic strength of our civil sectors. Unless we learn to harness our collective strengths and put them to work for our collective security, we will surely lose both over the long run.

Fifth and finally, the American public must be assured that our Defense Department is not being flagrantly wasteful. Surely it is not perfect in its acquisition policies. There is no valid reason, however, to single out the Department of Defense as the big waster among American government and private sector enterprises. It isn't. It is the product of our American culture and of our American style of government. To expect it to perform in an un-American manner appears to be the height of politically inspired hypocrisy. Surely the Defense Department can be accused of being 1, 2, or maybe even 3 percent inefficient. So is most every American enterprise. But it is not 10, 15, or 20 percent inefficient by any standard.

The simple fact of the matter is that our national security cannot be guaranteed over the long haul unless the Department of Defense receives additional funding—sizable additional funding—on a continuing long-term basis. Equally important, our national security cannot be guaranteed over the short haul unless we modernize our strategies and demonstrate our commitment to them through supplemental expenditures in the immediate future—within FY 1980. Considering the relatively modest sums involved, the nation can clearly afford what is required. As a matter of fact, it cannot afford not to afford it.

15

SAM NUNN

Defense Budget and Defense Capabilities

Soviet military investment. Changes in U.S. government expenditures. The current military imbalance. Ways to resolve the national security problems. NATO and Japan. Deficiencies in the all-volunteer force. The military manpower situation.

It is apparent that the trends in our national security posture in the last decade have not been favorable when compared to the effort of the Soviet Union and when measured against the tasks assigned to our military forces by reason of our national commitments. We have reached a point in our history where our vital interests, as defined by treaty commitments and economic and political realities, far exceed our military capabilities.

As we discuss and debate the future, it is important that the American people and their leaders in government understand what has occurred in the past ten to fifteen years and where we stand today.

U.S.–USSR DEFENSE SPENDING

First, we must recognize what has happened over the last decade in the military balance between the United States and the Soviet Union.

The adjacent bargraph chart (Figure 1) depicts the net assessment in billions of dollars of total U.S. and Soviet defense activities from 1968 through 1978. It is based on a detailed and comprehensive analysis by the Rand Corporation and was validated by Secretary of Defense Brown during the Strategic Arms Limitation Talks II (SALT II) hearings. Soviet defense programs show a steady increase during the period and are larger than those of the United States. The Kremlin has sustained steady real increases in military outlays for ten to fifteen years, while the United States has maintained a steady pace in decreasing real military expenditures. In the early 1970s our paths crossed; the Soviets continued to climb and we continued to descend.

Since 1970 the Soviet Union has invested a total of $104 billion more than the United States in military equipment and facilities and $40 billion more in research and development. Soviet foreign policy, invigorated by this relentless military buildup and the uncertain American response to it, is seeking to gain a stranglehold over the economic foundations of Western prosperity and military power.

The massive differences in spending on real military investment should come as no surprise to those who have been

Figure 1
Total U.S. and Soviet Defense Activities:
Net Assessment

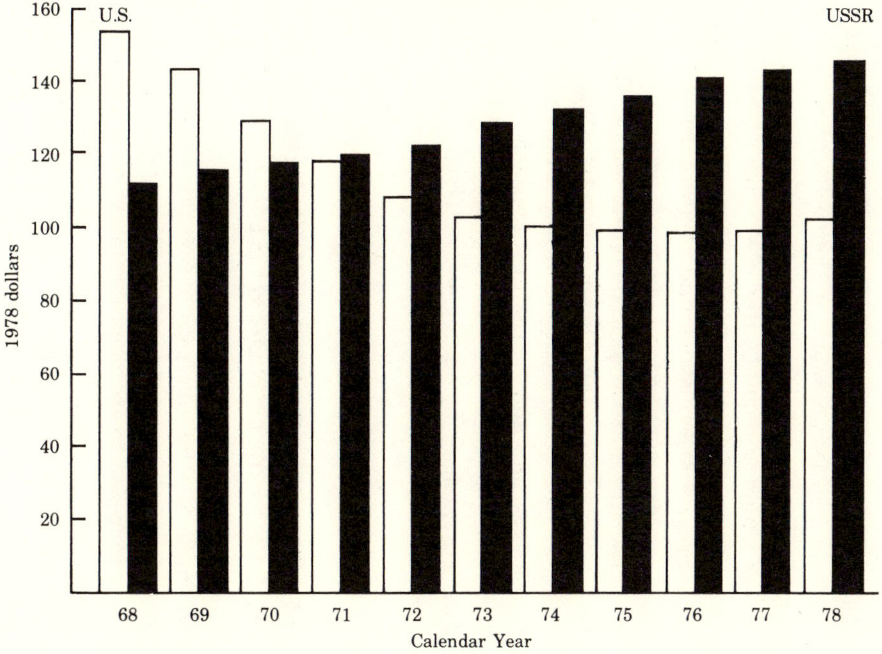

monitoring the introduction of new Soviet weapons systems—four new intercontinental ballistic missiles (ICBMs), the Backfire bomber, the SS−20, missile submarines and submarine-launched ballistic missiles (SLBMs), new tanks, new armored combat fighting vehicles, new air defense systems, and whole new classes of ships.

If our own Department of Defense had at its disposal the funds representing the disparity in investment between the Soviet Union and the United States over the last half-dozen years, it could have purchased the following: all 244 B−1 bombers, all MX missiles and shelters, the 13 Trident submarines programmed to date as well as the Trident I missiles, all 7,000 XM−1 main battle tanks, 500 advanced attack helicopters, 7,000 new infantry fighting vehicles, and a fleet of new tactical airlifters. It also could have bought about 400 F−14s and 800 F−18s to fully modernize naval air for the carrier forces, and it could have modernized all U.S. Air Force tactical air by adding 400 F−15s, 1,250 F−16s, and 400 A−10s.

SHIFTS IN FEDERAL SPENDING FOR MILITARY AND DOMESTIC PROGRAMS

We must also be cognizant of how our federal spending practices have changed, especially with the advent of a tremendous increase in social programs in the 1960s. There is no question that federal spending has increased in all areas, including national defense; however, as social and domestic programs have proliferated, the percentage increases in spending in these areas offer some shocking statistics. For example, in 1965 federal budget outlays for health were $1.7 billion, yet by 1979 health expenditures had risen to $50 billion, a percentage increase of over 2,800 percent. Likewise, in this same period our expenditures for social service programs increased by over 2,200 percent, and for welfare programs, by over 800 percent. Defense spending, however, in the same 1965–1979 period rose from $49.578 billion to $117.681 billion, a percentage increase of only 137 percent.

From the mid-1950s to the mid-1960s defense and nondefense areas had approximately equal shares of the budget. The nondefense areas have skyrocketed since that time, while there has been a steady decline in military budgets. This shift would be understandable and even acceptable if the Soviets were on the same treadmill, but this is not the case.

Defense Budgets

The defense budget represents the foundation of our national security policy. It must provide for the capabilities to meet the requirements of these policies. It must provide the forces; it must equip those forces; it must support those forces.

For fiscal year (FY) 1980, the president requested $135 billion for the Department of Defense and for 1981, $158 billion. Although a large sum of money, after inflation is taken into account the FY 1980 request is less in real dollars than the defense budget of FY 1965. The FY 1981 request is about 5 percent higher than the 1965 level after inflation is taken into account. This long-term decline has resulted in smaller forces and in the purchase of fewer weapons. U.S. capability rests on a declining number of personnel, ships, aircraft, and survivable strategic forces, while Soviet capability rests on increasing force levels backed by long-term increases in defense spending.

It is interesting to compare actual U.S. procurement levels today with procurement levels in 1964. In weapons procurement, the president has requested 342 fighter/attack aircraft for fiscal year 1981. This compares with 627 in 1964 —over a 45 percent reduction. The number of new ships

or conversions has decreased from 75 in 1964 to 19 in
FY 1981—a 75 percent reduction. There is one attack submarine requested for FY 1981 compared with six in 1964—
an 83 percent reduction. Ninety-four new helicopters are requested for FY 1981 compared with 1,600 in 1964—over a 90
percent reduction.

These raw numbers do not, of course, tell the story as to
quality differences, but they do indicate a trend that has
been brought about by budgets as well as by inflation and
technological change.

The American gift for technological innovation has
enabled us to produce the most sophisticated systems in the
world. The present challenge is also to use our know-how and
technology to build durable weapon systems that can be
maintained in the field and afforded in sufficient numbers to
carry out the nation's defense missions. The world's most
sophisticated fighter plane cannot defeat Soviet airpower if it
is constantly in the shop for repairs. Nor can the world's
greatest tank prevail if outnumbered five to one.

We also have fewer forces in being. Military personnel
strength has been reduced by over 600,000 since the 1964
pre-Vietnam levels. The number of navy ships has dropped
from 917 to 477. The number of air force aircraft has
dropped from 14,900 in 1964 to 9,300. The number of troops
we have deployed overseas has declined from 719,000 in 1964
to 466,000 today. The levels of forces the United States now
maintains is substantially below the levels during the
twenty-five years of the Cold War. In many instances, our
current procurement levels are barely keeping pace with attrition.

The Result of Input and Output—
a Shifting Military Balance

Input in terms of dollars into defense budgets and output in
terms of procurement, research and development, and readiness determine our military capabilities.

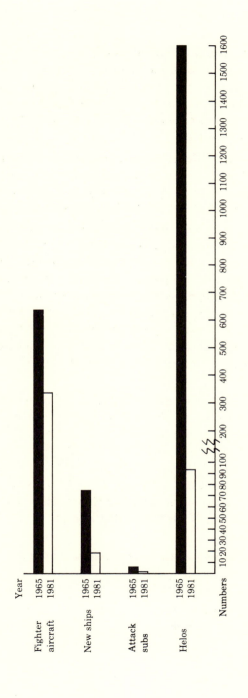

Figure 2
Procurement: 1964 v. 1981

A totalitarian government would never admit in public its military weaknesses. In a democratic society, however, if we are going to engage in a meaningful debate on national security goals, missions, and budgets, we must candidly recognize the weaknesses in our current posture and the adverse trends we face.

• First, we have lost strategic nuclear superiority, and during the next five to seven years our strategic position will be something less than essential equivalence. We are now in a tenuous position that I would characterize as clinging parity.

• Second, the Soviets have achieved an advantage in long-range theater nuclear forces in Europe. The North Atlantic Treaty Organization's (NATO's) theater nuclear weapons are too limited in range and too vulnerable to preemption. NATO's general purpose forces are not trained for sustained combat in a nuclear or chemical environment. NATO's nuclear modernization program adopted in December 1979 recognizes this serious imbalance and is designed to correct it, but the gap will continue through at least the first half of the decade.

• Third, NATO has a questionable capacity to sustain a conventional defense of Europe because of continuing severe shortages in available stocks of ammunition and war reserve equipment, a lack of sufficient strategic sealift and airlift resources, and the absence of a reliable manpower mobilization base. To put it simply, the United States no longer has strategic nuclear superiority, but this fundamental change is not reflected in NATO's theater nuclear and conventional force posture.

• Fourth, because of the shortages in strategic lift, the U.S. capability to rapidly deploy sizable forces to the Indian Ocean, the Middle East, or elsewhere is questionable at best.

• Fifth, the chronic shortages in funding for training, operations, and maintenance that have plagued all the services during the past decade have reduced the readiness of much of our force structure. While there is no political lobby for readiness, there is no military substitution fot it.

• Sixth, our dwindling navy today is spread too thin. With the West growing more dependent on foreign sources of oil, the U.S. Navy is being given more missions and more responsibility with fewer ships. We cannot continue to expand naval requirements while reducing naval capabilities.

The easy way out would be to pretend this situation does not exist, or to ask for some new study to tell us what our defense needs are. That is the way to avoid difficult decisions. Unfortunately, this is the way we have stumbled into past confrontations and conflicts; there were too many who preferred to see no threat to freedom because to admit such a threat implies a willingness to undertake the sacrifices to combat it.

WHERE DO WE GO FROM HERE?

The military problems we face have been fifteen years in the making and cannot be resolved overnight. But the word must go out to our allies and adversaries alike: the slumber is over; America has awakened. That is the real significance and importance of the defense budget plans and figures that will be considered by the Congress in the upcoming months.

Figure 3 displays the Department of Defense budget for 1960 through 1985 (as projected in the president's FY 1981 budget). These levels are in FY 1981 constant dollars—that is, they are adjusted for inflation. Post-Vietnam decreases in the budget are clear. Between 1975 and 1979 there has been some improvement, but higher than anticipated rates of inflation have eliminated the budget growth often predicted when a budget is submitted. In 1980 and in future years, if inflation is higher than reported, the same leveling process would happen.

The Carter administration's five-year defense plan reflects a realization of the adverse defense trends that have taken place and calls for real increases in defense spending and capability in the coming years.* The five-year plan contains some particularly important initiatives designed to modernize our theater nuclear forces and to enhance our ability to respond rapidly to contingencies in the Middle East and the Persian Gulf.

We will begin slowly to reverse the adverse trends if we (1) maintain at least the growth rates projected in the budget, (2) direct this growth to military investment and add increases where necessary for inflation, and (3) add to the ability of these dollars to buy real defense capabilities by finding efficiencies in other areas.

It should be apparent to all objective observers that we have serious national security problems. There is no cause, however, for scare tactics or panic. I am not suggesting sudden massive increases in defense spending. Our defense budgets must, however, demonstrate a solid commitment to modest but steady increases in defense spending for the foreseeable future. They must demonstrate to the world that America has awakened from her long slumber and will remain awake and alert for the 1980s and beyond. We must demonstrate that we are totally committed to provide for our national security. We have gone far too long a time without that demonstration.

It is obvious that the United States cannot, without spending more on defense than we have during the past decade:

---

*EDITOR'S NOTE: As this book went to press, it appeared that the "real increases" were slipping considerably as a double result of inflation: firstly, because the rate of inflation was higher than projected and thus eroded the increases, and secondly, because the budget-cutting in the revised 1981 budget, prompted by the soaring inflation, would not leave defense spending immune—as the president himself made clear. How much of the "real increases" would be left was not certain, however.

- assure essential equivalence at the strategic nuclear level;
- redress the theater nuclear imbalance in Europe;
- contribute to the creation of a truly formidable NATO conventional deterrent;
- expand the capabilities of our navy;
- establish a flexible, mobile combat force;
- increase the readiness of our existing forces.

A REVISED FREE WORLD STRATEGY

Whether the increase in the U.S. defense budget over the next five years is 3 percent, 5 percent, 7 percent, or even 10 percent, the United States cannot do it alone. These challenges must be met in concert with our allies in the free world. This is underscored by the recent developments in Iran and Afghanistan.

Thirty-five years after World War II, America is at a crossroad regarding her national security goals. We came out of that war largely self-sufficient and with overwhelming military and economic strength. Much of the rest of the world was in ruins. Our allies needed us more than we needed them and our adversaries feared and respected us. The world is now a different place.

Russia has built a massive military machine; Western Europe and Japan are economic superpowers; the United States has lost its nuclear dominance and has become economically dependent on overseas sources for oil and for many key raw materials.

The time has come to recognize that this fundamental shift has altered our traditional military requirements and has imposed upon the Atlantic alliance and our Pacific allies the need for greater investment in defense and for greater military specialization and cooperation.

NATO was created as an instrument to protect Western Europe from a direct military attack by the Soviet Union, yet the security of Western Europe today is just as sensitive to events in the Middle East and in the Indian Ocean as it is to events along the German border. The same can be said of Japanese dependence on these areas. The economies of Western Europe and Japan are even more dependent on Persian Gulf oil than we are.

The United States possesses inherent advantages in strategic and theater nuclear arms, in naval power, and in the ability to project military force in areas distant from Europe.

Our NATO allies, for political as well as military reasons, are not in a position to unilaterally guarantee their own securities against nuclear threats or against threats to their economic lifeline outside of Europe. We must remain the leading partner in these areas, but our partners must help.

Our NATO partners enjoy a natural advantage in conventional ground and tactical air forces confined to the European theater. The United States alone has never been in a position to guarantee the conventional defense of Western Europe, and NATO has never felt the necessity of providing essential equivalence in the conventional arena because of America's nuclear guarantee. Owing to shifts in the strategic balance, this complacency must end. Soviet essential equivalence in the nuclear balance must be met by NATO essential equivalence in the conventional balance. America should be a contributing partner, but our European allies must become leading partners in achieving essential equivalence in the conventional arena.

While we should continue to carry out our share of the NATO five-year defense plan, the United States must for the foreseeable future devote an increasing proportion of our defense effort to upgrading and expanding our navy and air force for contingencies outside of Europe. The sealift and airlift enhancement program designed for mobile forces will also greatly increase our ability to carry out our NATO commitments. The sea lanes in the Indian Ocean are as vital to Europe as are the highways and railroads in Central Europe. Only with America as the leading partner can we defend the former. Only with the Europeans as leading partners can we defend the latter.

Japan too must be prepared to assume a substantially larger responsibility for her own defense against immediate threats to her own territory. The United States should not seek to substitute improved Japanese military power for the U.S. military presence in Asia. Improvements in Japan's self-defense efforts, however, may permit U.S. forces to shift more of their attention to other priority missions such as defense of U.S. and Japanese sea lines of communication at extended distances from Japan, particularly in the Indian Ocean.

The United States has of necessity been the leader of the free world in military matters since World War II. We must continue to lead, but in the context of a maturing partnership cognizant of the fundamental changes that have occurred in the last decade.

Our challenge is to consider these fundamental changes and to develop national security goals which are clearly understood by the American people. We can no longer rely primarily on nuclear dominance and slowly mobilized industrial capacity to deter war. We must take a fresh look at our national security goals in close consultation with our allies. We must also take a fresh look at our own military personnel situation.

MANPOWER PROBLEMS—THE WEAK LINK OF U.S. READINESS AND DETERRENCE

Nothing has a more direct and immediate impact on our military capabilities and readiness than the status of our military personnel system. With the existing critical problems of the all-volunteer force (AVF) and the dim outlook for its future, the current personnel system is weakening daily, presenting the most serious challenge in our overall national security area. The AVF is the weakest link in our chain of military capability, readiness, and deterrence.

Despite the institution of the AVF under the most conducive circumstances—large youth population, weak economy, high unemployment, lower force levels, and high first-term pay—it is an experiment that has failed the tests of its framers and, more important still, it has failed to meet our military requirements.

Despite massive recruiting efforts and funding, the AVF has failed to provide sufficient quantity or quality of personnel to man our active and reserve forces. None of the active forces were able to meet strength levels in 1979, and the National Guard and reserve forces are woefully short. The U.S. Army alone will try to recruit one-third more recruits this year to maintain strength; in order to reach this quota, it has deliberately lowered quality standards. A critical situation is the shortage of medical personnel in both active and reserve forces, a shortage which would have a crippling effect during wartime.

Despite predictions of the framers of the AVF, the attrition or washout levels of first termers has been inordinately high. In the army alone, almost 38 percent left prior to completing their initial term of service in 1979.

Despite the plans of the framers of the AVF, peacetime registration was terminated by President Ford in 1975 and the nation's ability to mobilize and to provide trained manpower for combat is woefully deficient.

Despite the expectations of the framers of the AVF, the costs associated with maintaining a volunteer force have been significantly higher than expected and the cost savings contemplated from less turnover have not been realized. In 1964 manpower costs accounted for 48 percent of the defense budget. If this manpower proportion had remained constant at the 48 percent level between 1970 and 1978, we would have had an additional $100 billion in today's dollars to spend on military investment and readiness.

The end result is the enormous difference in levels of capital investment between the United States and the Soviet Union. Any defense budget must provide, on the one hand, for investment for weapons modernization and replacement. Over 70 percent of Soviet defense spending is devoted to capital investment—to the purchase of new weapons and to research and development. The other 30 percent is for operating expenses. In stark contrast, the cost of operating existing U.S. forces (military personnel, operations and maintenance, retired pay) gobbles up a staggering 56 percent of the defense budget, leaving less than 44 percent for investment to buy equipment and facilities for the future.

Alternatives

Several schools of thought are actively debating alternatives to the AVF. These include substantially increased funding and benefits, a return to some form of draft, or a national service program. The Carter administration opposes all of these alternatives and maintains that the all-volunteer force is working well. This is a position that may be politically comfortable but has no analytical credibility. The administration gradually is beginning to admit some problems and is now engaged in what could be described as "creeping candor."

One school of thought proposes massive infusions of pay as the solution to make the AVF succeed. In January 1977 the Congressional Budget Office issued a report on the *Costs of Defense Manpower* which projected significant shortages in the supply of recruits for the military services in the 1980s and discussed budget options. According to that report: "If the armed forces try to make up for these shortages with across-the-board pay increases, by 1985, they could add up to

$8 billion per year (in 1977 constant dollars) over today's manpower costs without any addition to military forces."

More recently, former Secretary of Defense Melvin Laird outlined ten specific actions as a minimum to try to make the AVF work. These include a 17 percent across-the-board pay raise. The Laird proposals would cost about $8 to $12 billion annually, not counting future inflation.

The "funding solution" involves huge sums of money without any real assurance that this investment would be successful. However, if it is the will of the American people that substantially increased manpower costs should be accepted in an effort to maintain our defense forces, then it should be recognized that such additional costs must be added to the five-year defense plan. These additions must not be funded by reductions in investment and readiness. If the increased funds for manpower are taken from the procurement and research and development accounts as they were from 1972 to 1978, the Soviets will attain military superiority by virtually every measure during the 1980s.

To the extent that additional funds are available for increased pay in the military, the priority and the emphasis must be on the career military force. I also believe that additional benefits for new recruits should be devoted primarily to educational incentives rather than to increases in pay. According to the preponderance of testimony before the Armed Services Committee, educational benefits could do much more to enhance the quality of accession than increased pay.

Recruiting for the volunteer force has been emphasized so much that the ratio of average pay for careerists to average pay for first-term military personnel has declined by 50 percent in the past fifteen years. This "front loading" of pay, bonuses, and benefits has a psychological effect on careerists, particularly on those in the higher enlisted ranks who see that most of their career progress occurs in the first five years of their service. The army is now short by 15,000 noncommissioned officers and the navy is critically short of chief petty officers as well.

The Warner/Nunn amendment, which passed the Senate on 4 February 1980, was designed to provide increased allowances and benefits for career personnel. It provides for a new variable housing allowance that will increase the allowance to military personnel who are ordered to high costs areas and must live off base. It provides for increases in sea pay, flight pay, basic allowances for subsistence, and for higher reimbursements for moving expenses for those who are ordered to change assignments. These increases are designed to increase the retention of the trained career force, particularly of those classified as E−4 to E−9.

Another school of thought advocates a return to some form of the draft. The draft as it was operated in the past was inequitable, and certainly we would not want to repeat the experiences of the Vietnam era. General Bernard Rogers, former Chief of Staff of the Army and now Commander of NATO, suggests a limited draft for short periods of time designed to form a large pool of pretrained manpower in the event of mobilization. This approach might also provide the needed stimulus for volunteers to join the active and reserve forces, but would of course bring out all of the arguments against compulsory military service.

It would also address one of the most pressing military manpower problems—the lack of trained personnel in case of a mobilization to augment current forces and to serve as replacements in the early stages of a war. As a primary source of this manpower we rely on the individual ready reserve, which is composed of people who have completed active duty and served the remainder of their military obligation without additional training but with a commitment to return to active duty in case of an emergency. For the army alone, that pool of manpower is short about 300,000 men. A new draft directed towards this problem would involve service of four to six months for active-duty training; the remaining period of military service could be served without attendance at drills but would require periodic refresher training and a commitment for mobilization early in an emergency. This would impose a much smaller burden on young people than the two-year draft and would solve some of the current problems. Obviously, the arguments made against any form of compulsory military service would apply in opposition to this plan.

Another alternative suggestion is advocated by Congressman Paul N. McCloskey. It would institute a national service system in which all young people would be asked to serve either in the military or in a civilian position. This is an extremely equitable concept which I support philosophically, but which I believe would take several years to implement in an effective and efficient fashion. Cost estimates are large and in some instances exceed $20 billion.

The challenge would be in providing the kinds of meaningful civilian jobs that would fulfill our national needs as well as satisfy the service orientation of our youth. Although this alternative does not appear to be a realistic short-term solution to the AVF problems, we should not dismiss the possibility of implementing such a program in the future. The continuing proliferation of youth-oriented employment, educational, and social programs calls with increasing urgency for their more efficient organization and coordination.

Other alternatives which should be considered involve educational incentives. The federal government now provides a substantial amount of loans and scholarships for the education of many young people. Is it unreasonable to expect a commitment for at least reserve service in return? One of the most heavily subsidized educational programs is in fact the education of physicians. Yet our active and reserve components are so short of military doctors that, in case of war, many young people will die or be permanently crippled unnecessarily just because there will be no doctors to treat them early in an emergency. We also need to review how these educational programs can be used as an incentive to attract people to volunteer for military service, thereby drawing higher quality people to serve in return for a substantial benefit.

We no longer have the luxury of the ostrich approach of burying our heads in the sand and ignoring the facts and the problems. We must begin to work on solutions to the manpower problems if the weakest link in the national security chain is to be reinforced.

There has lately been a clearer identification of the overall problems in our national security area than at any time in recent years. This has been accompanied by a growing willingness on the part of the American people to support reasonable efforts to solve these problems.

CONCLUSION

We have been guilty of misplaced priorities. We have usurped areas of government responsibility that are best left to local and state governments and neglected our responsibilities in areas which are uniquely the constitutional responsibility of the central government—specifically, national defense. It is time to reorder our priorities. Regaining the military strength needed to preserve our freedom and this democratic republic will not be achieved by complacency, wishful thinking; nor will it be achieved without sacrifice and determination. It will be accomplished by men who refuse to place the defense of this nation below any other priority.

That has been America's creed for two hundred years, and we have not traveled from the Boston Tea Party to setting foot on the moon because we are made of putty. I am confident that we have the courage, the will, and the determination to meet the challenge of the 1980s.

Discussion:
Part III

Discussions at the Belmont House conference (December 1979) included, in addition to the authors of this book, the following participants: Richard Allen (Potomac International Corporation), Angelo Codevilla (Senate Select Committee on Intelligence, Office of Senator Malcolm Wallop), Fleming Fuller (Documentary Department, KRON–TV), Eric Hemel (economist, Office of Senator Patrick Moynihan), Charles Kupperman (Research Director, Committee on the Present Danger), Robert Osgood (Professor of International Relations, School of Advanced International Studies, Johns Hopkins University), Dale Tahtinen (Reagan for President campaign), and Victor Utgoff (representative of Zbigniew Brzezinski, National Security Council). These excerpts pertain to subjects discussed in Part III.

ON ALLIANCES

ADELMAN: The Iranian crisis has raised interesting points about the NATO alliance. One is the question of burden sharing—whether the alliance is only a military endeavor or whether it spills over into the political, economic, and emotional realms. And secondly, relatedly, whether the geographic confines of NATO are as traditionally defined or spill over to wherever Western interests are affected—most obviously, in the Persian Gulf.

And on neither of those questions has there been any clear answer. The actions of the Europeans have been, however, in accordance with what we wanted them to do. Now it may be that when the screws are tightened there will be a split in our interests and actions, but that remains to be seen.

Japan is different. The Japanese bought up plenty of the 30 million barrels that were destined for the United States at very high prices. I would look at their tendency since World War II of concentrating on a yen-dimensional foreign policy and really looking at the world in terms of an economic empire.

They think about security very peripherally, and think that the United States will take care of it at that. And generally when any kind of crunch has come they have really backed off from any kind of confrontation. The Iranian crisis was really no different from a lot of their actions in the past, like the MiG–25 incident in 1976. Before that time they had press censorship, in effect, by their own press starting in 1972 on articles against Peking for fear of alienating their new Chinese friends. In 1977 when their plane was hijacked in Bangladesh about the same time a German plane was hijacked, the Japanese quickly gave ransom to the hijackers in Bangladesh while the Germans more courageously shot out the hijackers in Somalia. Now what we can do to get the Japanese involved in their defense is firstly, more defense cooperation on the nuts and bolts level that really has been talked about for so many years —operational joint maneuvers and joint sharing of technology, for example.

Secondly is the further offset of expenses for U.S. bases in Japan. Thirdly is implanting the idea of a national security account. But basically this is to be a new account, because this .9 percent of their GNP for defense has become such a clear reference point that it would be too politically dramatic to surpass the 1 percent mark. Also into this new national security account could be folded that military budget with stockpiles for food and oil and other things. This is something that the Japanese are going to have to decide, obviously.

The fourth, and I think most promising of all, would be to really press Japan to bolster strategically important countries in an economic way. Japan just this year has started to give aid in long-term loans in Egypt and Turkey, and I think this is a very, very promising sign. It does not threaten the countries around Asia who still do remember the Japanese military with fear.

NITZE: Isn't it true that the problem that the Japanese have is (a) a political problem domestically, and (b) a lack of any clear sense of how they could usefully make a greater contribution?

ADELMAN: I don't think so. It has been clear for many years that they could do more on their air defense and on surveillance of their sea-lanes.

ROWEN: They have not perceived any great threat, and there has been a tacit agreement on the part of the United States that there is no great military threat.

NITZE: That must be a tacit agreement on the part of the United States, for it has long been clear that we alone could not assure the security of the lines of communication to Japan against a serious threat.

ZUMWALT: In my estimate, we will not be able to handle a western Pacific military contingency.

ROWEN: The Japanese have not perceived that as a serious threat. They have talked about it some, but they have never really felt that this was a very probable threat. Pressures that we might have exerted on the Japanese we always drew back from.

ADELMAN: Because of the Japanese reactions or lack of doing what we say?

ROWEN: I think it was both an agreement with the Japanese that the probability of Russian moves in the Pacific was low plus the political cost to pushing hard on Japan.

ALLEN: Japan did, after all, benefit from the security umbrella that was provided free of charge.

The Japanese, given their peculiar nature and outlook, found that it was in their own best interest to create the prosperity sphere that they had sought to create by military means—this time by hard work, diligence, exports, and the like. No one ever challenged any of this.

One of the great economic success stories of the Vietnam war was the flooding of PXs with Japanese merchandise and the acquisition of consumer electronics by our fighting men in Southeast Asia.

Then some very serious shocks did come. August 15 of 1971: the new economic policy closing the gold window; the textile shock, which has been a sort of continuing one. With this administration particularly, the tremendous and massive shock in the energy field that was administered by the Carter administration, particularly on the issue of the nuclear reprocessing plant, to a Japan that had irrevocably made the choice to be nuclear and to have a plutonium future.

All of a sudden that was yanked out. Finally the administration caved in because it had no other choice. It adopted some face-saving measures. But I would say that the Japanese mood over the course of the last eight years has very little to be confident in with respect to the United States. I will stop there.

ZUMWALT: The Japanese have two recent examples of how our umbrella can disappear. In the Yom Kippur war we drew down forces from the Seventh Fleet in order to project power into the Indian Ocean. And again today, for the same reason in the Iranian crisis, we have no western Pacific capability. So they must be able to observe for themselves that the umbrella is a very sometime thing.

I think we do have to urge the Japanese to do more. And the Japanese will only do more once the objectives are clearly defined for them and the pressure is applied to get them to perform in accordance with those objectives. When they truly come to believe that it is in their national interest to behave in a given mode, they will do so fast. The industrialists of Japan are ready to go and to produce and to export weapons, and to pierce the mythical 1 percent ceiling. There is no question about that.

ROWEN: Those commitments have to appear to be in the Japanese interest. This is more probable now, because they can see the disappearance of the American forces. They should see that this may be a more or less permanent feature because of the pressures on us elsewhere.

So I am somewhat optimistic about being able to work out a joint strategy with them in time.

KEMP: At what point is there going to be a domestic reaction against the fact that allied defense expenditure—in particular, that of the Japanese—is so low? But if we put pressure on Japan to increase its defense expenditure, how do we really want to see that go? There are some very serious trade-offs here. There are risks involved in encouraging Japan to build up too much. On the other hand, there are clear advantages in having Japan do a lot more in certain arenas—maritime capabilities come to mind. But then it is a question of whether, in fact, they would go along with it.

In the past, when the United States tried to dictate to allies how one should divide up the defense supply, there has usually been some rather nasty backlash as Mr. McNamara found out early in the mid-1960s.

ZUMWALT: We really face a range in dealing with that problem. It is very easy to get Taiwan and South Korea to increase their defense budget, and it has been very difficult to get Japan to undertake more than just very, very modest increases. They are still just a little above 1 percent of their GNP. And the problem we have had is that we can't get their military and their civilians really to talk together in a serious way. Civilians have so distrusted their military that it hasn't been the kind of two-way, back-and-forth that we have in this country.

An ideal division of labor would be to have them merely subsidizing *our* defense budget. But that is politically preposterous.

KEMP: If we demand that the Japanese do more, and if they start to increase their budget as much as they are capable of, and if there is a shift in their political perspective, we have to face the reality that we would now be dealing with a situation of equals. They will have more autonomy; they will be more independent; they will be able to take foreign policy initiatives that up to now they have not taken. It raises a whole new ball game politically.

ROWEN: But the essential requirement is that we work out carefully what it is that we want them to do—sit down and work it out with them. The approach should be almost the opposite of that which we have sometimes taken, which is to urge them in a general way to spend more money on defense. They have never seen that as being useful.

On the other hand, if there are specific things to be done which are urgent, it will probably turn out—on a broader definition of defense—that they will be spending more.

SULLIVAN: I think you can raise a scan around the world and find many other countries who have future potential usefulness which we have neglected. You could start with Brazil. I think our acquiescence to the Brazilian cancellation of our mutual defense treaty a few years ago, at the beginning of this administration, was a step in the wrong direction. China must be considered. I think Indonesia has more to offer. I think we have neglected the base structure that Australia could provide in that part of the world. I think we have been negligent in encouraging the Spanish to move more rapidly toward NATO now that their regime has changed. I think we have neglected some countries in the northern tier of Africa, from Morocco to Tunisia and Sudan. We have been slow in picking up on Somalia in the years since the Soviets got out.

As countries emerge from Third World status and go from developing to developed, there is very little to draw them to the Communist fold at that time; in the main, you are looking at countries who may flirt with this kind of instability and revolutionary preference on the way up the ladder.

We may not have a nuclear umbrella by which we can protect these people any more, but we certainly have an economic game in which they eventually want to play. I believe that we have to look at such alliances in the future perhaps a little differently than we have in the past. We are not really offering marriage for life, but looser, less binding relationships, as it were. Some of these countries, when they are at the right stage in their development, will think that is fine.

The Soviets look at it this way. They are far less concerned about whether their alliances persist beyond five or ten years, and they are perfectly willing to move from one to another. What they are interested in is a certain number of bases at any particular time.

We have to move in that same direction. We are going to find that such alliances are not going to insure commonality of approach on everything from human rights to nuclear proliferation. But they are going to be useful in some limited context and I think we should be looking to take advantage of those contexts in a somewhat different way. I believe this is part of changing our national strategy and our attitude towards the accumulation of allies.

IKLÉ: Japan is a special case, nonetheless. It is bigger than the others. I think the important question is whether we may not be running out of time to consult with and cooperate with the Japanese to turn around their contribution on defense. If things go badly in the next few years, the disincentives for their turning around may be stronger than the incentives to do so and we may have really a rather short period where this can be accomplished—all because of their projected fear of the Soviet superiority. There could be so strong a disincentive that they become Finlandized, at least as far as their increasing their defense budget is concerned.

ALLEN: How do we find incentives for people emerging into modern industrial status? Could we talk for a moment about the political requirements to achieve that? After three years of holding people like the Brazilians, the Chileans, the Argentines, and others at a distance because of human rights blemishes or whatever other deficiencies, what sort of strategy could we devise for helping them out without hurting our own standards and interests? This goes beyond any particular administration.

SULLIVAN: But this administration has done something rather odd for the United States. It has put ideology first over politics, in some cases it has put politics over economics, and it has surely put economics over military factors. We have an unusual ranking of our four factors of national strength, if you will.

What I am suggesting is that it is time to back away from ideology and human rights as the top priority. In some cases we may also have to back away from political purity as No. 2. The one that then pops to the top is not military: it is economic. It seems to me that the best way back into some of these countries is through stronger economic ties first, with political ties second, then perhaps military ties third, letting this ideological thing drift away completely.

ALLEN: That, for example, requires an enormous act of political courage. Just take South Africa as another. These are a whole new set of requirements facing us for the 1980s and those are essentially political requirements, aren't they?

SULLIVAN: Yes, and I think we have to substantially broaden our view of what we think is acceptable politically in the world.

CODEVILLA: I think that the problem has not been solved. The United States has long used economics as the top incentive to convince nations to join the American club. But this has not worked terribly well, because the regimes of the Third World are not quite so interested in enriching themselves as they are in staying in power. The United States cannot or has not been willing to supply the kind of support that they want. We can give them everything except what they really want, while the Soviet Union is quite willing to give them precisely what they want and can threaten them with what they fear.

I think that the military factor has been much undervalued. Give foreign nations the finest rhetoric. Shower them with economic benefits such as can only come from the West. Then put them in front of the fact of growing Soviet power in their area. Let them remember that the Soviet Union gives military and political help to keep friendly regimes in power, let them remember the fate of people like Afghanistan's Amin whom they deposed, let them remember the sad fate of American allies—and I don't think you are going to have much of a contest now.

I think that we are deluding ourselves unless we begin to think of these problems in very, very harsh terms.

SULLIVAN: It isn't clear that the Soviets have been all that successful in maintaining friendly governments in all of these countries; they have been thrown out of several places.

ZUMWALT: Their batting average is still going up enough for baseball, and definitely is better than ours.

SULLIVAN: What we are talking about here are some of the increasing subtleties of dealing with what is still primarily a Soviet threat. The question is whether you have to deal with it head-on or whether you have to deal with it indirectly. For instance, the best defense of NATO now is not to pour tanks into Europe. It is to make sure that the Middle East oil doesn't dry up. These things are becoming somewhat more indirect.

MARSHALL: What do you propose to remedy any weakness in the Pacific?

ZUMWALT: A greater fraction of her GNP invested by Japan in defense, a better tying together of defense arrangements and facilities there among South Korea, Japan, Taiwan. Based on what I heard from the Chinese Communist leadership when I was there, we have the opportunity to work both sides of the Chinese fence—as long as it is a part of a defensive alliance to stop the Soviets and obviously not an attempted political arrangement between those two, we could make progress.

I am worried about the political background where any critical facilities are, such as in the Philippines with Marcos. What is his long-term survivability and what can policy do to try to improve that situation?

As I see it, we have in the Pacific, through the mechanism of the Commander in Chief, Pacific (CINCPAC), a capability, if we want to use it, of getting together a series of arrangements through which CINCPAC—sometimes *de facto*, sometimes *de jure*—can begin to create a real Pacific infrastructure. We don't have one today, in my judgment. We have people going independently, nations going independently, not in any way thinking about how what one nation does in its facilities or its policies can support another nation's requirements, and so forth.

I think that CINCPAC would become—in a planning role—the kind of person that the NATO commander has always been, with joint planning, common facilities common logistics, and so forth.

ON THE NAVY

IKLÉ: I see at least three points. One is the trends in naval power, which in a way are turning more sharply downward than they are in strategic forces. They are more deleterious — and also we must say that our lenses are fogged now in the naval area as they were in the strategic area by SALT. So the question is more sharply posed as to why politically, by default, we took the decision to let our naval forces role downhill.

Secondly is the overemphasis, to put it too briefly, on the central front, which of course would absorb so much of our shrinking naval assets if in a conflict we were to try to protect the sea lines of communication. I would not necessarily go along with Bing West saying that the central front is the most improbable battlefield. But rather that in that battlefield, if it should become one, there are deeper problems which the concentration of naval forces would not solve. The deeper problems, of course, have been presented by Van Cleave's discussion of the strategic situation in the mid-1980s. Let us always remember the continuing folklore of NATO, that if the conventional forces cannot succeed, then we go to "first use of nuclear weapons." And that is a complete clash with the reality of the weakness of our nuclear forces that we heard about this morning.

I do think, though, that there is a problem of moving away too deliberately from the emphasis on the central front, because this could politically be very upsetting to the Germans, where the nervousness comes close to the surface and sometimes above the surface.

The third point is the question of whether a limited war with the Soviet Union is credible. Because if it is not, then I immediately jump to the next question: is the *alternative* to a limited war credible? I am also a bit less sanguine that in the time of need and crisis countries like Egypt, Israel, and Turkey will come to our rescue. This troubles me, and I would like it to emerge here in the discussion. So I see more merit in being able to fight a limited engagement with the Soviets than perhaps West indicated in his abbreviated presentation.

BURT: I think that Bing West is absolutely correct in saying that the Carter administration has pursued a slightly refurbished version of the 1969 strategy. They have taken a very narrow view toward U.S. global commitments and tended to concentrate on the Soviet front.

That narrow view, I think, is part of a number of different things. Not, I think, just of a perceptual view of worldwide situations and dangers that exist or might emerge. It was very much a reaction to Vietnam and a feeling that shoring up our relations with other democratic governments and people in Europe was probably the least controversial step one could take in a defense program. As soon as one began thinking of using military power elsewhere, in particular in the Third World, all kinds of questions were raised.

So in some ways one could argue that the focus on Europe was not really based on any kind of strategic argument. It is really the only place that the administration could spend money without feeling a great deal of guilt. That means that the money that has been spent on Europe has not been terribly well spent.

But one can fall into the same trap that the administration did when it decided that it would try to compartmentalize its focus on one geographical region and narrowly define "central front" and ignore other problems—suggesting that the solution to de-emphasize the central front is not feasible because the military and strategic relationships between the central balance in Europe and, most obviously, the flanks are very clear.

The military problem in northern Norway and the eastern Mediterranean is very serious. No one suggests, for instance, that some form of military balance exists in northern Norway. In fact, it is the linkage between northern Norway and the central front which provides a degree of deterrence.

So any defense planner is always confronted with the problem of deciding where he is going to put his forces. If the central front gets too weak, then we tend to decouple—not in the conventional nuclear sense but in the geographical sense—these areas from the center. In thinking about new problems in the gulf, we are going to have to recognize that there is a relationship between military problems in the Persian Gulf and in Central Europe.

I would not want a situation to arise where the West and NATO became so weak in the center region that we might be unwilling, in this instance, to react to a problem in the gulf for fear that it might trigger Soviet military pressure in Central Europe. I think that the relationship—the link or the overall umbrella—is a very important one to keep in mind. And we have to be careful to avoid adopting an either/or on which to decide where our emphasis must lie. I think we have to be responsive to the threat and recognize that by and large our strategy and limited resources have by necessity forced us to pursue a policy of extended deterrence.

WEST: I would argue that there are certain things we could do toward the *northern* flank that for a marginal billion dollars could actually be better for the *central* front than putting that marginal billion dollars into the central front directly. So, while the extended deterrent can cut the other way, it has seldom been looked at that way. Maybe I was reacting too strongly to the central front because the emphasis has been so much there.

The pressure is on us—when the number of leaks in the dikes compares with the number of funds we have—to get our allies to do really quite a lot more. For instance, in the case of Japan, they are concerned about their oil situation. They recognize that the United States is doing something by moving forces to the Persian Gulf. We are moving these forces from the western Pacific, although there is uncertainty about North Korea. So one of the things that is important for our agenda is to find what nations like Japan can do — in ways which might be politically tolerable — to deal with the wide range of global challenges. We may not find the Japanese sending naval forces to the Persian Gulf. We could find, within the next few years, a commitment by Japan to do much more in the western Pacific. Up until now it has been politically impossible.

KEMP: We must consider the nature of a global war. A "limited" global war is an artificial concept. The more important distinction is between a nuclear and nonnuclear global war. If it is nonnuclear, what we have to think about is how that war might terminate and what the definitions of victory and defeat would be. I think it is plausible to think in Bing West's terms of a global, nonnuclear, U.S.–Soviet confrontation. In this case, the real estate one controls when the whistle blows is going to be a very important factor in determining the negotiations after the war.

It is to guard against this type of situation that we must have the capability to prevent the Soviet Union walking into vacuums that could occur because our forces could not get there. For in this type of war, even a token capability in areas such as the Persian Gulf, Africa, and parts of Asia is better than nothing. This, of course, is an ideal role for the U.S. Marine Corps within the context of the rapid deployment capabilities.

We must not present the Soviets with a free ride. Unfortunately, this is the present situation in the Persian Gulf. In a global war, we cannot assume that the Soviet Union can bring all its resources to bear in every critical area. They too have problems elsewhere, and therefore even token forces are of some use.

ZUMWALT: The naval point of view for a number of years has been that you simply do not have enough capabilities to deal with the maritime problem in a global war with maritime problems. It has been U.S. policy to give priority to the central front, thus giving the near certainty that we would have to abandon the western Pacific and the eastern Mediterranean. Even then, we may or may not be able to sustain the central front after fearsome losses at sea.

Now look at the capability of the Soviets with their battle groups all over. We have fairly well disassembled our worldwide base infrastructure while the Soviets, having increasingly built land facilities and long-range naval air bases, have quite an infrastructure throughout the globe—continually extended to new client states. They therefore are quite flexible with regard to where they make their mischief.

ON THE BUDGET

ZUMWALT: The question of the relationship between strategic and general purpose force expenditures is tough unless we throw in enough money to take care of both, which is really what we ought to do. I advocate that defense budgets should be going up to 7 percent of our GNP, as opposed to the present 4.8 percent or so; that would generate about $50 billion a year additional which would then begin to give us progress in regaining parity on the strategic side and the capability to deal with Soviet probes on the general purpose force side.

If we have to talk about a lesser amount of money, then I think you would find a major split within the military. I have always been on the side that says we have got to worry about the strategic first. I think the majority of senior military come out just the opposite of that. The majority senior military say, "We don't want to fight a nuclear war, so let's take care of the general purpose side first." I don't think we will choose to risk using the general purpose forces if we don't regain parity on the strategic side.

SULLIVAN: By when could you apply that extra money? By the time you could reasonably do it, you probably are no longer talking 7 percent but a more modest increase as a fraction of GNP.

CODEVILLA: Herman Kahn once asked an audience what the GNP of the United States was in 1940. The answer came back somewhere around $275 billion. What was the defense budget of the United States in 1942? Answer, $275 billion. What is the GNP of the United States today? At that time, it was about $1.5 trillion. He said, "What do you think we could buy in the way of defense for $1.5 trillion?"

I am wondering why it is that people think it would be difficult to increase defense spending by something like $50 billion within a year of two. There are no technical reasons other than the procedures that we have developed within the Defense Department for slowing down technological innovations and for throttling new programs. Of course there are political obstacles to increasing defense spending, but they proceed from judgments regarding the degree of danger to the country. Technical factors begin to be considered when perceptions of danger are low. When people perceive danger, they don't talk of the dollar sums and they don't talk of percentage increases. Rather they ask how many and what kinds of weapons are needed to do a certain kind of job.

SULLIVAN: There nevertheless are going to be procedures within the *Congress* to consider the rate at which they will accept higher expenditures in this area in view of what it does to the national debt and to spending in other areas. But if you wait two or three years, you might go up $60 billion. At that time this will not be anywhere near 7 percent of the GNP, though.

I think almost everybody agrees that unless some candidate really goes off the deep end and says we need an extraordinary tax cut, we are looking forward to a period of surpluses by the 1984–1985 time period. An interesting thing has happened. The existence of the budget committees has essentially arrested the growth in nonappropriated "entitlement" expenditures of the federal government, which had grown from 35 percent of the federal budget in about 1955 to about 60 percent in 1970.

But since 1972 or 1973 there actually began to be a very slight turndown in the fraction of federal expenditures for entitlements. That means that the discretionary federal spending is going up at about the same rate now as tax receipts, rather than becoming a smaller and smaller fraction of tax receipts. As a result of that, within a few years an extra $30 billion in some annual appropriation may not be hard to accommodate.

ZUMWALT: I fear that there is a very real prospect that this promised 4 or 4.5 percent increase will end up being no increase. One authority in the Pentagon has calculated that we will be lucky to get a half-percent real increase out of the 4.5 percent because inflation is going to be 13 percent instead of the 9 percent the president's numbers were based on.

SULLIVAN: The White House does have the right to go back to Congress for a supplement to take care of increased inflation. They did that last year and they can probably do it again. The president promised to go back in for more if his inflation numbers were wrong, so you can't accuse him of chicanery at this point. He can't go around saying that inflation is going to be 15 percent. And he has promised to go back in—as he did last year—for another $3.5 billion to try to compensate for higher inflation.

The last point that I try to raise is that the country has got to come to grips with the fact that a modest, sustained increase in the national debt is not going to drive us to the poorhouse. If you look at the national debt as a function of

GNP, it has decreased every year since 1945. If you look at the cost of servicing that debt, it has decreased every year since 1945 with the exception of one year when the interest rates went up so very rapidly.

ROWEN: It is a mistake to address the narrow technical issue of the national debt; it is more important to look at the overall allocation of resources in society and not ask, "Do the resources exist for the purpose of allocating a good deal more to defense?"—because they clearly do; but to look at what is changed in the overall pattern, the allocation of these resources since, say, 1950, when we had an increase in spending for defense from roughly 5 percent to 14 percent of GNP for defense over the course of only two years.

The total government spending—federal, state, and local—was around 20 percent of GNP; today it is about a third.

Given the resistance to tax increases spreading from California, it may take great pressure to reallocate away from other public purposes in order to get a large increase in defense. That does not mean that it cannot happen; but remember that we have a virtually no-growth economy, and that is an important difference. The United States economy had its usual business cycle fluctuations during the 1940s and 1950s and later, but the basic trend was strongly upwards. Productivity was growing rapidly. Incomes were growing rapidly. Defense increased very substantially during the 1950 to 1952 period; it was possible for all boats to float on a rising tide. There was a reallocation away from the private sector to the public sector in percentage terms, but the total economy grew rather rapidly so that there was hardly any absolute decline in private consumption during that period.

What would be required today to get a large defense increase? It would have to come in substantial measure out of transfer payments because the transfer payment component has grown so large. This has been the growth sector.

It would mean reduction in many benefits and conceivably a reallocation in Social Security, that most untouchable of the benefit categories. In the longer run, we can get the economy back on a higher growth path and that has to be attended to. But doing that also means a reallocation of resources towards saving and investment.

SULLIVAN: The problem—and opportunity—is that for every successive inflationary year taxes go up by a third of the amount of that inflation. So in fact, if taxes are going up, receipts are going up—not by conscious decision but by default. And that does create available funds to be spent somewhere.

Now if we have a couple of years of 10 percent inflation, federal taxes will go up by about 5 percent. Five percent is about $30 billion. If you take that $30 billion and put it in defense rather than decreasing taxes, and if you permit the national debt to grow at the rate of $20 billion in that year, in very oversimplified terms you have your $50 billion.

ROWEN: Two percent of the GNP is only 2 percent. The United States is a rich country, and we can find 2 percent, if it is important enough, other than via inflation. But it is really a serious mistake to underestimate the conjunction of forces that is coming to bear right now.

There was a close vote in the Senate about two weeks ago, when Senators Roth and Domenici proposed a restriction on the total amount of the GNP which the federal government in the aggregate would be allowed to spend. We have a no-growth economy. We have inflation increasing taxes; precisely the effect these folks are trying to roll back. We are going to remain in a no-growth economy unless we can also do something about reallocating resources away from government and away from consumption to savings and investment.

Increasing defense through inflation runs counter to another very important objective, and one in the long run that is essential if we are to have a strong economy—getting inflation down.

SULLIVAN: I think that the problems this country is confronted with on the military side, on the investment side, and on the energy side, are such that we are going to have to increase the federal fraction of spending. You just can't have it both ways. Our taxes are lower than in any of the major industrial countries.

The resistance to federal spending is reasonably selective, and this groundswell coming from California was certainly not against defense spending.

HEMEL: The only sensible approach I see is that defense realists have to persuade fiscal conservatives that the logical way to approach this is not to freeze or reduce the federal share of GNP generally, but to freeze the nondefense share of GNP. You have to do this, or there will be so much political inflexibility that the kind of defenses you are talking about will never occur.

SULLIVAN: My projection assumes that the federal share of entitlements stays constant, because I believe that is very close to where we are. I then project a 10 percent growth in the nondefense discretionary expenditures and look at what was then left for growth in defense expenditures. But clearly, if we are going to get the additional defense money, we will have to tighten our belts in some respects. People have got to change their aspirations.

FULLER: There are a couple of things that have come up in regard to budget considerations. It occurs to me that we have the potential, we have wealth, essentially, to do anything. But at the same time, does it not behoove us to be considerate of cost in that we have to deal with the public's perception of what is being done and to sell them in an ongoing manner in regard to these programs? For example, it seems that Congress often, of its own volition, seizes upon certain weapon systems that it perceives as being symbolic of progress or a step in the right direction—the *Nimitz* class carrier, to me, comes to mind. I am concerned about its vulnerability and its appropriateness today, and yet these systems are urged upon us and promulgated, even though they are hideously expensive. Perhaps we should be thinking more in terms of greater number and more redundancy and overlapping and more dispersed systems. And, of course, the MX racetrack deployment scheme which, I think we can assume if the thing is ever built, we are going to be talking more like $100 billion instead of $30 billion when the final tab comes in. What a cynical exercise that is, and what a terrible thing it is even to suggest to the public that we allocate our precious resources for such a finite system which is so far down the road.

ZUMWALT: I think the points you make are good. I think that it is incumbent upon us to be responsible in what we advocate. You didn't quite say this, but I think you were hinting at the fact that it is a shame that this thing is being put forward as a nonserious proposition just to get SALT II ratified. Two members of the White House staff told me that was the president's reason. At least one of us has a witness that Paul Warnke assures people not to worry about the MX—it will never be built. Now that is even worse. That is pretending that you are going to spend money wrongly in order to avoid spending money properly.

ROWEN: Another point has to do with possible triggering events. If you take a look around various parts of the world and project ahead for four or five years the behavior we have seen on the part of the Soviet Union in the last four or five years, then the American public will presumably be very upset and willing to spend much more on defense.

The Afghanistan move is certainly major and might well be a triggering event.

But the Yemens, Libya, Iraq, Iran itself, other possibilities exist in the Middle East, possibly in the near future. In Europe there remains the important candidate of Yugoslavia. In Southeast Asia the Russians clearly are getting much closer to Vietnam and Vietnam may move against Thailand. In the Caribbean and Central America we may see a visible Cuban/Soviet involvement more widely. In sub-Saharan Africa I suppose there are several possibilities. Any one of these may not be a very high probability. Integrated across the whole, major developments look likely.

So there likely will be further triggering events. Whether our political system, which is in a sensitized state now to Soviet moves, will respond in a modest way or strongly to these events is hard to say, but we will not lack triggers.

THOMPSON: The problem is, how many more potentially "triggering events" can we stand before it is too late to do any good by reacting? Ambassador François de Kose used the metaphor last year of the game of chess in which the queen gets to so commanding a position that all remaining plays really are superfluous; you throw in the game. Are we coming to that point very shortly, wherein a few critical moves could cause a number of key countries to throw in the towel and see the hopelessness of any further resistance?

IKLÉ: Should we react to triggering events? I want to go back to Paul Nitze's caution about our reacting in the Middle East. What do we do in the event of a post-Tito Soviet invasion of Yugoslavia? I can see the National Security Council saying, "Let us not send any assistance to the Yugoslav partisans. We may get involved. Obviously we can't win there. We knew that in Czechoslovakia and Hungary." Or we can say, "Let us not argue. Let's send them some aid, whatever the consequences."

In the present situation we would scrupulously refrain from aiding the partisans. In a larger global context, as I was trying to explain, I think that would be the wrong decision. We should move in with assistance and be prepared to lose on that battlefield in order to trigger the larger reaction that is needed to halt the further deterioration in the correlation of forces.

ADELMAN: It is pretty depressing when you get to the point where you want some kind of a defeat, no matter how little it may be, to waken people up.

IKLÉ: No, we don't *want* a defeat. We want an engagement. It would be better to win in Yugoslavia. But you have to be prepared to lose locally.

SULLIVAN: Wars have been fought that way for generations as a means of finding enemy concentrations.

THOMPSON: What is the great line of Wellington's at the battle of Malplaquet, "If we continue to have defeats like this, the victory will assuredly be ours." In any case, it is highly pertinent.

KEMP: Much depends on where a triggering event comes from. If it were an event in the Pacific, for instance, is it conceivable that you could have that type of increase in the budget without talking about Japan? It seems to me that, within the country as a whole, the demand that Japan should increase its defense expenditure is the price that would have to be paid if the trigger event was Korea. Meantime, the president has changed his rhetoric. He originally wanted to cut the defense budget by 7 percent.

SULLIVAN: If the president is successful in getting his newly proposed increases, he will not intersect the projection of the Ford increases until 1985. And in the meantime he will not have spent $60 billion that the prior administration thought was necessary.

So he will still be $60 billion behind in defense investment over that eight-year period. And I would argue that the same administration that projected a 2.5 percent increase a year in 1975 would now be projecting something much higher.

THOMPSON: But the president did speak a couple of weeks ago, in mid-December, for the first time about the momentum in the Soviet buildup. It was a fairly strong statement of the Soviet threat.

IV

An American Strategy
for the 1980s

16

CHARLES BURTON MARSHALL

Strategy:
The Emerging Dangers

The meaning of "strategy" v. its interpretation. Vital interests as causes for war or peace. The U.S. and the USSR. Factors affecting U.S./Soviet strategy. The UN Charter. Strategic nuclear power and SALT. The present strategic imbalance. The importance of the military.

On a later winter day in 1946 Secretary of State James F. Byrnes, extemporizing at a staff meeting, called for a change in perspective about the Soviet Union. It was high time, he said, to quit regarding that country as a basically well-disposed partner needing only to be dissuaded, by patience and examples of forbearance, from occasional lapses into waywardness. Instead, he went on, the United States should thenceforth recognize in the Soviet Union a deliberate and methodical antagonist in world affairs—one requiring to be countered. No one else with such station in U.S. councils of policy had ever said such a thing before, according to the late Charles E. Bohlen, who recalled having sensed one of history's turning points at the moment of hearing the secretary's utterance.

The problem at that moment concerned Soviet actions in retaining, beyond a promised withdrawal date, its military control established during World War II over the northwestern reach of Iran and in stirring up and supporting a separatist rebellion spearheaded by local Communists. Faced by U.S. opposition, the Soviet Union, sidetracking its ambition to annex Iranian Azerbaijan, withdrew its forces from Iran.

Further contentions followed, however, over subjugation of Soviet-occupied lands in Eastern Europe, over the futures of occupied and divided Germany, Austria, and Korea, of occupied Japan, of Turkey and Greece, and over a choice between international rivalry and international controls in the new and militarily important field of nuclear technology. Other U.S. officials one by one came around to the view expressed by Secretary Byrnes—President Truman himself among them in the spring of 1947. The pervasive contest over policy thereupon got a name—the Cold War. In two more years the Soviet Union emerged as a nuclear rival to the United States.

In response to the unfolding adversary relationship, the United States government created an array of institutions unprecedented for times of peace. These pertained to continuous consideration, at the presidential level of authority, of all aspects of security policy; to coordination of martial preparations and activities in all environments of war; to ongoing collaboration among the military chiefs of all the uniformed services; to gathering and analysis of foreign intimes beyond recall, people had been producing, exchanging, and consuming goods and services without having a generic term for the essence of their activities. Then in the late 1700s savants began to give order to pertinent precepts under a Greek label. Thus economics and economists appeared. Back to unrecorded antiquity human aggregates had been generating, fixing, packaging, and deploying energy — solely muscular energy in early epochs — and using weapons to bring it to bear on enemy targets and to discharge it against them with destructive design. After their entry into recorded history four thousand or more years ago such activities became a focus for numerous theorems and maxims, but efforts to systematize ideas about matching means and ends in the anticipation and conduct of major hostilities waited until the stimulus provided by the Napoleonic epoch. Again a Greek designation was adopted. Ponderers and practitioners alike came to be known as strategists. Thenceforth, as in economics, scope and content have varied with the times. Tracing all the permutations would be beyond the limits of available space and my learning, but three stages of definition are worth recalling.

For Carl von Clausewitz, a pioneer strategic thinker (his *On War* retains eminence after a century and a half), strategy was the art and science of managing military engagements sequentially with a view to victory conceived as success for the policy ends of war (Clausewitz 1976, p. 87) — in distinction from tactics, pertaining to the conduct of military engagements one by one. For Alfred Thayer Mahan, who was still unfamiliar with Clausewitz's writings at the time of producing *The Influence of Sea Power upon History* nine decades ago and thereby establishing himself as this country's original strategic theorizer, a definition of strategy confined "to military combinations . . . embracing fields of operations . . . regarded as actual or immediate scenes of war" (Mahan 1941, p. 22) was inappropriate for naval matters, where to wait upon hostilities before attending to conditions for victory would be to wait too long. Edward Mead Earle's delineation in 1944, enlarging upon Clausewitz's restrictive conception and Mahan's insight, does well enough for present purposes—subject to certain supplementary observations.

To quote from Earle's foreword to *The Makers of Modern Strategy* (1944, p. viii),

as war and society have become more complicated . . . strategy has of necessity required increasing consideration of nonmilitary factors, economic, psychological, moral, political, and technological. Strategy, therefore, is not merely a concept of wartime, but is an inherent element of statecraft at all times. Only the most restricted terminology would now define strategy as the art of military command. In the present-day world, . . . strategy is the art of controlling and utilizing the resources of a nation—or a coalition of nations—including its armed forces, to the end that its vital interests shall be effectively promoted and secured against enemies, actual, potential, or merely presumed. The highest type of strategy— sometimes called grand strategy—is that which so integrates the policies and armaments of the nation that the resort to war is either rendered unnecessary or is undertaken with the maximum chance of victory.

One might extend Earle's list of components, adding, for example, covert operations and the arcane arts of finding out what goes on on the other side of the hill. The conception there expressed, however, is comprehensive. Warmaking capabilities are seen to embrace a miscellany of considerations beyond military matters. Strategy, moreover, is discerned as integral to maintaining peace even as to the conduct of war. Peace and war, both related to problems of coming to terms with adversaries, are put in perspective not as wholly disjoined slabs of reality but as distinguishable conditions reflecting differing combinations of similar factors.

Earle's delineation links strategy to success. Applied in the world of action, however, strategy may also have to do with frustration and defeat and with necessities which they entail for trimming ends to fit means. One finds a hint of that aspect in Clausewitz's *On War,* where one is assured that emphasis on war as an instrument of policy, lest it become an endeavor in useless destruction, "does not imply that the political aim is a tyrant." Rather, Clausewitz observed that policy "must adapt itself to its chosen means, a process which can radically change it." According to Clausewitz, "War, and the commander in any specific instance, is entitled to require that the trends and designs of policy shall not be inconsistent with these means. That, of course, is no small demand" (1976, p. 87). As I understand the gist, civil authority is obligated to take into account limitations and requirements inherent in military instruments, and military leadership imposes a duty to press that consideration on civil superiors.

Earle's inclusion of "political" in a list of nonmilitary components of strategy invites a question. Politics is not a separable category of existence and activity—a pigeonhole. The term conveys overlap, fusion, and interplay, and the mental function called for is synthesis as distinguished from analysis. In that respect, politics resembles strategy. The words are forest words, not tree words. The concerns which they label require, in Edmund Burke's phrase, a combining mind.

Earle's reference to "vital interests" also calls for elucidation, for the phrase lies at the center of problems of peace and war and the precept of coherence in policy. The term "interest," derived from a Latin root for being between, expresses linkage from mind to object. At the mind end, the implied quality is readiness to be concerned. At the object end, the essence is perceived value—meaning the worth of something measured in other things also of worth to be put at risk, deferred, diminished, or even renounced if necessary for attaining or retaining that object. In the realm of strategic responsibility, such matters as interests, concerns, and expendability are palpable, not merely notional. The phrase "vital interests" indicates concern so intense and valuation so high as to impel decision-making—if necessary for the object involved—to risk, to defer, or even to sacrifice peace and its enjoyments.

Nothing is ever at hand to give *a priori* guidance to decision-makers in determining vitalness in the relevant sense. A vital interest represents an asset or a desideratum so classed by being affirmed as distinguished from being tested by litmus paper or checked against a catalog. The issue involved in classifying an interest as a vital interest is protean. It hinges on will and on calculation of means. The test of resolution is willingness and ability to pay the entailed price.

A question of primacy and derivativeness as between a nation's grand strategy and its vital interests is imponderable. These matters are integral to each other, whether in war or in peace. The related generalizations which I am about to affirm hold up despite a complicating tendency for warring sides to load on bonus effects as war aims and despite variations between one war and another in range and intensity of issues at stake.

An absence of mutually contradictory interests deemed vital by opposed sets of decision-makers denotes peace between organized societies, no matter how extensively and sharply their preferences may diverge. Mutual contradiction between interests deemed vital by decision-makers on the respective sides is what undoes peace and induces war. War breaks down and peace is enabled to resume upon renunciation by one side or the other—whether due to faltering will or failing means or both in combination—of interests once deemed to require being fought for. The renouncing side's strategy has failed. That side is the loser. A strategy may fail without being tested in war, however. That happens when want of means forecloses an organized society from classifying disputed interests as vital and forces it to yield, without fighting, what it would have fought over if it could.

In dealing with potential enemies—the heart of preserving peace—*the essence of avoiding war without capitulation lies in correctly identifying vital interests and in making their*

standing as such known to the putative enemy. Making one's
vital interests known involves, beyond simply declaring one's
purposes, a manifestation of one's command of means to vin-
dicate one's purposes. The essence of prevailing in war, if
forestalling efforts fail, is also in identifying correctly one's
vital interests and in having the will and commanding the
means to uphold them. In my understanding, such is the import of Earle's emphasis on the continuing applicability of
strategy through peace and war.

THE UNITED STATES AND
THE SOVIET UNION

In broad terms, the situation obtaining since the United
States undertook to fit its policies and institutions to that
comprehensive conception of strategy has been characterized by three main circumstances—two of them traceable
to the course and outcome of World War II and the third
stemming from a much longer past. First, two countries—
the United States and the Soviet Union—though not
necessarily or precisely equal, are in a class apart from all
others and superior to them in scope and resources for projecting influence beyond their own spans of jurisdiction. The
second relates to development and accumulation of pro-
digious mechanisms of warfare in instant readiness and with
the capability to project hugely destructive charges of energy
to targets thousands of miles distant—appropriately called
strategic arms because of their calculable potential to settle
the outcome of war with initial salvos sufficient to disable the
targeted country from carrying out a strategy. The preemi-
nence of the two superpowers extends to nuclear and rocket
technologies basic to that mode of warfare, so that each has
been the other's only plausible opponent for all-out
hostilities. The third circumstance is a fundamental an-

tithesis between images of the future reflected in the respective superpowers' external policies.

U.S. resources to manage the interplay between the counterposed superpowers has included a wide range of intellectual capabilities. Acuteness of thought on strategy in a battery of concerned professional and scholarly institutions and the range, volume, and quality of pertinent literature produced here are unique among all countries in any age, according to a judgment 'conveyed to me recently by a newly retired chief of strategic intelligence for a friendly government. He—I must leave him unnamed—added a rueful prediction: the approaching strategic defeat of the United States would be examined and portrayed with a thoroughness and an insight never heretofore brought to bear on a great event. While reluctant to accept his dour forecast, I understood the basis—as he explained it—for his misgivings. As a strategic competitor, so he said, the United States is handicapped by its remembered past; its commitment to a strategic approach to upholding peace on acceptable terms accordingly has been—and persists in being—too contingent and too much affected by vain hopes.

In considering the relevance of that view, one must distinguish between experience and assumptions. No proverb is more dubious than the one identifying experience as the best teacher. Experience surely excells inexperience as a preceptor. Some people, however, may learn its lessons all too well while others may learn nothing whatever from experience or may even accept instruction quite at variance with it. American experience concerning war—and therefore strategy— and the prevailing American perspective on that experience have long been at variance with each other and perhaps remain so.

The role of hostilities in shaping the American nation was manifest from the beginning. Covert operations abroad instigated by the Committee on Secret Correspondence of the First Continental Congress antedated the assertion of inde-

pendence. Opportunities and requirements accompanying a
military alliance with France prompted the Second Continental Congress to stake "our Lives, our Fortunes, and our
sacred Honour" on the proposition of severing ties to the
British crown. A claim to "full Power to levy War" was integral to the independence asserted, and vindication of it
came as a by-product of a far-flung war centered in Europe.
Subsequent wars substantiated the nation's right to conduct
maritime commerce, expanded its territorial base across a
continent, and maintained its integrity against secession.
Expansive effects of military success on perceptions of vital
interest were illustrated in wars against Mexico and Spain,
just as the reductive effects of battlefield reverses thereon
were exemplified in the War of 1812. The Confederacy's
debacle brought a lesson in the folly of omitting military
counsel from the meshing of means and ends in war, for no
commander or staff was in a position to tell civilian authority
in Richmond of the depth of the South's plight in late 1864,
thereby to avert hopeless perseverance into the final
destructive phase.

For all such demonstrations of the import of war and its
lessons in the American past—one could go on and on with
examples—my introductory courses in American history,
taken in high school in 1926 and in college in 1928, skipped
over the war intervals as parentheses in national experience.
Peace was normal. Wars were embarrassments and devian-
cies. They represented breakdowns of norms and interruptions to the general course of reality.

The gaps represented no mere school teachers' fancy but a
widely held American attitude traceable back to the nation's
beginnings. Alexander Hamilton spoke for a distinct
minority in anticipating for the United States a full share of
"the vicissitudes that have been the common lot of nations."
In the prevailing assumption, the United States was to be a
special case, its specialness inhering in exemption from external strife. As explained in Felix Gilbert's *To the Farewell*

Address (1961, pp. 44–75), every other country's interest in the survival and prosperity of the United States was assumed. The privileged country's destiny was to be an exemplar of peace for all nations. A succession of decades in a strategic backwater, under no pressure from enduring enemies, seemed to confirm the belief. Wars were interruptions. Any need for thinking how to win them could wait upon their advent. Preserving peace was a matter of preventing breakdowns. The way to prevent them was to encourage cooperation, communications, commerce, and the like, to center attention and energy on peaceful pursuits as distinguished from the arts of war. Conceptually, peace and war became disjoined slabs of reality.

However implausible I, for one, find it because it implicitly discounts the pervasiveness of cupidity in human affairs, the notion of a nonstrategic basis for peace has proved durable. It not only survived but indeed throve upon the twentieth century's two world wars. Each of those wars in turn was portrayed by U.S. leadership as the one last interruption— with perpetual peace to follow. Materializing that dream became the paramount end of U.S. policy in both wars. The core idea in the League of Nations Covenant of 1919 and the United Nations Charter of 1945 is that every signatory nation forswear belligerent initiatives. That obligation universalized—and taken at face value—would logically liberate every nation from anxieties likely to tempt it to foment preemptive war. By rational inference, the problem of conflicted versions of vital interests would be disposed of, for no nation would ever be compelled to defend interests for which no other nation would ever launch hostilities. The implicit promise of boundless tranquility would be made doubly sure by having every nation take a vital interest in having the concept work—and thus be disposed to take hostile action against any putative transgressor. In the perfected version, every organized society would be in a mood to fight for—and only for—preservation of peace, and only would-be transgressors would have to worry about enemies. The technically correct designation for that circular prescription to universalize peace is collective security. The UN Charter is the embodiment pertinent here.

In taking up the tasks of putting together a strategic basis to maintain acceptable conditions for peace with the Soviet Union and other countries in its sway, U.S. policymakers, in the main, regarded the pertinent undertakings as necessary roundabout steps toward vindicating the nonstrategic vision of peace in the UN Charter. The ultimate goal of strategy was perceived as a situation putting an end to all need of strategy.

In the prevailing interpretation the obstacle was the Soviet Union. The regime there had, as it were, unilaterally amended the charter, a result of looking at the world through the lens of Marxism-Leninism. In that view the causes of conflict were wicked outlooks, values, and interests knotted into the fabrics of societies not in the Marxist-Leninist mold. Advancement of peace required eradication of such perversities. With that accomplished, universal tranquility would reign; but meanwhile the Soviet Union, cast as the exemplar and agent of historic necessity, would exert unremitting hostility—geared to opportunism—against exponents of futures at variance with the Marxist-Leninist formulation, including preeminently the United States.

The obstacles posed by Soviet power so motivated were regarded as formidable but, over some undefined span of time, not insuperable. While avowing and demonstrating willingness to engage in mutually helpful endeavors, the United States would firmly oppose Soviet designs for aggrandizement. For countering the Soviet pushiness, the United States had at its disposal a general reservoir of strength thus described by the British historian Robert Payne early in the Cold War (1949, p. 7):

America bestrides the world like a Colossus; no other power at any time in the world's history has possessed so varied or so great an influence on other nations. . . . Half the wealth of the world, more than half the productivity, nearly two-thirds of the world's machines are concentrated in American hands; the rest of the world lies in the shadow of American industry.

U.S. resources included unchallengeable ascendancy in military aviation and in naval power over every ocean and a long headstart in nuclear technology providing strategic leverage susceptible of being brought to bear in deterring military initiatives at lesser levels of force. All such elements of strength—by being brought to bear in denying the Soviet Union opportunities to enlarge its sphere of influence and dominion—would serve to deprive the ruling group there of its sense of historic momentum and thereby to undo its confidence in Marxist-Leninist dogma as an infallible key to the future. Frustrated in designs for redoing other societies in the Soviet image and enticed by the rewards of amicable collaboration, the ruling group would eventually be rendered amenable to the version of peace documented in the UN Charter.

The thought of vindicating the UN Charter as the goal of U.S. strategic endeavors was registered in a miscellany of executive and congressional pronouncements, treaties of alliance, mutual defense agreements, and foreign aid contracts. President Truman so portrayed U.S. purposes in making war in defense of South Korea. The concept reechoed fifteen years later in President Johnson's call to war over South Vietnam (1965, pp. 606, 609) "to oppose the effort of one nation to conquer another . . . because our own security is at stake." His summons invoked what he called "a very old dream . . . of a world where disputes are settled by law and reason" to the exclusion of force, and added, "we have the power and opportunity to make it real."

Power and opportunity obviously proved illusory in that last instance. Under canons of strategy, the folly of asserting a vital national interest in the future of a remote land— whence the United States avowedly wished to extricate itself—against an adversary bent on possession is incontestable. The resulting defeat by a Soviet proxy was the most emphatic in American experience with war—that of the Southern Confederacy excepted. A more pertinent consideration here, however, is how the United States has fared in a wider scope with strategic designs to bring the Soviet Union around to collaboration in a dream of peace in the mode of the charter.

The weight of evidence on that question up to now is not encouraging—notwithstanding a multiplicity of agreements and efforts in the field of U.S.–Soviet peaceful collaboration. The Soviet Union continues to see the external world—and to shape policies and actions—according to Marxist-Leninist dogma. Over the years the ruling group has spun off an array of doctrinal corollaries asserting for the Soviet Union a prerogative and a historic duty to maintain the irreversibility of Marxist-Leninist orientation wherever imposed and a concurrent right to interpose in events and to guide trends in situations wherever occurring beyond the Marxist-Leninist realm. The abiding aim, as put by the Soviet foreign minister, is "visible preponderance" from which "to lay down the direction of world politics" (U.S. House of Representatives 1979, pp. 431–34).

One must dismiss as wishful and fatuous the assertion of Secretary of State Cyrus Vance, in an interview published in *Time* for 24 April 1978, of the harmony of "dreams and aspirations on the most fundamental issues" between the respective chiefs of state, presidents Carter and Brezhnev. Antithesis of purpose between the superpowers persists. The military aspect of the relationship has altered drastically. The causes of the shift are inseparable from the superpowers' contrasting images of the future.

That divergence was reflected in contrasting ways of saying "never again" after the crisis in 1962 precipitated by the United States' timely discovery of a Soviet attempt in stealth to emplace nuclear missiles in Cuba to offset a U.S. advantage in strategic nuclear arms. Following forced retraction of their missiles, Soviet policymakers vowed never to be caught thereafter at a disadvantage. They instead proceeded methodically to overtake the U.S. strategic lead so that in future confrontations they could exert pressure to give way due to their strategic superiority. U.S. policymakers, on the other hand, discerned an opportunity to pursue, in a new formulation, the enduring aspiration for a nonstrategic basis for general peace.

That notion carried U.S. strategic policies onto another tangent and to consequences of great moment. The concept developed over several ensuing years called for both superpowers to settle for equilibrium in strategic nuclear capabilities at a level to ensure reciprocal unacceptable damage in a hypothetical nuclear exchange. For fear of an utterly devastating retaliation, neither side would ever dare a first strategic nuclear strike. Second or third strikes would accordingly become logically impossible. The nuclear threat overhanging international politics would be dissipated. An environment auspicious for peaceful settlements by negotiation would be fostered. The nub was, in a sense, to foreclose clashes of vital interests between the superpowers by disabling them both from so defining and pressing the interests in dispute.

To exemplify forbearance and to afford the Soviet Union opportunity for catching up—if it wishes—so as to set conditions for such a strategic standoff, the United States in the middle 1960s throttled down on strategic nuclear power. In a similar mood, the United States subsequently decided to restrict accuracy in guidance systems for its submarine-launched strategic nuclear missiles so as to blunt their effectiveness against hardened military targets.

As so often in human affairs, it was easy to believe that what was in mind was also in the cards. U.S. devotees of arms control counted on the Strategic Arms Limitation Talks (SALT), begun a decade ago, to serve as a seminar for

educating the Soviet Union to align itself with the U.S. view.
As a pedagogical effort, SALT has fizzled. The Soviet Union
has held to its opposing notion on how to forestall superpower clashes of vital interests: by unilaterally disabling the
United States for so defining and pressing its preferences in
disputes with the Soviet Union. In the first round of SALT
ending in 1972 the Soviet Union pocketed, with alacrity but
without gratitude, the concession of a sizable U.S. technological headstart in defenses against intercontinental missiles —
a concession made in expectation of encouraging Soviet acceptance of U.S. ideas about a standoff in offensive strategic
capabilities. In the second round concluded in 1979 the
Soviet Union has made manifest its ambition to nail down
strategic nuclear preponderance, not necessarily to foment
war but surely to settle into a superior position for facing
such an extremity and thereby to have the upper hand in
contests of purpose stopping short of war.

Only recently Secretary of Defense Harold Brown (1979, p.
7) expressed himself as disposed to bank on the SALT process as "the foundation for progress in establishing an enduring political relationship with the Soviet Union that
reduces tensions, and sets important visible boundaries to
our ideological, and our political and military competition."
To say such a thing, however, is to mistake a wish for a fact.
SALT has proved serviceable to the Soviet version of strategy
and has disserved the United States. Not surprisingly, in
view of a long diplomatic record concerning strategic
negotiations, a decade-long effort to regulate hardware
aspects of strategic competition without an accommodation
on broad purposes has come to a dead end.

The country's predicament is aggravated by the effects of
long overreliance on the notion of mutual strategic deterrence. Its war-making capabilities for lesser levels of combat
have been permitted to sag—for why worry about means for
conducting wars destined never to occur? This has contributed to wide alienation of the American middle class

from the military aspects of national existence in overreaction—I think it is that—to the strategic debacle of South Vietnam. Whatever the causes, the armed services have fallen seriously below standards in number and quality necessary for meeting commitments.

THE U.S. DILEMMA

The situation now upon the United States, entirely at variance with its experience, is that of being pressed upon by a determined and resourceful adversary power with advantages at its disposal of being in a palpably superior military position. The stakes are not marginal concerns to be bargained over in a mood of give and take, but are basic to the characters of the two societies concerned. The problem for the United States is not how to avoid war—for war is ever avoidable by merely giving in—but how to avoid being defeated case by case through having been deprived, in a situation of visible strategic inferiority, of ability in extremity to define preferences cogently as vital interests. A word for that eroded capacity is prestige, meaning the faculty for being taken seriously on serious issues. Its essence may be illustrated by recalling a geneticist's experiment in crossing a tiger with a parrot. On being asked about the results, he said, "When it talks, I listen." For a country to lose that faculty for getting itself listened to is for it to be deprived of the capacity to avoid fateful junctures of having to choose between resorting to war under adverse circumstances and having to back down.

Reversing adverse strategic trends is an essential component—necessary but not of itself sufficient—in the task of restoring the United States to a proper position in world affairs. Much else must be done to correct a general tackiness that has come to characterize the conduct of external affairs. Such reformative work can scarcely be undertaken, however, by a government continuously subjected to surprise and forced to scramble from predicament to predicament in a manner that is bound to continue to be the lot of the United States in a protected position of strategic inferiority. Professor Karl W. Deutsch once wrote (1953, p. 53), "A 'sovereign government' is defined as one which is 'not subject to effective coercion by another power.' " In that essential sense, U.S. sovereignty is at stake.

The Soviet Union can be counted on to use intimidation to try to prevent the United States from going ahead with any efforts to right adverse strategic trends. Themes to be stressed are already amply evident. One theme posits strategic equilibrium as a present reality, an allegation supportable by citations from highest U.S. authority. On that premise, any attempt to improve the U.S. position militarily is assailable as aggressive. A companion theme already places the United States in a position of irreversible strategic disadvantage, so that attempted extrication is construed as foolhardy and impermissible. The counterposed themes can be played upon simultaneously.[1] Soviet discourse has been giving increasing weight to the second theme: stressing the necessity of U.S. accommodation to the circumstance of having already lost out in strategic competition with the Soviet Union. The recurring expression of scorn for the United States as a demonstrably inferior military factor is novel.[2]

Great danger for the United States—as well as huge expense—in trying to recoup strategically is surely in prospect. The choice, however, is not one between peril and safety or between expenditure and saving. The choice is between two forms of danger and between two kinds of costliness. In making such choices, an active course seeking to maintain some purchase on events is preferable to supine acceptance of defeat. For this country to elect the preferable course and carry through on it, however, will require of the nation the sort of wisdom expressed by a statesman of another era:

The commonest error ... is sticking to the carcasses of dead policies. When a mast falls overboard, you do not try to save a rope here and a spar there, in memory of their former utility; you cut away the hamper altogether. And it should be the same way with a policy. But, it is not so. We cling to the shred of an old policy after it has been torn to pieces, and to the shadow of the shred after the rag has been torn away. And therefore it is that we are now in perplexity. (Cecil 1924, 2:145)

One thing to be jettisoned is the mental baggage that has encumbered the U.S. approach to strategic arms negotiations. Secretary Brown's current annual review of the U.S. strategic position provides an example of diffidence to accept what is manifest in that connection. It describes as "unclear" the United States government's perception of Soviet perceptions—the perception on which the effectiveness of the U.S. strategy of mutual deterrents hinges—and calls pertinent Soviet doctrinal presentations "murky." The analysis finds in conclusion "little evidence of any Soviet view ... that assured destruction as a strategy would be a positive good" and acknowledges "suggestions"—suggestions only—that Soviet intentions are to be able to prevail in any strategic nuclear exchange and thus to be in position to regain cumulatively in contests of purpose short of strategic warfare (U.S. Department of Defense 1980, pp. 82–83).

Soviet doctrinal presentations actually are unequivocal. Any remnant of unclarity in U.S. comprehension of Soviet strategic perceptions—given such an amplitude of evidence—only reflects possessiveness for customary illusions. Such reluctance in the face of the incontrovertible reminds one of Groucho Marx in an old movie cleaning his spectacles after catching sight of a homely girl.

17

PAUL H. NITZE

Policy and Strategy from Weakness*

The drawing power of Western and Soviet cultures. Clausewitz on strategy. The balance of forces—military, economic, political/psychological. Hardware and manpower problems.

My purpose in these comments is to consider what sort of strategy we as a nation can adopt, given our circumstances and limitations. We will consider the correlation of forces as well as the inherent limitations on our use of force. But first,

*EDITOR'S NOTE: Paul Nitze's chapter consists of a revised version of his extended comments on national strategy made at the Belmont House conference (December 1979), and was not written in article form.

though the need for a national strategy is obvious and compelling, strategy cannot be understood in a policy vacuum. Strategy must be in support of policy, so the precondition for having a strategy is to have a policy. We must—as a precondition for a consideration of strategy—thus go back to policy, about which several critical points need to be made.

First, what is implied by a policy? A policy has to be on behalf of some "we"; thus we must be specific about what "we" it is we have in mind when we discuss a policy. In the present context, the "we" which is to be discussed is the United States as a nation. This implies a people, a territory, and a culture. It is to that "we" that U.S. policy relates. That is the primary "we"; but that "we" tends to expand out over others that are similarly minded and who, to a greater or lesser degree, face the same kind of threat. With respect to these one hopes for considerable convergence, and for an expansion from the core "we" to a larger "we." The converse objective is a narrowing of the "they"—the "they" that oppose the concepts of our "we." "They" in this instance are the men in the Kremlin (and the people whom they control) who are trying to expand their "we," which is to us a "they."

The object of policy is to preserve the base, in the sense of the people and the territory and the culture of the "we," and to have it expand outward and to reduce the threat presented by the "they."

Examining our aspirations as a culture is important to understanding the "we." Those aspirations have been so extensive in the past that we may have to trim some of them in the future. I was asked a question recently: "Am I optimistic or pessimistic?" To make a sensible answer, however, one has to be very specific about the context. If the question is, "Do you think that American culture has a better chance of surviving into the long-range future than the Kremlin ideology?"—I think it does. I think American culture is more complex, more humane, more deeply based than that of the Kremlin. Today its attractive power is greater around the world, even —or especially—amongst Communist youth. We are not as concerned as we once were by the attractive power of Communist doctrine to our youth, whereas the Russians are more worried about the attractive power of Western culture to their youth than they were ten or twenty years ago.

A further question, however, is what part of Western culture is going to survive? Is it going to be merely Coca-Cola, the slot machine, and porn culture, or is it going to be something which has in it a greater content of deeper values such as those that motivated the founding fathers of this country? What part of Western culture is going to survive, and what is its quality, is, I think, what the contest is all about.

Now as to strategy. Clausewitz (1976) emphasized the interaction between policy and strategy. His first point is that strategy should be aimed at furthering the policy of the state. He makes the further point that in the "pure" theory of war there is a tendency for war to reach the highest level of violence technically possible at the time. But then he goes on to say that no war has ever been fought pursuant to "pure" theory; that in all actual cases, because war is conducted in pursuit of policy, policy tempers the conduct of war. Everybody conducts a war for policy ends and therefore tries not to let it get to the full, ultimate violence of which it is capable.

Clausewitz makes a second point—that *war exists for the benefit of the defender*. The aggressor would always prefer to enter your country unopposed. Being the defenders, therefore, we have some choice as to the when and where of the initiation of war—because a war is not likely unless we propose to defend. War is ultimately the last defense of the initially weaker or less aggressive state.

In discussing the distinction and interrelationship between strategy and tactics, the third point Clausewitz makes is that in strategy *all factors bearing upon the correlation of forces are important at all times*. There is no strategic distinction between those forces that are committed at a given time and those that are uncommitted. They all have their strategic relevance, as the *possibility* to move and to commit uncommitted forces bears upon the strategic situation, even if they are as yet not committed.

In tactics, however, you worry about the reverse; namely, the uncommitted forces, because generally there is little to be gained by reinforcement of a lost engagement. What counts is what was initially committed to that particular tactical operation.

A fourth preliminary point is that any strategic view has to deal with appreciation of *all* the factors of the correlation of forces as they exist today and as one believes they are going to exist five years from now, ten years from now, and at other relevant times in the future.

Further, one should take into account the evolution of strategic ideas since Clausewitz's time. For instance, Edward Mead Earle (1944) extended the concept of strategy as Clausewitz developed it with a concept of grand strategy applicable in peace as well as in war. He included, in addition to the military factors, all the nonmilitary factors that bear upon the relative power position of potential opponents, including the economic, political, psychological, geographic context. It was Earle's view that it is only in *peacetime* that one in fact puts together all the various elements which will bear upon the situation in a potential military conflict, and that the true test of grand strategy is in the management of those forces—all those factors—so that one avoids a war and still sustains the pursuit of his objectives.

THE CORRELATION OF FORCES

What can one say about the correlation of forces today in the broad Edward Mead Earle sense? Reviewing the current situation, one must conclude that that correlation is today unfavorable, and that over the next five years it will probably become more unfavorable.

The Military Balance

Let us first look at the major components of the military balance. It is widely acknowledged that Soviet military effort has been increasing cumulatively year by year over the last fifteen years, and in recent years has exceeded that of the United States by wide margins. In percentage of gross national product it is now double or triple our own. In dollar equivalents it is estimated to exceed ours by 40 percent. In terms of hardware procurement and research and development their effort exceeds ours by an even greater margin. The president's proposed budget increases will not reverse these trends in the future.

If there were a strategic nuclear war, U.S. fatalities might be between five and twenty times those of the Soviet Union, depending on the way in which such a nuclear exchange came about. It is hard to conceive of a possible scenario which would not end up with more powerful Soviet than U.S. strategic nuclear forces remaining after the exchanges as well as faster Soviet recovery times.

With the continuing deployment of the MIRVed (multiple independently targeted reentry vehicles), accurate, mobile, rapidly reloadable SS–20s and Backfire and Flogger bombers, the theater nuclear balance has also swung to a position adverse to the United States.

The conventional force balance on the Euro-Asian land mass has favored the Soviet side ever since World War II. With the decline in the combat quality of the U.S. Army since Vietnam and the institution of the volunteer army, that balance has become even more negative.

On the oceans, whether the balance is favorable or unfavorable depends on what part of the ocean one is talking about. In the eastern Mediterranean, I would suggest that it has been negative from our standpoint for some period of time and that it is becoming negative in the western Mediterranean, depending upon what happens, for instance, in Libya. If the Russians were to have planes based in Libya, I believe that no part of the Mediterranean would be tenable for us today. There are other areas where our naval position is not tenable today if the Russians decide to oppose it. There *are* still other areas of the ocean where it remains favorable to the United States. I believe that one cannot say that the overall naval force balance, when one looks at the totality thereof, is favorable. Moreover, one cannot turn the situation around in any short time period such as five or even ten years. It is a longer-term project than that to get a country's naval posture turned around.

THE NONMILITARY COMPONENTS

The Edward Mead Earle (1944) concept of strategy suggests that we also analyze the nonmilitary components of the correlation of forces.

Economics and Energy

Overall, the U.S./European/Japanese economic structure is much more powerful and productive than that of the USSR and its client states. Western markets are the dominant markets and the dominant source of industrial and consumer goods and services. It is in this context that the significance of energy becomes apparent.

It is a problem almost as serious as the military problem, both because of the vulnerability of our oil supply and that of our allies and because of its impact on the inflation rate. I support Henry Rowen's point that some of the things we are doing about energy, such as subsidizing consumption, make our energy problem worse, not better. If we had to cut down oil consumption by 20 to 40 percent in the United States, it could be done. If we look back to the period not very long ago when we consumed only 60 percent of the oil that we consume today, we realize that those were not bad years at all. We now know more about energy conservation and conversion to other energy sources than we did then.

If the choice in solving our energy problem were to be viewed as one between using force in the Middle East or going without Middle East oil imports, the latter would clearly be the better choice. It is extremely difficult to see any circumstance, in light of the existing military balance in the world, in which the use of U.S. forces in the Middle East in combat against Soviet forces would be successful in assuring continued oil imports from that area. On the other hand, the risks of disaster in such an operation are real.

I think the measures which should be taken in connection with energy and inflation are all technically possible. Politically, however, they are extremely difficult. Considering the seriousness of the situation, radical remedies cannot be excluded, but alternatives must be realistically weighed against each other.

THE POLITICAL/PSYCHOLOGICAL COMPONENT

The next point, the political/psychological component of the correlation of forces, flows from what I said earlier about the character of the "we" and particularly the extended "we." *The political/psychological contest is at the heart of the struggle to extend the "we" and narrow the "they."* In Iran a principal problem is that the Russians have handled their policy with greater skill than we have in the psychological sense. Mohammedanism has no affinity with Russian Communist doctrine. Normally one would have thought that the religious people of Iran would have been frightened of Moscow, more so than of us. But they are not. The Russians have played to Iranian psychology better and much more subtly than we have. In any case, the Iranian mobs are screaming against the United States. We constitute no threat to Iran. Iranians are not concerned that we might move in tomorrow or the next day, while for centuries they have been very much worried that Russians would do so.

I have taken perhaps a most difficult place as an example. If one considers other places, it would seem to me that we have much better chances of winning the psychological battle if we work at it. But we have not organized to work at it. In fact, we did the reverse. We became apologists for the Soviet Union. We have not devoted ourselves to trying to optimize the spread of the "we" and a contraction of the "they." We simply have not seriously addressed ourselves to the problem. In this arena, our stance has been governed more by domestic political considerations than by foreign policy considerations.

Now that the Third World bloc has been shaken by the occupation of Afghanistan, many things are feasible which for some time were not. For a number of years a majority of the United Nations member nations were primarily motivated by gains anticipated from squeezing the United States. It was then impossible to rally a majority in the UN General Assembly for resolutions consistent with the basic principles of the charter. Today it is again possible to do so. From the political/psychological standpoint, it is much more practical to add weight to a majority in support of the principles of the UN Charter acting together against a violator of those principles than to seek widespread support for policies identified as being purely U.S. policies.

BACK TO STRATEGY

Let us turn from the correlation of forces and its elements to certain more specific points concerning strategy. The first one is the time period at which one has to look. I think one should look at it in something like five-year segments: five years, ten years, and fifteen years in the future. It is important to look at these long time intervals because—at least in the military field—you cannot do much to change the balance in less than ten or fifteen years.

Priorities

In allocating resources for the development of military forces far in the future, questions arise as to relative priority between elements. In my view, highest priority should go to the strategic nuclear umbrella. It is the area in which we have had and still have some competitive advantage. And it is not that costly; it represents less than 15 percent of the defense budget. Moreover, we cannot use any of our other military forces in combat against the Russians without having confidence that we have a strategic nuclear umbrella adequate to control escalation. I therefore see but little argument against the proposition that the first priority should go to the strategic nuclear field.

The second priority should go to the navy. Overseas operations cannot be logistically supported unless we can maintain the necessary sea lanes of communications. Airlift is inherently inadequate for sustained logistic support; it requires more weight of fuel than it can lift.

Should correct decisions be made with respect to priorities, it is still necessary to correctly allocate resources among all the segments. It is generally true that the last increment to the highest priority category is not as important as the initial segment of lower priority categories. Even if we move resolutely and wisely to correct the adverse trends in the military component of the correlation of forces, this will take time, and the balance at any given time in the future cannot be predicted with certainty.

CONDUCTING POLICY FROM RELATIVE WEAKNESS

In more general terms, we have to deal with the fact that at least for some years we will be conducting strategy from relative weakness. In the past, most people looking at strategy have assumed it would be conducted from a position of strength. Few have looked at the art of conducting strategy from relative weakness. If one looks at history, no country has emerged as a great country that has not lived through periods of great weakness and has shown it can conduct strategy from weakness and recover.

Communist doctrine has a clear set of instructions on the conduct of policy from weakness. If the correlation of forces is favorable—and Communists use the term "correlation of forces" in about as broad a sense as Earle does—then the Kremlin must exploit that favorable correlation, take action, and nail down potential advantages while they are available. If the correlation of forces is against them, they must throw dust into the enemy's eyes while they establish the preconditions for reversing the trends. The correlation of forces must again become favorable before forceful action can prudently be taken. By analogy, we should recognize that the correlation of forces now is negative for us, that it is going to be negative for the next five years at least, and that the object of policy should be to throw dust in the enemy's eyes while getting on with reversing the trends and making them positive.

For the next five or ten years the cutting edge of throwing dust in the enemy's eyes must be in the psychological field. From that standpoint the Iranian hostage crisis has helped us pull together with our allies and has weakened the unity of the Third World in building a coalition against us. From that standpoint, it hasn't been all negative.

On the subject of the neutron bomb, we should have turned that around into a devastating attack on the Soviet Union with respect to the SS−20 and into a complete defense for the neutron bomb. The relative probable civilian casualties from one neutron bomb and an SS−20 warhead is on the order of one to 100,000. They are just not in the same ballpark. Here we let the Russians get away with a tremendous propaganda campaign around the world in which the neutron bomb is described as a weapon of "mass destruction" and the SS−20 as being better than sliced bread.

The threshold test ban has also given us some important opportunities which we have not taken. I am told that there are clear-cut violations of the ban, yet nobody in the executive branch of the government says much about them. They say that perhaps our measurement techniques are not accurate. Of course they are not accurate within a factor of two, but in estimating these violations we have already made allowance for an inaccuracy factor of two. Otherwise we would not have been confident that they were violating it. I gather that the Soviets are also testing the SA−10 radars against incoming reentry vehicles in violation of the antiballistic missile treaty.

Another example of throwing dust in the enemy's eyes is the suggestion above that we capitalize on the new attitudes in the Third World and put renewed emphasis upon support for the basic principles underlying the UN Charter. Those principles, including the prohibition on the use of armed force except in individual or collective self-defense and the prohibition on interference in the internal affairs of other states, can be of enormous help to us during the coming period of danger.

One final point about this. When one is throwing dust in the enemy's eyes, one may not want to be explicit about how these things are assessed. For example, in the case of European theater nuclear modernization, the political purposes alone are perhaps sufficient for going ahead despite the low priority it may deserve on purely military grounds. But we must first do the military analysis in a hard, rigorous way before making such political decisions. Otherwise we will not know what we are doing. Maintaining the alliance structure is politically important despite the fact that the alliance may be in no position to engage successfully in hostilities on the continent of Europe during the next five to ten years. But I am not at all sure this should be proclaimed from the rooftops. In any case, our European allies are even less prepared to confront Soviet forces in military action than we are. The interrelationships between the psychological part of it and the underlying military part of it are extremely complex.

Throwing sand, of course, is only a short-term expedient. A prime requirement in improving the correlation of forces over the longer term is to reverse the adverse trends in the military balance, particularly in the strategic nuclear and naval balance areas. The debate on the creation of forces, however, has been too narrowly drawn. Much of the recent debate has been on whether to ratify the Strategic Arms Limitation Talks treaty, or how to base the MX, and things of that kind. But there has been little debate on things that are just as important—for example, selective service. The manpower problem is as crucial as the hardware problem and presents inherently greater difficulties. Eventually we are going to have to consider the problem of civil defense, which plays a critical role in the strategic balance. I know it is politically a most difficult issue, but it is the most cost-effective and perhaps the most important action we could take in cor-

recting the strategic nuclear balance and therefore the overall military balance.

Beyond the creation of forces is the problem of what we
should do about the *use* of military force, particularly in the
near term, while our strategic objective must be drawn and
pursued from relative weakness. Much of the recent public
debate has focused on the circumstances under which we
might deploy forces, as for the defense of Saudi Arabia or
Egypt, or for whatever crisis abroad one may wish to propose.

The most important question may be whether, in the next
five to ten years, there are *any* circumstances under which it
would be wise for the United States actually to commit military forces in combat with Soviet forces on the periphery of
the Eurasian landmass. From Riga to Baku, from Tashkent
to Vladivostock, Moscow can project power outward from interior lines, as in Afghanistan where the recent completion
of tunnels, railroad depots, and bridges enabled the Soviet
Union to move in so short a time the massive forces required
for its invasion. The United States cannot counter such
moves militarily today, if indeed it ever could on the conventional level.

If it could counter them at the conventional level, the
strategic nuclear balance has shifted so that any such moves
on the Eurasian landmass would be affected by Soviet escalation control: that is to say, Soviet nuclear predominance carries the implied threat of an ability to escalate a conflict up
the nuclear ladder just as the U.S. predominance in the
Cuban missile crisis in 1962 implied such a threat to the
Soviet Union.

The situation in the 1980s will require that we understand
our limitations and the constraints on our use of military
power. There is no inherent reason, save a willful—and we
hope unlikely—desire of the Soviet Union to confront us
militarily in the near future, why we as a nation cannot conduct policy from an honest appraisal of our current position
while refashioning our policies and forces and thus improve

our position eventually to an honest parity. My view is that there is no good alternative to such a policy and that we must start now.

Discussion:
Part IV

Discussions at the Belmont House conference (December 1979) included, in addition to the authors of this book, the following participants: Richard Allen (Potomac International Corporation), Angelo Codevilla (Senate Select Committee on Intelligence, Office of Senator Malcolm Wallop), Fleming Fuller (Documentary Department, KRON–TV), Eric Hemel (economist, Office of Senator Patrick Moynihan), Charles Kupperman (Research Director, Committee on the Present Danger), Robert Osgood (Professor of International Relations, School of Advanced International Studies Johns Hopkins University), Dale Tahtinen (Reagan for President campaign), and Victor Utgoff (representative of Zbigniew Brzezinski. National Security Council). These excerpts pertain to subjects discussed in Part IV.

ON STRATEGY

IKLÉ: One has to ask oneself why things are not being changed. The problem is in part psychological, to be sure, but predominantly political. I feel one of the best explanations of that has been provided by Senator Moynihan in his discussion of attitudes of the people who staff the agencies, whether it is a United States UN mission, the U.S. Internal Communication Agency, the Voice of America, or the attitudes toward what used to be ineptly called covert action. Since it is embedded in the staffing in and outside of Washington, it is not so easily cured. It will be difficult to mobilize all this quickly.

The second explanation is the obsession of the administration with SALT. The administration was unwilling to jeopardize the treaty's fate by revealing Soviet violations of the test ban treaty, or the extension of the Brezhnev doctrine to Afghanistan until it was invaded on a scale that couldn't be hidden. We have long had the idea of freedom being on the rise, people longing for freedom, people longing for modernization. Carter continually talks about the wave of freedom and the wave of human rights sweeping the world, but I have yet to be shown where this wave is manifesting itself. I don't see any progress or yearning for modernization, in our sense of the word, especially with respect to events in the Persian Gulf recently.

NITZE: Note that I used neither the word freedom nor democracy. It is clear that our founding fathers had no intention of building a democracy in the Greek sense of the word. They were conscious of the responsibilities of freedom as well as the license of freedom. Talk about human rights in the president's terms generally does not reflect deep insight into what it is all about. It does not reflect the point that John Adams understood so well, namely, that if the alternatives are chaos or some degree of order, then order is more important. He said that the first task is to avoid chaos and assure some kind of an orderly society. If the foundations of an orderly society are assured, then one ought to strive to make it as diverse and free as one can.

If you are trying to run a country like Uganda, you cannot do it with British parliaments or American political parties. It will not work that way.

ADELMAN: Does strategy sometimes dictate giving up vital interests?

MARSHALL: If the United States were in a position successfully to use military force in Iran, it would do it. But it cannot do it. We would regard this as a vital interest impinged upon. There is no litmus paper test for a vital interest. Vital interests are those that you will sacrifice peace for. This is not *a priori* to policy. Policy is the process of determining what you can make your vital interest.

ADELMAN: Yes, but Nitze's line of argument raises the question of whether we will have any vital interests over the next five years, given our weakness.

NITZE: Our national interests have a hierarchy. The peak of that hierarchy is the integrity of the nation itself and of its territory. Then you try to spread out from there, to the extent you have the means to do it successfully and whether the correlation of forces is such that you can do it.

OSGOOD: Until recently we have been discussing how to improve the correlation of forces in a period of history in which we all recognize there is a considerable imbalance between the total resources of power that we have available to us, including the public will and the national leadership, and the magnitude of our policy objectives and our definition of our security interests.

The problem is more serious than we think because, although it is essential in this period to improve the correlation of forces starting with the strategic balance, even that is not going to bring our resources of power into balance with our very extended conception of our security interests, our involvements in the world, and our policy objectives.

One of the things a strategy should do is to bring these things into balance on the grand level. Ever since around 1950 the rate of expansion of our security objectives has far outstripped the expansion of our resources of power, and the correlation of forces has gotten worse and worse. To fill in the gap there have been a number of strategies and a number of expedients and lots of tactics and, above all, an evolution of assumptions about the nature of the world which would, we hope, eliminate the problem.

One set of strategies was developed during the Kennedy administration in which, in essence, we tried to build situations of local strength and stability in the Third World, both through economic aid and by expanding our overseas local war intervention capabilities. It had worked in Europe. We have seen the limits of that strategy, given the expansion of the international system in the Third World, the increasing incidence of local conflict, the instability that will not be eliminated by economic aid or any of the other instruments of policy that we thought of in the period.

Another strategic idea for closing this gap was regionalism, relying more heavily on regional balances of power, perhaps with dominant ascendent middle-range powers, which Brzezinski called the "new influentials." The only really new and promising regional development that I see is ASEAN, and that is a long way from having the kind of military significance that would act as a surrogate of power for the United States.

I thought that the Nixon-Kissinger administration made a good try at a strategy for closing this gap between power resources, on the one hand, and policy or security objectives on the other. Firstly through détente, which I believe did enhance American and European security in Europe. It did not, however, come close to applying to the Third World, where I believe as late as the Moscow Confernce in 1972

Henry Kissinger really believed that there was some prospect of extending the rules of the game to the Third World.

Another aspect of the Nixon-Kissinger strategy was to rely more heavily on surrogates of power. The most notable of those was Iran —enough said. Another aspect was the creating of the trilateral balance by bringing China into the game. I believe that on balance that had a good effect, though we have not begun to realize some of the dangers of it in the long run; but it still does little to help redress the correlation of forces in the central balance of the international system. It does not alleviate our problem in the Third World, which is where an important part of our problem of imbalance exists as long as we define our interests as extensively as we do.

The Carter administration's approach is trying to close the gap in part by getting on the "right side" of change in the Third World and all that. This, I think, has been counterproductive. There is another strategic idea which was just hinted at as a tactical expedient in the short run, and that was retrenchment, by which I mean actually defining U.S. interests in a more limited extent while assuming away the Soviet threat. But these expedients, strategies, and assumptions will not come close to closing the gap, in the grand strategic sense, between power resources and security objectives.

There is one other logical measure that one might consider in the long term in a grand strategic sense, and that is the partial devolution of power from the United States and its major allies. This is in the global sense our one great potential and unused power asset, and yet we will all recognize the tremendous problems of a successful devolution of power because, among other things, the conditions for success include several things that are very difficult to combine. I think, first, our allies would have to be quite convinced that we are not going to take care of their vital interests. Otherwise they do not have the incentive to take up the balance. At the same time, they should not be so convinced of our

declining power—so lacking in confidence in our power—
that they will simply opt out of the game.

So, although I think in the long run a partial devolution of
power is the only real way short of redefining our vital interests in a more limited fashion to close this gap, it seems to
me the problems are immense in doing that. Leonard
Sullivan alluded to another possibility, which is in effect acquiring new allies on the basis of their redefinition of their
security interests. But I am skeptical of that because I do not
see the candidates who will line up with the United States in
terms of convergent security interests, as far as their partici-
pating in order-keeping arrangements even within their own
regions.

NITZE: It seems to me that Robert Osgood has very
cogently summarized the history of the evolution of U.S.
strategic ideas over the past ten years. But his analysis rests
on the various strategic assumptions made by successive
leaders during that period. In other words, the policymakers
have assumed that only Europe and Japan were important,
that the Middle East was not a vital interest, or that
regionalism could replace U.S. influence, etc. I would suggest
that to base strategy on hopeful assumptions is not apt to
work. You have to base strategy and policy on judgments and
the judgments have to be geared into what the facts are—
either the present facts or the facts that you can anticipate
you can in some way create or that somebody else will create.
But you cannot just assume things that are not supported by
the facts of the real world without running into disaster. The
assumption was made that Europe and Japan were our only
two vital interests, and beyond that just some kind of half a
war potential was to be provided, but clearly not in the Middle East. As was brought out earlier, the key to Europe and
probably to Japan *is* the Middle East. Europe and Japan can
hardly maintain their independence if the Middle East falls
under Russian control. Therefore the Europe/Japan—only

assumption was an assumption which did not correspond to fact.

I think it is essential that we abandon this business of considering that useful strategies and policies can be based on unrealistically hopeful assumptions. We must first be clear about our purposes and then develop strategies which correspond to objective assessment of the external world and of our capabilities to influence the evolution of that world.

SULLIVAN: I wonder if in fact we can have any future if we pursue a policy of retrenchment, and if we continue to view the situation in the world as the United States versus the Soviets. It strikes me that Paul Nitze's remarks underplay what I consider to be the vital necessity to keep a full coalition among the Western states to achieve our objectives. I simply do not believe that you can ever give up many important interests worldwide and still have a successful United States. So I think the policy objectives have to include some understanding of the needs and the attractions of other countries that have to work with us.

The second point is that the correlation of forces has larger political, economic, and ideological vectors than I had previously thought. It strikes me that one of the problems in this country that puts us at an enormous disadvantage is that we have no effective governmental mechanisms for internally reconciling our diverse national interests. One wonders if our economic policies, military security policies, ideological policies, and political policies can work unless they are far better orchestrated than they have been in the past. This has been a huge Soviet advantage in that they have within their hierarchy the mechanisms for drawing consistently from these four different vectors and operating or orchestrating them together. We even lack the mechanism to do that—not only the understanding but the mechanism. For instance, we have at least three branches of the government with different interests in the sharing of technology, and essentially no mechanism is there for assuring consistency among the three different branches.

HEMEL: I thought one of the arguments for a U.S. military presence in Korea was not that our twenty thousand or thirty thousand troops would tip the balance if there were a war, but that it would raise the stakes and thereby prevent a war. I just wonder why that same line of reasoning would not apply to the Middle East.

NITZE: As you remember, what I questioned was whether we should commit forces in a situation involving potential conflict with Soviet forces on the Eurasian landmass without a pretty solid line of retreat. Now that is not the same thing as saying we should not deploy task forces, because we might deploy a task force in support of political objectives rather than with the view that we would use that force in actual combat with forces of the Soviet Union. The principle remains, however, that to bluff is dangerous. It is justified *only* occasionally.

ROWEN: Isn't it also true that Korea is a particular area which *is* defensible? It is not so clear that some of these areas are going to be defensible.

NITZE: In Korea we were not intending to use those forces against the USSR if we could help it. But in any such area you want to be sure that you have a line of retreat.

HEMEL: Why?

NITZE: Because otherwise you are likely to be defeated. At this stage of the game it is not wise to go into a situation where we would be defeated or where we could get into a nuclear war. A nuclear war would be tragic beyond belief, particularly a nuclear war that we lost. That would result in the destruction of all values. Suicide is not a basis for policy.

KEMP: Just on this issue of the Eurasian landmass, I am assuming that you mean literally the Eurasian landmass. You would leave out Africa, you'd draw the line at the Suez Canal, and maybe at some of the islands of Southeast Asia.

NITZE: I am not sure that I would leave out the Suez Canal. The Suez Canal can probably be dominated by potential power from the USSR. If it were a theater nuclear war, the SS–20 and the Backfire bomber would probably dominate the Suez Canal. You just do not want to be in the Suez in that kind of an engagement. If the contest were limited to conventional weapons, it might be a standoff, depending upon a number of variables. This illustrates the importance of maintaining an adequate strategic deterrent to assure escalation control.

KEMP: I think we do have to be very explicit about where we could or could not put up a stand in the conventional arena in the next several years. But I think that one comes to the conclusion that we cannot do anything unless we do something about the few remaining allies and friends we have in these regions of the world. One of the most depression things about the current administration's policies is its policy towards Korea and Turkey and, to a lesser extent, to the Middle Eastern countries. I would think I would be more optimistic and say that if we do give really active support to our friends of the region, then, in anything short of a nuclear war, it is a problematic calculation as to how it would come out. We could rely on a forward support, and in that kind of situation I think one does have to take into account what the respective stakes are. What is going to be the most threatening to the Soviet Union, and therefore the issue it is most likely to escalate, is conflicts right along its border. Northern Iran would be very dangerous from that perspective in every sense. The farther you go away from the Soviet border, the less inclined they will be to push this thing to the point of global confrontation. In that context, if you stop to look at the map of the Eurasian landmass, there are areas where they do not have as yet the type of protection which guarantees that sort of victory under all circumstances. They may be approaching that, but they certainly haven't got that now, and I don't think they will in the next five years.

Therefore I guess I come down slightly more optimistic than Nitze, but with the premise that the relationship with friends is more important perhaps even than military capabilities in the short run.

WEST: For at least the next five years, if the Soviets have to pass over a wide body of water—say, over five hundred miles—they are probably in trouble, if you believe that you can have a limited war with them that would be conventional. The Backfire does not exist in the numbers to be a genuine naval threat for several years. In the interim they are using a 1958 production Badger which is so slow that U.S. interceptors could defeat it.

The military battle is important, and it has been greatly neglected in the last fifteen years. But there is a broader system here which has not been emphasized enough but which goes beyond the military problem. This important, broader point is that we are involved in part in a contest of social and cultural systems. And in this psychological, propagandistic, moralistic realm we ought to encourage a human rights focus—not necessarily Carter's—where it exists, say, in South Korea, perhaps in Brazil. My feeling is that some human rights commitment is very important for us in trying to build a serious, tough, if not formal alliance system in the Third World.

COSTICK: My discussions with people from the Defense Advanced Research Projects Agency involved in certain projects have led me to the conclusion that some of the key enterprises are suffering for a lack of funds. The projects in question are related to the strategic umbrella, the various aspects of the ABM program including high energy lasers, the satellite defense system, and so on. These are the areas which I would consider of utmost importance and priority, and I think $5 billion annual increase in defense expenditures must include funds for those projects. We must have an ABM system on the shelf available for rapid deployment.

Another important question concerns the so-called "China card." Under what circumstances should it be played, how, and for what purpose? What could increase the Soviet perception of growing threat from Communist China? What could be done to concentrate Soviet attention on mainland China, even to the extent of provoking Soviet military operations—including preemptive strike?

To gain the necessary time to overcome our strategic deficiencies, I believe it should be the United States' objective to get the Soviet Union tied down on the Chinese mainland. I think that the Soviets are aware of the problem. It would probably set them back twenty years and it would give us the breathing spell needed to achieve the strategic superiority we've enjoyed in the past.

Playing *this* Red China card could be enormously important. This does not mean that we should not also support anti-Soviet guerrilla forces in Yugoslavia, Afghanistan, Angola, Ethiopia, and so on.

There are differences in the local cultures. Some people fight; some people do not. I am convinced that the Soviets are aware, for instance, that in Yugoslavia there would be a fight. And even if it won this fight, a spill-over effect would hurt the Soviets in other areas. We should generate similar problems for them in other areas.

KEMP: I think one has to make a distinction here between long-term and short-run objectives in playing these cards. I don't like the term "card" anyway. It assumes that the Chinese are inert and will allow themselves to be played.

My observation on that would be that for the next ten years, so long as we are so dependent on the Middle East, we have to be very careful. China is one issue on which the Soviet Union is paranoid; they are scared of what might eventually happen along that border. And it is precisely in those sorts of circumstances, where the Soviet Union is fearful of a war with China and where we are actively supporting the Chinese one way or another, that they may play the Middle East "card." If they do, there will be nothing we can do to stop them. In that case, it seems to me, they could split the alliance.

In thinking about China, one is thinking about a very long haul with countries involved other than the United States. We do not need to rush in with a host of military systems. If we are going to rush in at all, we should rush in with nuclear weapons. That is the only true quick fix, it seems to me, that we can give the Chinese that is going to make any dent at all in what the Soviet Union could bring to bear in a war with China.

COSTICK: From my perception of the international facts, the Soviet Union will move into the Middle East no matter what. In the short run, domestic pressures will make them take military initiatives; their energy situation will considerably worsen. If they do nothing, their economic growth as a result would be arrested. Problems in Eastern Europe, which relies on the Soviet Union for its energy needs, will start to surface. There will be cracks in the structure. The Soviets cannot afford it.

In the long run, however, given the continuation of established trends and Soviet ideological imperatives, the takeover of the Middle East will be only a question of time unless the constellation of forces changes in favor of the United States.

Regarding Communist China, obvious direct U.S. involvement is not necessary. Making Red China a menace to the Soviet Union could be accomplished by so-called "peaceful means"—and in fact these are already taking place in the forms of scientific and technological exchanges, transfer of key technology, and sale of manufacturing equipment and scientific tools. What Communist China needs is easily disguised under dual-purpose technology. Acquisition of so-called dual-purpose technology would make their missiles reliable and accurate and their nuclear warheads clean. On the other hand, through scientific and technological exchange they can acquire the enhanced radiation weapon technology, which in fact they may have already received from the United States. Anyhow, some two and a half years ago Hua Guo Feng stressed to his colleagues in China that acquisition of enhanced radiation warhead technology from the United States stands on the highest scale of his priority list.

V

Epilogue

18

W. SCOTT THOMPSON

Toward a Strategic Peace

Foreign policy in the current administration. The need for leadership. National security—quick fixes and long-term measures. The soldier, the diplomat, and national policy. The adaptability of nations. Two opposed views of international conflict.

The message of this book, we have noted, is not a macho call to arms. Most of the contributors have watched the decline of America's defenses for long enough to know that a turn-around will not come from inflated rhetoric and the sound of impending doom. This is rather a set of sober essays and discussions whose intent it is to show the depth of the present national security dilemma along with the problems within our immediate competence to remedy. Many of our contributors thus wrote hopefully.

As this book was in preparation, the American public was waking up to the message our contributors had been delivering during the past several years. But the reveille has been confused. The public learns one day that America's interests are deeply enough engaged in a foreign crisis to warrant stern presidential rhetoric. The public is told that we have endured the worst crisis since World War II; war has been threatened. But what we have done about it in fact, in military terms—as part of an overall attempt to control inflation by reducing federal spending—is to cut the defense increases planned in autumn 1979. (Continued high rates of inflation will further erode real defense spending.) The implications of all this become evident by noting that as a result of the invasion of the Republic of Korea in 1950, which was a less serious matter from a strategic point of view, the United States tripled its defense budget.

It became apparent within a few months of the Afghan invasion that nothing of the administration's thinking about Soviet policy, in any authoritative sense, had changed. Additions to the military budget were not being considered; indeed, the wages of inflation would soon be eroding the modest increases decided on during the autumn of 1979. Sources close to high administration officials ventured their opinion that, at the top, the administration considered the Soviet move a protective reaction to prevent instability in Soviet Central Asia rather than a move likely to lead to further aggression. This was itself an illogical sequence since, in an intrinsically unstable region, the result of a protective reaction is a wider perimeter in need of further protection, and thus further expansion. Not one official of the Carter administration has been replaced subsequent to the invasion, revealing better than any other indicator that no real change of heart has occurred.

There is something far worse to contemplate. Presumably unconsciously, some administration leaders soon began the process of intellectual accommodation which many had predicted would start once the Soviets moved in earnest on vital Western interests. For it seemed clear that the Afghan invasion was a near direct product of a Soviet calculation of American weakness; America's unwillingness to stand up to Soviet aggression was made abundantly evident in three years of nonreaction to increasingly blatant moves. In its latter days, moreover, repeated American failure to respond was a conscious policy, as it seems Moscow realized, not a trap or a trick as Soviet commentators at first suspected. But now American advocates of continuing nonresponse were in fact suggesting that it was those who had consistently advocated increased military strength and will who were responsible for the Afghan invasion. They argued that the "hawks" had stymied American cooperation with the Soviet Union in matters of arms control and trade, and thus Moscow was induced to move as it did in Afghanistan.

The declaratory policy flowing from such a belief is clear: namely, the assertion that we now have sufficient military strength, that we need do nothing militarily in response to the invasion. "On that premise," as Charles Burton Marshall put it, "any attempt to improve the U.S. position militarily is assailable as aggressive." But the evidence is now overwhelming and abundant that we are *not* strong enough, that we in no way can deliver on the admonitions delivered by the president to the Soviets. Under such circumstances, the only alternatives are defeat in war or defeat in peace through appeasement. Since the latter is less costly, it is the likely outcome if we continue on the present course. Current policy thus appears ready to accommodate Moscow in the first instance by not remedying our military deficiencies, which will in any case make it impossible for us to do what we have determined not to do, namely, to respond militarily whenever Moscow nibbles—or bites—away at our interests. And meantime we will use strong rhetoric with regard to further Soviet advances.

THE COMPLEXITIES OF THE PROBLEM

Small wonder the public is confused. A growing chorus of outside experts testifies to our weakness and to our inability to resist Soviet expansion unless our defenses are strengthened. Even candidates of the ruling party challenging the incumbent accuse Jimmy Carter of weakness—while proposing defense cuts. Well-intentioned opposition candidates have proposed the movement of U.S. forces to places in or near the Middle East where there is no base to receive them. Several have suggested a quarantine of Cuba, overlooking the fact that the blockade of 1962 required almost two hundred ships—which today could not be spared from our substantially smaller navy without voiding most of our commitments in distant seas, including especially those in the Indian Ocean.

Americans have never experienced weakness and helplessness in foreign policy. Frustration, yes, as in Vietnam; or indifference, as at so many foreign conflicts in the past two centuries in which America's vital interests were simply not engaged. But now, while a weak administration with a deserved reputation of "dovishness" purports to draw a line against further Soviet expansion, America's most reputable hawks in fact counsel prudence of the most compelling sort, at least until our military capability is substantially rebuilt.

No one is giving the American people an authoritative lead. The contributors to this book underline how little of a strategic sense inheres in the American psyche, thanks to our geographic isolation and lucky history. Combined with the crisis of leadership, this absence of strategy (and of a strategic guide) is a critical deficiency. For with leadership from someone sure in his moves and certain of his direction—Franklin Roosevelt comes to mind—the American people have never failed to face up to their international responsibilities.

Possibly the most important thing to be gleaned from these essays and discussions, then, is a sense of the complexity of our strategic dilemma and of how all the major weaknesses we have identified—energy dependence, lack of ships, tanks, planes, deterioration of our alliances, and so forth—negatively reinforce each other and compound the problem. But until a President of the United States can state clearly and emphatically our strategic imperative and the priorities it implies, it is unlikely we will rebuild a cogent strategy. If this volume gives no easy formulae for simplifying our national security dilemma, it is not for lack of guides to improving our strategic position. These come out at three levels: damage limitation, the short-term quick fix, and the long-term basic correction.

(1) Damage limitation is simply a "Band-Aid" treatment to stop the surface bleeding of the body of American defense programs and services. This hemorrhaging began in the late 1960s as our armed forces absorbed all the marginal defense dollars in waging an unpopular and (in the event) losing war. As we have seen, it came to a halt in 1975–1976, but then worsened dramatically in 1977. On the bleeding went until the autumn of 1979, by which time even the most anti-defense minded of senators were forced by the evidence of the Soviet buildup to endorse an increase of our defense spending.

From all appearances, the period of outright hemorrhaging is over, if only because strong-willed senators forced the president and his administration to accept the notion of some defense increases. The question then becomes: what can be done in the short term to improve our position? We find both political and military prescriptions in this study, not all of which elicited agreement from each of the participants in this project. All agree that our intelligence mechanism could be swiftly reconstructed. But it was not self-evident to everyone, for instance, whether improvement of relations with India is possible, given the immediacy of Pakistan's needs. Nevertheless, attention to the possibilities helps us to realize that a program to enhance our position involves work in every geographic corner of the globe. And India is too large to ignore, too long connected with us for us to relinquish hope. Clearly much can be done to utilize the capabilities of our allies, as many of our contributors note. Not enough is ever made of the direct contributions important allies like France can (and to an extent already do) bring to alliance capabilities in critical theaters like the Indian Ocean, where it has the largest surface fleet.

(2) At the military level, numerous quick fixes are possible — and urgently needed. Foremost is a hardening of our command and control network, currently vulnerable to a Soviet attack. As foreshadowed earlier, even our ability to communicate with our submarines in a nuclear environment is in doubt.

Next would be the immediate commencement of the shell-game program of multiple vertical shelters for our Minuteman missiles. With this, additional holes would be constructed for each missile site, and Soviet war planners would be unable to determine in which one the transportable missile was located. Unlike the so-called racetrack scheme proposed by the administration for deployment with the new MX missile much later in the decade, the shell game could begin today. Merely adding one extra hole per missile cuts its vulnerability in half, while the full program of twenty holes per missile improves security enough to put us back on the road to functional parity. The program proposed here would also be substantially cheaper than the proposal of the administration, which was devised to meet Soviet SALT-inspired objections to the simple and effective shell game. Numerous other programs have been discussed in these pages.

(3) Proponents have never seen quick fixes as substitutes for basic and long-term remedies. With technologically sophisticated defense systems, lead times are long and indeed have lengthened. In the first place, programs to deploy the MX missile system and the Trident submarines have been grievously delayed—and can be speeded up; but we will still not have them in full complement before the end of the decade. Even these programs, however, miss the real point about long-term prospects. Research and development on strategic systems (on which the Soviets have been spending thrice our budget) must, in the second place, be substantially increased for the follow-on to these 1970s-based technologies. We are nowhere near a decision on whether, for example, to work toward smaller, better dispersed submarines as opposed to continuing the program of large Tridents. The cause of this failure is that our national attention has been absorbed in debate over whether America should even have weapons systems comparable overall to those of the Soviet Union—that is, whether we should work to regain rough parity with Moscow, which we have plainly lost. While the Soviet elite optimized defense planning, America debated SALT, sought ways to constrain its friends and even its allies from purchasing advanced arms, attempted to punish other allies who (with the decline of a credible American defense umbrella) sought to develop their own nuclear defense, and in various other ways worked against its own security.

There is still a third echelon of long-term development needs, discussed herein by Geoffrey Kemp. Space and ocean-based technologies could maximize America's remaining technological superiority. Space-based lasers may or may not be practicable in the 1980s, but some leading scientists clearly think they can add a vital dimension to our defensive capabilities. The national discussion of our security has not reached this level of discourse, while all available evidence shows Soviet research surging forward on each of these fronts.

THE CHALLENGE OF STATECRAFT

We opened this volume by presenting a spectrum of the means of foreign policy, by making a distinction between the roles of soldier and diplomat in the execution of foreign policy—a term we take in its broadest sense to include national security concerns as well. By posing the distinction as we did, a balance was implied between the claims of diplomacy and armed force.

One may wonder whether such fairly represents the real world. Against the harsh realities of Soviet control of Afghanistan's high ground, how much will diplomacy be able to do in South Asia? Of how much interest to Moscow's Politburo is a United Nations vote sharply condemning the Soviet Union for its aggression—against the fruits of that aggression still savored and maintained, which include preeminently the fear and awe permeating chanceries everywhere, but also include the new strategic advanced position commanded despite the fierce resistance of Afghan patriots? In situations of equality, diplomacy is useful, and nations skilled in its use may avert crises for a time. Democracies will surely wish to try diplomacy before any resort to force.

But to what extent can diplomacy (or, as it is often put today, politics) substitute for the potential or actual role of force? Just after the Afghan invasion one columnist noted that he had hitherto hoped that the Soviets would not use their accumulating military power for political advantage — on the absurd assumption that there had ever been any other Soviet motive for its accumulation on which we could play. Indeed, one of the highest officeholders in the present administration argued in a brief to his candidate during the 1976 campaign that the burden of American diplomacy had to be to convince the Soviet Union not to use its growing military superiority for political purposes. In such a world of fantasy, what possible interest would American diplomacy be to tough Soviet negotiators accustomed to dealing with the world of fact rather than with that of the manipulation of verbiage? American strength had become, according to a candid Soviet KGB spokesman, a "strength of words" (see Marshall, Chapter 16, note 2).

Yet contributors to this volume have properly emphasized the political challenge ahead; indeed, given the long lead times to rebuild our military strength, *politics is the one avenue of safe contestation for us in our competition with the Soviet Union.* Paul Nitze argued, for example, that once again such avenues as the General Assembly of the United Nations were open to us since the Soviet Union has so flagrantly violated the norms of the UN Charter. And such political moves—Olympic boycott is a still better example—if and only if played to the accompaniment of a steady military buildup at home, will clearly give the Soviet Union pause as to the utility of continuing or extending its aggression, especially as it considers the absolute absence of any internal Afghan support for its invasion of that land.

So too can the rise of Islam be used to the mutual benefit of Islamic states and the West. This unprecedented and powerful movement spreading from Southeast Asia to the Maghreb has as its aim its own cultural and religious purposes, some of them perhaps antithetical to those of the West. But this movement, the result of pride issuing from the great rise in oil prices and of humiliation from Arab defeats at Israeli hands, is far more antithetical to Soviet purposes and potentially a great danger to Soviet internal stability as well. Nowhere in the Soviet Union are demographic forces more powerful than in Soviet Central Asia. American policy, if visibly built on a growing foundation of strength, can harness these forces to mutually beneficial ends. Until the politics of weakness is put aside, Persian Gulf powers will continue to stand at arms' length from us, refusing to permit the deployment of our forces on their territory. How indeed could we expect them to consider our commitment credible in the light of our recent behavior in Vietnam, Iran, and elsewhere? But convinced that we have staying power in sufficient amount to deter a Soviet attack (or Soviet-supported proxy attack), Saudi Arabia and the other friendly Persian Gulf states would undoubtedly grant to us the use of facilities that would make it possible for us to enhance their now-threatened security as well as to defend the oil lifelines of the West.

Thus soldier and diplomat are indeed still complementary arms of policy. It is not an either/or question. It is one of meshing the two, but there must be a critical mass of military power for dealing with most crises—the necessary if not always sufficient ingredient. In the absence of adequate military power, diplomatic action is of doubtful utility as an antidote or substitute. For if it comes to that, as Clausewitz wrote, "the decision by arms is for all operations in war, great and small, what cash settlement is in trade."[1]

There is also a psychological dimension with respect to third party reactions to the unnaturally weak—and the increasingly powerful—adversaries. It is not accidental that mobs in vulnerable Pakistan burned down the American embassy, not the Soviet one, even as the great and threatening buildup of Soviet forces in Afghanistan began to be visible. Several months later the Pakistani government turned down a $400 million American aid offer because—self-evidently—it added more political vulnerability to the Soviet Union than military capability to resist. Soviet power was credible.

What will clarify the position and rally America in these confused circumstances of today? Afghanistan was no Pearl Harbor—though ironically Soviet control of that strategically located country endangered America's world-wide interests and threatened its industrial capacity far more than had that attack on U.S. territory and the resultant loss of lives and ships in 1941. For—and the point is worth dwelling on—Pearl Harbor alerted the nation massively and swiftly. Today it is difficult to conceive of a similar attack on American interests that could awaken the nation so cost-effectively, doing so little damage to our powers of quick recovery. The overthrow of the Saudi family in that oil kingdom by radical soldiers of the Qaddafi sort (or worse, of the Yemeni sort under the direct influence of Moscow) might wound our alliance system fatally, given the differential of oil dependence between Western Europe, Japan, and ourselves of which Henry Rowen writes herein. It would lack the immediacy of Pearl Harbor, while the damage to our industrial potential would be an order of magnitude greater. Around the globe one sees the same relationship. Most of the moves of which the Soviet Union is now capable along its periphery—an invasion of Iran, a reinforcement of a North Korean attack on the Republic of Korea, a move into Baluchi Pakistan, or probes in Berlin—would do vast damage to the Western system. Their effect would be irreversible today and in the near future, but would hardly constitute a *casus belli* to an American administration which has already permitted the even more harmful invasion of Afghanistan to pass by without military riposte.

There is another spectrum pertinent to statecraft which we must consider here, that of the degree of a state's adaptivity. Nations must adapt to new internal and new external circumstances. To the extent that they do not adapt, they begin to deteriorate as politico-security systems; their economies decline or their borders become permeable. Their international standing slides as their performance at home—and their ability to sustain their vital interests abroad—decline. Prosperity and the fructification of one's external interests is the objective, but survival is the bottom

line. On a continuum, one polar extreme is extinction—not a
theoretical point in a period in which South Vietnam ceased
to exist, Laos and Cambodia lost their independent identity
such as it was, and Pakistan lost over half its population—
while at the other extreme is the progressive enlargement of
one's own security perimeter, like Rome two millenia ago,
Moscow today. This measure is largely indifferent to the internal values of states, to their representativity of moral virtue so long as a regime can maintain order; it has to do with
how leaders align these internal characteristics with the opportunities abroad, meshing the two as advantageously as
possible.

America today is plainly near the maladaptive end of the
spectrum, with its defenses eroded, its alliance system
weakened, its internal structures increasingly uncompetitive
and incapable of adjusting themselves to new realities, and
its will and spirit enfeebled. The Soviet regime is by contrast
near the adaptive end of the continuum, despite the irrele-
vance of its ideology and its lack of internal popular support.
This is because the Soviet Union's own nature and ideology
are more congruent with the difficult present stage of adjustment in the Third World, where violence and struggle are
more the *leitmotif* than are human rights and political
development, and it is because the Soviet leaders have better
understood the nature of the role of power in the world
system and have thus been better able to manipulate the nations of Western Europe whose geography gives Russian
military power an immediate salience. Even Moscow's con-
torted understanding of how America works is less confused
than that of many American leaders of the Soviet system,
the proof of which lies in how well each elite predicts the
other's actions.

America has been speaking loudly while carrying a small
stick. "Drawing a line" for the protection of the Persian
Gulf—a line across which Soviet forces have been warned
not to go, as administration spokesmen have repeatedly been

putting it—illustrates the paradox of recent U.S. strategy. For the Soviets have already made the key move in South Asia, advancing their forces to the point where their tactical air power has Persian Gulf oil and airfields within range. The American response has been entirely nonmilitary, and manifestly unsuccessful.

CONCLUSION

Our prescription? Develop strong nerves and speak softly while rebuilding our defenses—something which may take ten or even fifteen years. And we must think strategically. This means we must connect the diverse parts of *our* strategy: a naval buildup in the Indian Ocean once we have ships and sailors in adequate number; psychological warfare in Central Asia, where even the frequency of our radio broadcasts has been cut back in recent years; theater nuclear modernization in Europe to bolster allied confidence; enhanced military cooperation with Japan; enlarged military exercises and cooperation with allies everywhere. Our "intermediate" intelligence capability for covert operations where these are appropriate must be restored. A diplomatic campaign against Soviet aggression throughout the Third World must be mounted. Perhaps most important, the draft must be restored. And we must craft this all into an integrated whole for increasing our own and our allies' confidence in our staying power.

And it means we must connect—and resist—the diverse parts of Soviet thrusts wherever they appear: military moves met—*where an escape hatch exists* in case Soviet forces confront us—with military resistance, Soviet propaganda moves relentlessly shown for what they are, and their covert moves exposed however much this may compromise prospects for arms control agreements (in such contrast to

specific administration cover-ups for Soviet violations of détente these past several years). Soviet military developments
should be graphically exposed through publication of aerial
photography[2] to raise Western elite consciousness of the
threat of Soviet power. We should put intense pressure on
Third World countries to break the stranglehold which committed Soviet allies now have on the so-called nonaligned
world, and we should work, through peer pressures, to induce
Soviet Third World allies to cut back on the military pri-
vileges granted to the Soviet armed forces in those states.

Doing all these things will be difficult for the American
psyche which, as noted, has had little experience with
strategy—and therefore little appetite for it. In *Defending
America* (1977) Marshall hit upon the central problem in
considering the nature of peace—what makes it possible and
what sustains it. There is a widespread view in Washington
and elsewhere that the United States and the Soviet Union
have the same interest in preserving peace. But this view
represents a fundamental, critical misunderstanding. At one
level, it is true, we have similar views: each views peace as a
desirable state, but the agreement is fortuitous and trivial
because the *reasons* underlying the views are very different.

On the one hand, Americans, inspired by the Enlighten-
ment belief in progress, assume that others have noble intentions and share our vision—especially our commitment to a
world that tolerates diversity. In this view, peace will result
in improved communication and trust. In this view, we seek
no fundamental change in our adversaries: we take their intentions as noble, and our commitment to diversity is
tolerant of their different social and economic systems.
Peace, in these circumstances, is natural; war, a horrible
deviation.

The Soviets' view is the very opposite of this. In their view,
peace is obstructed by *intrinsic flaws* in our system and in us,
and therefore peace can only come when they have reformed
us, changed us fundamentally. Their commitment to this

task is all the more compelling when it is seen as the instrument and fulfillment of historical necessity. Peace, in the American sense, is thus not a natural state, while conflict is inherent to the Soviet view of historical process.

Nor does our view of peace find much support in history. Even more important, it is a view which has dangerous implications when posed against an adversary with a *principled commitment* to force change upon us—change, indeed, which is considered essential to long-term peace.

In practice, our nonstrategic view of peace has been redeemed in recent years only by retreat. As Clausewitz is quoted earlier, war exists for the benefit of the defender; he initiates war by deciding at what point to stop retreating and defend. Since stability and certainty are as important in relations between nations as in relations between people, peace through retreat only encourages more aggression as the aggressing party seeks to know where that point is—where the defending party will defend an interest, if necessary by force.[3] A strategic concept of peace maintains a clear definition of interests. Though these may change, in the end defining national interests involves some calculus of cost and benefits: how much is any particular interest worth to us? It is a calculus which, as an important element, must also include judgment of national will.

Thinking strategically far transcends the question of whether we are to be hawks or doves. It has to do with whether we are to pursue our objectives—at whatever level we have decided to place these—intelligently and in proportion to our means. We have presumably realized that our aims, our policy, must ironically be lowered, even as we substantially increase defense spending. That means lowered not only with regard to the ways in which we enhance our security and that of our allies, but with regard to what we can accomplish in the fields of nonproliferation, human rights, or even racial integration in Africa or elsewhere until our house is strong and in order. For our political aims have been too high. As has been argued, these have risen even as our military means have declined. If we are to return to an adaptive foreign policy mode, one in line with reality, our leaders will have to husband our resources carefully and use them sparingly only where success has a fair chance. Our rhetoric and our means must be in line, must be seen to be consonant; our leaders must be clear of focus and our people awake to how much must be accomplished in a short time. Both because of the size of the decline in our internal capabilities and of the growth of the threat facing us, America now has its greatest challenge in history.

NOTES

1. W. Scott Thompson: "Introduction"

1. The peace following the 1973 treaty was not going badly, after all, until Watergate made retaliation for the other side's infractions impossible. See Frizzell and Thompson (1979).

2. E. H. Carr (1956), a generation ago, wrote that it is in the nature of things that "the intellectual should find himself in the camp which seeks to make practice conform to theory; for intellectuals are particularly reluctant to recognize their thought as conditioned by forces external to themselves, and like to think of themselves as leaders whose theories provide the motive force for so-called men of action."

3. For an elaboration of this argument, with supporting data, see Jones and Thompson (1978).

2. Elmo R. Zumwalt, Jr.: "Heritage of Weakness: An Assessment of the 1970s"

1. The most recent official estimates are from Burton (1979).

2. The SALT II treaty permits the USSR to maintain the numerical advantage in strategic launchers through 1985 by the artifice of not counting the 375 strategic Backfire bombers the USSR will have.

3. See Nitze (1979a).

4. For one such set of calculations, see Nitze (1979b).

5. Dr. Brown's statement is cited in an article by Lacouture (1979, p. 30).

6. Recent reports are that Dr. Brown is advocating that the United States, beginning in 1985 and completing in 1989, build a five-ship forward deployed capability to land a marine brigade of equipment and thirty days' supplies.

7. Memorandum of conversation dated 3 July 1977.

8. This statement is quoted in Garrett (1979).

9. For a pathbreaking analysis of these activities, see Dismukes and McConnell (1979).

10. During three weeks in South Africa in February 1977, the author asked a score of black leaders, individually, what the children were doing. A number reported that children were in the black front-line countries, Algeria, or the USSR, receiving Marxist military training.

11. In a leadership succession crisis, the winner typically is the Praesidium member who allies himself with the military establishment against the advocates of increased emphasis on soft goods. See Zumwalt (1962).

12. Quotations from Burton (1979).

5. William R. Van Cleave: "Quick Fixes to U.S. Strategic Nuclear Forces"

1. This is the conclusion of the two-part analysis by "Galen" (1979).

2. Concerning B−1 derivative options, for example, *Aviation Week* (27 August 1979) reported that the U.S. Air Force is not interested because it is "concerned that any aircraft development would impinge on the MX deployment because of the cost impact of multiple strategic programs."

7. Albert Wohlstetter: "Half-Wars and Half-Policies in the Persian Gulf"

1. See JCS 1769/1, "Report by the Joint Chiefs of Staff, April 29, 1947," reprinted in Etzold and Gaddis (1978, p. 72).

2. For an excellent summary Soviet statement of these themes, see the article written by Sergei Losev (1980, p. 28), director general of the official Soviet news agency Tass.

3. Aron said it meant "en bref, accepter l'inacceptable."

4. See also "A Fine French-German Duet with a Few Fuzzy Notes." *The Economist* (9 February 1980), pp. 43−44.

5. See the program advanced by Abdul Rahman Mansouri, first deputy foreign minister, in an interview with a *Wall Street Journal* staff reporter: "Saudi Leader Urges Three-Point Program for Mideast Stability." Compare the anonymous Saudi policymaker reported in the *New York Times* (27 February 1980): "We are trying very hard to get the Russians out of the Arab world. How could we condone the presence of another major power in the region?"

6. For one among many recent reports of such hopes among Western officials, see Richard Burt in the *New York Times* (23 December 1979).

7. Some of the nonmilitary goods have a formidable potential for military application. The highly enriched uranium which the French announced they will sell and deliver to Iraq for the purposes of nuclear "research" has only the remotest application in the civilian economy of Iraq, but such concentrated fissile material is the most important and hardest to produce component of nuclear weapons and can be quickly incorporated in a weapon assembly. Highly enriched uranium makes feasible weapons of the simplest design—the gun as distinct from the implosion-type essential for plutonium.

8. Speech 6 January 1980 by Iraqi President Saddam Husayn over Iraqi national radio and television network on the 59th anniversary of the formation of the Iraqi army; place not given.

9. One convenient summary of this debate is provided by Richard Burt (1980).

9. Miles M. Costick: "Soviet Military Posture and Strategic Trade"

1. Jack Vorona (1979), Assistant Vice Director for Scientific and Technical Intelligence, Defense Intelligence Agency.

2. Background information is contained in Center for Strategic Studies (1976, pp. 13−31); Harvey et al. (1972, p. 219); Costick (1978).

3. The Coordinating Committee of the Consultative Group of Nations. Membership consists of NATO nations less Iceland, plus Japan. Its purpose is to regulate exports of strategic products to Communist governments.

4. This information was provided by a German intelligence source; also by somewhat incomplete information found in the *San Jose Mercury* (28 August 1968), and by Sutton (1973, p. 204).

11. Henry S. Rowen: "The Threatened Jugular: Oil Supply of the West"

1. The IEA Sharing Agreement for cuts beyond 7 percent of imports calls for sharing the shortfall (after mandatory consumption reductions) proportionately on the basis of pre-embargo net import levels.

2. For an analysis which emphasizes the basic stability of the countries of the Persian Gulf region, especially those on the Arab side, see Noyes (1979).

3. The problem can be viewed somewhat differently. For instance, if even in an emergency we believed we could cut back along a "flatter" trajectory than that represented by d_s, i.e., one closer to d_1, then we could wait for the crisis to hit before cutting back. Much public discussion of the "nonessentiality" of many types of automobile use suggests a widespread belief that gasoline consumption could be cut with relative ease in a crunch. Given the deep adaptation of our economy to the automobile, this inference seems doubtful.

A different argument for rejecting cuts now is that doing so may not greatly reduce the need for further necessary cuts in a crisis. This can be seen if we regard all of the oil consumed by the United States and its allies (about 39 million barrels per day) as in a common pool. In such a case the reduction in U.S. noncrisis consumption does not necessarily reduce the crisis demands as shown in Figure 1 because of the crisis needs of the participants in the larger pool. This perspective implies, correctly, the need for overarching international cooperation in the common good—both in noncrisis and crisis periods.

4. A poor second-best would be a tax on gasoline. It is a poor alternative to a tariff because it would affect only one category of use of oil, into which uses it would cut deeply. According to James Sweeney (1980), savings from a modest extra gasoline tax—e.g., $0.50 per gallon—would be small because improvements in auto efficiency standards are yielding most of the fuel savings that would be generated by such a tax at this level. Large fuel savings require a much larger tax—say, of $1.00 per gallon.

5. This calculation assumes that uncertainty about the depth and extent of the crisis enables us only to draw down one-half of the SPR; if we can use it more efficiently, its value would be even greater, but perfect efficiency in use should not be assumed. A 3.3 million barrel per day cut implies a reduction of about 8 million barrels per day—40 percent—of total Persian Gulf supplies.

16. Charles Burton Marshall: "Strategy: The Emerging Dangers"

1. For example, see Soviet Foreign Minister Andrei Gromyko's pronouncement reported in *The New York Times* (19 February 1980).

2. A notably harsh expression of this theme in an interview with an unnamed Soviet diplomat (unofficially identified as Boris Davydov, head of the KGB contingent in the

Soviet Embassy in Washington) appeared in *Die Welt* (Bonn) on 4 January 1980. The theme was explicit in an interview of President Brezhnev reported in *The New York Times* on the same date. *Pravda* for 29 January 1980 further elaborated the theme, according to the *Washington Star* (31 January 1980).

18. W. Scott Thompson: "Toward a Strategic Peace"

1. As Hans Rothfels has noted, Engels found this thought "particularly suggestive. Even though cash settlement and battle may rarely occur, everything is directed toward them. If they occur they decide everything" (Rothfels 1971, p. 104).

2. Such publication has been fiercely resisted by the intelligence community on the grounds that it would reveal intelligence method to the Soviet Union. There is a trade-off, however, between that danger and the danger that the American public will otherwise not fully comprehend the need for a massive program to counter Soviet war preparations.

3. This is true irrespective of an aggressor's motivations—whether the Soviets are "actively aggressive" or "acting only from weakness." If anything, there are good reasons for believing that a nation acting from internal weakness—as many current doves argue about the Soviets—will be *more* aggressive in seeking to clarify uncertain relationships than a nation acting from internal strength.

REFERENCES

Adelman, Kenneth L. 1978. "Seminar in African Diplomacy." *Harper's* (September).

Aron, Raymond. 1979. "From American Imperialism to Soviet Hegemonism." *The Washington Quarterly* (Summer).

Borchgrave, Arnaud de. 1978. "A Fresh Warning." *Newsweek* (17 July).

Brown, George. 1979. *United States Military Policy for FY 1980.* Washington, DC: U.S. Government Printing Office.

Brown, Harold. 1979. "Address to the Counsel of Foreign Relations, New York, 5 April 1979." News Release No. 153–79. Washington, DC: Office of Assistant Secretary of Defense (Public Affairs).

Bundy, William. 1974. "International Security Today." *Foreign Affairs* 53, 1 (October).

Burt, Richard. 1980. "Does the U.S. Have Muscle to Back Carter Doctrine?" *New York Times* (29 February).

Burton, Donald F. 1979. Testimony as Chief, Military-Economic Analysis Center, Office of Strategic Research, National Foreign Assessment Center, before the Subcommittee on General Procurement, Committee on Armed Forces, U.S. Senate (1 November).

Canby, Steven. 1974/75. *The Alliance and Europe: Military Doctrine and Technology.* Adelphi Paper 109 (Winter). London: International Institute for Strategic Studies.

Carr, E. H. 1956. *The Twenty Years Crisis.* New York: Macmillan.

Cecil, Lady Gwendolyn. 1921. *Life of Salisbury.* London: Hodder Staughton.

Center for Strategic Studies. 1976. *The Soviet Military Technological Challenge.* Washington, DC: The Center for Strategic Studies, Georgetown University (September).

Clausewitz, Carl von. 1976. *On War.* Ed. Michael Howard and Pater Paret. Princeton, NJ: Princeton University Press.

Collins, John M. 1978. *American and Soviet Military Trends.* Washington, DC: Center for Strategic and International Studies.

———. "Petroleum Imports from the Persian Gulf: Use of U.S. Armed Force to Ensure Supplies." Issue Brief IB79046. Library of Congress, Congressional Research Service (21 May).

Congressional Joint Economic Committee. 1979. *Soviet Economy in a Time of Change.* Washington, DC: U.S. Government Printing Office.

Costick, Miles M. 1976. *The Economics of Détente.* Washington, DC: Heritage Foundation.

———. 1980. *The Soviet Military Power and Western Technology.* Washington, DC: Institute on Strategic Trade.

———. 1978. *The Strategic Dimension of East-West Trade.* Washington, DC: Institute on Strategic Trade.

Currie, Malcolm R. 1976. *Program of Research, Development, Test and Evaluation, FY 1977.* Washington, DC: Department of Defense.

Defense Agency (Tokyo). 1978. *Defense of Japan.* Tokyo: Defense Agency (July).

Deutsch, Karl W. 1953. *Nationalism and Social Communication.* Cambridge, MA: MIT Press.

Dismukes, Bradford, and McConnell, James, eds. 1979. *Soviet Naval Diplomacy.* New York and Oxford: Pergamon Press.

Earle, Edward Mead. 1944 (1971). *The Makers of Modern Strategy.* Princeton, NJ: Princeton University Press.

Edwards, I., Hughes, M., and Noren, J. 1979. "U.S. and U.S.S.R.: Comparisons of GNP." In Congressional Joint Economic Committee, *Soviet Economy in a Time of Change.* Washington, DC: Government Printing Office.

Etzold, Thomas H., and Gaddis, John Lewis, eds. 1978. *Containment: Documents on American Policy and Strategy.* New York: Columbia University Press.

Fisher, Dan. 1980. "Russia Urges Europe Parley on Mideast Oil Security." *Los Angeles Times* (1 March).

Frizzell, D. C., and Thompson, W. Scott, eds. 1977. *Lessons of Vietnam.* New York: Crane, Russak.

Fukuyama, Frank. 1980. "Iraq and Kuwait: Past Policies and Future Options." PAN Heuristics OSD—78—9—9 (Marina del Rey, California, revised February).

"Galen, Justin." 1979. "The SALT Decade: Accepting Soviet Strategic Superiority." *Armed Forces Journal International* (May, June).

Garnett, John, ed. 1970. *Theories of Peace and Security.* London: Macmillan.

Garrett, Banning. 1979. "China Policy and the Strategic Triangle." In Kenneth A. Oye, Donald Rothchild, Robert J. Lieber, eds., *Eagle Entangled: U.S. Foreign Policy in a Complex World.* New York: Longman.

Gilbert, Felix. 1961. *To the Farewell Address.* Princeton, NJ: Princeton University Press.

Graham, Daniel O. (Lt. Gen.). 1976. "U.S.—Soviet Military Balance—Who's Ahead?" *The Reader's Digest* (September).

Harvey, Mose L., et al. 1972. *Science and Technology as an Instrument of Soviet Policy.* Coral Gables, FL: Center for Advanced International Studies, University of Miami.

Herr, Robert. 1979. "Spengler in Moscow." *The New Republic* (31 March).

Iklé, Fred Charles. 1977. "The Export of American Technology: A Threat to United States Security?" In *Transfer of Technology to the Soviet*

Union and Eastern Europe, Selected Papers. Washington, DC: Permanent Subcommittee on Investigations, U.S, Senate.

International Institute for Strategic Studies. 1979. *The Military Balance, 1979–1980.* London: International Institute for Strategic Studies.

Johnson, Lyndon B. 1965. "Pattern of Peace in Southeast Asia." Address at The Johns Hopkins University, Baltimore, MD, 4 April 1965. *Department of State Bulletin* 52, No. 1348 (26 April).

Jones, T. K., and Thompson, W. Scott. 1978. "Central War and Civil Defense." *ORBIS* 22, 3 (Autumn).

Kennan, George F. 1962. *Russia and the West, under Lenin and Stalin.* Boston: Little, Brown.

Korniyenko, A. (General Major). 1969. "The Economic Bases of the State's Military Power." *Military Thought,* No. 8.

Lacouture, John E. 1979. "Seapower in the Indian Ocean: A Requirement for Western Security." *U.S. Naval Institute Proceedings* (August).

Lehman, John. 1979. "A Symposium." *Washington Quarterly* (Winter).

Losev, Sergei. 1980. "Carter Wants a Confrontation." *U.S. News and World Report* (11 February).

McCarthy, Eugene. 1978. "Look, No Allies." *Foreign Policy,* No. 31 (Spring).

McNamara, Robert. 1966. "The Story of Robert McNamara: Report on Washington's Most Controversial Figure." *U.S. News and World Report* (25 July).

Mahan, Alfred Thayer. 1941. *The Influence of Sea Power upon History, 1660–1783.* Boston: Little Brown.

Meyer, Cord. 1979. "How Russia Narrows the Technology Gap." *The Washington Star* (27 April).

Middleton, Drew. 1977. "U.S. Held to Maintain Lead over Soviet in Strategic Arms." *The New York Times* (3 October).

Morishima, Michio. 1978. "A Newer Theory of the 'New Defense Plan.'" *Bungei Shunju* (July).

Mork, Knut Anton, and Hall, Robert E. 1979*a* . "Energy Prices and the U.S. Economy in 1979–81." Working paper MIT−EL 79−043WP (August). Cambridge, MA: MIT Energy Lab.

———. 1979*b*. "Energy Prices, Inflation, and Recession, 1974–1975." Working paper 369 (July). Washington, DC: National Bureau of Economic Research, Inc.

Nitze, Paul H. 1979*a*. Testimony before Armed Services Committee, U.S. House of Representatives (15 November).

———. 1979*b*. Statement to Committee on Armed Services, U.S. Senate (9 October).

Noyes, James. 1979. *The Clouded Lens.* Stanford, CA: Hoover Institution Press.

Oye, Kenneth A., Rothchild, Donald, Lieber, Robert J., eds. 1979. *Eagle Entangled: U.S. Foreign Policy in a Complex World.* New York: Longman.

Payne, Pierre Stephen Robert. 1949. *Fabulous America*. London: Gollancz.

Reston, James. 1980. "Moscow's Costly 'Victory.'" *New York Times* (6 January).

Rothfels, Hans. 1971. "Clausewitz." In Edward Mead Earle, *The Makers of Modern Strategy*. Princeton, NJ: Princeton University Press.

Rowen, Henry S., and Weyant, John. 1980. "The Optimal Strategic Petroleum Reserve Size for the United States." International Energy Program (Stanford University) discussion paper (October).

Slocum, Walter. 1971. *The Political Implications of Strategic Parity*. Adelphi Paper 77. London: Institute of Strategic Studies.

Sokolovskiy, V. D., ed. 1968. *Soviet Military Strategy (Voyennaya Strategiya)*. 3d ed. Moscow: Voyenizadat.

Stengel, Donald E. 1974. *International Economic Policy*. Testimony before the Subcommittee on International Trade, U.S. House of Representatives. Washington, DC: U.S. Government Printing Office.

Sutton, Antony C. 1973. *National Suicide*. New Rochelle, NY: Arlington House.

Sweeney, James. 1980. "Effect of Federal Policies on Gasoline Consumption." *Resources and Energy* (forthcoming).

Thompson, W. Scott. 1978. *Power Projection*. New York: National Strategic Information Center.

Tuohy, William. 1979. "Iran Reports Iraqi Attack on Oil Region." *Los Angeles Times* (15 December).

U.S. Department of Defense. 1978. *Annual Report: Fiscal Year 1979*. Washington, DC: U.S. Government Printing Office.

————. 1979. *Annual Report: Fiscal Year 1980*. Washington, DC: U.S. Government Printing Office.

————. 1980. *Annual Report: Fiscal Year 1981*. Washington, DC: U.S. Government Printing Office.

U.S. House of Representatives. 1979. "Soviet Diplomacy and Negotiating Behavior: Emerging New Context for U.S. Diplomacy." *House Documents*, No. 96–236, 96th Congress, 1st Session.

U.S. Senate, Committee on the Armed Services. 1979. *Military Implications of the Treaty on the Limitation of Strategic Offensive Arms and Protocol Thereto (SALT II Treaty)*. Hearing 17–18, 23–24 October. Washington, DC: U.S. Government Printing Office.

U.S. Senate, Permanent Subcommittee on Investigations. 1977. *Transfer of Technology to the Soviet Union and Eastern Europe, Selected Papers*. Washington, DC: Permanent Subcommittee on Investigations, U.S. Senate.

Van Cleave, William R., and Thompson, W. Scott. 1979. *Strategic Options for the Early Eighties: What Can Be Done?* National Strategy Information Center publication. White Plains, MD: Automatic Graphic Systems, Inc.

Vorona, Jack. 1979. *Statement on Acquisition of Soviet Military Systems.* Before the Subcommittee on Procurement, Senate Committee on Armed Services, 8 November. Washington, DC: U.S. Government Printing Office.

Wakaizumi, Kei. 1978–1979. "Japan's Passive Diplomacy Reconsidered." *Asia Pacific Community* (Winter).

Warnke, Paul. 1977. "The Real Paul Warnke." *The New Republic* (26 March).

Zumwalt, Elmo R., Jr. 1962. "The Problems of Succession in the USSR." Doctoral thesis, National War College.

ABOUT THE AUTHORS

KENNETH L. ADELMAN, Senior Political Scientist at the Strategic Studies Center of SRI International and Adjunct Professor at the Defense Intelligence School, is a former assistant to the Secretary of Defense. A member of the International Institute for Strategic Studies (London), he is the author of numerous articles on U.S. intelligence and foreign policies published, most recently, in *Foreign Policy, International Security, Africa Report, ORBIS, Current History*, and *Policy Review* .

RICHARD R. BURT was assistant director of the International Institute for Strategic Studies (London) until 1977 when he became National Security Affairs correspondent at the *New York Times* Washington Bureau. A former Advanced Research Fellow at the Naval War College and Defense Adviser to the Wednesday Group, U.S. House of Representatives, he is the author of many published articles and Adelphi papers on defense budgeting and new weapons technology.

MILES M. COSTICK is president of the Institute on Strategic Trade and has served as special and legislative assistant in both houses of the U.S. Congress. He is the author of *The Economics of Détente, The Strategic Dimension of the United States Computer Exports to the U.S.S.R.*, and *The Strategic Dimension of East-West Trade*, and of articles published in *The Journal of Law and Economics, Defense and Foreign Affairs Digest*, and *The Wall Street Journal*, among other publications.

ROBERT F. ELLSWORTH, Managing Director of Robert Ellsworth and Company, is a former member of Congress. He was in the Department of Defense as Deputy Secretary and Assistant Secretary, and served as U.S. Ambassador to NATO from 1969 to 1971. He is currently a director of the Atlantic Council of the United States and the American Council on Germany, a governor of the Atlantic Institute, and a member of the Council on Foreign Relations and the International Institute for Strategic Studies (London).

FRED C. IKLÉ is chairman of the Conservation Management Corporation in Washington, DC, a member of the Executive Panel of the Chief of Naval Operations and of the International Research Council, Center for Strategic and International Studies, Georgetown University. He is on the boards of directors of the International Peace Academy, the European-American Institute for Security Research, and the Hudson Institute. A former Director of the Arms Control and Disarmament Agency and professor of political science at MIT, Dr. Iklé is the author of *How Nations Negotiate, Every War Must End*, and of articles on SALT and on the U.S. military posture published in *Fortune*.

GEOFFREY T. H. KEMP, consultant to the Department of Defense, to the Georgetown Center for Strategic and International Studies, The Brookings Institution, the Hudson Institute, and the RAND Corporation, is Associate Professor of International Politics at The Fletcher School of Law and Diplomacy, Tufts University. In 1976, with the Committee on Foreign Relations of the U.S. Senate, he was responsible for the study *U.S. Military Sales to Iran* published by the Subcommittee on Foreign Assistance. The author of a number of published articles and chapters in studies on armaments and the arms race, his most recent publication is *Arms Transfers to the Third World: The Military Buildup in Less Industrial Countries*, co-edited with Uri Ra'anan and Robert L. Pfaltzgraff, Jr.

EDWARD N. LUTTWAK is Senior Fellow, Center for Strategic and International Studies, and Research Professor, Georgetown University, and is consultant to the U.S. Department of Defense. A contributor to the institute's publications *Defending America* (1977) and *The Third World* (1978), he is also the author of *Coup d'état, a Practical Handbook*, published in fourteen languages, *Strategy and Politics*, "SALT and the Meaning of Strategy" in *The Washington Review of Strategic and International Studies*, and "The American Style of Warfare and the Military Balance" in *Survival*.

CHARLES BURTON MARSHALL, until 1975 Professor of International Politics at The Johns Hopkins School of Advanced International Studies, is a consultant on strategic matters. He has been staff consultant to the Committee on Foreign Affairs of the U.S. House of Representatives and was a member of the Policy Planning Staff at the U.S. State Department. His writings include *The Limits of Foreign Policy* and *The Exercise of Sovereignty*, and he is the author of "National Security: Thoughts on the Intangibles" in the institute's 1977 book on *Defending America: Toward a New Role in the Post-Détente World*.

PAUL H. NITZE, 57th Secretary of the Navy and former Deputy Secretary of Defense, represented the Secretary of Defense in the U.S. Delegation to SALT I from 1969 to 1974. He is chairman of Policy Studies for the Committee on the Present Danger and also chairs the Advisory Council of The Johns Hopkins School of Advanced International Studies. His positions with the U.S. State Department include service as deputy director of the Office of International Trade Policy, deputy to the Assistant Secretary of State for Economic Affairs, and director of the Policy Planning Staff. He is author of a chapter on nuclear strategy in the institute's book entitled *Defending America* (1977).

SAM NUNN, senator (D) from Georgia, insisted as a member of the Armed Services Committee that the administration increase defense spending before he would consider supporting the SALT II treaty. Supporter of a strong national defense posture along with efficiencies in defense spending and management, he chairs the Armed Services Subcommittee on Manpower and Personnel and the Permanent Subcommittee on Investigations.

HENRY S. ROWEN is Professor of Public Management at the Graduate School of Business, Stanford University, and principal investigator fo the Stanford International Energy Program. A former president of the RAND Corporation, he is Chairman of the Executive Panel, Office of the Chief of Naval Operations, and a member of the Defense Science Board, Department of Defense, the Council on Foreign Relations, and the International Institute for Strategic Studies (London). He wrote the initial chapter in the institute's *Options for U.S. Energy Policy* (1977), contributed to the forthcoming *Nonproliferation and U.S. Foreign Policy* edited by Joseph A. Yager, and is coauthor with Ryukichi Imai of *Nuclear Energy and Nuclear Proliferation: Japanese and American Views*.

LEONARD SULLIVAN, JR., is a former Assistant Secretary of Defense for Program Analysis and Evaluation, a position in which he served as one of the four principals of the Defense Systems Acquisition Review Council. He is an independent consultant on matters of national security and a resident consultant for the Center for National Security Research at the Systems Planning Corporation in Washington, DC. Major studies to which he has contributed include "The National Strategy Review," "The Potential Use of American Intervention Forces in the Next Decade," "Soviet Perceptions of Arms Control and the Correlation of Forces," and "The Impact of Precision-Guided Munitions on NATO Conventional Capabilities."

W. SCOTT THOMPSON is Associate Professor of International Politics, Fletcher School of Law and Diplomacy, Tufts University, and Visiting Fellow at the Center for International Affairs, Harvard University. A former assistant to the Secretary of Defense, he is consultant to the U.S. Navy, the RAND Corporation, and a member of the editorial boards of *ORBIS* and the *International Security Review*. He is the author of the monograph *Power Projection*, and coeditor with William Van Cleave of *Strategic Options for the Early Eighties*. He wrote a chapter on "The Projection of Soviet Power" in the institute's book *Defending America* (1977), and edited the 1978 publication *The Third World: Premises for U.S. Policy*.

WILLIAM R. VAN CLEAVE is Professor of International Relations, director of the Defense and Strategic Studies Program, and 1979–1981 Associate of the Annenberg Center for the American Experience at the University of Southern California. He is chairman of the Strategic Alternatives Team, a member of the Board of Directors of the Committee on the Present Danger, and serves on the editorial boards of *ORBIS*, the *Strategic Review*, and the *International Security Review*. A member of the first SALT delegation from 1969 to 1971 and a special assistant in the office of the Secretary of Defense, in 1976 he was part of the "B TEAM" charged with reviewing national intelligence on Soviet strategic capabilities and objectives.

FRANCIS J. WEST, JR., director of Strategic Research at the Naval War College, is a former assistant to the Secretary and Deputy Secretary of Defense and consultant to the Secretary of the Navy. A specialist in systems analysis and in defense and national security policy, his writings include the 1978 U.S. Navy publication *Sea Plan 2000—Naval Force Planning Study*.

ALBERT WOHLSTETTER, University Professor and Fellow of the Center for Policy Studies at the University of Chicago and Sometime Fellow of All-Souls College, Oxford University, is a member of the Chief of Naval Operations Executive Panel. He has twice been awarded the Department of Defense Medal for Distinguished Public Service—the first person not employed by the department to be awarded this honor and the only one to receive it twice. His experience includes many years of research on problems of arms and arms control, on protecting strategic forces and stabilizing deterrence, and on NATO policy in Europe and north Asia. His many publications include the chapter "Racing Forward or Ambling Back?" in the institute's *Defending America*, a number of articles published in *Foreign Policy*, and the forthcoming book *Swords from Plowshares*.

ELMO R. ZUMWALT, JR., Admiral, U.S. Navy (Ret.), was Chief of Naval Operations from 1970 to 1974. He had previously organized and directed the navy's Systems Analysis Division and served as Deputy Scientific Officer to the Center for Naval Analyses. He is known for his work in modernizing the navy and increasing the fighting capabilities of the U.S. fleet by outfitting its ships with sophisticated and efficient weapons. He is the author of *On Watch* and of numerous articles and commentaries published nationwide.

INDEX

PUBLICATIONS LIST*

THE INSTITUTE FOR CONTEMPORARY STUDIES

260 California Street, San Francisco, California, 94111

Catalog available upon request

BUREAUCRATS AND BRAINPOWER: GOVERNMENT
REGULATION OF UNIVERSITIES
$6.95. 171 pages. Publication date: June 1979
ISBN 0−917616−35− 9
Library of Congress No. 79−51328
Contributors: Nathan Glazer, Robert S. Hatfield, Richard W. Lyman,
Robert L. Sproull, Paul Seabury, Miro M. Todorovich, Caspar W.
Weinberger

THE CALIFORNIA COASTAL PLAN: A CRITIQUE
$5.95. 199 pages. Publication date: March 1976
ISBN 0−917616−04−9
Library of Congress No. 76−7715
Contributors: Eugene Bardach, Daniel K. Benjamin, Thomas E.
Borcherding, Ross D. Eckert, H. Edward Frech III, M. Bruce Johnson,
Ronald N. Lafferty, Walter J. Mead, Daniel Orr, Donald M. Pach,
Michael R. Peevey

THE CRISIS IN SOCIAL SECURITY: PROBLEMS AND PROSPECTS
$6.95. 214 pages. Publication date: April 1977; 2d ed. rev.,
1978, 1979
ISBN 0−917616−16−2/1977; 0−917616−25−1/1978
Library of Congress No. 77−72542
Contributors: Michael J. Boskin, George F. Break, Rita Ricardo Campbell,
Edward Cowan, Martin S. Feldstein, Milton Friedman, Douglas R.
Munro, Donald O. Parsons, Carl V. Patton, Joseph A. Pechman,
Sherwin Rosen, W. Kip Viscusi, Richard J. Zeckhauser

DEFENDING AMERICA: TOWARD A NEW ROLE IN THE
POST-DETENTE WORLD
$13.95 (hardbound only). 255 pages. Publication date: April 1977 by
Basic Books (New York)
ISBN 0−465−01585−9
Library of Congress No. 76−43479

*Prices subject to change.

519

Contributors: Robert Conquest, Theodore Draper, Gregory Grossman,
Walter Z. Laqueur, Edward N. Luttwak, Charles Burton Marshall,
Paul H. Nitze, Norman Polmar, Eugene V. Rostow, Leonard Schapiro,
James R. Schlesinger, Paul Seabury, W. Scott Thompson, Albert
Wohlstetter

THE ECONOMY IN THE 1980s: A PROGRAM FOR
STABILITY AND GROWTH
   $7.95. 300 pages. Publication date: June 1980.
   ISBN 0-917616-39-1
   Library of Congress No. 80-80647
Contributors: Michael J. Boskin, George F. Break, John T. Cuddington,
Patricia Drury, Alain Enthoven, Lawrence J. Kotlikoff, Ronald
I. McKinnon, John Pencavel, Henry S. Rowen, John L. Scadding,
John B. Shoven, James L. Sweeney, David Teece

EMERGING COALITIONS IN AMERICAN POLITICS
   $6.95. 524 pages. Publication date: June 1978
   ISBN 0-917616-22-7
   Library of Congress No. 78-53414
Contributors: Jack Bass, David S. Broder, Jerome M. Clubb, Edward H.
Crane III, Walter De Vries, Andrew M. Greeley, S. I. Hayakawa,
Tom Hayden, Milton Himmelfarb, Richard Jensen, Paul Kleppner,
Everett Carll Ladd, Jr., Seymour Martin Lipset, Robert A. Nisbet,
Michael Novak, Gary R. Orren, Nelson W. Polsby, Joseph L. Rauh,
Jr., Stanley Rothman, William A. Rusher, William Schneider, Jesse
M. Unruh, Ben J. Wattenberg

FEDERAL TAX REFORM: MYTHS AND REALITIES
   $5.95. 270 pages. Publication date: September 1978
   ISBN 0-917616-32-4
   Library of Congress No. 78-61661
Contributors: Robert J. Barro, Michael J. Boskin, George F. Break,
Jerry R. Green, Laurence J. Kotlikoff, Mordecai Kurz, Peter
Mieszkowski, John B. Shoven, Paul J. Taubman, John Whalley

GOVERNMENT CREDIT ALLOCATION: WHERE DO WE GO
FROM HERE?
   $4.95. 208 pages. Publication date: November 1975
   ISBN 0-917616-02-2
   Library of Congress No. 75-32951
Contributors: George J. Benston, Karl Brunner, Dwight M. Jaffe, Omotunde
E. G. Johnson, Edward J. Kane, Thomas Mayer, Allen H. Meltzer

NATIONAL SECURITY IN THE 1980s: FROM
WEAKNESS TO STRENGTH
$8.95 (paper). 500 pages. Publication date: May 1980
ISBN 0−917616−38−3
Library of Congress No. 80−80648
$19.95 (cloth). 500 pages. Publication date: June 1980
ISBN 0−87855−412−2. Available through Transaction Books,
Rutgers−The State University, New Brunswick, NJ 08903
Contributors: Kenneth L. Adelman, Richard R. Burt, Miles M. Costick,
Robert F. Ellsworth, Fred Charles Iklé, Geoffrey T. H. Kemp,
Edward N. Luttwak, Charles Burton Marshall, Paul H. Nitze,
Sam Nunn, Henry S. Rowen, Leonard Sullivan, Jr., W. Scott
Thompson, William R. Van Cleave, Francis J. West, Jr.,
Albert Wohlstetter, Elmo R. Zumwalt, Jr.

NEW DIRECTIONS IN PUBLIC HEALTH CARE: AN EVALUATION
OF PROPOSALS FOR NATIONAL HEALTH INSURANCE
$6.95. 277 pages. Publication date: May 1976
ISBN 0−917616−00−6
Library of Congress No. 76−40680
Contributors: Martin S. Feldstein, Thomas D. Hall, Leon R. Kass, Keith
B. Leffler, Cotton M. Lindsay, Mark V. Pauly, Charles E. Phelps,
Thomas C. Schelling, Arthur Seldon

NEW DIRECTIONS IN PUBLIC HEALTH CARE: A PRESCRIPTION
FOR THE 1980s
$6.95 (paper). 290 pages. Publication date: May 1976; 3d ed.
rev., 1980
ISBN 0−917616−37−5
Library of Congress No. 79−92868
$16.95 (cloth). 290 pages. Publication date: April 1980
ISBN 0−87855−394−0. Available through Transaction Books,
Rutgers—The State University, New Brunswick, NJ 08903
Contributors: Alain Enthoven, W. Philip Gramm, Leon R. Kass, Keith B.
Leffler, Cotton M. Lindsay, Jack A. Meyer, Charles E. Phelps,
Thomas C. Schelling, Harry Schwartz, Arthur Seldon, David A.
Stockman, Lewis Thomas

NO LAND IS AN ISLAND: INDIVIDUAL RIGHTS AND
GOVERNMENT CONTROL OF LAND USE
$5.95. 221 pages. Publication date: November 1975
ISBN 0−917616−03−0
Library of Congress No. 75−38415
Contributors: Benjamin F. Bobo, B. Bruce-Briggs, Connie Cheney, A.
Lawrence Chickering, Robert B. Ekelund, Jr., W. Philip Gramm,
Donald G. Hagman, Robert B. Hawkins, Jr., M. Bruce Johnson, Jan
Krasnowiecki, John McClaughry, Donald M. Pach, Bernard H.
Siegan, Ann Louise Strong, Morris K. Udall

522

NO TIME TO CONFUSE: A CRITIQUE OF THE FORD
FOUNDATION'S ENERGY POLICY PROJECT *A TIME TO
CHOOSE AMERICA'S ENERGY FUTURE*
$4.95. 156 pages. Publication date: February 1975
ISBN 0−917616−01−4
Library of Congress No. 75−10230
Contributors: Morris A. Adelman, Armen A. Alchian, James C. DeHaven,
George W. Hilton, M. Bruce Johnson, Herman Kahn, Walter J. Mead,
Arnold B. Moore, Thomas Gale Moore, William H. Riker

ONCE IS ENOUGH: THE TAXATION OF CORPORATE
EQUITY INCOME
$2.00. 32 pages. Publication date: May 1977
ISBN 0−917616−23−5
Library of Congress No. 77−670132
Author: Charles E. McLure, Jr.

OPTIONS FOR U.S. ENERGY POLICY
$5.95. 309 pages. Publication date: September 1977
ISBN 0−917616−20−0
Library of Congress No. 77−89094
Contributors: Albert Carnesale, Stanley M. Greenfield, Fred S. Hoffman,
Edward J. Mitchell, William R. Moffat, Richard Nehring, Robert
S. Pindyck, Norman C. Rasmussen, David J. Rose, Henry S. Rowen,
James L. Sweeney, Arthur W. Wright

PARENTS, TEACHERS, AND CHILDREN: PROSPECTS FOR CHOICE
IN AMERICAN EDUCATION
$5.95. 336 pages. Publication date: June 1977
ISBN 0−917616−18−9
Library of Congress No. 77−79164
Contributors: James S. Coleman, John E. Coons, William H. Cornog,
Denis P. Doyle, E. Babette Edwards, Nathan Glazer, Andrew
M. Greeley, R. Kent Greenawalt, Marvin Lazerson, William
C. McCready, Michael Novak, John P. O'Dwyer, Robert Singleton,
Thomas Sowell, Stephen D. Sugarman, Richard E. Wagner

THE POLITICS OF PLANNING: A REVIEW AND CRITIQUE OF
CENTRALIZED ECONOMIC PLANNING
$5.95. 367 pages. Publication date: March 1976
ISBN 0−917616−05−7
Library of Congress No. 76−7714
Contributors: B. Bruce-Briggs, James Buchanan, A. Lawrence Chickering,
Ralph Harris, Robert B. Hawkins, Jr., George W. Hilton, Richard
Mancke, Richard Muth, Vincent Ostrom, Svetozar Pejovich, Myron
Sharpe, John Sheahan, Herbert Stein, Gordon Tullock, Ernest
van den Haag, Paul H. Weaver, Murray L. Weidenbaum, Hans
Willgerodt, Peter P. Witonski

PUBLIC EMPLOYEE UNIONS: A STUDY OF THE CRISIS IN
PUBLIC SECTOR LABOR RELATIONS
$6.95. 251 pages. Publication date: June 1976; 2d ed. rev., 1977
ISBN 0−917616−08−1/1976; 0−917616−24−3/1977
Library of Congress No. 76−17444
Contributors: A. Lawrence Chickering, Jack D. Douglas, Raymond
D. Horton, Theodore W. Kheel, David Lewin, Seymour Martin
Lipset, Harvey C. Mansfield, Jr., George Meany, Robert A. Nisbet,
Daniel Orr, A. H. Raskin, Wes Uhlman, Harry H. Wellington,
Charles B. Wheeler, Jr., Ralph K. Winter, Jr., Jerry Wurf

REGULATING BUSINESS: THE SEARCH FOR AN OPTIMUM
$6.95. 261 pages. Publication date: April 1978
ISBN 0−917616−27−8
Library of Congress No. 78−50678
Contributors: Chris Argyris, A. Lawrence Chickering, Penny Hollander
Feldman, Richard H. Holton, Donald P. Jacobs, Alfred E. Kahn,
Paul W. MacAvoy, Almarin Phillips, V. Kerry Smith, Paul H.
Weaver, Richard J. Zeckhauser

TARIFFS, QUOTAS, AND TRADE: THE POLITICS
OF PROTECTIONISM
$6.95. 330 pages. Publication date: February 1979
ISBN 0−917616−34−0
Library of Congress No. 78−66267
Contributors: Walter Adams, Ryan C. Amacher, Sven W. Arndt, Malcolm
D. Bale, John T. Cuddington, Alan V. Deardorff, Joel B. Dirlam
Roger D. Hansen, H. Robert Heller, D. Gale Johnson, Robert O.
Keohane, Michael W. Keran, Rachel McCulloch, Ronald I.
McKinnon, Gordon W. Smith, Robert M. Stern, Richard James
Sweeney, Robert D. Tollison, Thomas D. Willett

THE THIRD WORLD: PREMISES OF U.S. POLICY
$5.95. 332 pages. Publication date: November 1978
ISBN 0−917616−30−8
Library of Congress No. 78−67593
Contributors: Dennis Austin, Peter T. Bauer, Max Beloff, Richard E. Bissell,
Daniel J. Elazar, S. E. Finer, Allan E. Goodman, Nathaniel H. Leff,
Seymour Martin Lipset, Edward N. Luttwak, Daniel Pipes, Wilson E.
Schmidt, Anthony Smith, W. Scott Thompson, Basil S. Yamey

UNION CONTROL OF PENSION FUNDS: WILL THE NORTH
RISE AGAIN?
$2.00. 42 pages. Publication date: July 1979
ISBN 0−917616−36−7
Library of Congress No. 78−66581
Author: George J. Borjas

WATER BANKING: HOW TO STOP WASTING
AGRICULTURAL WATER
  $2.00. 56 pages. Publication date: January 1978
  ISBN 0—917616—26—X
  Library of Congress No. 78—50766
Authors: Sotirios Angelides, Eugene Bardach

TAXING & SPENDING
  $15/one year, $25/two years, $4/single issue. For delivery outside the
  United States, add $2/year surface mail, $10/year airmail
A quarterly journal that analyzes the immediate and long-range effects of
  the tax limitation movement as well as the broad issues of national
  and local taxing and spending policy.